Reformed Historical Theology

Edited by
Herman J. Selderhuis

In co-operation with
Emidio Campi, Irene Dingel, Benyamin F. Intan,
Elsie Anne McKee, Richard A. Muller, and Risto Saarinen

Volume 74

Gregory David Soderberg

As Often As You Eat This Bread

Communion Frequency in English, Scottish,
and Early American Churches

Vandenhoeck & Ruprecht

With the kind support of Stichting Zonneweelde (Zonneweelde Foundation).

Bibliographic information published by the Deutsche Nationalbibliothek:
The Deutsche Nationalbibliothek lists this publication in the Deutsche Nationalbibliografie;
detailed bibliographic data available online: https://dnb.de.

© 2023 by Vandenhoeck & Ruprecht, Theaterstraße 13, 37073 Göttingen, Germany,
an imprint of the Brill-Group
(Koninklijke Brill NV, Leiden, The Netherlands; Brill USA Inc., Boston MA, USA;
Brill Asia Pte Ltd, Singapore; Brill Deutschland GmbH, Paderborn, Germany,
Brill Österreich GmbH, Vienna, Austria)
Koninklijke Brill NV incorporates the imprints Brill, Brill Nijhoff, Brill Hotei,
Brill Schöningh, Brill Fink, Brill mentis, Vandenhoeck & Ruprecht, Böhlau,
V&R unipress and Wageningen Academic.

Typesetting: le-tex publishing services, Leipzig
Cover design: SchwabScantechnik, Göttingen
Printed and bound: Hubert & Co. BuchPartner, Göttingen
Printed in the EU

Vandenhoeck & Ruprecht Verlage | www.vandenhoeck-ruprecht-verlage.com

ISSN 2198-8226
ISBN 978-3-525-56070-9

Table of Contents

Acknowledgements

This book a the slightly modified version of a dissertation that I defended in November 2021 to obtain the degree of Doctor of Philosophy at the Vrije Universiteit Amsterdam. I am indebted to numerous people for their encouragement and support. In particular, I am especially thankful for:

- two of my professors from my undergraduate days at New St. Andrews College: Christopher Schlect who sparked my love of church history, and Peter Leithart who helped me understand the centrality of the church and of the Lord's Supper.
- my supervisors of my PhD program at the Vrije Universiteit, Amsterdam, Prof. Gijsbert van den Brink and Prof. dr. Wim Janse who both provided enthusiastic support, guidance, and challenged me to reach a higher stage of academic research than I thought possible.
- the numerous other professors from the VU, Amsterdam, and fellow doctoral researchers that asked probing questions about my research at the annual "research days." Prof. dr. Erik de Boer was especially supportive of this project.
- Dr. Hermann Speelman, who generously shared his own research on this topic and provided suggestions for seeking a grant.
- my parents, who have always been supportive of whatever I was pursuing at the moment, including academic studies. My father asked many questions to help me keep thinking about how my research might relate to practical realities in the contemporary church.
- my children, who were never quite sure why their father was always heading off to the library or reading another book on historical theology. I was lucky enough to take most of my children to visit the wonderful country of the Netherlands, so hopefully that makes up for some of the other absences of their father while he pursued yet another footnote or source.
- my wife, Cynthia, who endured long years of a preoccupied and distracted husband while I worked on this project. I could not have completed this without her love, support, and capable handling of life on the home front.
- to the Fund 'Stichting Zonneweelde' whose generous grant helped fund the publication of the book.

Chapter 1
Communion Frequency and Reformed Identity

1.1   Introduction

The Reformed philosopher Nicholas Wolterstorff once claimed that there was "no more fundamental liturgical issue facing the Reformed churches today" than the issue of weekly communion.[1] Other sources suggest a growing interest in this issue. The introduction to a series of blogs on The Gospel Coalition's website noted that weekly communion was "becoming a badge of honor in a growing number of Presbyterian and Baptist churches."[2] The issue of communion frequency continues to be debated in the American Reformed churches.[3] While this is not just a "Reformed" issue, it raises fundamental questions about the nature of the Reformed tradition.[4] Does the historic Reformed tradition elevate the "Word" too

---

1 Nicholas P. Wolterstorff, "The Reformed Liturgy," in *Major Themes in the Reformed Tradition*, ed. Donald McKim (Grand Rapids: Eerdmans, 1992), 295.

2 Ray Van Neste, "Three Arguments for Weekly Communion," April 18, 2012 http://www.thegospel-coalition.org/article/three-arguments-for-weekly-communion [accessed May 5, 2015], Kenneth J. Stewart, "The Frequency of Communion Calmly Considered," April 18, 2012 http://www.thegospel-coalition.org/article/the-frequency-of-communion-calmly-considered [accessed May 5, 2015], Eric Bancroft, "We Celebrate the Lord's Supper Frequently But Not Weekly," April 18, 2012 http://www.thegospelcoalition.org/article/we-celebrate-the-lords-supper-frequently-but-not-weekly [accessed May 5, 2015].

3 In his study, J. Todd Billings stresses the importance of frequent communion: "At the Lord's Supper, nourishment is absolutely necessary for those who feed upon and abide in Christ, and if nourishment is central to a congregational practice of the Lord's Supper, then it is very hard to justify an infrequent celebration." *Remembrance, Communion, and Hope: Rediscovering the Gospel at the Lord's Table* (Grand Rapids: William B. Eerdmans Publishing Company, 2018), 182.

4 See Kenneth W. Wieting, *The Blessings of Weekly Communion* (Saint Louis: Concordia Publishing House, 2006) for a treatment of communion frequency from a Lutheran perspective. Joseph Dougherty traces the growth of frequent communion in the Roman Catholic communion in *From Altar-Throne to Table: The Campaign for Frequent Holy Communion in the Catholic Church*, ATLA Monograph Series, no. 50 (Lanham, MD: The Scarecrow Press and American Theological Library Association, 2010). Orthodox theologian Alexander Schmemann lamented the pattern of infrequent communion prevalent in most Orthodox churches, *The Eucharist: Sacrament of the Kingdom*, trans. Paul Kachur (Crestwood, NY: St. Vladimir's Seminary Press, 1987), 299–245. Robert Taft provides a far-ranging survey of communion frequency in history, including evidence from all branches of the Orthodox churches. He indicates that most Eastern Orthodox receive communion annually, or a few times a year. See Robert A. Taft, "The Frequency of the Eucharist Throughout History," in Maxwell Johnson, ed., *Between Memory and Hope: Readings on the Liturgical Year* (Collegeville, MN: The Liturgical Press, 2000), 93.

far above the "Sacraments"? What does it mean to partake of communion in a meaningful way? Has the Reformed tradition interpreted Paul's exhortation to "examine yourself" in an overly intellectualistic fashion? Can a ritual be repeated frequently, and yet not lose any sense of its profound meaning? On both sides of the issue, we find voices that critique, or affirm, various aspects of the Reformed tradition. The debate over communion frequency takes us to the heart of questions about religious identity.[5]

Questions about communion frequency also inevitably raise questions about history. Authors appeal to various practices or principles in Scriptural texts, to justify both frequent and infrequent communion. This study does not explore the Biblical data about the nature or ideal frequency of the Eucharist. Other studies have done that, though many fruitful lines of research still remain.[6] The goal here is to illuminate the historical backgrounds and contexts of communion frequency debates in the American Reformed tradition, especially in the Scottish frequency debates of the 1700s and early 1800s. In these debates, the main texts used in discussions about communion frequency are found in the New Testament books of Acts and 1 Corinthians, although many writers in favor of frequent communion appeal to the "dying words" of Jesus (Matt. 26:26-29; Mark 14:22-25; Luke 22:14-20; 1 Cor. 11:23-34). Since we typically respect the dying words of our friends, how much more should we respect Jesus' last command to observe a meal in his remembrance? The examples of the early church's eating and worshipping together in Acts are also key texts in this debate. Although Acts 2:42-47 and Acts 20:7 depict the early disciples engaged in worship, fellowship, care for each other, and the "breaking of bread," interpreters disagree on whether these early gatherings are normative for the church, and whether they set a pattern that should be followed every time the church gathers. Authors also debate whether the "breaking of bread" refers

---

5 It should be noted that I personally favor the practice of frequent communion. This project began as a defense of the practice of weekly communion. However, through further research, and following the suggestions of my advisers, the project became one of historical analysis. It is hoped that this study will enable others to dispassionately study the development of communion frequency patterns and polemics in Reformed churches and, ultimately, make informed choices on communion frequency within their own contexts.

6 In addition to Billings, *Remembrance, Communion, and Hope*, see Max Thurian, *The Eucharistic Memorial*, trans. J.G. Davies, Ecumenical Studies in Worship, no. 7 and 8 (Richmond: John Knox Press, 1960), 2:125–128; J.-J. von Allmen, *Worship: Its Theology and Practice* (New York: Oxford University Press, 1965), 147–157, 238–39, 312–314; Peter J. Leithart, *The Kingdom and the Power: Rediscovering the Centrality of the Church* (Phillipsburg: P&R Publishing, 1993), chap. 6; Jeffrey J. Meyers, *The Lord's Service: The Grace of Covenant Renewal Worship* (Moscow: Canon Press, 2003), chap. 12; Michael S. Horton, "At Least Weekly: The Reformed Doctrine of the Lord's Supper and of Its Frequent Celebration," *MJT* 11 (2000), 147–169; *People and Place: A Covenant Ecclesiology* (Louisville: Westminster John Knox Press, 2008), 135–141.

to communion, a regular meal, or both. 1 Cor. 11 plays an especially prominent role in communion frequency polemics. The phrase "as often" in 1 Cor. 11:25-26 is interpreted in various ways. Paul's warning to observe the Lord's Supper in a "worthy" manner makes this discussion a matter of great importance. Many authors cite 1 Cor. 11:29-30 as they warn their readers of the dire consequences of not coming to communion in a worthy manner. The Passover and other feast days of the Old Testament also figure prominently in arguments about frequency. Patterns of fasting and feasting in the Old Testament are interpreted in various ways, depending on the aims of each writer.

All of this might sound subjective and arbitrary. How can different authors interpret the same texts in such diverse ways? Examining the history of communion frequency debates is thus a helpful case study of hermeneutical priorities and the interpretive lens that authors bring to the text of Scripture. It also illustrates the fact that liturgical practices are inextricably connected with specific historical times, and certain places. To appeal to the past reveals a certain understanding about the claim of the past on our present. For theologians, pastors, and preachers Scripture is not merely history, of course. Christians have always looked upon the Scriptures as divinely revealed precepts and principles that must inform their lives. However, interpreters do not agree on exactly how the past impinges upon the present. For example, how do the rituals of the Jews relate to the worship of the Christian church? In the communion frequency debates that disturbed Scottish Reformed churches in the eighteenth century, opponents of frequent communion felt most at home in the Old Testament. For authors like John Thompson, John Anderson, and Alexander Duncan, the Passover stood as a divinely instituted *infrequent* sacrament. Since they also accepted the notion that the Lord's Supper primarily fulfills the Passover, then the details of Passover observance become prototypical of Christian participation in the Eucharist.[7] On the contrary, Scots Reformed authors who argued for *frequent* communion focused primarily on New Testament texts and argumentation, and tended to view any appeal to the Old Testament as a return to the "shadows" of the Law.[8] Some, like Thomas Randall, went so far as to claim some form of "special revelation" from Christ to the apostles regarding communion frequency.[9] Randall

[handwritten marginal note: hermeneutical priorities]

---

7 John Thomson, *Letters addressed to the Rev. John Mason, M.A. of New-York, in Answer to his Letters on Frequent Communion* (Glasgow: William Paton, 1799; Troy: R. Moffitt & Co., 1801), 25–26; John Anderson, *Communion Seasons Defended: A Scriptural Response to John M. Mason's "Letters on Frequent Communion"* ed. Sean McDonald (Grand Rapids: Torwood Press, 2013), 8–9; Alexander Duncan, *A Disquisition on the Observance of the Lord's Supper* (Edinburgh: George Kline, 1807), 8–14.

8 John Erskine, *An Attempt to Promote the Frequent Dispensing of the Lord's Supper* (Kilmarnock: J. Wilson, 1803), 55.

9 Thomas Randall, *A Letter to A Minister from his Friend, Concerning Frequent Communicating, Occasioned by the late Overture of the Synod of Glasgow and Air upon that Subject* (Glasgow, 1749), 7.

was able to make this claim because, to him, the New Testament texts definitely portray the apostolic church observing weekly communion.

Nor does the question of history and its claim on the present apply only to Scriptural history. Since rituals define religious communities, our rituals can connect us to a "family of faith" in the past. Some Christian authors writing about communion frequency are quick to identify with their historical family, while others want to distance themselves from the past. Proponents of frequent communion tend to have a more positive view of the church in history and point to many examples of frequent communion in the early church, as well as in certain Protestant Reformers. Those who question frequent communion typically have a dim view of the historical church, at least before the Reformation. They quickly point out the many "errors" (judging from a strict Protestant perspective) that also existed in the early church, tendencies that seemed to culminate in the medieval Catholic church. They note, quite rightly, that Roman Catholic apologists also appeal to early traditions (whether written or unwritten), and so are skeptical of nebulous appeals to the "early church." This difference in views of history also affects how current churches make sense of their own "family history" in the more recent past.

This dynamic plays out when considering the influence and example of John Calvin, as it relates to contemporary communion practice and the theology of the Eucharist. It is common knowledge that John Calvin expressed his desire for weekly communion in various publications but was unable to persuade the magistrates of Geneva to implement it.[10] However, does this argument presuppose a certain understanding about Reformed identity? Are Reformed churches all "Calvinian"? Should Reformed communities desire to identify so closely with just *one* theologian, no matter how brilliant or influential? Reformed churches are not named after a single man (like Luther) and the tradition has always been more diverse, with many equally influential theologians. For a tradition that prides itself on its supposed reliance on the Scriptures, a simple appeal to the opinions of only one theological authority can seem precarious. Opponents of frequent communion are quick to point to other Reformers who did not share Calvin's opinion on weekly communion.

The question of communion frequency, then, inevitably involves us in questions of church history and historical theology.[11] It is therefore valuable to survey arguments about communion frequency from a historical perspective. The goal is not

---

10 In treating Calvin below, his more nuanced view of communion frequency and preparation for communion will be highlighted.

11 On the topics of "church history" and "historical theology" see James E. Bradley and Richard A Muller, *Church History: An Introduction to Research, Reference Works, and Methods* (Grand Rapids: Wm. B. Eerdmans Publishing Co., 1995) as well as Jaroslav Pelikan, *Historical Theology: Continuity and Change in Christian Doctrine*, Theological Resources (New York: Corpus Instrumentorum, 1971).

to proclaim either side as the "winner." Christian theology is always a conversation with the past, and historical theology is a record of that conversation. Ideally, if pastors, ministers, church leaders, and lay people can listen sympathetically to the conversation about frequent communion in the past, they will be enabled to make wise decisions about communion frequency in the churches of the present.

1.2 Research Goals, Methodology, and the Significance of the Project

The goal of this research project is to analyze the backgrounds of the debate over weekly/frequent communion in Anglo Saxon parts of the Reformed tradition, from the perspective of historical theology. The movement towards weekly communion gained significant traction in American Presbyterian churches during the twentieth century, but it remains controversial in some circles. A vocal minority of popular authors, as well as several scholars, advocate for the institution of weekly communion. While the official documents and liturgies of mainline Presbyterian and Reformed churches in recent years have tended to move in the direction of more frequent communion, actual liturgical practice tends to lag.[12] In more conservative churches, weekly communion can be seen as "sacramental" and dangerously reminiscent of Roman Catholicism. For many, to practice weekly communion contradicts essential features of the Reformed tradition.

From the perspective of historical theology, this study is relevant because it will provide the first systematic examination of the debate, particularly in the Anglo-American tradition. For Reformed theology, this study is significant because it re-examines many of the standard assumptions about the purpose of communion by revisiting the sources. For Reformed churches, this study will provide a much-needed resource for conducting the ongoing debate on weekly communion in a historically sound and informed way. For ecumenical theology, the issue is significant because many branches of the Christian church, such as Lutheran, Roman Catholic, and Orthodox, have struggled with the issue of communion frequency as well, and this study makes it possible to compare the causes and backgrounds of this phenomenon.

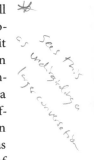

This study focuses on a central research question: *What patterns of communion frequency characterized the sixteenth-century Swiss Reformed, English Puritan,*

---

12 See James F. White, *The Sacraments in Protestant Faith and Practice* (Nashville: Abingdon Press, 1999), 88 and Ronald P. Byars, *Come and See: Presbyterian Congregations Celebrating Weekly Communion* (Eugene: Cascade Books, 2014).

Scottish Reformed, and early American Reformed communities?[13] This entails a consideration of three sub-questions:

1. How were patterns of communion frequency shaped and impacted by historical, political, and ecclesial considerations?
2. Since the desire for church discipline and proper participation have also been key concerns for Reformed communities, how did these priorities impact communion frequency?
3. Although communion frequency was a concern for many in the Reformed tradition, it assumed central importance in a series of pamphlets and essays written by Scottish Reformed authors in the 1700-1800s. What were the key exegetical and polemical strategies of these debates? What can contemporary churches learn from them, as leaders today seek to make wise choices in the matter of communion frequency?

This project adopts a geographical and chronological approach, since this unearths some of the differences and similarities in argumentative strategies as well as the lines of influence across various parts of the Reformed communities in the Continent, the British Isles and in the American colonies. It focuses on original sources that dealt with the issue of frequent communion, with one exception: to survey attitudes towards frequent communion in the Reformation period, it mainly relies on Reformation scholars, sampling the results of sound research that has already been done. Thus, in order not to re-do the work of previous scholars, I have not investigated the primary sources of the 16th century Reformers whose views are rendered in Chapter 2. However, primary sources from the English Puritan and Scottish Reformed traditions form the backbone and largest portion of material, since the issues of communion frequency and proper participation in the Eucharist were an important aspect of these movements.

1.3   Scope of Research

During the course of research, it became apparent that the late seventeenth century and early eighteenth century were pivotal moments for communion frequency debates in Scottish Protestant churches and English reforming churches, on both sides of the Atlantic.

---

13 Unfortunately, the Dutch tradition cannot be examined here. There are many fruitful areas of influence and correlation between the Dutch Reformed churches and every aspect of this research project, but that work must be taken up by those more familiar with the sources in the Netherlands. The same applies to other trajectories of the Reformed tradition, such as in France, Germany, Hungary, South Africa, South Korea, and other parts of the world.

Thus, this period is crucial for understanding the backgrounds of communion frequency practices, and polemics, in contemporary American Reformed churches. The issue of communion frequency usually centers on a perceived tension between purity and frequency. It is the tension caused by emphasizing two things at the same time—the need to commune more frequently, as well as the need to be morally and spiritually prepared for communion. This tension has manifested itself in all branches of the Christian church but was thrown into high relief because of various priorities and emphases of the Reformation and the reforming movements it inspired. *The center of the issue*

Focusing on the late 1600s, the 1700s, and early 1800s, yields a wealth of material and provides realistic and logical bookends for this project. Additionally, focusing on the tension between purity and frequency brought further definition to the research question, because it was then easier to sift through the various arguments and polemics on both sides of the communion frequency issue. Rather than attempting to analyze every single argument, or source, this project surveys and summarizes the interplay of the ideals and priorities of authors and traditions in the matter of communion frequency, especially as it relates to spiritual preparation and ecclesiastical discipline. As Amy Plantinga Pauw notes, the Lord's Supper became a primary locus where the dual priorities of the Reformed communities were held in a somewhat uneasy tension.[14]

This project focuses specifically on sources that explicitly argue either for, or against, frequent communion in the Scottish, English, and early American Reformed churches. It also utilizes sources that illuminate the broader questions of church discipline, ecclesial purity, and proper preparation for communion. Since most of these sources proliferated in the 1700s and late 1800s, this forms the central period of the research project.[15] The issue of communion frequency became more

---

14 "In Calvin's Geneva and in the Puritan society Edwards longed to restore in New England, the church was to exist both as an established institution demanding the allegiance of everyone *and* as a community set apart by its distinctive life. The church strives for comprehensive membership *and* for visible holiness. The interplay of these aims can be seen in Reformed theologies of the Lord's Supper. The emphasis on church as mother led Calvin to call for frequent celebrations of communion to nurture and strengthen faith, while the stress on church as bride encouraged an ongoing concern, though variably enacted, to fence the table against all who would pollute it by their unworthiness. In Edwards's church in Northampton, the clash between views of the Lord's Supper as nourishment for the spiritually weak and as love feast for none but the truly faithful brought an acrimonious end to his pastorate." Amy Plantinga Pauw, "Practical Ecclesiology in Calvin and Edwards," in Thomas Davis, ed., *John Calvin's American Legacy* (Oxford: Oxford University Press, 2010), 97.

15 Unless otherwise indicated, the spelling of early modern sources has been standardized. Additionally, texts in the 1700s and 1800s made generous use of italics. Most of these have been changed into regular font.

pressing in the late nineteenth century, gained momentum with the liturgical renewal movements of the twentieth century, and shows no signs of abating. However, fully analyzing those sources and that era must wait for a further research project. This project lays the foundation for future research by surveying the tensions between purity/preparation and frequency, stemming from the Reformation, and exploding into widespread controversy in the 1700 and early 1800s. This period of debate and controversy forms part of the essential backdrop for later developments in the twentieth and twenty-first centuries.

This study begins with a presentation of the views of representative Continental Reformers on the issues of communion frequency and church discipline (Chapter 2). It continues with the beginnings of the Reformation movement in England and Scotland (Chapter 3), examining the origins of the differences between the respective reform movements in both countries, especially in relation to communion frequency and the role of church discipline in the Church of Scotland. Further developments in post-Reformation England and Scotland are treated next (Chapter 4), with particular attention to the growth of the Puritan movement and its stress on preparation for communion. The growth of Reformed churches and Puritan communities on both sides of the Atlantic are summarized next (Chapter 5), highlighting the influence of Scottish immigrants to the Americas. The communion frequency debates within various Scottish Reformed churches, which included writers in America, is then surveyed (Chapter 7), along with a comparative analysis of the rhetorical and polemical strategies utilized in the debates. The conclusion (Chapter 7) summarizes the study and offers a final analysis and reflection on the relevance of this research for contemporary churches and church leaders.

There are many areas for further research. This study only sketches a broad outline, and many gaps remain to be filled. For instance, further research can also explore the similarities and contrasts between English Dissenters/Puritans and authors within the Established church on the issue of communion frequency. As scholars continue to notice shared concerns and beliefs between Dissenters and the developing Anglican church, beliefs and practices about communion frequency are a promising field that could demonstrate commonalities on the level of everyday experience in parishes, and not just in theology and ecclesiology.[16]

More research is also needed on developments in America. As Doug Adams comments, "[W]e know that communion was very frequent in seventeenth and eighteenth centuries and infrequent as churches developed in the nineteenth century; but we do not know fully enough when and how such changes occurred across

---

16 See Hunt, "The Lord's Supper in Early Modern England," 39–83 for more on the similar concerns of those who remained within the Church of England and Puritans on the issue of communion frequency. Further research can explore these connections and contrasts.

the country."[17] In the same way, the Dutch tradition (as well as many other branches of the Reformed tradition) have not been treated here.

Further studies should examine how communion frequency changed, or was impacted, in other Reformed communities throughout Europe, and beyond. In particular, the relationships between the English Puritans and the Dutch are numerous. Are there parallels, and/or contrasts, with how English Puritans and the Dutch Reformed thought about and practiced communion? This study lays the foundation for many other fruitful lines of research.

---

17 Doug Adams, *Meeting House to Camp Meeting: Toward a History of American Free Church Worship From 1620 to 1835* (Saratoga: Modern Liturgy-Resource Publications and Austin: The Sharing Company, 1981), 16.

Chapter 2
Communion Frequency in the Late Medieval Period and the Sixteenth-Century Continental Reformed Reformation

2.1   Introduction

This chapter will discuss both the eucharistic theologies and the communion practices of some key figures of the Reformed Reformation.[1] The overall focus of this book is the history of communion frequency debates, especially as they came into sharp focus in the 1700s in Reformed churches in Scotland, England, and the Americas. This necessitates a limited scope for this introductory overview.[2] It is

---

1 Since Carter Lindberg introduced the term "Reformations" in 1996, scholars have continued to debate the appropriate terminology to describe the momentous religio-political changes in sixteenth-century Europe. See Lindberg, *The European Reformations*, 2nd ed. (Chichester: Wiley-Blackwell, 2010), xii–xiii, xv, 1–22. Carlos Eire notes that the emphasis on multiplicity "emerged principally from historians who ceased focusing on theology and the institutional history of churches and turned their attention instead to social, cultural, economic, and political issues" and from "historians who no longer sought to prove that a particular church or tradition was in sole possession of the Truth, with a capital T," in *Reformations: The Early Modern World, 1450–1650* (New Haven: Yale University Press, 2016), x. Although acknowledging the complexity and interrelatedness of reform movements in the early modern period, my sympathies lie with Euan Cameron, who uses "the Reformation" to indicate "a particular process of change, integrating cultural, political, and theological factors in a way never seen before and rarely since." He argues that "this process cannot simply be equated with the corresponding movements in Catholicism," in *The European Reformation*, 2nd ed. (Oxford: Oxford University Press, 2012), 1. At the end of his study, Cameron notes the existence of many "paradoxes" in the "course of the Reformation." Yet, "[d]espite its internal feuds and inconsistencies, and the infinitely diverse social and political contexts in which it was adopted, there was an essential, underlying coherence to the Reformation process" (436). So also, Markus Wriedt, "I opt for the use of the term Reformation in its singular sense to describe the complex developments within the sixteenth and seventeenth centuries. There might be parallels in other times and locations, but I would not like to extend the meaning of Reformation to these contexts, for it weakens the limiting structure of the definition and with that its effective use." "How to Bring About a Reformation: A critical re-consideration about most recent theories in Historiography," Public Lecture: Marquette University, Milwaukee WI, October 13, 2005, 24. Here, I will endeavor to use terms that reflect both the plurality, as well as the basic underlying unity of vision, among the Protestant Reformers. This is similar to Diarmaid MacCulloch's usage of "Reformation," with the stated understanding that it includes both Protestant and Catholic reforms, in *The Reformation: A History* (New York: Penguin Books, 2003), xix.

2 To speak of the "Reformed tradition" is an unfortunate necessity. Obviously, there is a great deal of diversity and multiformity among Reformed churches, yet there is a basic family resemblance. In this book, "Reformed" refers to churches that trace their ancestry to the Swiss reform movement,

impossible to thoroughly examine every sixteenth-century figure on the issue of communion frequency here. The research focus entails selection of those Reformation thinkers who figure prominently in the developing tradition. In other words, this overview of the sixteenth century Reformation is limited to those thinkers who had the most impact on later polemics and practices. This can be determined—however imprecisely—by how often they are quoted in later polemics, and also by the lasting influence of ecclesiastical structures or liturgical practices that they and their followers instituted. Much as the "early church," or "apostolic church" functioned as a norm for the Reformers, so Calvin, or the "best Reformed churches" functioned as norm in later communion frequency polemics.[3]

This chapter, then, is an exercise in "Reformation reception history." The emphasis is not on exhaustively detailing the views of the sixteenth-century Protestant Reformers, or on arriving at new conclusions. Rather, the focus is on sketching some of the main points of their beliefs on eucharistic frequency, on the importance of preparation before receiving the Eucharist, and how those beliefs were transmitted to later generations of pastors, theologians, and laypeople in churches that identified with the Reformed tradition.

Accordingly, John Calvin's eucharistic theology will be briefly outlined and his desire for weekly communion will be explored in depth. Other key figures, such as Huldrych Zwingli, Johannes Oecolampadius and Martin Bucer, will also be surveyed. In doing so, the close relationship between theological argumentation, socio-political contexts—often the local government played a crucial role in settling the frequency debate—and the weight of liturgical traditions will be considered. However, the issue of communion frequency must also be situated firmly in the context of the proper reception of the sacrament, which requires an understanding of theories of "Reformed Church Discipline."[4] The Reformers struggled with a con-

---

influenced especially by Calvin and Zwingli. Indeed, the tensions between these two figures continue to manifest themselves in current communion frequency debates in American Reformed churches. For an attempt to define "Reformed theology" in a way that does justice both to its unity and plurality, see Gijsbert van den Brink and Johan Smits, "The Reformed Stance: Distinctive Commitments and Concerns," *Journal of Reformed Theology* 9 (2015): 325–347.

3 See Esther Chung-Kim, *Inventing Authority: The Use of the Church Fathers in Reformation Debates over the Eucharist* (Waco: Baylor University Press, 2011) and also Gregory Soderberg, "Ancient Discipline and Pristine Doctrine: Appeals to Antiquity in the Developing Reformation," (M.A. thesis, University of Pretoria, 2006). Specific examples of how later Reformed and Protestant polemicists appealed to Calvin and the sixteenth-century Reformers will be given below.

4 The term "Calvinist" misleads here because it "obscures the fact that its true origins lie not with Calvin but in the writings of Johannes Oecolampadius and Bucer, and in their attempts to recreate what they considered to have been the institutions of the primitive Christian Church." Michael F. Graham, *The Uses of Reform: 'Godly Discipline' and Popular Behavior in Scotland and Beyond, 1560–1610* (Leiden: E.J. Brill, 1996), 1.

stant tension between advocating more frequent communion, while also desiring people to commune properly. As a result, the issue of *how* one should commune tended to assume priority over the question of how *often*.

Because of its limited focus, this chapter makes generous use of secondary sources, while endeavoring to let various sixteenth-century figures speak for themselves when possible. Because of this project's overall focus on the backgrounds of the communion frequency debate in American Reformed churches, the emphasis is on sources in English.

2.2   Aspects of Communion Frequency in the Context of the Protestant Reformation

To understand the issue of communion frequency in the various Protestant movements, we must briefly sketch the pre-Reformation context.[5] Since patterns of worship and communion frequency were quite similar throughout late medieval Europe, this section will take a broad perspective, while also highlighting specific features of worship in the British Isles. While several factors contributed to the religious upheavals in sixteenth-century Europe, the issue of worship played a central role. According to McKee "[t]he sixteenth-century Reformation is most often remembered as a reform of theology or church politics, but it was also and especially a reform or worship."[6] Those who eventually became labeled as "Protestants" viewed the medieval Mass as a corrupt and blasphemous act. In their efforts to "purify" this rite, the Reformers focused on what the rite did, and what it was, rather than issues of frequency. However, most of the Reformers argued for frequent communion in one sense, because they generally proposed more frequent communion than the customary annual reception.

As the Reformers pursued their vision of creating a renewed Christian society, they faced the daunting task of restructuring the beliefs and rituals that held communities together.[7] Cameron writes "[m]edieval Christianity formed a vast,

---

5 For more detail, see Gary Macy "The Medieval Inheritance," in *A Companion to the Eucharist in the Reformation*, ed. Lee Palmer Wandel (Brill: Leiden, 2014), 15–37.

6 Elsie Ann McKee, "Reformed Worship in the Sixteenth Century," in Lukas Vischer, ed., *Christian Worship in Reformed Churches Past and Present* (Grand Rapids: William B. Eerdmans Publishing Company, 2003), 3.

7 This was especially true of community festivals like Corpus Christi. See John Bossy, *Christianity in the West 1400–1700* (Oxford: Oxford University Press, 1985), 71. So also Cameron: "In general, many of the most popular activities of late medieval religion depended on doing something, on participation, activity, movement, essentially on experiencing an event fraught with sacral power, more than on learning or understanding a message." *The European Reformation*, 14.

diverse, and seamless texture."[8] At the center of it all was the Eucharist. Bossy rejects Protestant-centric interpretations of the traditional mass: "Despite the complaints of liturgists and reformers, it was not a contradiction that mass should be offered by the priest alone, in a ritual language, largely in silence and partly out of sight, and yet embody or create the sense of collective identity."[9] This sense of collective identity increasingly took the form of the identification of the priest with Christ, and the identification of the people with the priest. Therefore, as the priest communed daily with Christ, the people present at the mass also communed with Christ.[10]

The origins of infrequent communion in the Christian church are somewhat shrouded in mystery.[11] Assuming the weekly, or even perhaps daily, patterns of communion in the early Christian communities, what accounts for its decline? The complete history of communion frequency is outside the scope of this project, but several factors contributed to the decline of oral reception of the Eucharist. Rigorist standards for worthy reception in the patristic era probably played a role.[12] Additionally, the institutionalization of the church after Constantine created a substantial group of catechumens who delayed baptism and thus were dismissed from the church gatherings before the Eucharist.

To partake in communion was a serious undertaking in late medieval Christianity. It required proper preparation, which included confession to a priest, performing

---

8 Cameron, *The European Reformation*, 11.

9 Bossy, *Christianity in the West*, 67.

10 "Increasingly, limitation of celebration to one mass a day, except on Christmas, was developing … And it was also increasingly necessary to claim that the mass had effect *ex opere operato*, as a ritual which was effective independently from the priest's character and virtue. Throughout the next centuries this regular priestly celebration was used as an argument for infrequent communion by the laity, inasmuch as the priest communicated daily for all Christians." Miri Rubin, *Corpus Christi: The Eucharist in Late Medieval Culture* (Cambridge: Cambridge UP, 1991), 50. Wandel agrees, "The ever closer identification of the priest with the Eucharist seems to have had as one of its consequences the decline in lay participation in the Mass." *The Eucharist in the Reformation*, 32–33.

11 See Taft, "The Frequency of the Eucharist Throughout History," 77–96.

12 "Saints Jerome and Augustine deferred to the communicant's own judgment. Jerome, however, may have insisted upon abstention from sexual intercourse as a way to prepare oneself for Communion; this very notion could easily have contributed to the decline in recourse to the sacrament, yet the notion prevailed in the Middle Ages. John Chrysostom demanded of the communicant 'sincerity and purity of soul' (Hom. III in Eph.)'. He was combating pervasive Arianism and so emphasized the divinity and remoteness of Christ." Dougherty, *From Altar-Throne to Table*, 2. Dougherty relies here on Thomas Scannel, "The History of Daily Communion," in *Report of the Nineteenth Eucharistic Congress, Held at Westminster from 9th to 13th September 1908* (London: Sands, 1909) and E. Dublanchy, "Communion eucharistique (fréquente)." *Dictionnaire de théologie catholique*, Paris: Letouzy et Ané, 1929.

any penance that was prescribed by the priest, and fasting before communion.[13] This point is important because sixteenth century reforms took place in a context in which people were accustomed to a process of preparation before communion. One aspect that made the Protestant movement different than previous reform movements was its insistence that every baptized adult should commune, and that they should do so more frequently than had been the custom in medieval Europe.

In late medieval Europe and the British Isles, lay participation in communion fell to such an extent that the Fourth Lateran Council (1215) had to mandate annual participation.[14] Aside from priests and some mystics, most Christians did not commune frequently.[15] Although a precise pattern of cause and effect is difficult to prove with certainty, a theology of visual reception (or "spiritual communion") of the Eucharist also developed in the late medieval period. As Ellwood states: "The host was for most people a divine epiphany, and the infrequency of actual reception of the sacrament only increased the popular sense of reverence for the eucharist."[16] This understanding of visual reception stemmed from an Augustinian and neo-Platonic physiology. According to Miles, Augustine (drawing on Plato) believed vision was made possible by a "ray" projected through the human eye, creating a back-and-forth movement.[17] Such a belief obviously would render the act of gazing upon the Eucharist a deeply spiritual, and physical, event. As Davies summarizes: "To see the sacred Host became the principal, if not the exclusive,

---

13 Alec Ryrie, *The Age of Reformation: The Tudor and Stewart Realms 1485–1603* (New York: Routledge, 2013), 18.

14 Norman P. Tanner, *Decrees of the Ecumenical Councils*, vol. I, (London: Sheed & Ward, 1990), 245.

15 According to Cameron: "Penance was typically administered yearly to laypeople; those same laypeople might take the Eucharist (as opposed to hearing and watching Mass said without receiving) once a year in the Easter season or, for the very committed, perhaps three or four times a year." *The European Reformation*, 12. Ryrie summarizes: "All this meant that receiving communion was a rarity. The obligation on all good Christians was to do so once a year, at Easter; more frequent communion was a rarefied practice for the unusually pious." *The Age of Reformation*, 18.

16 Christopher Ellwood, *The Body Broken: The Calvinist Doctrine of the Eucharist* (New York: Oxford University Press, 1999), 14.

17 "In the theory of vision described by Augustine, the most influential Christian author of the medieval and reformation periods, a fire within the body–the same fire that animates and warms the body–is collected with unique intensity behind the eyes; for an object to be seen by a viewer, this fire must be projected in the form of a ray that is focused on the object, thereby establishing a two-way street along which the attention and energy of the viewer passes to touch its object. A representation of the object, in turn, returns to the eye and is bonded to the soul and retained in the memory." Margaret R. Miles, *Image as Insight: Visual Understanding in Christianity and Secular Culture* (1985; repr., Eugene: Wipf and Stock Publishers, 2006), 7. See also Miles, "Vision: The Eye of the Body and the Eye of the Mind in Augustine's *De Trinitate* and Other Works," *Journal of Religion*, no. 2 (April 1983): 125–142.

concern of worshippers in the High Middle Ages."[18] People went to great lengths to run from church to church, to see as many elevations of the Host as possible. They also "insisted on glass chalices in order to have ocular demonstration of the miracle effected by consecration."[19]

This emphasis on *visual* eucharistic participation, rather than actual oral reception, was reinforced by popular beliefs, such as that "one is protected from sudden death and blindness on a day one has seen the sacrament, or that one does not age in the time spent regarding the host."[20] The Reformers confronted a situation where there existed a close and clear connection between infrequent communion and a heightened level of spiritual experience. There were also other ways for the laity to encounter the spiritual presence of Christ besides oral reception of communion, even though these other ways were clearly not on the same level. They could eat some of the blessed bread that was distributed at the end of mass. Or they could receive the kiss of peace and the blessing of the priest.[21] Additionally, the passing of the "pax" became widespread in late medieval times as a substitute for communion.[22] Though later Reformers harshly criticized the late medieval church for its eucharistic practices, it does not appear that the average parishioners believed they were living in spiritual poverty. Rather, they were surrounded by many opportunities to see, hear, taste, and even touch, symbolic words, actions, and objects that were all infused with some degree of Christ's presence and power.

There were isolated movements and individuals which advocated or practiced frequent communion before the Reformation.[23] Some medieval mystics advo-

---

18 Horton Davies, *Worship and Theology in England*, vol. 1, *From Cranmer to Baxter and Fox, 1534–1690* (Grand Rapids: William B. Eerdmans Publishing Company, 1970, 1975; combined edition 1996), 140.

19 Davies, *Worship and Theology in England*, vol. 1, 140. Davies is drawing primarily here from Hermanus A. P. Schmidt, *Introductio in Liturgiam Occidentalem* (Rome: Herder, 1960).

20 Ellwood, *The Body Broken*, 14.

21 Rubin, *Corpus Christi*, 73.

22 "The pax entered Roman liturgies around the year 1000 and particularly in the monastic milieu, but entered parish usage particularly in the later centuries, as substitute for reception of communion. This was usually an object as round and smooth as the host, made of wood or precious metal, and inscribed with a crucifixion scene or the Lamb of God. This was passed down from the celebrant to his attendant clergy, and to the congregation, to be touched and kissed as a token of charity, before all attention returned to the altar to view the priest's sacrifice." Rubin, *Corpus Christi*, 74.

23 Bossy, *Christianity in the West*, 72. Thomas à Kempis (1379/80–1471) exhorts his readers to partake of communion often in Book 3 of *The Imitation of Christ*. According to Richard Viladesau, the Florentine reformer Savonarola (1452–1498) also advocated more frequent communion, but not for all. He believed that too frequent reception for the average layperson would be dangerous, since reception must always be preceded by confession and some sort of separation from the world. See his *The Triumph of the Cross: The Passion of Christ in Theology and the Arts* (Oxford: Oxford University Press, 2008), 93.

cated or practiced frequent communion.[24] Other individuals, like Margery Kempe (c. 1373–c. 1440), practiced weekly communion, which most likely produced negative feelings from others around her, who could not, or did not, commune as frequently.[25] However, as Duffy notes "frequent communion was the prerogative of the few."[26] In a context of infrequent communion, more frequent communion marked someone as different from the community. For most people who communed annually at Easter, this high point of the Church year was important for reinforcing and strengthening the social bonds of the community.[27]

Additionally, the Bohemian reform movement of the later 1300s also stressed frequent communion.[28] The community in Prague established by reformist priest Jan Milíč Kroměříž (d. 1374) included an emphasis on frequent communion. This movement continued and gained momentum from scholars at the Prague University "notably in Mathias of Janov's monumental *Regulae Veteris et Novi Testamenti*, as well as the writings of Adalbertus Ranconis, Matthew of Cracow, and Henry of Biterfield."[29] Holeton relates that the movement continued to grow and gain ecclesiastical support until "by the early years of the fifteenth century, frequent communion (at

---

24 For the views and communion habits of some mystics, see Rubin, *Corpus Christi*, 316–19, and 64–66 for other medieval authors and their opinions about communion frequency.

25 Eamon Duffy cites Kempe in the context of showing how the medieval Eucharist created a sense of community: "It is true that frequent reception of communion probably did encourage religious individualism, as it certainly often sprang from it. Margery Kempe's weekly reception, representing a claim to particular holiness of life, marked her off from her neighbours, and was almost certainly resented by them." *The Stripping of the Altars: Traditional Religion in England 1400–1580* (New Haven: Yale University Press, 1992; 2nd ed. 2005), 93.

26 Duffy, *The Stripping of the Altars*, 93.

27 Duffy, *The Stripping of the Altars*, 93. Duffy is writing primarily about England. The situation does not appear much different in medieval Scotland. Although there are some instances where medieval Scottish liturgical and ceremonial practices differed from that of England, "[n]one of this evidence, however, can be construed to prove that the devotional life of Scotland was exceptional in comparison with that of the rest of Europe. It must be assumed, for example, that although the laity were excited by the display of the consecrated sacrament and despite efforts to encourage regular communication, most of them—perhaps the bulk of the adult population—only communicated at Easter." James Galbraith, "The Middle Ages," in Duncan Forrester and Douglas Murry, eds., *Studies in the History of Worship in Scotland* (Edinburgh: T. & T. Clark, 1984), 25.

28 "The practice by Hussites in the late fourteenth century of offering communion in both kinds and frequent communion to the laity was a statement of their criticism of the church, and of the clerical privilege enshrined in its rituals. It was against the idolatry of lay gazing—that private contemplation of the eucharist at elevation—which was the most common eucharistic encounter of most layfolk, and in favour of frequent and spiritually regenerating communion, rescued from clerical mystification, that Matthew of Janov and Jan Hus directed their practices." Rubin, *Corpus Christi*, 72–73.

29 David R. Holeton, "The Bohemian Brethren," in Geoffrey Wainwright and Karen B. Westerfield Tucker, eds., *The Oxford History of Christian Worship* (Oxford: Oxford University Press, 2006), 312.

least weekly and often daily) was widespread throughout Bohemia."[30] This directly influenced the beginnings of the movement to reintroduce the eucharistic cup to the laity.[31]

To conclude, Christian worship in late medieval Europe involved a rich tapestry of opportunities to experience the spiritual power of the Eucharist, whether through actual oral reception, visual reception, or through one of the other substitutes such as the blessed bread, the priest's blessing, or the passing of the pax. Although there were various movements before the Reformation which advocated more frequent communion, the issue of communion reception took center stage in the Reformation.

2.3 Reforming Communion Frequency

The Reformers generally believed that both clergy and laity should receive both elements and should commune more frequently than in the past. Senn points out that the Reformers' beliefs about *who* should participate in the Eucharist gave the issue of frequency a greater urgency.[32] While some Reformers argued for weekly communion, other patterns prevailed.[33] However, most of the Reformers failed to persuade their communities to participate in communion as often as they wished: "In practice, general custom would lag far behind the theological aspirations of the reformers, and enforcing frequent communion would prove extremely difficult."[34]

Just as there was no uniform eucharistic theology among the Reformers, there was also variety in communion frequency in the emerging Protestant groups.[35] Calvin

---

30 Holeton, "The Bohemian Brethren," 312.

31 "Inspired by the pastoral success of the frequent-communion movement and supported by the extensive collections of texts—biblical, patristic, scholastic, and canonical—that had been compiled to justify it, some theologians (notably Jakoubek of Stříbo and Nicholas of Dresden) began promoting the restoration of the chalice to the laity." Holeton, "The Bohemian Brethren," 312–313.

32 He notes that the Reformers "all subscribed to the view that there should be no masses without communicants. So the frequency of reception of communion in the Reformation Churches became tied to the frequency of celebration of Holy Communion." Frank C. Senn, *A Stewardship of the Mysteries* (New York: Paulist Press, 1999), 99.

33 Euan C. Cameron summarizes: "Luther envisaged a regular weekly communion, as of old, though whether all the congregants were expected to take communion so often is doubtful. Zwingli expected the evangelical communion to be offered perhaps three or four times a year. Calvin saw a weekly communion as ideal, though it was hard to enforce this in practice. All deplored the Catholic custom of receiving only once a year, at Easter, and simply hearing Mass the rest of the time." *The European Reformation*, 190.

34 Cameron, *The European Reformation*, 190.

35 See Philip Benedict, *Christ's Churches Purely Reformed: A Social History of Calvinism* (New Haven: Yale University Press, 2002), 500–501, for a summary of the communion practices of various

did not achieve his stated desire for weekly communion, and the compromise that emerged in Geneva prescribed quarterly communion. As Benedict summarizes: "Communion three or four times a year became the norm in most other continental Reformed churches as well, although the sacrament was celebrated monthly in Basel, Nassau-Dillenberg, and among English and New England Congregationalists, and six times yearly in Hungary and certain Dutch cities."[36]

Thus, while there was no normative pattern for communion frequency among sixteenth century Protestants, the eucharistic theologies and practices of individual Reformers and the cities in which they ministered can be examined. The city councils—especially in Switzerland—often determined communion frequency, just as they legislated other aspects of the Reformation.

The next sections will examine the eucharistic views and practices of selected Reformers. It is by no means an exhaustive survey.[37] Rather, it attempts to sketch some of the main figures and distinctive features of the Reformed tradition that was then transmitted to England, Scotland, and the early American colonies.

European Reformed churches, especially in regard to receiving communion sitting or standing around a table.

36 Benedict, *Christ's Churches Purely Reformed*, 502.

37 One Reformer who deserves further study in this area is Peter Martyr Vermigli (1499–1562). Joseph C McClelland's foundational study claims that Vermigli was in favor of frequent communion: "Although Peter Martyr does not state so explicitly as Calvin that the Eucharist should be celebrated 'at least every Sunday', this is his constant presupposition." *The Visible Words of God: An Exposition of the Sacramental Theology of Peter Martyr Vermigli A.D. 1500-1562*, (Grand Rapids: Wm. B. Eerdmans, 1957), 255–256. McClelland focuses on Vermigli's teachings on liturgical almsgiving and maintains that Vermigli envisions this as occurring in the context of the weekly Eucharist. In his *Treatise on the Sacrament of the Eucharist* (1549) Vermigli does make a few statements regarding communion frequency: "Therefore whoever does not reject a holy life (I mean life eternal and most happy), must he not cherish the Eucharist above all things? Will he not embrace it as a sweet pledge of his salvation? Will he not use it in the congregation of the saints as often as it is given? Indeed he will, if he ponders these matters earnestly within himself." Vermigli, *The Oxford Treatise and Disputation on the Eucharist*, trans. and ed., Joseph C. McClelland, The Peter Martyr Library, ser. 1, v. 7, Sixteenth Century Essays & Studies, vol. 55 (Kirksville, MO: Truman State University Press, 2000), 11. He also censures the Catholic view of the Eucharist because it causes men to come to communion "less frequently." By contrast, Vermigli argues that "there is no profit [in the Eucharist] unless they communicate." Vermigli, *Treatise*, 44.

2.4   Johannes Oecolampadius (1482–1531)

Johannes Oecolampadius played a role in the reformations of both Augsburg and later Basel.[38] In Basel, at least, it seems that weekly communion was the ideal. In a letter to Sebastian Hubmaier (1525), Oecolampadius discusses infant baptism and describes his ideal eucharistic service. Writing about "De ritu coenae dominicae," he assumes the Eucharist has a regular place in worship and also manifests his strong desire to guard the purity of the Supper.[39] Oecolampadius was among the first of the Reformers to argue for "fencing" the table, a feature that Calvin and others implemented and enforced. This entailed warning their congregants about

---

38 See Gordon Rupp, *Patterns of Reform* (Philadelphia: Fortress Press, 1969), part I, for a helpful overview of Oecolampadius in English. Ernst Staehelin's works are still foundational. See his *Das Theologische Lebenswerk Johannes Oekolampads*, QFR 21 (New York: Johnson 1939), and his two volume *Briefe Und Akten Zum Leben Oekolampads: Zum Vierhundertjahrigen Jubilaum der Basler Reformation herausgegeben von der Theologischen Fakultät der Universität Basel*, QFR, Bd. 10, 19 (Leipzig, 1927; New York, London: Johnson, 1971). Also helpful are Ed L. Miller, "Oecolampadius: The Unsung Hero of the Basel Reformation," *Iliff Review* 39, no. 3 (Fall 1982): 5–24; Thomas A Fudge, "Icarus of Basel? Oecolampadius and the Early Swiss Reformation," *JRH* vol. 21, no. 3, (October 1997): 268–284; Nicholas Piotrowski, "Johannes Oecolampadius: Christology and the Supper," *MAJT* 23 (2012): 131–137; Jeff Fisher, "The State of Research of the Basel Reformer, Johannes Oecolampadius with a Focus on the History of Biblical Interpretation," (unpublished paper, 2009, accessed July 20, 2016. https://www.academia.edu/986421/The_State_of_Research_on_the_Basel_Reformer_John_Oecolampadius_1482-1531_with_a_Focus_on_the_History_of_Biblical_Interpretation) and Eric W. Northway, "The Reception of the Fathers & Eucharistic Theology in Johannes Oecolampadius (1482–1531), with Special Reference to the *Adversus Haereses* of Irenaeus of Lyons," PhD diss., (Durham University, 2008). Fisher also provides a helpful biography and summary of research in *A Christoscopic Reading of Scripture: Johannes Oecolampadius on Hebrews* (Göttingen: Vandenhoeck & Ruprecht, 2016), 13–32.

39 "After the confession, gospelling, hymns and prayers and after the Trisagion, I would have a period of silence appointed in which each might fervently meditate within himself on the Passion of the Lord. Then the words of the Lord's Supper appointed for the rite should be read publicly and intelligibly, and when these have been read, again a great silence for meditation and the giving of thanks. Afterwards should come the Lord's Prayer, and when this is over, the communicants should be summoned to the Lord's Supper, having first been admonished by the minister that each shall examine and judge himself. And if anybody is present who has been admonished by the Church the second or third time according to the Lord's command he should be repelled from the table until there is sure proof of his penitence, and he is reconciled. Then when they have received communion with the exhortation to charity and care of the poor, the congregation might depart in peace." Rupp, *Patterns of Reform*, 26, translating from the original in Staehelin, ed., *Briefe und Akten zum Leben Oekolampads*, vol. I, QFR 10, no. 239: Jan. 18, 1525. Staehelin points out that, at the time of writing, Oecolampadius was still a "Predigtvikar" and did not have any real influence over the order of the Mass or Lord's Supper. However, the letter does give us a record of Oeoclampadius' ideals, which he tried to implement later in Basel.

the dangers of coming to communion without repentance, as well as barring the unrepentant from participation.

According to Philip Schaff, when Protestant worship was officially established in Basel (April, 1529), this included "weekly communion in one of the city churches," although Schaff does not explain this further.[40] Nelson Burnett clarifies that urban and rural churches in the region of Basel held communion three times a year, at Christmas, Easter, and Pentecost. In the city itself "it was held in one of the four parish churches" in a weekly rotating cycle.[41] Olaf Kuhr argues that this Basel *Reformation Ordinance* of 1529 possibly influenced Farel and Calvin's 1537 *Articles concerning the Organization of the Church and of Worship*, which they submitted to the Genevan town council.[42]

Later periods of Basel's history also provide evidence about communion practices. In 1543, some Zurichers visited Basel and then reported to Bullinger that the cathedral preacher Oswald Myconius was teaching a deviant doctrine of the Lord's Supper. Bullinger sent a concerned letter to Myconius, who then responded with a written sermon, protesting his orthodoxy. In this context, Burnett mentions that "[s]ince the Lord's Supper was celebrated monthly in the cathedral, Myconius had frequent opportunity to preach on the sacrament, and so, with regard to its doctrinal content, Myconius's sermon can be assumed to be an accurate representation of his teaching."[43] Thus, whatever the actual practice in 1529, it seems that by 1543, monthly communion was the norm, at least in the cathedral where Myconius preached. Additionally, pastors in the rural areas around Basel struggled to convince their parishioners to attend communion even three times a year because the late medieval pattern of annual communion at Easter continued to dominate. Pastors endeavored to bring their people to more frequent communion throughout the

---

40 Philip Schaff, *History of the Christian Church*, vol. VIII, 3rd ed., rev. (Charles Scribner's Sons, 1910; reprint, Grand Rapids: Wm. B. Eerdmans Publishing Company, 1977), 114.

41 Amy Nelson Burnett, "The Social History of Communion and the Reformation of the Eucharist," *Past & Present*, no. 211 (2011): 114, citing the Basel *Reformation Ordinance* of 1529 in *Aktensammlung zur Geschichte der Basler Reformation in den Jahren 1519 bis Anfang 1534*, 6 vols., ed. Emil Dürr and Paul Roth (Basel: Verlag der historischen und antiquarischen Gesellschaft Universitätsbibliothek Basel, 1921–50), vol. 3, Nr. 473, 395–96.

42 Olaf Kuhr, "Calvin and Basel: The Significance of Oecolampadius and the Basel Discipline Ordinance for the Institution of Ecclesiastical Discipline in Geneva," *Scottish Bulletin of Evangelical Theology* 16 (1998): 23. Kuhr also points out other striking similarities between the documents, which suggest clear lines of influence from Basel to Geneva. For more detail, see Kuhr, *Die Macht des Bannes und der Busse: Kirchenzucht und Erneuerung der Kirche bei Johannes Oekolampad (1482 – 1531)* (Bern New York: P. Lang, 1999).

43 Amy Nelson Burnett, *Teaching the Reformation: Ministers and Their Message in Basel, 1529-1629* (Oxford: Oxford University Press, 2006), 61.

1500s and into the early 1600s, when they began to see more increased attendance at communions.[44]

2.5   Martin Bucer (1491–1551)

To understand the Strasbourg reformer Martin Bucer, it is important to remember that Bucer wrote in a time before confessional lines had hardened.[45] Bucer was not simply a proto-ecumenist, willing to go to endless lengths to gain eucharistic agreement. Bucer's thought developed in response to political and ecclesiastical realities.[46] However, it is also true that Bucer often confused others, and James Kittelson suggests that Bucer may not have totally understood his own eucharistic opinions.[47] Nevertheless, Bucer was firmly committed to the doctrine of justification

---

44 Nelson Burnett, *Teaching the Reformation*, 244.

45 See Nicholas Thompson, "Martin Bucer," *A Companion to the Eucharist in the Reformation*, 75–95 for an overview, as well as the careful study of Ian Hazlett, "The Development of Martin Bucer's Thinking on the Sacrament of the Lord's Supper in its Historical and Theological Context," PhD diss., (Westfälische Wilhelms-Universität zu Münster, 1975). Peter Matheson also helpfully elucidates the motivations and priorities driving Bucer's efforts of reform and ecumenical mediation in "Martin Bucer and the Old Church," D. F. Wright, ed., *Martin Bucer: Reforming Church and Community*, 5–16. G.J. van de Poll notes the specific nature of Bucer's eucharistic thought, as well as the close link between church discipline and communion for Bucer: "Bucer's attitudes towards the opposing parties in the Supper-strife of the sixteenth century cannot be described as merely conciliatory, in search of a formula which could be accepted by both parties; on the contrary, we are here confronted with a third factor in the Protestant doctrine on the Eucharist, in which Bucer gradually developed a doctrine that distinctly loosened itself from Luther and Zwingli. This development, the traces of which we [see] in his liturgy, must be seen in close connection with the development of his church-, discipline- and office conception." *Martin Bucer's Liturgical Ideas: The Strasbourg Reformer and His Connection with the Liturgies of the Sixteenth Century* (Assen: Koninklijke Van Gorcum, 1954), 81.

46 Nicholas Thompson summarizes: "If we are to understand Bucer's eucharistic theology properly, we have to remember that he worked and wrote as confessional boundaries were *beginning* to harden. Because he did not take a permanent schism for granted, he was ready to engage in verbal and theological experiments that seemed tendentious, and even dishonest, to later generations of confessionalized Protestants. However, if his eucharistic thought is understood in its historical context and in close connection with his broad ecclesiology, it will be seen to have its own integrity" ("Martin Bucer," 95). See also Ian Hazlett, "Bucer" in *The Cambridge Companion to Reformation Theology*, David Bagchi and David C. Steinmetz, eds. (Cambridge: Cambridge University Press, 2004; reprint 2013), 105–107, for the theological and epistemological commitments underlying Bucer's ecumenical efforts.

47 James Kittelson, *Toward an Established Church: Strasbourg from 1500 to the Dawn of the Seventeenth Century* (Mainz: Verlag Philipp von Zabern, 2000), 50. For more on Bucer's development and influence see John W. Riggs, *The Lord's Supper in the Reformed Tradition*, Columbia Series in Reformed Theology (Louisville: Westminster John Knox: 2015), 74–80 and Amy Nelson Burnett,

by faith and was willing to tolerate differences in the understanding and practice of the Lord's Supper.[48]

There are indications that Bucer desired weekly communion, but only partially succeeded in attaining this ideal.[49] Bruno Bürki argues that, in Strasbourg, Bucer had to settle for a system of rotating Eucharists, so that each parish church would celebrate the Supper on every fourth Sunday. However, the cathedral where Bucer pastored held the Supper every week.[50] Nichols also suggests that Bucer tried to institute weekly communion, though unsuccessfully.[51] Hughes Oliphant Old concurs.[52] This is confirmed by several different lines of evidence.

First, in *Grund und Ursach* (1524), Bucer and the other pastors of Strasbourg propose a Sunday liturgy in which the observance of the Lord's Table appears to be normative and assumed.[53] The Strasbourg Reformers stress that the sacrament should only be held on Sundays, when the whole congregation can gather together,

---

"The Myth of the Swiss Lutherans: Martin Bucer and the Eucharistic Controversy in Bern," *Zwingliana* 32 (2005): 45–70.

48 According to Thompson: "Bucer did not regard the Eucharist as a central article of Christian faith. Thus he did not require his theological counterparts to agree with him on the finer details of sacramental theology, provided they were united on the 'chief article,' the doctrine of justification. For Bucer this meant not only God's forensic justification of undeserving sinners, but also their growth in love of God and neighbor. The resulting 'edification' of a community in love meant that a genuinely catholic church must tolerate the weakness of those who had saving faith in Christ but had not come to a fuller knowledge of the truth revealed in scripture" ("Martin Bucer," 75–76). See also Brian Lugioyo, *Martin Bucer's Doctrine of Justification: Reformation Theology and Early Modern Irenicism* (Oxford: Oxford University Press, 2010).

49 Howard Hageman claims that the "Strasbourg liturgy of 1538 still held to the weekly service of Word and Sacrament" but does not offer any sources for this assertion. See *Pulpit and Table: Some Chapters in the History of Worship in the Reformed Churches* (1962; repr., Eugene: Wipf and Stock Publishers, 2004), 25.

50 Bruno Bürki, "The Reformed Tradition in Continental Europe," in *The Oxford History of Christian Worship*, 442. See also Bard Thompson, *Liturgies of the Western Church* (1961; reprint, Philadelphia: Fortress Press, 1980), 160–61 and Nelson Burnett, "The Social History of Communion and the Reformation of the Eucharist," 114, citing *Martin Bucers Deutsche Schriften*, ed. Robert Stupperich et al., 17 vols. (Gütersloh, 1960-), v, 32–3.

51 James Hastings Nichols, *Corporate Worship in the Reformed Tradition*, (Philadelphia: The Westminster Press, 1968), 56. He also notes: "But the Eucharistic order remained, even when it was reduced by lack of congregational participation to a 'dry Mass.' The minister conducted the service, with the exception of the reading and preaching of the Word, from the table." This detail is important to remember, especially when considering claims that the Reformed service became simply a "preaching service."

52 Hughes Oliphant Old, *Holy Communion in the Piety of the Reformed Church*, ed. Jon Payne (Powder Springs, GA: Tolle Lege Press, 2013), 25.

53 Bard Thompson, *Liturgies of the Western Church*, 161–62. There are questions of authorship, however. Regarding *Grund und Ursach*, Hazlett notes that while it "was officially a collective publication of the Strasbourg preachers explaining their reforms in detail," there is fairly certain evidence that Bucer

as opposed to the previous practice of priests saying the mass and communing every day by themselves.[54] They acknowledge that there are "some truly pious men, well versed in Scripture, who prefer that the Lord's Supper should be observed rarely," and they realize that some people do not feel worthy to partake, which they attribute to the "old, erroneous belief."[55] However, they maintain that the only thing required is "that one should believe he has been redeemed by the death of Christ, and desire only to be strengthened by God in such a faith, and in love for the neighbor."[56] They state quite strongly "[t]his is the interpretation which every Christian should hold when he goes to the Lord's Supper *as often as it is served*, and if he does not hold this interpretation, then he is not a true Christian ..." (italics added).[57] This leads to the next reason the Strasbourg ministers advocated the whole congregation gathering and partaking together—the ban.

For the sixteenth century Reformers, the question of proper communion was paramount. Accordingly, *Grund und Ursach* also proposes instituting the "Christian ban," to exclude the unrepentant from both the Supper and the Christian fellowship.[58] Although Bucer and the other Strasbourg pastors present this as their ideal, they also display pastoral wisdom and acknowledge that not everyone felt comfortable enough, or worthy enough, to take communion every Sunday. Additionally, they recommend discouraging some people from partaking for a time, until they have more exposure to correct preaching of the Word. They look forward to further reformation and leading from God, where the church can more closely approach the ideal of weekly communion.[59]

Third, further evidence about communion frequency in Strasbourg comes from a French college student studying there in 1525. He wrote to the Bishop of Meaux, describing a Sunday morning worship service which included the sacrament of communion. He gives no indication that this is unusual, or different from a typical

---

"composed at least the sections on the Lord's Supper." "The Development of Martin Bucer's Thinking on the Sacrament," 85.

54 They write, "the Lord's Supper is a bond of Christian community through which we, like Christ, that is through Him and for His sake, have all things in common, and so it has been customary with us to observe the Lord's Supper only on Sundays when the whole congregation partake with the minister." Ottomar Fredrick Cypris, "Basic Principles: Translation and Commentary of Martin Bucer's *Grund und Ursach*, 1524," Th.D. diss., (Union Theological Seminary, 1971), 141. Original text is found in *BDS* I:194–278.

55 Cypris, "Basic Principles," 144–145.

56 Cypris, "Basic Principles," 144.

57 Cypris, "Basic Principles," 144, italics added.

58 Cypris, "Basic Principles," 145.

59 Cypris, "Basic Principles," 146–149. See also Nelson Burnett's commentary on *Grund und Ursach*, in *The Yoke of Christ: Martin Bucer and Christian Discipline* (Kirksville: Sixteenth Century Publishers, 1994), 28–29.

Sunday service.[60] Additionally, in 1530, Bucer produced the *Confessio Tetrapolitana* or *Vierstädtebekenntnis*, aided by Wolfgang Capito and Caspar Hedio, to submit to Emperor Charles V at the Imperial Diet of Augsburg.[61] The Tetrapolitan Confession represented Strasbourg, Constance, Memmingen, and Lindau, and defended the reforms undertaken in those cities. In Chapter 15, "Of the Eucharist," the authors make a brief mention of how the reforms in their cities entail more frequent communions than before.[62]

Finally, Bucer's ideal of frequent communion also surfaces in some of his works, such as his *Brief Statement or Instruction on How the Sick should be Visited by the Ministers of the Church and the Procedure to be Followed in their Homes*. Although the precise date of composition is unknown, scholars believe it was written before Bucer's exile to England in 1549.[63] Regarding the Supper and its reception by the sick, Bucer writes that we "should receive these his great and precious gifts as frequently as possible with sincere devotion and utter thankfulness," although he does not specify exactly what he means by "frequently."[64] In his last book, *De Regno Christi*, published in 1557, Bucer maintains that churches have the right to order their elements and forms of worship—including the sacraments—in the way they

---

60 William Maxwell, *The Liturgical Portions of the Genevan Service Book* (Westminster: Faith Press, 1931; 1965), 29–30.

61 See James T. Dennison, Jr., ed., *Reformed Confessions of the 16th and 17th Centuries in English Translation: Volume 1, 1523–1552* (Grand Rapids: Reformation Heritage Press, 2008), 137–139 for the background and context of the confession.

62 "For with the greatest earnestness our men always teach and exhort that every man with simple faith embrace these words of the Lord, rejecting all devices and false glosses of men, and removing all wavering, apply his mind to their true meaning, and finally, with as great devotion as possible, receive these sacraments for the quickening nourishment of their souls and the grateful remembrance of so great a benefit; as is generally done now among us more frequently and devoutly than heretofore." Dennison, Jr., ed., *Reformed Confessions of the 16th and 17th Centuries in English Translation: Volume 1, 1523–1552*, 159.

63 See D.F. Wright's introduction in *Common Places of Martin Bucer* (Abingdon: Sutton Courtenay Press, 1972), 429.

64 Wright, ed., *Common Places of Martin Bucer*, 433. See also Wim Janse, 'Controversy and Concordance between Calvin and Westphal on the Communion of the Sick,' in: *Calvinus clarissimus theologus. Papers of the Tenth International Congress on Calvin Research* (Göttingen: Vandenhoeck & Ruprecht, 2012), 159–179, footnotes 42 and 48. According to Janse, "Calvin must have recognized his own thoughts in Westphal's criticism. He had become acquainted with sick-bed communion, and learned to value it, probably as early as his stay in Basel in 1535–1536, certainly in Strasbourg 1538–1540. There, unlike Basel, the ceremony was linked to the (monthly) celebration of the Eucharist: on the same day that the congregation celebrated the sacrament a deacon was deputized to visit the sick, together with some members of the congregation." 42.

deem best, appealing to 1 Cor. 14:40 and its stress on doing everything "decently and in order."[65]

Although Bucer greatly valued the Eucharist, communion frequency was not the main goal of his reforming efforts—*pure* and *proper* communion dominated Bucer's writings. In his "Brief Summary of Christian Doctrine," prepared in 1548 to distinguish the Strasbourg reform from both Anabaptist teaching as well as the Catholic-friendly Augsburg *Interim* of 1548, Bucer does not mention the issue of frequency at all.[66] On the contrary, he stresses the need for proper preparation to receive communion.[67] Like most early modern theologians, he focuses on the theological and metaphysical nature of the Eucharist, rather than how often it should be observed.[68]

Additionally, like other sixteenth-century Reformers, Bucer worked within a context where he had to gain the approval and support of local city governments.[69] Because the magisterial Reformers believed that the civil magistrates held an authority given to them by God, this created an expectation that the civil authorities would, in turn, seek to govern according to God's revealed will. Thus, even if various Reformers believed that more frequent communion was expedient and desirable,

---

65 "In this matter, Christ's churches must have their freedom so that each may define the content and method of presentation of sacred readings, interpretations of Scriptures, catechizing, administration of the sacraments, prayers and psalms, and similarly the public correction of sinners, imposition of penance, and reconciliation for those who have satisfied the churches by doing penance, all in such a way as each church judges to be of greatest profit for its people, so that as a result of these activities they may be moved to a true and living repentance, and strengthened and advanced in the faith of Christ." Bucer, *De Regno Christi*, in *Melanchthon and Bucer*, Wilhelm Pauck, ed., (Philadelphia: The Westminster Press, 1969), 256.

66 Wright gives the full English title as "A Brief Summary of the Christian Doctrine and Religion Taught at Strasbourg for the Past Twenty Eight Years, together with a Reply from the Preachers of Strasbourg to a Defamatory Writing Accusing them without a Shadow of Truth of the Spirit and Teaching of the Anabaptists; and [the question] Who is Competent to Reform the External Ceremonies of Divine Worship" in *Common Places of Martin Bucer*, D.F. Wright, ed., 75; original title: *Ein Summarischer vergriff der Christlichen lehre vnd Religion die man zu Strasburg hat nun in die xxviij jar gelehret...* (Strasbourg: Wendelin Rihel, 1548).

67 "The minister, following the example and command of our dear Lord, should there prepare the participants in all seriousness and with true devotion, by means of straightforward instruction derived from the holy Scripture, to partake of the holy sacraments. (To this end it has long been the practice to read to the people the writings of the prophets, apostles and evangelists.)" Wright, ed., *Common Places of Martin Bucer*, 86.

68 Wright, ed., *Common Places of Martin Bucer*, 87.

69 Martin Greschat discusses Bucer's conception of church and the civil government in "The Relation Between Church and Civil Community in Bucer's Reforming Work," in Wright, ed., *Martin Bucer: Reforming Church and Community*, 17–31. See also Bernd Moeller, *Imperial Cities and the Reformation: Three Essays*, ed. and trans. H.C. Erik Midelfort and Mark U. Edwards, Jr. (Fortress Press, 1972; Durham, NC: Labyrinth Press, 1982).

this belief was held in check by their desire to work within the boundaries of the God-ordained civil authorities. Yet, the Reformers were not simply passive subjects, waiting for the civil authorities to act. Greschat points out that Bucer developed and "adapted" his theology of the state very specifically to give the authorities of Augsburg license to implement reform, and also to reject the alternatives of Sebastian Franck's "spiritualist" separation of church and state, as well as to oppose the Catholic resistance to change.[70] Additionally, Willem van 't Spijker demonstrates how the necessity of ecclesiastical discipline gradually assumed greater importance in Bucer's thought. He also shows that, while Bucer did not succeed in fully implementing his ideals of discipline, John Calvin did, during his pastorate of the French exiles in Strasbourg.[71] This is important to note because the issue of preparation for communion and church discipline played an increasingly important role in Reformed discussions of communion frequency.

2.6   Huldrych Zwingli (1484–1531)

It is difficult to separate the Zwingli of later interpreters from the historical Zwingli.[72] It is especially difficult for English speakers, since so few of his works have been translated. Nevertheless, an attempt must be made, because of Zwingli's foundational importance in the Reformed tradition, and because of his lasting influence in the issue of communion frequency.

Gordon Wakefield provides a typical summary of Zwingli's order for the Lord's Supper: "The Zwinglian rite is bare, lacking the numinous, with no heavenly dimension, nor sense of the communion of saints. There is no consecration, no intercessions. No longer is Communion the Sunday service. It is confined to four times a year. And communion is to be received sitting, a practice which originated with Zwingli."[73] This is a somewhat dim view but is a common characterization.[74]

---

70 Greschat, "Relation," 21.

71 Willem van 't Spijker, "Bucer's influence on Calvin: church and community," in D. F. Wright, ed., *Martin Bucer*, 35–41. In this instance, van 't Spijker describes a relationship of "mutual influences" between Bucer and Calvin, 40.

72 B.A. Gerrish helpfully summarizes the differences between Luther and Zwingli in their understanding of "sign" as applied to the Eucharist, while interacting with two innovative interpreters of Zwingli (Julius Schweizer and Jacques Courvoisier). See "Discerning the Body: Sign and Reality in Luther's Controversy with the Swiss" in Gerrish, *Continuing the Reformation: Essays on Modern Religious Thought* (Chicago: University of Chicago Press, 1993), 57–75.

73 Gordon S. Wakefield, *An Outline of Christian Worship* (Edinburgh: T&T Clark, 1998), 73.

74 Hageman also has no sympathy for Zwingli: "The divorce of Word and Sacrament, the transformation of the Sunday service into a sermon, the quarterly celebration of the Supper—these were Zwingli's deliberate design, a cultus derived directly from his creed. In it he has left a lasting mark on the

Alternatively, Wandel points out the positive features of Zwingli's liturgy: "Zwingli called for a fundamental rethinking of the function of the Eucharist and formulated a liturgy in which the congregation participated actively, both vocally and in the action of Communion itself: in taking the bread in their own hands, in breaking off pieces, and themselves putting the bread in their mouths."[75] In contrast to Luther's liturgy, where the clergy retained control of the elements and placed them in the mouths of the people, Zwingli created a liturgy where the people participated more. Jim West notes how unusual it was for Zwingli to give the women in the church a prescribed role in the communion service, when he wrote a liturgy which proposed men and women alternatively reciting portions of the liturgy.[76]

Bard Thompson also describes Zwingli's eucharistic liturgy positively:

> Whatever defects there may have been in Zwingli's eucharistic theology and liturgy, the occasion was anything but a bare memorial. The Zurich liturgy of 1535 spoke of it as 'a great holy mystery.' Not in much speaking or teaching, not in a profusion of ceremonies, but in monumental simplicity and stillness, this liturgy gave expression to the central affirmations of Zwingli's eucharistic theology: contemplation, fellowship, thanksgiving, and moral earnestness.[77]

As with many other Reformers, one cannot easily summarize Zwingli's eucharistic theology.[78] Later assessments of Zwingli tend to focus on what Zwingli denied,

---

worship of all the Reformed churches." *Pulpit and Table*, 21. Horton is slightly more charitable: "One's view of the efficacy of Communion largely determines one's views concerning frequency. It is not surprising that a more Zwinglian approach, which emphasizes the subjectivity of the believer and the community, will yield a more introspective Eucharistic practice. To the extent that the Supper is considered a divine gift, its frequent celebration is likely to be affirmed." *People and Place*, 137.

75 Lee Palmer Wandel, *The Eucharist in the Reformation* (Cambridge: Cambridge University Press, 2006), 74.

76 Jim West, introduction to *Huldrych Zwingli: The Implementation of the Lord's Supper* (Occasional Publications of the Pitts Theological Library), http://pitts.emory.edu/files/publications/ZwingliLordsSupper.pdf, 5, accessed December 29, 2016.

77 Bard Thompson, *Liturgies of the Western Church*, 146. D.H. Tripp also provides a more balanced summary of Zwingli: "He did not, in his own mind, reduce the Eucharist to a mere act of remembrance, but affirmed a spiritual impartation of Christ in the sacramental action, although his doctrine was never clear to Luther (nor to many others, in his own time and since). He also introduced a new emphasis on the Eucharist as an act of fellowship, in which Anabaptist influence may perhaps be seen." "Protestantism and the Eucharist," in Chelsyn Jones, Geoffrey Wainwright, and Edward J. Yarnold, eds., *The Study of Liturgy* (New York: Oxford University Press, 1978), 255.

78 Carrie Euler, "Huldrych Zwingli and Heinrich Bullinger," *A Companion to the Eucharist in the Reformation*, 57–74.

rather than what he affirmed.[79] Zwingli heavily emphasized the "communal and commemorative function of the sacraments."[80] He often uses the word *commemoratio* because communion was a "reenactment" of the Last Supper, and it was "a ritual that brought the Christian community together."[81] With this understanding, observing communion infrequently might actually serve a positive purpose. To celebrate communion four times a year would highlight its distinction from both Catholics and Anabaptists and would also "reinforce the communal nature of the sacrament."[82] So it seems inaccurate to characterize Zwingli's view as "mere memorialism." As Bruce Gordon summarizes: "Zwingli's liturgical drama was far more powerful than a mere act of memory; it was a profound and largely traditional expression of the command to imitate Christ."[83]

After a detailed summary of how various scholars have interpreted Zwingli, Riggs concludes: "A general summary of secondary scholarship on Zwingli's eucharistic theology would be that no one should assume that Zwingli was merely a 'memorialist.'" He clarifies further: "Characterizing Zwingli as memorialist must be carefully shown and not merely assumed."[84] In regard to communion frequency, Zwingli's views appear to have developed over time—a statement that is perilously close to a platitude when discussing the Reformers, but it bears repetition since they have so often been treated as static figures, opposed to each other and their various opponents in polemical works.[85]

Zwingli's first venture into liturgical revision resulted in the *De canone missae epicheiresis*, published in 1523. Nathan Mitchell highlights Zwingli's liturgical creativity, as well as his fidelity to the catholic tradition in the *Epicheiresis*. Zwingli composed four original eucharistic prayers and combined them with the standard

---

79 According to Euler, "It is true that Zwingli and his followers interpreted the "This is my body" figuratively (to mean "This *signifies* my body") and denied all possibility of a corporeal presence in the bread and the wine, but they never believed the Supper to be an "empty" ritual, devoid of emotional or spiritual impact." She also notes that, at the end of his life, Zwingli was moving towards a "more positive notion" of what the Eucharist was, "a communal and spiritual eating of Christ that could strengthen faith." ("Huldrych Zwingli and Heinrich Bullinger"), 58.

80 Euler, "Huldrych Zwingli and Heinrich Bullinger," 59.

81 Euler, "Huldrych Zwingli and Heinrich Bullinger," 62.

82 Euler, "Huldrych Zwingli and Heinrich Bullinger," 63. She adds: "(The more frequently it was celebrated, the less likely the entire community would participate each time.)" This is a common sentiment in discussions about communion frequency.

83 Bruce Gordon, *The Swiss Reformation* (Manchester: Manchester UP, 2002), 67.

84 Riggs, *The Lord's Supper in the Reformed Tradition*, 58.

85 "Scholarship has generally accepted an approach to Zwingli's eucharistic theology that divides his work into three periods: his early writings up to 1524, prior to the controversies with Luther; a middle period running from Zwingli's letter to Alber (1524) up to (or, for some scholars, through) the Colloquy at Marburg (1529); and a final period from Marburg through Zwingli's death (1529–31)," Riggs, *The Lord's Supper*, 58.

preface and Sanctus.[86] However, in Zwingli's later reforms, the centrality of the Eucharist was replaced by an emphasis on the faithful participation of the believing community.[87] In the *Aktion oder Brauch des Nachtmahls* (1525) Zwingli states "[w]e will follow this practice, as far as it will please our churches, four times a year, namely, Easter, Pentecost, harvest time, and Christmas."[88] In fairness to Zwingli, it should be noted that even this scheme of infrequent communion was more frequent than his congregation was used to: "The Eucharist would be held four times a year (four times as often as medieval laity had been obliged to communicate)."[89]

However, this does not mean there was no sense of communion in the Zurich observances of the Lord's Table. Peter Opitz claims that Zwingli has unfairly been viewed primarily through the lens of his controversy with Luther, which complicates the task of understanding Zwingli's broader theology of the Eucharist.[90] Zwingli states that the ceremonies prescribed in *Aktion oder Brauch des Nachtmahls* are "beneficial and fit for the human heart in fostering the spiritual remembrance of Christ's death, the increase of faith and brotherly fidelity, the improvement of life, and the prevention of depravity."[91] According to Opitz "[t]he center of Zwingli's theology of the Lord's Supper was, that the present congregation, gathered around the Lord's table, hears the 'living invitation of God' and therefore will be at the right place, to get a living experience of the presence of God and of salvation."[92]

---

86 "Ironically, then, it was Zwingli the 'symbolist' who (…), preserved the eucharistic prayer tradition familiar to Catholics. Indeed, taken together (as they were meant to be), Zwingli's four prayers created a strikingly good anaphora resembling classic models such as the Liturgy of St. James." Nathan D. Mitchell, "Reforms, Protestant and Catholic," in Geoffrey Wainwright and Karen Westerfield Tucker, eds., *The Oxford History of Christian Worship*, 324.

87 Mitchell, "Reforms, Protestant and Catholic," 324.

88 West, ed., *Huldrych Zwingli: The Implementation of the Lord's Supper* http://pitts.emory.edu/files/publications/ZwingliLordsSupper.pdf, 8, accessed December 12, 2016.

89 D.H. Tripp, "Protestantism and the Eucharist," 255.

90 Peter Opitz, "At the Table of the Lord: To Zwingli's View on the Lord's Supper," 1, accessed December 12, 2016, https://www.academia.edu/5802889/At_the_Table_of_the_Lord_To_Zwinglis_View_on_the_Lords_Supper.

91 West, ed., *Huldrych Zwingli: The Implementation of the Lord's Supper* http://pitts.emory.edu/files/publications/ZwingliLordsSupper.pdf, 7, accessed December 12, 2016.

92 Opitz, "At the Table of the Lord," 1–2. See also Wim Janse: "To Zwingli, the Holy Supper was, in order: a commemorative meal (*Gedächtnismahl*), an emphasizing of the brotherly communion (*Gemeinschaftsmahl* in a horizontal sense: *communio sanctorum*), and a pledge or oath of faith and allegiance to Christ (a confessional and a commitment meal). For the latter aspect Zwingli used the beautiful term *Pflichtzeichen* (literally: "pledge sign"). The *Pflichtzeichen* was the oath that Swiss mercenary soldiers, whose military allegiance changed every year, swore on the colours of the war lord who had enlisted their services, as a pledge to do battle on his behalf only. This was how Zwingli liked to see the Holy Supper: as a *distinctivum* or a sign by which the participants distinguished themselves from the world, and committed themselves to the service of Christ," "Calvin's Doctrine of the Lord's Supper," *Perichoresis*, vol. 10, Issue 2 (2012): 141.

Nelson Burnett has drawn attention to the historical context of Zwingli's plan for communion, especially in relation to the Anabaptist movement. She argues that quarterly communion reinforced the "communal aspect" of the Lord's Supper in Zurich.[93] Significantly:

> Up until May 1524 Zwingli had still accepted the idea that the Lord's Supper could be held after any regular preaching service for those who desired to communicate. His adoption of a more restricted celebration of the Lord's Supper was done in reaction to the separation of the Anabaptists from the Zurich Church, especially as this break was demonstrated by their private practice of communion.[94]

The Zurich Anabaptists started holding communion in a simplified ceremony that emphasized the unity of their community. They also desired to establish more frequent communion, along with implementing the disciplinary procedures of Matthew 18.[95] For the Anabaptists, their observance of the Supper both clearly defined who was part of their fellowship and emphasized their separation from the rest of the wider Zurich community. Their communions were both frequent and private, held in homes.[96] Nelson Burnett suggests that Zwingli's plan of quarterly communion was a direct response to the Anabaptist movement. It would "publicly demonstrate the unity of the entire *Gemeinde* as both ecclesiastical and civil community."[97] As laid out by Zwingli: "Individuals could communicate only on those days specified by the leaders of Church and State, and always together with everyone else from the community. The Lord's Supper according to the Zurich liturgy was a public statement of Christian and communal identity in the face of Anabaptist separatism."[98]

Along the same lines, Opitz maintains that the doctrine of "reconciliation" is foundational for Zwingli's eucharistic theology. Because we are reconciled with Christ, through faith, we are brought into a powerful dramatization, and actualization, of this spiritual reality in the Supper. Through the rituals of eating and drinking with each other, and through passing the bread around by hand—which was revolutionary at the time—the Supper brings about reconciliation among the church community.[99] This visual symbolism and its practical ramifications would

---

93 Nelson Burnett, "The Social History of Communion and the Reformation of the Eucharist," 112–13.

94 Nelson Burnett, "The Social History of Communion and the Reformation of the Eucharist," 113.

95 Nelson Burnett, "The Social History of Communion and the Reformation of the Eucharist," 113.

96 Nelson Burnett, "The Social History of Communion and the Reformation of the Eucharist," 113.

97 Nelson Burnett, "The Social History of Communion and the Reformation of the Eucharist," 113.

98 Nelson Burnett, "The Social History of Communion and the Reformation of the Eucharist," 114.

99 Opitz, "At the Table of the Lord," 3. Also, "Zwingli names what happens during the Lord's Supper, a 'realization' or an 'assurance' of the reconciliation of the person with God. The Lord's Supper is

mitigate against any understanding of the Supper as a sacrificial act, or any view that exalted the pastor above the people in a mediatory role.

Opitz summarizes the sense of "horizontal" communion that characterized Zwingli's communion service:

> A real living experience of God's salvation cannot be produced by men, neither by bishops nor by Reformed church leaders. But it can be expected, where it is promised. The aim of Zwingli's liturgy of the Lord's Supper was exactly this. And the table was the point where the vertical, spiritual dimension, and the horizontal, human dimension, could meet. The reproach of 'spiritualizing' the Lord's Supper may be correct in some cases, but certainly not in the case of Huldrych Zwingli.[100]

Whatever the extent of the development in Zwingli's thought, it did not affect communion frequency in Zurich. The Zurich churches continued to observe communion four times a year throughout Zwingli's time there. After Zwingli's death, the Zurich theological tradition continued developing, although perhaps in ways Zwingli would not have condoned. However, it is important to separate the actual ideas of Zwingli from the later trajectory that some of his ideas may have taken. Although Zwingli and his practice at Zurich may fall short from the ideals of proponents of frequently communion, it is still true that it was a major achievement to institute quarterly communion in a context that was used to annual communion.

---

thus a celebration of an event that has occurred and is therefore essentially a thankful, joyful and confessional meal." 4. See also Opitz, "The Swiss Contribution to the Reformation Movement": "Zwingli's communion liturgy provided that the bread be passed around in the community and that everyone break off a piece thereof. This was a revolution in view of the sacramental piety of that time, which was deeply rooted in the church's liturgical life as well as in the perception of the general public. Zwingli justified this rite with the following argument: if everyone passes the bread on to the next person, it may bring about reconciliation between two antagonized neighbours during the communion. Therefore, communion would have induced something important as a meal of reconciliation. By the same token, Zwingli argued against the exclusion from communion: the Lord's supper as a celebration of reconciliation could also be a place where impenitent sinners may return and repent. Therefore, nobody should be excluded from partaking in communion." 5, accessed December 12, 2016, https://www.academia.edu/15358770/The_Swiss_Contribution_to_the_Reformation_Movement.

100 Opitz, "At the Table of the Lord," 8.

2.7   Heinrich Bullinger (1504–1575)

As Zwingli's successor as the Antistes (head) of the Zurich church Heinrich Bullinger saw himself as the guardian of Zwingli's memory and legacy.[101] Although at one time Bullinger was eclipsed by other Reformers, scholars continue to find evidence of his immense influence. His published works far out-stripped Zwingli's, and Bullinger commanded respect and influence in the international Protestant community, especially through his theological works and expansive letter-writing network.[102] Especially relevant to the purposes of this study is Bullinger's impressive position of respect and influence among the English Reformers, and thus on the American Reformed churches.[103] Additionally, since many English Marian exiles took refuge in Zurich, it seems reasonable that Zurich's communion practices would take on an idealized status, perhaps as a standard to judge the English church. What were Bullinger's views, and what was Zurich's communion frequency pattern during his ministry there?

Bullinger addresses communion frequency in his *Decades*. The Decades were translated into English in three editions (1577, 1584, and 1587) and circulated widely in England.[104] The Fifth Decade is devoted to the topic of the sacraments and discusses communion frequency directly in the ninth sermon.[105] Bullinger

---

101 Bruce Gordon, "Introduction," in *Architect of Reformation: An Introduction to Heinrich Bullinger, 1504–1575*, ed. Gordon and Emidio Campi (Grand Rapids: Baker Academic, 2004), 24.

102 Bruce Gordon writes: "By the time of his passing he was one of the best-known reformers in Europe. The extent of his international network of contacts is indicated by the 12,000 letters that have survived and are being edited in Zurich ... Bullinger corresponded with the leading reformers of England, France, the Empire, Eastern Europe, the Netherlands, and Scandinavia. Many of his correspondents, such as those in England, had stayed in his house as religious refugees whilst others simply knew him as the wise patriarch of the Reformed church." *Architect of Reformation*, 21. See also Benedict, *Christ's Churches Purely Reformed*, 59–60 for Bullinger's published literary output and 63–65, for a summary of his letter-writing influence.

103 "Many of Queen Elizabeth's first generation of bishops had had direct experience of Zurich and kept in regular contact with Bullinger and his associates, writing urgently for advice about the issues troubling their church and receiving a steady stream of counsel in return." Benedict, *Christ's Churches Purely Reformed*, 64. Additionally, Archbishop Whitgift made Bullinger's *Decades* "required reading for a large class of the clergy (1586)." John T. McNeill, *The History and Character of Calvinism* (New York: Oxford University Press, 1954), 310.

104 *The Decades of Henry Bullinger, Minister of the Church of Zurich*, The Fifth Decade, H.I. trans. Thomas Harding, ed., (Cambridge: The University Press, 1852; reprint New York: Johnson Reprint Corporation, 1968), xxvii.

105 For the historical backdrop to the sacramental sections of the *Decades*, see Euler, "Huldrych Zwingli and Heinrich Bullinger," 69–70. Bullinger possibly withheld publishing portions of his text because of tensions with the Lutherans and because he was in the midst of negotiating the *Consensus Tigurinus* with Calvin. For Bullinger's eucharistic theology in general see Euler, "Huldrych Zwingli and Heinrich Bullinger" and John Riggs, *The Lord's Supper in the Reformed Tradition*, 103–111.

carves a carefully articulated middle position between the extremes of infrequent and frequent communion, concluding that both honor God, as long as people commune in faith. Bullinger endeavors to appreciate the good intentions of those on both sides of the issue:

> They that celebrate the supper of the Lord upon certain and ordinary times of the year, would not have it brought into contempt or loathed by reason of the daily frequenting. For they have some consideration of their own people; and they would have the supper to be celebrated worthily, and that the people may have a desire unto it. But they that celebrate very oft, they suppose it an unmeet [unfit] thing, that good things, by often frequenting them, should be despised, for the better the thing is, the oftener, say they, it is to be used. Both these sorts desire to serve the Lord, and would have that to be done to great and good effect, which the Lord hath left free.[106]

Bullinger also stresses the need to prepare oneself spiritually before communion. He recommends that all "are to be admonished, that every man descending into himself to prove himself, and afterward so eat of this holy bread and drink of this holy drink, that he eat not and drink not thereof unworthily unto his condemnation."[107]

During Bullinger's ministry, the Lord's Supper was celebrated three or four times a year in Zurich. It was observed on the "three or four most significant festivals of the church year and had nothing to do with the weekly rhythm of worship."[108] After Zwingli's death in the disastrous Battle of Kappel (1531), an internal civil war between Catholics and Protestants, the reformation in Zurich remained in a precarious position. Throughout his life, Bullinger had to negotiate with a city council that wanted no more of the fiery preaching that had characterized Zwingli's ministry.[109] It appears that the liturgical reforms were also less than successful. Diethelm notes that "the attempt to retain only feast days that could be justified

---

106 *The Decades of Henry Bullinger*, 424. The preceding sentences are also revealing: "Furthermore, how many times in a year the faithful ought to receive this sacrament of the Lord's supper, the apostles have given forth no commandment, but have left it indifferent unto every church's discretion. For what is more plain than that which St Paul hath said: 'As often as you shall eat of the this bread, and drink of this cup, you shall declare the Lord's death until he come?' For the Lord (as the same apostle setteth it down), first commanding, said: 'Do this, as oft as you shall drink it, in remembrance of me.' Howbeit, let no man think, that the celebration of the Lord's supper is left so freely unto him, that he need never to receive it; for that were no lawful liberty, but most unlawful licentiousness." (424–425).

107 *The Decades of Henry Bullinger*, 425.

108 Roland Diethelm, "Bullinger and Worship: 'Thereby Does One Plant and Sow the True Faith,'" in *Architect of Reformation*, 146.

109 Gordon, "Introduction," in *Architect of Reformation*, 19, 22.

from the Bible could not be sustained, and in Zurich we find celebrations for the Apostles, as well as the patron saints of the Grossmünster, Felix and Regula."

This context helps explain a letter Bullinger wrote in 1567. As Diethelm summarizes: "In reply to a question from Konrad Ulmer, the head of the church in Schaffhausen, who wanted to know why the Swiss Reformed did not celebrate the Lord's Supper weekly, as the Lutherans and Calvinists did, Bullinger admitted that weekly celebration was certainly justifiable on theological grounds, but after forty years he had no desire to alter the established practice, as this could lead to renewed controversy."[110] At the time of this letter, Bullinger was near the end of his life, and had lost his wife and only daughter in the plague in the 1560s. After a lifetime of controversy, his reluctance to challenge the *status quo* (as seen in the Fifth Sermon of the *Decades* and in his reply to Ulmer) is quite understandable. Despite Bullinger's prominence and influence, he is not quoted much in later communion frequency polemics. That honor goes to John Calvin.

2.8   John Calvin (1509-1564)

In comparison to the many controversies Calvin tackled in his lifetime, the issue of communion frequency did not receive as much of his attention as other issues. This, no doubt, reflects the fact that there was no notable opponent arguing for infrequent communion, and also that there were many other matters of great concern which demanded Calvin's time and attention. Calvin's stated preference for frequent communion can be briefly summarized.[111] After a summary of Calvin's statements on communion frequency, they will be situated within his broader ideals for ecclesiastical discipline. It becomes apparent that Calvin was willing to sacrifice frequency for sake of proper preparation, which could imply that frequency was not an unqualified blessing in Calvin's mind.[112]

---

110 Diethelm, "Bullinger and Worship," in *Architect of Reformation*, 146.

111 G.S.M. Walker summarizes: "For to him [Calvin] the Lord's Supper was central in the church's life, and up to the last edition of the *Institutio* he pleaded for its weekly celebration." G.S.M. Walker, "The Lord's Supper in the Theology and Practice of Calvin." in G.E. Duffield, ed., *John Calvin*, Courtenay Studies in Reformation Theology, (Appelford: The Sutton Courtenay Press, 1966), 131. See also Wandel, *The Eucharist in the Reformation*, 171–172, especially her conclusion that, "Frequent communion, therefore, for Calvin was essential to one's growth as a Christian—it transformed one's being and epistemology."

112 For Calvin's view of the Eucharist in general see the following: Julie Canlis, *Calvin's Ladder: A Spiritual Theology of Ascent and Ascension* (Grand Rapids: Wm. B. Eerdmans Publishing Co., 2010); Ralph Cunnington, "Calvin's Doctrine of the Lord's Supper: A Blot Upon His Labors as a Public Instructor?" *WTJ* 73 (2011): 215–36; Thomas J. Davis, *The Clearest Promise of God: The Development of Calvin's Eucharistic Teaching*, AMS Studies in Religious Tradition 1 (New York:

In the *Institutes* (1559), Calvin devotes four sections specifically to the question of communion frequency: "Now, to get rid of this great pile of ceremonies, the Supper could have been administered most becomingly if it were set before the church very often, and at least once a week."[113] The phrase "at least" is interesting here. Would Calvin approve of daily communion, or communion more often than on Sundays? In the next section, Calvin argues specifically against the late medieval practice of annual communion and presents his own construction of how communion patterns developed throughout history.[114] He appeals to Acts 2:42 and "Paul" (without citing a particular verse) and states: "Thus it became the unvarying rule that no meeting of the church should take place without the Word, prayers, partaking of the Supper, and almsgiving." He maintains that this apostolic pattern "remained in use for many

---

AMS Press, 1995); idem, *This Is My Body: The Presence of Christ in Reformation Thought* (Grand Rapids: Baker Academic, 2008); B.A. Gerrish, *Grace and Gratitude: The Eucharistic Theology of John Calvin* (Eugene: Wipf and Stock, 2002, 1ˢᵗ ed. 1993); idem, "Gospel and Eucharist: John Calvin on the Lord's Supper," in *The Old Protestantism and the New: Essays on the Reformation Heritage* (Chicago: The University of Chicago Press, 1982); Wim Janse, '12. The Sacraments', in *The Calvin Handbook*, ed. Herman J. Selderhuis (Grand Rapids: William B. Eerdmans, 2009), 344–355, in particular 351–355: '12.4. The Lord's Supper'; Keith A. Mathison, *Given for You: Reclaiming Calvin's Doctrine of the Lord's Supper* (Phillipsburg: P&R Publishing, 2002); John R. Meyer, "*Mysterium Fidei* and the Later Calvin," *SJT* 25 (1972): 393–411; John W. Riggs, *The Lord's Supper in the Reformed Tradition*; Ronald S. Wallace, *Calvin's Doctrine of Word and Sacrament* (Eugene: Wipf and Stock, 1997, 1ˢᵗ ed. 1953); Herman Speelman, "Weekly at the Lord's Table: Calvin's Motives for a Frequent Celebration of the Holy Communion," in *Liturgy and Ethics: New Contributions from Reformed Perspectives*, Pieter Vos, ed. (Leiden: Brill, 2018), 149–174.

113 John Calvin, *The Institutes of the Christian Religion*, [= *Instit.* hereafter] ed. John T. McNeill, trans. Ford Lewis Battles, 2 vols., LCC (Philadelphia: Westminster Press, 1960), 4.17.43. McNeill's commentary is interesting here: "Calvin was among the earliest to urge Communion as frequently as this." 1421, n. 39. But it is not clear whether Calvin was "among the earliest" of the Reformers, or of other Christian writers as well, since McNeill then discusses communion frequency in the Roman Catholic tradition, and the calls for more frequent communion in the Jansenist movement. Since Calvin predates Jansenism, McNeill seems to imply that Calvin was one of the first early-modern writers to advocate frequent communion.

114 Although the main text for the topic of communion frequency is the *Institutes*, as well as some of Calvin's shorter writings, this must be balanced by an awareness that Calvin's theology went through a process of development. Like other sixteenth-century writers, Calvin was more interested (and angry) about what the Eucharist was, theologically and metaphysically, and not how often it should be observed. Wim Janse summarizes the development in Calvin's thought: "Calvin's doctrine of the sacraments shows successively Zwinglianizing (1536–1537), Lutheranizing (1537–1548), spiritualizing (1549–1560), and again Lutheranizing (1561–1562) accents," in *The Calvin Handbook*, 345. For more details see Janse, "Calvin's Eucharistic Theology: Three Dogma-Historical Observations," in Herman J. Selderhuis, ed., *Calvinus sacrarum literarum interpres: Papers of the International Congress on Calvin Research* (Göttingen: Vandenhoeck & Ruprecht, 2008), 37–69. For Calvin's early development, and the possible influence of Melanchthon, see Richard A. Muller, "From Zürich or from Wittenberg? An Examination of Calvin's Early Eucharistic Thought," *CTJ* 45 (2010): 243–255.

centuries after."[115] Calvin also offers a panoramic statement of the importance and benefits of frequent communion:

> Rather, it was ordained to be frequently used among all Christians in order that they might frequently return in memory to Christ's Passion, by such remembrance to sustain and strengthen their faith, and urge themselves to sing thanksgiving to God and to proclaim his goodness; finally, by it to nourish mutual love, and among themselves give witness to this love, and discern its bond in the unity of Christ's body. For as often as we partake of the symbol of the Lord's body, as a token given and received, we reciprocally bind ourselves to all the duties of love in order that none of us may permit anything that can harm our brother, or overlook anything that can help him, where necessity demands and ability suffices.[116]

After appealing to a series of "ancient canons" that deal with the duty of participation in the Eucharist, Calvin enlists support from Augustine and Chrysostom (two of his favorite fathers).[117] Interestingly, the quotes from Augustine speak more directly about the *variety* of communion reception in the North African churches—some "partake daily … others receive them on certain days … elsewhere, only on Saturday and Sunday," which, again, raises the question of whether Calvin would approve of more-than-weekly communion?

In the next section, Calvin makes his well-known claim that the custom of taking communion once a year is a "veritable invention of the devil," and then offers some conjectures about the source of this practice, and its misuse and development in the Catholic church. He reiterates his conviction that "the Lord's Table should have been spread at least once a week for the assembly of Christians, and the promises declared in it should feed us spiritually. None is indeed to be forcibly compelled, but all are to be urged and aroused; also the inertia of indolent people is to be rebuked. All, like hungry men, should flock to such a bounteous repast."[118] He detects the "artifice" of the devil in introducing this custom of infrequent communion, because it makes people "slothful" the rest of the year. He closes with another quote from Chrysostom, where Chrysostom laments the reluctance of people to partake of

---

115 Calvin, *Instit.* 4.17.44.

116 Calvin, *Instit.* 4.17.44.

117 Calvin, *Instit.* 4.17.44–45. See the Battles-McNeill *Institutes*, 1423–1424, f.n. 43 and 44 for full citation details. See also Anthony N. S. Lane, *John Calvin: Student of the Church Fathers* (Grand Rapids: Baker Books, 1999) for more detailed studies of Calvin's use and knowledge of patristic sources.

118 Calvin, *Instit.* 4.17.46.

communion.[119] However, Chrysostom laments that people do not come to the "daily" offering. Through quoting Chrysostom and Augustine with approval, is Calvin tacitly acknowledging the legitimacy of daily communion?

Answering this question involves understanding Calvin's view of weekly, as opposed to daily, worship. In his treatment of the ten commandments in the *Institutes*, Calvin distinguishes between various aspects of the fourth commandment. He maintains that the coming of Christ has abolished the "ceremonial" part of the fourth commandment. However, this does not mean that the commandment is meaningless for the church. As Calvin writes: "Although the Sabbath has been abrogated, there is still occasion for us: (1) to assemble on stated days for the hearing of the Word, the breaking of the mystical bread, and for public prayers; (2) to give surcease from labor to servants and workmen."[120] He maintains that these two purposes still apply in the church. Furthermore "[m]eetings of the church are enjoined upon us by God's Word; and from our everyday experience we well know how we need them."[121] Calvin anticipates a possible objection "[w]hy do we not assemble daily, you ask, so as to remove all distinction of days? If only this had been given us! Spiritual wisdom truly deserved to have some portion of time set apart for it each day. But if the weakness of many made it impossible for daily meetings to be held, and the rule of love does not allow more to be required of them, why should we not obey the order we see laid upon us by God's will?"[122] Calvin displays pastoral sensitivity in his prescriptions for worship and for communion frequency. Although he acknowledges that daily worship is the ideal, he is content to be governed by the "rule of love," which makes allowances to the "weakness" of many.[123]

The same approach emerges in Calvin's "first" *Catechism* (1538). After the coming of Christ, the two purposes of the Sabbath are that "on set days we gather together to hear the word, to break the mystical bread, to pray publicly; secondly, that servants and workers be given surcease from their toil." The ideal is daily worship "[y]et such is our weakness that it cannot be arranged for meetings of this sort to take place daily."[124]

---

119 *Calvin, Instit.* 4.17.46. The quote is from Chrysostom's *Commentary on Ephesians*, chap. 1. hom. iii.4. McNeill indicates that this quote was added in the 1543 edition of the *Institutes*, while the previous material in section 46 dates to the original 1536 edition.

120 Calvin, *Instit.* 2.8.32.

121 Calvin, *Instit.* 2.8.32.

122 Calvin, *Instit.* 2.8.32.

123 Much has been written and claimed regarding Calvin's view of the Sabbath and its continuing significance for the church. See the careful study of Richard B. Gaffin, Jr., *Calvin and the Sabbath: The Controversy of Applying the Fourth Commandment* (Mentor: Ross-shire, 1998; repr. 2008).

124 I. John Hesselink, ed., Ford Lewis Battles, trans. *Calvin's First Catechism. A Commentary* (Louisville, KY: Westminster John Knox, 1997), 13.

We see the same general pattern of teaching in Calvin's second catechism. Reid titles it *Catechism of the Church of Geneva*.[125] God rested on the seventh day to give us an example, so that we might be "formed in his image."[126] We do this by meditating on the "works of God," and "crucifying our flesh." This is the true meaning of the Sabbath day, although we should do this continually "because of our weakness one special day is appointed." What should we do on this day? The "child" answers: "The people are to meet for the hearing of Christian doctrine, for the offering of public prayers, and for the profession of their faith." Conspicuously absent from this list is any mention of the Lord's Supper. However, in response to the question of how much of the commandment still applies to Christians, the "minister" in the catechism responds: "Not to neglect the sacred ordinances which contribute to the spiritual polity of the Church; especially to attend the sacred assemblies for the hearing of the Word of God, the celebration of the mysteries, and the regular prayers as they will be ordained."[127]

Calvin summarizes the continuing significance of the Sabbath in the *Institutes*:

> First, we are to meditate throughout life upon an everlasting Sabbath rest from all our works, that the Lord may work in us through his Spirit. Secondly, each one of us privately, whenever he has leisure, is to exercise himself diligently in pious meditation upon God's works. Also, we should all observe together the lawful order set by the church for the hearing of the Word, the administration of the sacraments, and for public prayers. In the third place, we should not inhumanly oppress those subject to us.[128]

Here Calvin explicitly includes participation in the sacraments as part of true Sabbath observance. Calvin believed in the continuing significance of the Sabbath as a stated weekly time (or more often if possible) that could include the Eucharist. Although Calvin does not say much about communion frequency in his treatment of the Sabbath, his last word on the fourth commandment stresses frequent worship. He writes "in order to prevent religion from either perishing or declining among us, we should diligently frequent the sacred meetings, and make use of those external aids which can promote the worship of God."[129] No doubt he intended to include the Eucharist under the heading of "external aids."

---

125 He notes that there is no firm date for this second catechism: *Calvin: Theological Treatises*, ed. and trans., J.K.S. Reid, Library of Christian Classics, vol. XXII (Philadelphia: The Westminster Press, 1965), 83.
126 Reid, *Calvin: Theological Treatises (Catechism)*, 112.
127 Reid, *Calvin: Theological Treatises (Catechism)*, 113.
128 Calvin, *Instit.* 2.8.34.
129 Calvin, *Instit.* 2.8.34.

Calvin also more extensively addresses the topic of communion frequency and preparation in his 1540 *Petit traicté de la saincte Cene du nostre Seigneur Jesus Christ* (or, *Short Treatise on the Holy Supper of our Lord and only Savior Jesus Christ*). He wrote this treatise to map out a middle position between the available eucharistic options. He wanted to explain the Protestant view of the Eucharist, rebut the Roman view, and attempt to find common ground between the extremes of Luther and Zwingli.[130]

Calvin begins the treatise by considering *why* Christ instituted the Lord's Supper. The Supper is a means of spiritual nourishment: "But as the life into which he has regenerated us is spiritual, so the food for preserving and confirming us in it must be spiritual."[131] Furthermore "all Scripture tells us that the spiritual bread by which our souls are maintained is the same Word by which our Lord regenerated us."[132] Then why do we need the Eucharist? Is it something distinct from the Word? The Eucharist is given to us because, the "Father, of his mercy, not at all disdaining to condescend in this matter to our infirmity, has desired to attach to his Word a visible sign, by which he represents the substance of his promises, to confirm and fortify us, and to deliver us from all doubt and uncertainty."[133] Calvin presents three reasons why the Lord has given us the Supper. As a seal of the promises of the gospel, to incite thankfulness for his goodness to us, and to motivate us in holy living, and "particularly to unity and brotherly charity, as is specially recommended to us."[134]

---

130 Ellwood notes that the tract was the "first occasion on which his [Calvin's] attention was given over wholly to the topic" of the Eucharist, and was also "Calvin's first attempt to give a comprehensive account of his sacramental position in the French language." *The Body Broken*, 56. See also Joseph Tylenda, "The Ecumenical Intention of Calvin's Early Eucharistic Thought," in B.A. Gerrish, ed., *Reformatio Perennis: Essays on Calvin and the Reformation in honor of Ford Lewis Battles* (Pittsburgh: The Pickwick Press, 1981); McNeill, *The History and Character of Calvinism*, 153; John R. Meyer, "*Mysterium Fidei* and the Later Calvin," 393–395, for more background on the context of the *Petit traicté* and for Calvin's early Eucharistic thought in general. Evidence for the ecumenical intention, and success, of Calvin's tract is seen in the fact that the Bremen pastor Albert Hardenberg, the crypto-calvinist pupil of Martin Bucer, submitted an anonymous translation of parts of the *Petit traicté* to the Lutheran magistrate of Bremen in 1548 in order to prove his own Lutheran doctrinal orthodoxy – which was accepted as orthodox by the Bremen magistrate. See Wim Janse, *Albert Hardenberg als Theologe. Profil eines Bucer-Schülers* [SHCH 57] (Leiden/New York/Köln: E.J. Brill, 1994), 471–477. See also Herman Speelman, *Melanchthon and Calvin on Confession and Communion: Early Modern Protestant Penitential and Eucharistic Piety* (Vandenhoeck & Ruprecht, 2016), 231–243 for more analysis.
131 Reid, *Calvin: Theological Treatises*, (*Petit traicté* = PT hereafter), 143.
132 Reid, *Calvin: Theological Treatises* (PT), 143.
133 Reid, *Calvin: Theological Treatises* (PT), 144.
134 Reid, *Calvin: Theological Treatises* (PT), 144.

Calvin presents a remarkable summary of his eucharistic theology: "Or to explain the matter more simply, as we in ourselves are lacking in all good and have not a particle of what might help us to salvation, the Supper is attestation that, being made partakers of the death and passion of Jesus Christ, we have everything that is useful and salutary for us."[135] Calvin is anxious to affirm that real *communion* occurs in the Supper.[136]

Because we have real communion with the risen Christ, we must approach the Table cautiously.[137] While we need to examine ourselves to determine "whether we have a true repentance in ourselves and a true faith in our Lord Jesus Christ," Calvin also cautions against the opposite extreme of overly-morbid introspection.[138] In summary, to "communicate worthily" means to eat in faith, trusting in Christ alone, while also recognizing our sinfulness and our deep need for the righteousness of Christ.[139]

Calvin maintains that we need to come to the Lord's Supper precisely *because* we are weak and sinful.[140] Although later generations of Calvinists seem to have struggled with the issue of proper preparation, and feeling unworthy to partake of communion, Calvin strikes a balanced, pastoral, note in this treatise.[141] Calvin exhorts his readers to come to the Table, no matter how they feel about their own

---

135 Reid, *Calvin: Theological Treatises* (PT), 145.

136 He claims that "all benefit which we ought to seek from the Supper is annulled, unless Jesus Christ be there given to us as substance and foundation of all. This agreed, we shall confess without doubt that to deny the true communication of Jesus Christ to be offered us in the Supper is to render this holy sacrament frivolous and useless—a blasphemy execrable and unworthy of attention." Reid, *Calvin: Theological Treatises* (PT), 146.

137 "It is, then, not without reason that Paul passes such grave condemnation on those who take it unworthily. For if there is nothing in heaven or earth of greater value and dignity than the body and blood of our Lord, it is no small fault to take it inconsiderately and without being well prepared. Therefore he exhorts us to examine ourselves well, in order to use it properly." Calvin, *Short Treatise* (PT), 149.

138 Reid, *Calvin: Theological Treatises* (PT), 150.

139 Reid, *Calvin: Theological Treatises* (PT), 150.

140 Reid, *Calvin: Theological Treatises* (PT), 152.

141 Calvin also writes: "When we feel within us a strong distaste and hatred of all vices, proceeding from the fear of God, and a desire to live well in order to please our Lord, we are fit to partake of the Supper, notwithstanding the vestiges of infirmity which we carry in our flesh. If indeed we were not weak, subject to mistrust, and imperfect in life, the sacrament would be of no service to us, and it would have been superfluous to institute it. Since then it is a remedy which God has given us to assist our frailty, to fortify our faith, to augment our charity, and to further us in all sanctity of life, so far from this making us abstain, we ought the more to make use of it, the more we feel oppressed by the disease." Reid, *Calvin: Theological Treatises* (PT) 152.

personal worthiness.[142] How often should we observe the Supper? Calvin's reply relates directly to the key point of investigation in this chapter:

> As to the time of using it, there can be no certain rule for all. For there are certain particular impediments which excuse a man for absenting himself. And besides we have no express command, constraining Christians to make use of it every day it is offered to them. However, if we have careful regard to the end for which our Lord intended it, we should realize that the use of it ought to be more frequent than many make it.[143]

Considering this emphasis on frequent communion in the *Institutes* and in the *Short Treatise*, it is interesting to compare Calvin's comments in his *Commentaries* on portions of Scripture that seem to suggest frequent communion. It is especially interesting to note how differently he approaches the text, as compared with later writers in the Reformed tradition. Where later writers quote various Biblical texts as dogmatically teaching or requiring frequent communion, Calvin seems to have a more balanced approach. Two portions of Scripture stand out because of their prominence in later Reformed communion frequency polemics: Acts 2:42-47 and 1 Cor. 11:23-33.

In his commentary on Acts, Calvin finds a clear reference to the Lord's Supper in Acts 2:42. This is a key verse, not only for Reformed theologies of worship in general, but also for later communion frequency debates.[144] He believes "breaking

---

142 Reid, *Calvin: Theological Treatises* (PT), 153.

143 Reid, *Calvin: Theological Treatises* (PT), 153. He continues: "For the more infirmity oppresses us, the more frequently we need to have recourse to that which is able and ought to serve to confirm our faith and further us in purity of life. Therefore, the custom ought to be well established in all Churches, of celebrating the Supper *as frequently as the capacity of the people will allow*. And each individual in his own place ought to prepare himself to receive it whenever it is administered in the congregation, unless there be some grave hindrance which compels him to abstain. Though we have no express command defining the time and the day, it should be enough for us to know that the *intention of our Lord is that we use it often*; otherwise we shall not know well the benefit which it offers us." (emphasis added).

144 The entirety of his comments is important because of this passage's continuing prominence in Reformed communion frequency polemics: "With regard to the apostles' teaching and to prayer, the meaning is clear. Fellowship and the breaking of bread may be understood in different ways. Some think that breaking of bread means the Lord's Supper, others that it refers to alms, others again that the faithful had their meals together in common. Some think that 'fellowship' (κοινωνία) is the celebration of the Holy Supper; I hold rather with those who believe that this is meant by the breaking of bread. For 'fellowship' (κοινωνία), without addition, is never found in this sense. I therefore refer it to mutual association, and other duties of brotherly fellowship. The reason why I would rather have breaking of bread to be understood here of the Lord's Supper is because Luke is recording those things which constitute the form of the church visible to the naked eye. Indeed, he defines four marks by which the true and genuine appearance of the church may be distinguished."

bread" refers to communion (*coena dominica*), but he does not stress the issue of frequency in this passage. While the Supper is important, he views it as one of the "four marks" which characterize the church. Frequency of communion was not on the forefront of Calvin's mind as he exegetes this verse. More important for him was to establish the corporate, public, nature of worship (prayer), and to argue for the priority of correct doctrine over religious rituals.

Another important Scriptural passage in later frequency debates is 1 Corinthians 11, particularly concerning Paul's commands for the Corinthians to "examine" themselves before participating in the Lord's Supper. How does Calvin approach this passage? Following Paul, Calvin highlights the very real danger of eating the Supper in an "unworthy" manner.[145] Calvin distinguishes between various degrees of sin and rebellion and warns that God will punish us, to the degree that we are unrepentant and continuing willfully in sin.[146] However, Calvin distances himself from the necessity of auricular confession and the intense interrogation of the conscience that apparently occurred occasionally in the late medieval church (Calvin calls it "torture"). Calvin presents a pastoral and practical summary of what it means to partake of the Supper in a "worthy" manner. It means we must come with "faith and repentance," but God does not demand a "perfect" faith. Our faith in Christ makes us worthy.[147]

Reformation Commentary on Scripture: Acts, Esther Chung-Kim and Todd R. Hains, eds., (Downers Grove: IVP Academic, 2014), 35; CNTC 6:85 (CO 48:57).

145 "To eat unworthily, then, is to pervert the pure and right use of it by our abuse of it." *Commentary on the Epistles of Paul the Apostle to the Corinthians*, John Pringle, trans. (Edinburgh: Calvin Translation Society; reprint Baker Books, 2005), 385.

146 "As, then, there are various degrees of *unworthy participation*, so the Lord punishes some more slightly; on others he inflicts severer punishment." *Commentary on the Epistles of Paul the Apostle to the Corinthians*, 385–86.

147 "If you would wish to use aright the benefit afforded by Christ, bring faith and repentance. As to these two things, therefore, the trial must be made, if you would come duly prepared. Under repentance I include love; for the man who has learned to renounce himself, that he may give himself up wholly to Christ and his service, will also, without doubt, carefully maintain that unity which Christ has enjoined. At the same time, it is not a perfect faith or repentance that is required, as some, by urging beyond due bounds, a perfection that can nowhere be found, would shut out for ever from the Supper every individual of mankind. If, however, thou aspirest after the righteousness of God with the earnest desire of thy mind, and, humbled under a view of thy misery, dost wholly lean upon Christ's grace, and rest upon it, know that thou art a worthy guest to approach that table—*worthy* I mean in this respect, that the Lord does not exclude thee, though in another point of view there is something in thee that is not as it ought to be. For faith, when it is but begun, makes those *worthy* who were *unworthy.*" *Commentary on the Epistles of Paul the Apostle to the Corinthians*, 388.

John 6 is another contentious passage in communion frequency polemics. Calvin believes that Jesus is referring primarily to eating by faith, not the Eucharist.[148] But he also believes that this passage points forward to the Eucharist. One of his main reasons for denying that the Eucharist is the main referent of the passage is the issue of child-communion. Calvin disagrees with the "ancients" in the early church who gave their children communion, believing it was essential to salvation. Calvin argues that John 6 "does not relate to the Lord's Supper, but to the uninterrupted communication *of the flesh of Christ*, which we obtain apart from the use of the Lord's Supper."[149] Commenting on verse 54 ("Whoever feeds on my flesh and drinks my blood has eternal life, and I will raise him up on the last day," ESV), Calvin clearly states "(…) it plainly appears that the whole of this passage is improperly explained, as applied to the Lord's Supper."[150] However, he also believes that this passage foreshadows the Lord's Supper.[151]

In commenting on John 6, Calvin mentions Augustine's reference to daily and weekly communion. While it is not possible to form strong conclusions from this passing remark, it is also true that Calvin mentions it in an approving way. When

---

148 "The inference which some draw from this passage—that *to believe in Christ* is the same thing as *to eat Christ*, or *his flesh*—is not well founded … I acknowledge that Christ is not eaten but by faith; but the reason is, because we receive him by faith, that he may dwell in us, and that we may be made partakers of him, and thus may be one with him. To *eat* him, therefore, is an effect or work of faith." *Commentary on the Gospel of John*, trans. William Pringle, (Edinburgh: Calvin Translation Society/ Grand Rapids: Baker Book House, 2005), 260.

149 *Commentary on the Gospel of John*, 265.

150 The next part of this passage is relevant as well, in light of later polemics: "For if it were true that all who present themselves at the holy table of the Lord are made partakers of his flesh and blood, all will, in like manner, obtain life; but we know that there are many who partake of it to their condemnation. And indeed it would have been foolish and unreasonable to discourse about the Lord's Supper, before he had instituted it. It is certain, then, that he now speaks of the perpetual and ordinary manner of eating the flesh of Christ, which is done by faith only. And yet, at the same time, I acknowledge that there is nothing said here that is not figuratively represented, and actually bestowed on believers, in the Lord's Supper; and Christ even intended that the holy Supper should be, as it were, a seal and confirmation of this sermon. This is also the reason why the Evangelist John makes no mention of the Lord's Supper; and therefore Augustine follows the natural order, when, in explaining this chapter, he does not touch on the Lord's Supper till he comes to the conclusion; and then he shows that this mystery is symbolically represented, whenever the Churches celebrate the Lord's Supper, in some places daily, and in other places only on the Lord's day." *Commentary on the Gospel of John*, 266. See also *Institutes*, 4.17.5, where Calvin also interacts with John 6, and says essentially the same things.

151 Commenting on verse 55: "Thus also in the Lord's Supper, which corresponds to this doctrine, not satisfied with the symbol of *the bread*, he adds also *the cup*, that, having in him a twofold pledge, we may learn to be satisfied with him alone; for never will a man find a part of life in Christ, until he has entire and complete life in him." *Commentary on the Gospel of John*, 267, and, commenting on verse 56—"the doctrine which is here taught is sealed in the Lord's Supper." 268.

taken together with his other famous statement, that the Lord's Supper should be held weekly "at least," it seems likely that Calvin would approve of more-than-weekly communion.

2.9   Church Discipline and Communion Frequency

It is misleading to focus exclusively on the question of communion frequency without also examining what various Reformers believed about the preconditions for participation in the Eucharist. Most significantly, this issue surfaces when we take into consideration various notions of church discipline and the structure of church government.[152] Early modern Reformers were not simply trying to purify the worship of the church. They were—in varying degrees—trying to reform society and construct cities and nations in accordance with the Word of God.[153] Hendrix refers to this as the "Christianizing" of Europe.[154] Understanding this overarching goal situates the importance the Reformers gave to ecclesiastical discipline.[155] The frequency of communion cannot be separated from the question of access to the sacrament. Since the Lord's Supper stood at the heart of the Christian community, questions of access and frequency were interconnected.

Furthermore, the question of access was bound up in the larger question of the relationships between church and the civic authorities. As different Protestant communities formulated various systems of church-state structures, this also affected the various pathways of access to communion.

---

152 Herman A. Speelman's comments on Calvin apply to other Reformers as well: "[I]t is difficult to provide a clear description of Calvin's vision of confession and ecclesiastical discipline without simultaneously discussing the Eucharist." *Melanchthon and Calvin on Confession and Communion*, 193. Elsie Ann McKee observes that the links between communion frequency and church discipline in the Reformed tradition have not always been clearly understood. But, understanding this connection "helps to illuminate the arguments over the (in)frequency of the celebration of the Supper, despite Calvin's expressed desire to the contrary." *The Pastoral Ministry and Worship in Calvin's Geneva* (Genève: Librairie Droz S.A., 2016), 248.

153 As Nelson Burnett observes: "While many of the laity may have seen the Reformation as an opportunity to throw off the regulations and requirements of the medieval church, the reformers themselves, especially those who had been influenced by the biblical humanism of Erasmus, were concerned with forming a new Christian society." "Church Discipline and Moral Reformation in the Thought of Martin Bucer," 440.

154 Scott H. Hendrix, *Recultivating the Vineyard: The Reformation Agendas of Christianization* (Louisville: Westminster John Knox Press, 2004), xvii–xxiii.

155 For a helpful summary of views on ecclesiastical discipline in the sixteenth century see Robert Kingdon, "Calvin and Church Discipline," *John Calvin Rediscovered: The Impact of His Social and Economic Thought*, ed. Edward Dommen and James D. Bratt (Louisville: Westminster John Knox Press, 2007), 29–31.

Reformers and the communities they worked within developed theories of church governance and discipline during their careers and in their various stages of reform. These theories of church discipline remained abstract theories in some instances, so it is tenuous to conclude too much about their impact on patterns of communion frequency. Other theories were implemented more successfully.[156] Since eucharistic practices and theologies are intimately bound up with issues of church discipline, some aspects of the differing views on the relationships between church, state, discipline, and the Eucharist will be surveyed briefly.

2.9.1 Zurich, Basel, and Strasbourg

Zwingli, to begin with, "based his theory on the conviction that the church and civil community formed a single corporate entity under the complete authority of the Christian magistrate."[157] As he wrote in 1531: "A Christian is nothing other than a faithful and good citizen, and a Christian city is nothing other than a Christian church."[158]

Oecolampadius advanced another approach. Although other Reformers were interested in the idea of "eldership" in the church, Oecolampadius was the "first

---

156 J. Wayne Baker discerns two major approaches—that of Zwingli (the Zurich tradition) and that of Oecolampadius, Farel/Calvin, and Beza (the Basel/Genevan tradition). As Baker summarizes: "The Zurich tradition was ably defended not only by Bullinger, but also by Wolfgang Musculus at Bern and by Thomas Erastus at Heidelberg. That tradition, however, came under increasing attack by the second Reformed tradition, as it was further developed by Guillaume Farel and John Calvin, and fully explicated by Theodore Beza. In the end, it was the position of Oecolampadius that became the Reformed approach to church discipline." "Church Discipline or Civil Punishment: On the Origins of the Reformed Schism, 1528–1531," *Andrews University Seminary Studies*, Spring 1985. vol. 23. no. 1, 18. However, this categorization may be too simplistic: "While this distinction is in many ways accurate, these two positions are better understood to represent different ends of a more variegated spectrum of Reformed opinion on church discipline in particular and the relationship of the church and state more broadly in the 16th century." Jordan Ballor and W. Bradford Littlejohn, "European Calvinism: Church Discipline," in: European History Online (EGO), published by the Leibniz Institute of European History (IEG), Mainz 2013-03-25. URL: http://www.ieg-ego.eu/ ballorj-littlejohnw-2013-en URN: urn:nbn:de:0159-2013032507 [2017-05-05]. Additionally, as these authors note, "recent scholarship increasingly suggests that other colleagues of Bucer, such as the Italian reformer Peter Martyr Vermigli and the Polish reformer Jan Łaski, (1499–1560), exercised an equally decisive influence on the development of Reformed discipline across Europe." However, because this study is limited to the reception and appropriation of the Reformers in later communion frequency polemics, Vermigli and Łaski cannot be treated here, as they do not figure prominently in later discussions.

157 Baker, "Church Discipline or Civil Punishment," 5. See also Moeller, *Imperial Cities and the Reformation*, 75–78.

158 ZW (Huldreich Zwinglis sämtliche Werke) 14, no. 6, 424, l.20–22, quoted in Speelman, *Calvin and the Independence of the Church* (Göttingen: Vandenhoeck & Ruprecht, 2014), 255.

sixteenth-century reformer to argue for an eldership which would administer discipline independent of civil authority," and he "insisted on autonomy for the church in the disciplinary sphere."[159] In 1530, he requested that the Basel city council institute a new type of church discipline.[160] Whereas Zwingli saw fundamental unity between church and city, he believed that "church and civil society were separate entities," [and] "that there was an essential difference between secular and ecclesiastical authority."[161] Oecolampadius wanted to exclude unrepentant sinners from the Lord's Supper. Accordingly, "the ban must be instituted under the control of the church."[162] For Oecolampadius, this issue concerned the health of the church: "Oecolampadius clearly felt that without such church discipline, the Reformed church was not fully reformed."[163]

Oecolampadius "attempted to enlist Zwingli's support, and Zwingli appears temporarily to have been at least partially persuaded by Oecolampadius."[164] However, through the influence of Berchtold Haller and Martin Bucer, and perhaps also the opposition of the magistrates of Zurich, Zwingli backed away from embracing Oecolampadius's plan. According to Baker, in 1530, Zwingli reverted to his original position. In a St. Gall synod on December 22, another pastor proposed implementing church discipline. Zwingli opposed this.[165]

Zwingli's successor, Heinrich Bullinger (1504–1575) developed his own distinctive view about church discipline and participation in communion.[166] Bullinger wrote to Haller in 1531: "I see excommunication to be nothing other than the public and Christian guarding of public virtue and Christian morals."[167] Bullinger, like many of the Reformers, framed much of his theology of church discipline in response to the early Anabaptist movement. As Baker summarizes: "The Anabaptists denied that the magistrate rightly exercised Christian discipline. Quoting Matt 18:17, they declared, 'The magistrate is not the church.' Bullinger countered

---

159 Graham, *The Uses of Reform*, 10.

160 Baker, "Church Discipline or Civil Punishment," 7.

161 Baker, "Church Discipline or Civil Punishment," 7.

162 Baker, "Church Discipline or Civil Punishment," 8.

163 Baker, "Church Discipline or Civil Punishment," 9. See also Hans R. Guggisberg, *Basel in the Sixteenth Century: Aspects of the City Republic before, during, and after the Reformation* (St. Louis, MO: Center for Reformation Research, 1982), 32.

164 Baker, "Church Discipline or Civil Punishment," 10.

165 Baker, "Church Discipline or Civil Punishment," 11–12.

166 For Bullinger on church discipline and the Lord's Supper, see Speelman, *Melanchthon and Calvin on Confession and Communion*, 170–171, 179, f.n. 41.

167 Baker, "Church Discipline or Civil Punishment," 13, quoting Heinhold Fast, *Heinreich Bullinger und die Täufer. Ein Beitrag zur Historiographie und Theologie im 16. Jahrhundert* (Weierhof [Pfalz], 1959), 173.

this argument by insisting that Christ used a synecdoche in Matt 18: "If the magistracy was gathered in Christ's name (Matt 18:20), then it could and should act as the agent of the church in matters of discipline."[168] Excommunication, or church discipline, was the responsibility of the civil magistrate. Benedict explains further that Bullinger believed that, when the magistrates were Christian, the more accurate model was the Old Testament structure "with pious kings overseeing the temple and punishing those who violated both tablets of the Ten Commandments."[169]

However, Bullinger did not equate excommunication with exclusion from the Lord's Supper. In his 1531 letter to Haller, he argued *against* the ban from the Eucharist. For Bullinger, the Eucharist "was for the consolation and healing of sinners."[170] Baker does not mention the wider context of Bullinger's difficult ministry in Zurich. After the death of Zwingli in the disastrous Battle of Kappel (1531), the Zurich city government wanted to move away from the heightened rhetoric that had, in their view, helped lead to the conflict. As part of his negotiations with the civil authorities, Bullinger agreed not to preach about public policy.[171] In effect, he seems to have agreed to a measure of separation between church and state. This may help explain his reluctance to link excommunication with spiritual matters in the church.

Another factor in his sometimes-tense relationship with the civil magistrate was Bullinger's assumption of "personal control over the clergy," a move which Bullinger made, according to Gordon, to maintain a level of "freedom" from the overreaching authority of the magistrate.[172] This "personal control" of the clergy meant that Bullinger had to routinely examine other pastors and investigate any trouble and help to resolve issues. According to Gordon "[t]his extraordinary level of activity reflected Bullinger's essential approach to church affairs: he made a strict division between the private and visible spheres of church life," and did not "probe too deeply" into what other pastors believed. He comments further: "This was a decision he would live to regret. Nevertheless, he took the same view on the wider church. Although his approach was heavily didactic, Bullinger argued that outward conformity was all that the church could demand; it could not know the thoughts of the heart."[173]

---

168 Baker, "Church Discipline or Civil Punishment," 13–14.

169 Benedict, *Christ's Churches Purely Reformed*, 54.

170 Baker, "Church Discipline or Civil Punishment," 14.

171 Bruce Gordon, "Introduction," *Architect of Reformation*, 75, 19 and Benedict, *Christ's Churches Purely Reformed*, 53–54.

172 Gordon, "Introduction," *Architect of Reformation*, 22.

173 Gordon, "Introduction," *Architect of Reformation*, 22. Gordon explains this "regret": two pastors under Bullinger's care, Lelio Sozzini and Bernardino Ochino, claimed Bullinger's approval of them, even while publishing "heterodox" material, "Introduction," 23.

This bifurcation between the outward and inward manifests itself in Bullinger's ninth sermon in the Fifth *Decade*, devoted to the Sacraments. After addressing the issue of communion frequency, Bullinger then describes who should participate in the Lord's Supper. He maintains that it is "to be given unto all faithful christian [sic] people, of what sex soever, men and women, high and low."[174] He goes on to say that the church ministers should not deny the Supper to anyone that comes forward to receive it, even as Jesus gave the original Lord's Supper to the traitor Judas. Bullinger strongly asserts that the presence of hypocrites at the Supper does not defile the faithful participants. In this, we see clearly Bullinger's distinctive view, among early modern Reformed theologians, that the Lord's Supper is for everyone.[175] He believed that the magistrate had a God-ordained role to uphold morality and order within the community, and that excommunication was a civil matter—not a church censure.[176]

According to Baker, "Oecolampadius was horrified by Bullinger's argument, perhaps particularly by Bullinger's labeling of his opposition as 'Anabaptist.'"[177] Furthermore "Oecolampadius felt that those, like Bullinger, who rejected the use of the ban did not understand either the purpose of the Supper or the nature of the church."[178] For Oecolampadius, the purity of the church was at stake: "It was true that the Eucharist was for sinners, but not for flagrant and public sinners; the Supper was for those who confessed Christ (Rom 10:9), not for the enemies of Christ."[179] These ideals were never recognized in Basel,[180] but many of Oecolampadius's views eventually took root in the Reformed tradition, through the influence of John Calvin and the Genevan church.[181]

---

174 *The Decades of Henry Bullinger*, 425.

175 *The Decades of Henry Bullinger*, 425–26.

176 See J. Wayne Baker, "Church, State, and Dissent: The Crisis of the Swiss Reformation, 1531–1536," *Church History*, (June, 1988), pgs. 135–152.

177 Baker, "Church Discipline or Civil Punishment," 15.

178 Baker, "Church Discipline or Civil Punishment," 16.

179 Baker, "Church Discipline or Civil Punishment," 16.

180 Nelson Burnett argues that in Basel, the pastors had "little coercive power in the exercise of church discipline. The task of moral oversight in Basel actually involved three different groups: pastors, lay ban brothers, and secular officials. Of these three groups, the pastors had the least amount of authority, so in practice the exercise of church discipline was not a significant component of pastoral care in Basel. Nevertheless, the exercise of discipline was important in theory, and the pastors themselves were concerned with the conduct of their parishioners," *Teaching the Reformation*, 249.

181 Baker, "Church Discipline or Civil Punishment," 18. See Olaf Kuhr, "Calvin and Basel," for more on the probable influence of Oecolampadius on Calvin regarding church discipline. See also Nelson Burnett, *The Yoke of Christ: Martin Bucer and Christian Discipline*, 56–58 for a succinct summary of Oecolampadius and his influence on Bucer; cf. Willem van 't Spijker, *The Ecclesiastical Offices in the Thought of Martin Bucer*, trans. John Vriend and Lyle D. Bierma (Leiden: E.J. Brill, 1996), 219–225.

Bucer's influence is also important to understand.[182] Although, like Oecolampadius, his plans for church discipline were not realized in his own context, Bucer had a profound influence on other churches and cities, primarily through Calvin, who took Bucer's ideas and implemented them in Geneva.[183] As Nelson Burnett highlights, Bucer developed a mature, holistic, conception of church discipline and formation. It was not only negative and punitive, but incorporated positive elements such as religious instruction, catechesis, pastoral examination, private confession of sins, public profession of faith, fraternal admonition, and participation in a community fellowship committed to holiness and informal discipline.[184]

Bucer laid out his vision in *Von der waren Seelsorge* (1538).[185] Here, he attempts to persuade his readers about the necessity and value of church discipline, both the informal care of Christians for each other, and the official actions and censures of an ecclesial body.[186] Bucer presents his understanding of how the church should function, pastorally and practically. A key concern is that people should be kept from participating in the Lord's Supper if they are not truly repentant.[187] Because

---

182 The most thorough treatment in English is Nelson Burnett, *The Yoke of Christ*. See also Moeller, *Imperial Cities and the Reformation*, 79–82. For Bucer's views on ecclesiology in general, Van 't Spijker's study, *The Ecclesiastical Offices in the Thought of Martin Bucer*, is also indispensable.

183 "Bucer's broad definition of church discipline reflects his concern that belief should influence behavior … all the elements of church discipline were intended to aid the internalization of moral norms and thus provide a standard for the individual Christian's behavior. In this respect, Bucer's ideas foreshadow some of the techniques used in the second half of the sixteenth century by Lutherans, Calvinists, and Catholics alike to shape the confessional identity of their members," Nelson Burnett, "Church Discipline and Moral Reformation in the Thought of Martin Bucer," *SCJ*, XXII, no. 3, 1991," 453–54. See also, Willem van 't Spijker, "Bucer's influence on Calvin," in Wright, ed., *Martin Bucer: Reforming Church and Community*, 36–37 for further instances of Bucer's influence on Calvin in the matter of church discipline.

184 Nelson Burnett, "Church Discipline and Moral Reformation in the Thought of Martin Bucer," 440. See also Van 't Spijker, *The Ecclesiastical Offices*, 473–474 for a summary of Bucer's views on church discipline. Bucer provides a succinct statement of his mature ecclesiastical discipline ideal in "A Brief Summary of the Christian Doctrine and Religion Taught at Strasbourg for the Past Twenty-eight Years," in *Common Places of Martin Bucer*, D.F. Wright, ed., 87–89; *Ein Summarischer vergriff der Christlichen lehre vnd Religion die man zu Strasburg hat nun in die xxviij jar gelehret…* [Strasbourg: Wendelin Rihel, 1548]. = Seebass, Bucer Bibliographie Nr. 183.

185 *Von der waren Seelsorge vnnd dem rechten Hirten dienst wie der selbige inn der Kirchen Christi bestellet vnnd verrichtet werden solle …* (Strasbourg: Wendelin Rihel, 1538). = Seebass, Bucer Bibliographie Nr. 81.

186 For "informal" church discipline, see Bucer, *Concerning the True Care of Souls*, Peter Beale, trans. (Edinburgh and Carlisle: The Banner of Truth Trust, 2009; repr. 2016), 5–7. The treatise focuses more on the official, ordained, ministry of the church, while continuing to stress the importance of every Christian caring for one another.

187 "Now, since the holy Supper is the most glorious and joyful remembrance and communion of the Lord, in which there is given and imparted the highest pardon, complete peace and perfect

Bucer values the Supper so highly, he desires everyone to be fully prepared to receive it: "It is obvious that people are still weak in their knowledge of Christ and have not yet been sufficiently taught concerning the kingdom of Christ, if they think that the holy Supper should not be withheld from anyone who desires it, and are not concerned what people are admitted to the highest communion of Christ and heavenly peace."[188]

Although, as said, Bucer could not fully implement his plans in Strasbourg, he had the opportunity to influence other churches, most notably the Hessian church in 1538. They requested his help, and he drew up ordinances to assist the process of reforming their churches. In these ordinances, which were approved in 1539, Bucer was able to fully implement his vision for church discipline because "the whole system of discipline, including the power of excommunication (*verbannung*), was placed in the hands of ministers, elders and superintendents."[189] Furthermore, he implemented a process of catechesis and pre-communion examination.[190] Bucer's program for the Hessian church foreshadowed later developments in the Reformed tradition: "Here, for the first time in the sixteenth century, was a system involving consistories with lay elders having the power to excommunicate—the type of church polity later established in Geneva, Scotland, the Huguenot churches of France, and other parts of Germany and the Netherlands."[191]

One innovation directly relevant to taking communion was *pre-communion confession and examination*. Although initially skeptical, Bucer warmed to the idea. Private confession divided Lutherans and followers of Zwingli.[192] Luther and his disciples encouraged private confession of sins, and absolution (in the sense of one believer assuring another of God's forgiveness—not a sacramental act),

---

communion with Christ and all his members, the Holy Spirit has ordained and always maintained in his churches that, although those who repent are always to be comforted with the grace of God and salvation of Christ and are to be encouraged to share in the communion of Christ, which alone brings true atonement for sin, yet they are to be excluded and kept away from the holy Supper until such time as they have demonstrated their repentance in true humility so that the church may completely pardon them and forgive their sins." Bucer, *Concerning the True Care of Souls*, 135–36.

188 Bucer, *Concerning the True Care of Souls*, 137.

189 Graham, *The Uses of Reform*, 14. Nelson Burnett also claims that the "Hessian disciplinary ordinance can be seen as the most complete statement of Bucer's views on Christian discipline," *The Yoke of Christ*, 119.

190 "Anyone wishing to participate in Communion had first to be catechized, and could not be guilty of any major public sin for which they had not performed some sort of repentance," Graham, *The Uses of Reform*, 14.

191 Graham, *The Uses of Reform*, 15. Notably, Bucer was able to convince Anabaptists in Hesse to reintegrate into the local church, precisely because of the promise of a stricter form of church discipline. See Lugioyo, *Martin Bucer's Doctrine of Justification*, 22.

192 Nelson Burnett, "Church Discipline and Moral Reformation in the Thought of Martin Bucer," 442.

but Zwingli sharply criticized this.[193] Zwingli "argued that a person's sins were forgiven as soon as he believed that God had forgiven them and was confident in that belief ... The Zwinglians also rejected the pre-communion examination as 'papistic.'"[194] The Reformers in Basel, on the other hand, had introduced, for the first time in the Protestant churches, the practice of examining children before their first communion.[195] Although different cities and theological camps addressed the issue differently, they all shared a basic concern to ensure that people received communion in the proper fashion.

In his early ministry, Bucer held to the common belief among many humanists that private confession was salutary and helpful, though they denied the need for sacramental confession to a priest.[196] As Bucer pursued unity with the Lutherans on the Eucharist more intentionally (culminating in the Wittenberg Concord of 1536), he also grew in his appreciation for the Lutheran position on private confession.[197] During this time, Bucer also began to advocate a pre-communion examination, which created conflict with his Zwinglian friends, Thomas and Margareta Blarer.[198]

In *De Regno Christi* (1550), one of his last writings, the mature Bucer returns to this theme and appeals to the example of the early church as he advocates catechesis before baptism and some form of examination before being allowed access to communion: "So it is also fitting that faithful ministers of Christ have evidence of true repentance for sins and a solid faith in Christ the Lord from the fruits of those to whom they offer the Eucharist." He supports this with a quotation from Chrysostom's Homily 83, *On Matthew*. He cites with approval the practice of deacons in Chrysostom's time, who patrolled the church doors to ensure that no "unworthy person approached" the Eucharist.[199]

---

193 Nelson Burnett, "Church Discipline and Moral Reformation," 442. For more on the Lutheran and Swiss positions on practices of private confession see Nelson Burnet, *The Yoke of Christ*, 19–25.

194 Nelson Burnet, *The Yoke of Christ*, 442.

195 Nelson Burnett, *The Yoke of Christ*, 24–25, referencing *Aktensammlung zur Geschichte der Basler Reformation in den Jahren 1519 bis Anfang 1534*, 3:389–390 (no. 473).

196 Nelson Burnett, "Church Discipline and Moral Reformation," 442–43.

197 Nelson Burnett, "Church Discipline and Moral Reformation," 443–44. She traces the development of Bucer's views on confession and absolution, motivated by his efforts to mediate between Zwingli and the Lutherans (in the wake of the Marburg Colloquy), 45–54.

198 Nelson Burnett, "Church Discipline and Moral Reformation," 444. Additionally: "By the end of the 1530s Bucer was advocating the introduction of the pre-communion examination in his own church in Strasbourg. The pre-communion examination, with its opportunity for private confession, counsel, and instruction, was in Bucer's eyes an ideal vehicle for pastors to meet with their parishioners and to teach them the moral implications of their Christian faith," ibid., 445. See also Nelson Burnett, *The Yoke of Christ*, 79–80.

199 *Melanchthon and Bucer*, ed., Wilhelm Pauck (Philadelphia: The Westminster Press, 1969), 237. Original in *Martini Buceri Opera Omni*, ed. Robert Stupperich, Series 2, vol. 15, *De Regno Christi*

This is significant, considering some claims that are made about Bucer and weekly communion. Although it seems that Bucer did favor frequent communion, he also advocated pre-communion examination. It is not clear whether this was ever actually implemented in Strasbourg or Augsburg, but it remains an important legacy of the Reformed eucharistic tradition. Oecolampadius, Bucer, and Calvin (as will be demonstrated below) advocated *both* frequent communion *and* diligent preparation and pastoral examination. These twin emphases have not often been held together in Reformed churches, though. Much of the Reformers' eucharistic and ecclesiastical theology remained unrealized, which must be kept in mind when appealing to their example or precedent.

— important to think through [handwritten margin note]

2.9.2 Worship and Church Discipline in Geneva

For Calvin, frequent communion and church discipline are both part of a healthy church and community. This is seen in his earliest proposals for restructuring church and society in Geneva.[200] But, his views on this matter developed over time, especially in the context of negotiating the reformation process in both Strasbourg and Geneva. Although the *Articles sur le Gouvernement de l'Eglise* (1537) were not fully adopted or approved by the Genevan magistrates, they do reveal Calvin's theological and ecclesiastical priorities.[201] In particular, Calvin is concerned to regulate and guard the purity of the Lord's Supper. These Articles are an important early indication of Calvin's dual priorities of both *frequent* communion and *pure* communion. He begins the Articles with these dual priorities:

> (…) it is certain that a Church cannot be said to be well ordered and regulated unless in it the Holy Supper of our Lord is always being celebrated and frequented, and this under such good supervision that no one dare presume to present himself unless devoutly, and with genuine reverence for it. For this reason, in order to maintain the Church in

---

Libri Duo, ed. Francois Wendel (Paris: Presses Universitaires de France; Gütersloh, Bertelsmann, 1955).

200 "From the very beginning, Calvin fought the desecration of the sacrament. He wanted the Lord's Supper to be celebrated frequently, although he did not view participation in it as a matter of course, without any form of supervision and discipline, which was emphasized already in his early articles 'Concerning the organization of the Church and of Worship in Geneva.'" Speelman, *Melanchthon and Calvin on Confession and Communion*, 22.

201 For the actual functioning of worship, see Elsie A. McKee, "Places, Times, and People in Worship in Calvin's Geneva," *Journal of the Institute for Christianity and Culture of the International Christian University*, no. 41, (Tokyo, Japan: 2010): 101–20 and Jung-Sook Lee, "Spiritual Renewal Through Worship Reform in Calvin's Geneva," *Torch Trinity Journal* 7 (2004): 123–139. For the overall political background, see Speelman, *Calvin and the Independence of the Church*, especially 63–67, for the 1537 *Articles*.

its integrity, the discipline of excommunication is necessary, by which it is possible to correct those that do not wish to submit courteously and with all obedience to the Word of God.[202]

Calvin advocates both frequent eucharistic celebration and pure and proper participation. These two concerns continue to drive his eucharistic theology and his practical ecclesiology. In these *Articles*, Calvin clearly states his preference for weekly communion.[203] However, Calvin is a realist. He recognizes that the people of Geneva may not be ready to suddenly start participating in a weekly Eucharist, without proper preparation and teaching: "But because the frailty of the people is still so great, there is danger that this sacred and so excellent mystery be misunderstood if it be celebrated so often."[204] Accordingly, the *Articles* recommend a compromise of monthly communion in a scheduled rotation among the three major churches in Geneva.[205]

Calvin continues his treatment of the Eucharist, and makes it plain that the purity of the Supper is paramount:

> But the principal rule that is required, and for which it is necessary to have the greatest care, is that this Holy Supper, ordained and instituted for joining the members of our Lord Jesus Christ with their Head and with one another in one body and one spirit, be not spoiled and contaminated by those coming to it and communicating, who declare and manifest by their misconduct and evil life that they do not at all belong to Jesus. For in this profanation of his sacrament our Lord is gravely dishonoured.[206]

To guard the sacrament, Calvin maintains that the church must enforce discipline and, if necessary, excommunication.[207] Calvin appeals to a series of Bible verses

---

202 Reid, *Calvin: Theological Treatises* (*Articles sur le Gouvernement de l'Eglise* = *Articles* hereafter), 48.
203 "It would be well to require that the Communion of the Holy Supper of Jesus Christ be held every Sunday at least as a rule. When the Church assembles together for the great consolation which the faithful receive and the profit which proceeds from it, in every respect according to the promises which are there presented to our faith, then we are really made participants of the body and blood of Jesus, of his death, of his life, of his Spirit and of all his benefits. (…) In fact, it was not instituted by Jesus for making a commemoration two or three times a year, but for a frequent exercise of our faith and charity, of which the congregation of Christians should make use as often as they be assembled, as we find written in Acts chap. 2, that the disciples of our Lord continued in the breaking of bread, which is the ordinance of the Supper. Such also was always the practice of the ancient Church," Reid, *Calvin: Theological Treatises*, (*Articles*), 49.
204 Reid, *Calvin: Theological Treatises*, (*Articles*), 50.
205 Reid, *Calvin: Theological Treatises*, (*Articles*), 50.
206 Reid, *Calvin: Theological Treatises*, (*Articles*), 50.
207 Reid, *Calvin: Theological Treatises*, (*Articles*), 50–51.

(Matt. 18, 1 Tim. 1, 1 Cor. 5) as well as to the example of the "ancient Church."[208] When one is excommunicated, that person is prohibited from communion, and other believers are to avoid "intimate dealings" with them, but they are expected to keep attending church and hearing the sermons, since the preached Word might convict them of their sins and bring repentance.[209] But Calvin does not simply focus on corrective discipline. He also recommends more constructively that the magistrates make a public profession of their faith, that psalm-singing be encouraged, and that children be catechized and examined.[210]

This emphasis on catechesis and proper preparation for communion was repeated in the 1541 *Ecclesiastical Ordinances*.[211] The section on the Eucharist begins with Calvin's characteristic plea for frequency: "Since the Supper was instituted for us by our Lord to be frequently used, and also was so observed in the ancient Church until the devil turned everything upside down, erecting the mass in its place, it is a fault in need of correction, to celebrate it so seldom."[212] Then it proceeds with what had become the "Genevan communion compromise," recommending monthly observance.[213] However, the *Ordinances* also stress the need for proper preparation and examination.[214] Again, Calvin's desire for frequent communion is carefully balanced by the conviction that we must come to communion adequately instructed and properly prepared.[215]

---

208 Reid, *Calvin: Theological Treatises*, (*Articles*), 51. Calvin lists three reasons for excommunication: to avoid dishonoring Jesus and his Church, to provoke the sinner to repentance, to warn others and keep them free from evil influences. Reid, *Calvin: Theological Treatises*, (*Articles*), 51.

209 Reid, *Calvin: Theological Treatises*, (*Articles*), 52.

210 Reid, *Calvin: Theological Treatises*, (*Articles*), 54.

211 According to Reid, these Ordinances were first drafted by Calvin and the other ministers of Geneva in September, 1541, and then formally adopted by the Genevan magistrates in November, *Theological Treatises*, 56. See also Karin Maag, *Lifting Hearts to the Lord: Worship with John Calvin in Sixteenth-Century Geneva* (Grand Rapids: Wm. B. Eerdmans Publishing Co., 2016), 148.

212 Reid, *Calvin: Theological Treatises*, (*Articles*), 66.

213 "Hence it will be proper that it be always administered in the city once a month, in such a way that every three months it take place in each parish. Besides, it should take place three times a year generally, that is to say at Easter, Pentecost and Christmas, in such a way that it be not repeated in the parish in the month when it should take place by turn," Reid, *Calvin: Theological Treatises*, (*Articles*), 67. This proposed system of rotating communions, similar to the pattern in Bucer's Strasbourg, was not approved by the Genevan city council. Instead, they implemented quarterly communion. McKee, *The Pastoral Ministry and Worship in Calvin's Geneva*, 255–56.

214 "The Sunday before the celebration, intimation is to be made, in order that no child come before it has made profession of its faith as proved by examination by the Catechism, and also that all strangers and new-comers may be exhorted first to come and present themselves at the church, so that they be instructed and thus none approach to his own condemnation," Reid, *Calvin: Theological Treatises*, (*Articles*), 67.

215 For concrete examples of the Consistory "fencing" the Table, see Karin Maag, *Lifting Hearts to the Lord*, 152, 154. As in other areas of doctrine and praxis, Calvin's attitude here developed over

One of Calvin's enduring legacies is the system of ecclesiastical discipline that he eventually established in Geneva.[216] According to Kingdon, this was the most controversial aspect of Calvin's 1541 church constitution, as well as the point on which Calvin was most adamant.[217] Although some scholars have suggested Anabaptist influence on Calvin during his pastorate in Strasbourg as a source for his theory of church discipline, it seems clear that Calvin arrived at his conclusions independently.[218] Bucer's influence on Calvin is also surely a factor.[219] Kingdon's often-repeated characterization of the Genevan Consistory as a "compulsory counseling service" captures an important aspect of Calvin's theological and practical understanding of ecclesiastical discipline.[220]

Church discipline obviously impacted participation in communion. Although the Genevan pastors recognized the desirability of more frequent communion, they also created disciplinary structures that necessarily limited eucharistic frequency. The 1541 *Ecclesiastical Ordinances* mandated that twelve elders be chosen so that

---

time. Speelman describes Calvin's early ministry in Geneva: "Because the Lord's Supper formed the visible core of religious life for Calvin, and because the government failed to do anything about the profanation of the Holy Supper, he grew in the conviction that it would be good for the preachers to be given some form of supervision in regard to the Lord's Supper." *Calvin and the Independence of the Church*, 95. He continues later (102), "Calvin's most important contribution to the rebuilding of the church's new life in Geneva was formed by his efforts to convince the council and population how important it was to maintain the sanctity of the Lord's Supper."

216 Speelman discerns a five-stage process, over 25 years, whereby Calvin more fully developed his theory and practice of penance, confession, and church discipline. That development is beyond the scope of this book, but the central motive behind this entire process was Calvin's desire to safeguard the purity of the Lord's Table. Because he believed communion was so important, he was also driven to implement systems of penance and preparation so people could come to the Table and reap the full benefits, while avoiding the judgment of God. See Speelman, *Melanchthon and Calvin on Confession and Communion*, 153–160 and chap. 8.

217 Robert Kingdon, "Calvin and the Government of Geneva," in *Calvinus Ecclesiae Genevensis Custos*, ed. Wilhelm Neuser (Frankfurt am Main: Verlag Peter Lang, 1984), 59.

218 Matthew Scott Harding, "A Calvinist and Anabaptist Understanding of the Ban," *Perichoresis*, vol. 10, Issue 2 (2012): 165–193. Calvin spent the years 1538–1540 in Strasbourg, but Harding points to clear advocacy of church discipline, and excommunication in particular, in Calvin's works *before* 1538.

219 Kingdon, "Calvin and Church Discipline," 30.

220 Kingdon, "A New View of Calvin in Light of the Registers of the Geneva Consistory," *Calvinus Sincerioris Religionis Vindex: Calvin as Protector of the Purer Religion*, Wilhelm H. Neuser and Brian G. Armstrong, eds., (Kirksville, MO: Sixteenth Century Journal Publishers, 1997), 23. Kingdon also comments: "In the Consistory the pastors joined the elders in what amounted to a combination counseling service and court," in "Calvin and the Government of Geneva," 64. See also Jeffrey R. Watt, *The Consistory and Social Discipline in Calvin's Geneva* (Rochester: University of Rochester Press, 2020).

"there be some in every quarter of the city, to keep an eye on everybody."[221] This was not simply motivated by a desire to be busybodies and pry into the private lives of the citizens. As Calvin expressed it in his order of worship, the *Form of Prayers and Manner of Ministering the Sacrament according to the use of the Ancient Church* (1540), the fundamental motivation was to preserve the holiness of the Lord's Supper. Calvin sternly warns the unrepentant to "abstain from this Holy Table, lest they defile and contaminate the holy food which our Lord Jesus Christ gives to none except they belong to His household of faith."[222]

Careful studies of the day-to-day functioning of the Genevan Consistory demonstrate a general pattern. People were summoned before the Consistory, questioned, and examined. If found guilty, the most common form of punishment was a public scolding, usually performed by Calvin, but not exclusively. After this admonition, or remonstrance, the matter was usually resolved. This was effective because of the "central role of public shaming in maintaining social discipline in sixteenth-century communities."[223] Because of the public nature of communion, with its close linkage to the Christian commonwealth, being barred from communion (in either suspension or excommunication) was a serious matter for most Genevans. One's standing in the church affected familial, business, and political relationships in the wider community. Accordingly, the Consistory devoted much of its time before the quarterly communion services to facilitating the reconciliation of offended parties, and to drawing up a list of those who were unrepentant, and thus barred from communion.[224] This work continued after the communion services, to make sure those who were still unreconciled could partake of the next communion.[225] This illustrates again the intimate connections between church discipline and communion frequency in Geneva.

Maag describes the eucharistic patterns of Reformation Geneva as follows: "The Genevan church year was shaped by the quarterly celebrations of the Lord's Supper, at Christmas, at Easter, at Pentecost, and in September. Each Lord's Supper service was preceded by a Sunday of preparation during which special sermons

---

221 Reid, ed., *Calvin: Theological Treatises*, 63–64. See also Kingdon, "A New View of Calvin in Light of the Registers of the Geneva Consistory," 21–22 for the structure and composition of the Consistory.

222 Thompson, *Liturgies of the Western Church*, 206.

223 Kingdon, "A New View of Calvin," 26.

224 Kingdom, "The Genevan Revolution in Public Worship," *Princeton Seminary Bulletin*, 20, no. 3 (1999): 278.

225 Kingdon, "A New View of Calvin," 30. Scott Manetsch suggests that the decline in ecclesiastical discipline after Calvin's death may have been linked to the "practical difficulties of enforcing discipline and restoring a growing number of people to the Lord's Supper," *Calvin's Company of Pastors*, 211.

were preached in the churches."[226] Calvin's preaching at these services was more passionate and fervent than usual. Terlouw suggests that Calvin's intensity in these preparatory sermons was a natural consequence of how seriously Calvin viewed the sacrament and the obligations of those who going to commune.[227] Prior to these four communions, the Genevan Consistory held special meetings to ensure that everyone repented of their sins and returned to fellowship with each other, and with the church. In 1550, the elders and other town officials visited houses before the Easter communion, questioning the residents about their readiness to participate in the communion.[228]

As McKee points out, this communal rhythm of preparing for, and observing the sacrament, formed the high point of both ecclesiastical and political life in many Reformed churches.[229] One of the factors contributing to this communal rhythm was that "by 1550 it [communion] came to be held only on Sundays ... Another was the characteristic relationship between the Lord's Supper and teaching/discipline in Geneva that led to a pattern of liturgical time which distinguished the Calvinist Reformed into the modern era. There was a distinctive liturgical rhythm which later generations would call 'sacramental seasons.'"[230] McKee is building on, and

---

226 Maag, *Lifting Hearts to the Lord*, 19. So also Manetsch, *Calvin's Company of Pastors*: "The rhythm of church discipline, of censure, repentance, and restoration, was tied closely to the quarterly communion cycle. The Consistory faced an especially heavy load of disciplinary cases in the weeks leading up to the four annual celebrations of the Lord's Supper, and a disproportionately large number of people were suspended from or restored to the sacrament of the Table during this period. To handle this increased workload, the Consistory met twice rather than once during the week prior to communion Sunday. Likewise, Geneva's church constitution required that ministers visit the households in their parishes during the weeks prior to the celebration of the Lord's Supper at Easter to ensure that all men and women who partook of the bread and wine possessed a basic understanding of the Christian message," 127. In addition, see Christian Grosse, *Les rituels de la cène: le culte eucharistique réformé à Genève (XVIe–XVIIe siècles)*, (Geneva: Librairie Droz, 2008), 443.

227 "The sanctity and dignity of the Lord's Supper had to be safeguarded since the holy sacrament required purification of body and soul. This is why Calvin, in the final part of his sermons [on the Sunday before communion services], in the context of application and exhortation, deliberately made use of the vehement tone." Arjen Terlouw (2018) "'Naturally More Vehement and Intense': Vehemence in Calvin's Sermons on the Lord's Supper," *Reformation & Renaissance Review*, 20:1, 70–81, DOI: 10.1080/14622459.2017.1419802.

228 McKee, *The Pastoral Ministry and Worship in Calvin's Geneva*, 264–66. Manetsch provides a helpful overview of the Consistory and its work of church discipline in *Calvin's Company of Pastors*, 182–220. See also Speelman, *Melanchthon and Calvin on Confession and Communion*, 218–219.

229 "For the Calvinist Reformed tradition, the practice of the Lord's Supper was much more than a single service on certain Sundays of the year; it was the central high point of liturgical time." McKee, *The Pastoral Ministry*, 263.

230 "In effect the four celebrations of the Lord's Supper shaped four seasons of special religious devotion. The Supper and its importance are illuminated by the rituals which came to be associated with it.

summarizing, the foundational research of Christian Grosse here. For the purposes of this study, it is especially interesting to note the similarities between the Genevan pattern of preparation, examination, and quarterly communion with what became the standard practice in the Scottish Reformed churches and the Scottish immigrant communities in the Americas. Since many English and Scottish reformers took refuge in Geneva, and other Swiss cities, during times of persecution, they no doubt took part in the Genevan "sacramental seasons" and were inspired by them in their continued efforts of reform when they returned to their homelands. Thus, the communion practices of Geneva influenced many other communities in Europe, and beyond.

In the context of this study, in can be concluded that Calvin thought that weekly communion was ideal, but not essential (it could be either more, or less, often). However, Calvin gradually came to hold that spiritual preparation and examination were indispensable for proper participation in the Lord's Supper, and for practical reasons this necessitated an infrequent communion-rhythm of at best 5–6 times a year per church. Just a few years before his death, Calvin wrote to another pastor in 1561:

> We are very pleased that the Supper is being celebrated every month [in the other pastor's church], provided that this more frequent use does not produce carelessness. When a considerable part of the congregation stays away from communion, the church somehow becomes fragmented.[231]

Calvin continues, relating the history of his own struggles with implementing more frequent communion:

> When I first came here [to Geneva], the Lord's Supper was observed only three times a year, and seven whole months intervened between the observance at Pentecost and at the Birthday of Christ. A monthly observance pleased me, but I could not persuade the people, and it seemed better to bear with their weakness than to continue arguing

---

These manifest an intensified attention to faith and practice on the part of the whole of Geneva for the week or even two before and sometimes after the actual service itself. Formally, there was supposed to be an announcement of the Supper on the previous Sunday, with some (limited) exposition of the meaning of the sacrament … That same Sunday before the Supper there was regularly an examination of the catechism for students who were considered ready to profess their faith." There would also be additional consistory meetings to deal with cases of church discipline before the Supper. McKee, *The Pastoral Ministry*, 263–64.

231 *Calvin's Ecclesiastical Advice*, Mary Beaty and Benjamin W. Farley, trans. and eds. (Louisville: Westminster John Knox, 1991), 96 [*Consilium*, Aug. 12, 1561, OC 10:213].

stubbornly. I took care to have it recorded in the public records, however, that our way was wrong, so that correcting it might be easier for future generations.[232]

McKee comments: "Calvin was apparently cautioning this correspondent not to sacrifice unity for the sake of frequency. While he continued to protest against the small number of times the sacrament was offered, the pastor accepted this accommodation as preferable to a conflict which might destroy the church. He chose his battles and determined to take his stand on preparation and unity."[233]

Because of this unflinching emphasis on moral purity when approaching the Lord's Supper, Kingdon argues that Calvin actually made the ceremony more meaningful and important than it had been:

> It is true that Calvin would have preferred communion more frequently than once every four months. But the city government made it clear that they did not want more frequent communion. Calvin bowed to their will on this point. The issue was not that important to him. It was not as important as the maintenance of discipline. Indeed it can be argued that Calvin made a virtue of necessity and made communion of greater importance than before, by demanding that everyone receive it, and by going to considerable lengths to see to it that recipients were in fact worthy.[234]

Although Calvin began his career trying to chart a middle course between the eucharistic theologies of Zwingli and Luther, his enduring legacy was in the matter of ecclesiastical discipline. Later generations of Reformed theologians would argue about the true nature of Calvin's eucharistic theology, but the prominence of Calvin's program of church discipline remained distinctive and influential.[235] Calvin's decision to accept quarterly communion in Geneva had "significant consequences, for the limitation of communion to four times a year turned the Genevan form of celebrating the Supper into a powerful tool for establishing group identity not only in that city but even more so in the French and Scottish Churches that looked to Geneva as their model."[236]

---

232 *Calvin's Ecclesiastical Advice*, 96.
233 McKee, *The Pastoral Ministry and Worship in Calvin's Geneva*, 256–57.
234 Kingdom, "The Genevan Revolution in Public Worship," 279.
235 Kingdon, "Calvin and Church Discipline," 25.
236 Nelson Burnett, "The Social History of Communion and the Reformation of the Eucharist," 114–15.

2.10   Conclusion

The relationship between church discipline and communion frequency highlights a tension within the Reformed tradition. Although the Reformers uniformly advocated more frequent oral (as opposed to visual) communion than had been typical practice in the late medieval church, they also argued, to varying degrees, for the implementation of church discipline. They did not simply argue for more frequent communion—they argued for more *faithful* frequent communion. For the Reformers, faithful partaking of communion required true faith and a life of obedience that manifested that faith. To ensure faithful partaking, the Reformers wrote catechisms and instituted set times and patterns for catechesis. They advocated pre-communion examinations by the elders. They also proposed various forms of church oversight, accountability, and disciplinary structures.

Although Reformers like Oecolampadius and Bucer did not live to see their ideals successfully implemented, it is important to remember and consider their views on discipline when inquiring about their views on communion frequency. In later debates, the Reformers were often appealed to in a simplistic fashion, which ignored the totality of their ecclesiological ideals and aspirations.[237] The question of development in Calvin's thought (e. g., is his insistence on frequent communion something peculiar to the young Calvin?) is answered by the pastoral realities of his *context*. In other words, although Calvin remained committed to an ideal of weekly, or more frequent, communion, he was also more and more willing to sacrifice frequency for due preparation, and it seems that the concern for such preparation gained prominence in Calvin's pastoral context. In any case, purity and the proper reception of communion became the priorities for Calvin.[238] The Genevan structures of church discipline also impacted participation in communion. Although Calvin, at least, desired more frequent communion, he also created disciplinary structures that necessarily limited eucharistic frequency. It would have been impossible to have weekly communion, given how much time the consistory needed to examine potential communicants and deal with cases of church discipline. The priority of purity and proper participation took precedence over frequency, or at least made frequent communion unrealistic and unattainable.

---

237 In the communion frequency debates of eighteenth and nineteenth centuries in the Scottish Presbyterian church, we find frequent appeals to Calvin on this issue. See Chapters 5 and 6, below.
238 "For Calvin, the Lord's Supper was a means of grace which should be celebrated as often as the whole church was prepared to commune ... However, when he became a pastor, Calvin recognized that the ideal frequency of the apostles would be virtually impossible in the circumstances he faced ... Reforming the practice required a balance between emphasizing the value of participating and the ways (re)defining worthiness, and it was lay people who most needed this kind of encouragement." McKee, *The Pastoral Ministry*, 250–51.

Appealing to the authority of "Calvin" reveals a peculiar dynamic. Robert Kingdon notes that:

> There are some interesting debates among the French Reformed in the seventeenth century on the question of whether elders should be entitled to assist in administering communion. Both sides appealed to the authority of Calvin. [One side appealed to Calvin's published writings, and the other appealed to his actual practice.] This is one point among many where it becomes clear that to understand the shape and nature of Calvin's influence, we need to consider his ministry as well as his books.[239]

In a similar fashion, those who favor more frequent communion can appeal to many sources in Calvin's writings, whereas those who oppose it can appeal to Calvin's practice of catechesis, examination before communion, and church discipline, as well as other instances in his writings where Calvin stresses purity and preparation. Thus, ironically, Calvin is quoted and appealed to by authors who later argued for more frequent communion in the English, Scottish, and early American contexts, as well as by those who wished to maintain the pattern of infrequent communion that developed. Those who desired weekly communion could quote Calvin in support of their views. However, the pattern of church discipline and emphasis on preparing people to receive communion, both intellectually, and spiritually, would prevail in Reformed churches.

---

239 Robert Kingdom, "The Genevan Revolution in Public Worship," 178.

Chapter 3
Communion Frequency in the Reformation in England and Scotland (1536–1603)

3.1   Introduction

The Scottish communion frequency debates of the 1700s and 1800s that spilled over into the Americas were inseparably connected with English reform movements of the 1600s. English authors were quoted and appealed to, alongside of Continental theologians like Calvin. Although the Protestant movements in Scotland and England traveled on different tracks in many instances, there were also countless ways in which the movements influenced each other.

The influence of the sixteenth century reforms in the British Isles spanned the Atlantic to directly impact the first American colonies and the churches in the New World. Many American Presbyterian churches traced their lineage to the era of the Westminster Assembly (1643–1653). Issues of adherence to, or departure from, the Westminster Confession disturbed branches of the American Reformed church, even into the present day. Beyond this issue of ecclesiastical identity, there is no doubt that Reformed churches have profoundly influenced and shaped American culture.[1] In many ways the influence of the British Puritan movements has affected American Reformed and Presbyterian churches even more deeply than the first generation of Continental Reformers.

This chapter will not attempt to offer a complete history of the British Reformation and various manifestations of English and Scottish Protestantism.[2] Rather, it will trace the twin themes of preparation/purity and communion frequency in British authors, especially in relationship to the Scottish Reformed church. It surveys the English Isles during the period 1536, when the stirrings of reform began with the passing of the Six Articles, to 1603, when James VI of Scotland became James I of England (3.2). It will examine the communion practices and theology of late medieval England, and then summarize the changes in theological understandings

---

1 See Thomas Davis, ed., *Calvin's American Legacy*; Bradley J. Longfield, *Presbyterians and American Culture: A History* (Louisville: Westminster John Knox Press, 2013); James H. Smylie, *A Brief History of the Presbyterians* (Louisville: Geneva Press, 1996); and Mark Knoll, *A History of Christianity in the United States and Canada* (Grand Rapids: William B. Eerdmans Publishing Company, 1992), 30–51.
2 For an overview of the current state of research, see Peter Marshall, "England," in David M. Whitford, ed., *Reformation and Early Modern Europe: A Guide to Research* (Kirksville: Truman State University Press, 2008), 250–272.

of communion in the early English Reformation. In particular, the growing concerns about protecting the purity of the church, and helping parishioners to come fully prepared to communion, will be highlighted. Developments north of the border will also be surveyed, as well as the founding documents of the Scottish Reformation, focusing on their statements about communion frequency (3.3). The various factors that contributed to the developing patterns of communion frequency in Scotland will be delineated. Many of the factors that affected communion frequency in England and Scotland were the same, or quite similar. Comparing them will facilitate a more comprehensive analysis of later communion frequency debates and practices.

3.2   Reformation and Communion Frequency in England

The scholarly interpretations of the upheavals in sixteenth century England and beyond are only slightly less contentious than the original events themselves.[3] Although no heretics are now burned at the stake, scholars offer conflicting readings of the immense changes in early modern English religion and society.[4] As Peter Marshall observes "the English Reformation, once an exclusively mid-Tudor business, has become a 'long Reformation,' and a process, not an event."[5] A major challenge to previous historiography has been the work of the "Catholic revisionists"—most notably Eamon Duffy, Christopher Haigh, and J.J. Scarisbrick.[6] The

---

3 "In a thirty-year period from the latter portion of Henry's reign to the opening of Elizabeth's no less than six varieties of Christian faith and practice successively prevailed in the English Church," William Crockett, "From the Reformation to the Eighteenth Century," in Stephen Sykes and John Booty, eds., *The Study of Anglicanism* (London: SPCK/ Fortress Press, 1988), 6. Euan Cameron comments on the contentious nature of the reform movements in England and Scotland: "England and Scotland were the most important, if not the only, kingdoms to adopt the south German or Swiss pattern of Reformation as their sole official faith. However, in both these countries the reformed settlement led to decades of controversy: not whether to allow Protestantism or not (as in France), nor yet what 'confession' to choose (as in the Palatinate), nor even (at first) how to keep doctrine pure (as in the intra-Lutheran feuds). The disputes were over how thoroughly 'reformed' the kingdoms were to be; how far the new creed could be enforced; and how the zealots' desire for thoroughness could be reconciled with a monarch's concern to keep the movement under rigid control. In both kingdoms the monarchy faced energetic voluntary Protestants striving to promote the 'confession' at the expense of the monarch's authority." *The European Reformation*, 391.

4 See Peter Marshall, *Heretics and Believers: A History of the English Reformation* (New London: Yale University Press, 2017) as well as Eamon Duffy, *Reformation Divided: Catholics, Protestants and the Conversion of England* (London: Bloomsbury, 2017), 1–15 for a provocative summary of Reformation studies in general, and of perspectives on the English Reformation (s) in particular.

5 Marshall, "England," 250.

6 "The effect of what some commentators have not hesitated to call 'Catholic revisionism' has been to deal a fatal blow to Whiggish and progressivist narratives of the early Reformation in England."

situation does not improve if we look later in English church history. Coffey and Lim note that "[d]efining Puritanism has become a favourite parlour game for early modern historians."[7] First, however, we will briefly mention some main contours of the English Reformation, from the passage of the Six Articles in 1536 to the beginning of Elizabeth's reign in 1558 (3.2) and then the Scottish Reformation (3.3). The goal of this chapter is to set the stage and describe part of the context of the later communion frequency debates of the 1700s and 1800s, on both sides of the Atlantic.

3.2.1   Key Aspects of the English Reformation

While the English Reformation forged its own path, it was by no means an isolated phenomenon. In the early years of the English Reformation, as on the Continent, communion frequency was not a central issue, and the nature of the Eucharist was a more pressing issue than the precise frequency of its reception. Like their counterparts on the Continent, many English Reformers were generally pursuing more frequent communion in a basic sense, compared to the infrequent oral reception of the Eucharist in the medieval period. Those advocating reforms of the church also pursued a goal of oral reception by the entire church, more frequently than in the past. Only later, in the 1700s and early 1800s, would even more frequent (i. e. weekly) communion become a concern (see Ch. 5 and 6).

As said, the English reforming movements did not exist in isolation from developments in Europe. Although Luther's writings infiltrated England slowly, eventually his books were ceremonially burned outside St. Paul's Cathedral in 1521 and bishop John Fisher preached for two hours against Luther's dangerous ideas. Furthermore, King Henry VIII penned a response to Luther's "heresy," which earned him the title "Defender of the Faith" from Pope Leo X.[8] But reforming ideas and ideals spread rapidly. A vibrant social network existed that united Reformers of all types throughout Europe and the British Isles. A few of the more obvious and pertinent examples include the Zurich church leader Heinrich Bullinger's popularity and

---

Marshall, "England," 252. See J.J. Scarisbrick, *The Reformation and the English People* (Oxford: Oxford University Press, 1984), Christopher Haigh, *English Reformations: Religion, Politics, and Society under the Tudors* (Oxford: Clarendon Press, 1993) and Eamon Duffy, *The Stripping of the Altars: Traditional Religion in England 1400–1580*.

7 *The Cambridge Companion to Puritanism*, ed. John Coffey and Paul C.H. Lim (Cambridge: Cambridge University Press, 2008), 1. Regarding theological labels, Marshall writes: "The tenor of much current work here is to point to the fluidity of religious positions in what was effectively a pre-confessional age. For the first half of the sixteenth century at least, 'Protestant' is an anachronistic term, and 'evangelical' better conveys a sense both of the linkages to pre-Reformation culture and of the nondenominational character of a fissiparous movement for religious renewal." Marshall, "England," 255.

8 Peter Marshall, *Heretics and Believers*, 125–26.

influence in England (especially through the translation of his *Decades* into English),[9] Thomas Cranmer's early travels to Germany, his extensive correspondence network with Continental Reformers, and his personal friendships with Bullinger, Martin Bucer, and Peter Martyr Vermigli (which resulted in Bucer and Vermigli taking positions at Cambridge and Oxford, respectively). During the brief reign of Edward VI, many other church leaders besides Bucer and Vermigli came to England from the continent, including the Polish nobleman and reformer Jan Łaski (John à Lasco), who presided over the Stranger church of Dutch and French refugees in London.[10] Conversely, those who were forced to flee England and Scotland during the reigns of Henry VIII and Mary took refuge in reforming communities on the Continent. When they returned, they came back to England and Scotland with fresh enthusiasm for the continued reformation of church and society.[11] The network of influences ran far and deep. Indeed, much of the tension between various parties and movements within Scotland, England, Ireland, and Wales was fueled by efforts to either reproduce (or not) reforming patterns on the Continent.[12]

The career of John Knox in particular, and the shape of the Scottish Reformation in general, exemplifies this pattern of Continental influence on the British Isles. Knox's life also illustrates the close connections between the reform movements in England and Scotland. Knox spent much of his ministry in England. He was a chaplain to Edward VI and was involved in the production of the 1552 Second Prayer Book.[13] Later, Knox was one of the refugees who fled to the Continent to

---

9 See Benedict, *Christ's Churches Purely Reformed*, 59.

10 Regarding the Edwardian reforms, Peter Marshall summarizes MacCulloch's contributions, especially "his insistence on the internationalism of mid-Tudor Protestantism. Far from being an insular process (geared ultimately toward the evolution of something called Anglicanism), the Edwardian reformation positioned itself at the heart of a beleaguered European Protestant movement. Cranmer maintained close relations with the great networker of the Reformed Protestant world, Heinrich Bullinger of Zürich." See his "England," 257. Marshall also points out how this approach complements the work of Andrew Pettegree, "who has highlighted the importance of the London stranger churches, as well as the myriad international connections of English Protestants under Mary." See Andrew Pettegree, *Foreign Protestant Communities in Sixteenth-Century London* (Oxford: Clarendon Press, 1986). For à Lasco, see Benedict, *Christ's Churches Purely Reformed*, 68–73.

11 A prime example of this is John Hooper, who spent time in Zurich being mentored by Bullinger, before returning to England. Hooper eventually became the bishop of Gloucester and was burnt at the stake during the reign of Queen Mary. See W. Morris S. West, "John Hooper and the Origins of Puritanism," *The Baptist Quarterly* 15, no. 8 (1954): 346–368.

12 "While specific points of influence on particular individuals may often be hard to pinpoint, it is nonetheless clear that continental thought had a decisive impact upon English thought at this time in terms of its general shape and emphases," Carl Trueman, "The Theology of the English Reformers," in *The Cambridge Companion to Reformation Theology*, 162.

13 Duncan B. Forrester, "The Reformed Tradition in Scotland," in Wainwright and Westerfield Tucker, *The Oxford History of Christian Worship*, 475.

escape Mary. After his experiences abroad, and after serving as one of the pastors of an English-speaking congregation in Geneva, Knox returned with fresh enthusiasm for the work of reform, as did many others. But the Scottish Reformation was not the work of John Knox alone. David Wright highlights the "communal" nature of the Scottish Reformation.[14] This collective, or communal, aspect is seen both in the actual liturgies and ecclesiastical documents of the Scottish reform movement, but also in the wider dependence of the Scottish Reformation on previous developments on the Continent, and in England.[15] This is obvious in the official liturgy of the Scottish Reformation, *The Forme of Prayers and Ministration of the Sacraments*, which was heavily influenced by the Genevan model. It was also printed along with Calvin's 1542 catechism, translated into English. Additionally, continental documents such as the First Helvetic and Second Helvetic Confessions were prominent in the Scottish Reformation.[16]

As on the Continent, the first generation of English Reformers, such as Thomas Cranmer, John Hooper, Nicholas Ridley, and others, stressed that the lay people of the church must be present to have a Biblical communion service.[17] This call for congregational communion was part of their understanding of the "catholicity" of the church. They appealed explicitly to the example of the early church and claimed that their practices were more in line with the "primitive" church.[18] The question

---

14 David F. Wright, "The Scottish Reformation: theology and theologians" in Bagchi and Steinmetz, *The Cambridge Companion to Reformation Theology*, 175–176.

15 "The relatively late date of its decisive Reformation Parliament in July and August 1560 reflected and facilitated the Reformed kirk's reliance on more original achievements elsewhere, in England and on the continent," Wright, "The Scottish Reformation: theology and theologians," 176.

16 The early Scots reformer, George Wishart, produced an English translation of the First Helvetic Confession and a 1566 General Assembly in Scotland gave the official stamp of approval to Bullinger's Second Helvetic Confession. Wright, "The Scottish Reformation: theology and theologians," 176–177.

17 "Here one can discern a common thread uniting the reforms of Luther, Calvin, Zwingli, and Cranmer: all four churchmen believed strongly that the communion of the people is, by dominical institution, absolutely integral to the eucharist—just as they believed that there can be no sacrament without the 'lively preaching' of the Word." Mitchell, "Reforms, Protestant and Catholic," 325. As Davies puts it: "They believed that the Mass is essentially a Communion service and that where there is no reception by the faithful there is no Communion," Horton Davies, *Worship and Theology in England*, vol. 1, 141.

18 Mitchell notes that, "although in the first Book of Common Prayer (1549) Cranmer retained the traditional form of a eucharistic anaphora for use during 'The Supper of the Lorde, and The Holy Communion, Commonly Called the Masse,' he carefully noted in the rubrics that 'agreeable to the usage of the primitive Church,' the minister 'shall always have some [others] to communicate with him,' and that he 'shall forbear to celebrate the Communion, except he have some that will communicate with him.'" Mitchell, "Reforms, Protestant and Catholic," 325, quoting *The First and Second Prayer Books of Edward VI*, intro. Douglas Harrison, Everyman's Library (London: Dent, 1910), 212.

this presented, and the problem it created, was how to educate, train, and teach their congregations about the essential nature of the Lord's Supper, and to dispel and discredit the teachings and practices of the Catholic church. Though the early Reformers may have believed in an ideal of weekly communion, they were quickly confronted by the monumental task of changing the minds and hearts of people who had worshipped in particular ways for generations—even centuries.

While the issue of communion frequency was not a central issue in the early stages of the English Reformation, the tensions that would later divide the English church so profoundly were already latent in the reforms of Thomas Cranmer and others. For a host of reasons, the English Reformers retained elements of the medieval Catholic church—episcopal government, most notably, and liturgical elements that had been rejected by many of the Continental Reformers, especially by the Swiss. Cranmer's *First Book of Common Prayer* (1549) endeavored to balance reforms of liturgy and doctrine, while also preserving the forms and structures of traditional Western worship. However, other Reformers wanted to go further in the work of reformation.[19] These two streams—liturgical conservatism, and a more thoroughgoing reform—would continue to flow turbulently through the English Church and would turn into an overwhelming flood in the wars of the 1600s.[20]

3.2.2 Communion Frequency in the English Reformation

The First Book of Common Prayer is ambiguous in its ideal for communion frequency.[21] It provides for communion to be observed on Sundays, but also on festivals, special days of devotion, and during the week. In analyzing Cranmer's eucharistic theology, Davies states that Cranmer desired weekly communion, but offers no specific proof.[22] MacCulloch finds a clue about communion frequency expectations in a royal proclamation that was issued in the wake of the political unrest in 1549, in which the future of the English Reformation was in doubt.[23] In a proclamation on October 30, 1549, Cranmer and the other Councilors reiterated the core beliefs and practices of English reform efforts. Those who opposed the reforms were to be imprisoned, and those who refused to contribute their share

---

19 Carl Trueman highlights the latent tensions in the reforming English Church, tensions that preview the course of the various controversies in the Church of England. He also notes John Knox's contribution to what would become the more extreme Puritan point of view; "The Theology of the English Reformers," in Bagchi and Steinmetz, *The Cambridge Companion to Reformation Theology*, 169–173.

20 Trueman, "The Theology of the English Reformers," 169.

21 According to Frank Senn, *A Stewardship of the Mysteries*, 108. He references the Everyman Library version of the First Prayer Book, 32ff.

22 Davies, *Worship and Theology in England*, vol. 1, 118. He repeats the same basic claim on 185.

23 See Marshall, *Heretics and Believers*, 328–337, for background on the political and religious situation.

towards purchasing the bread and wine for the weekly communion service were to be punished. MacCulloch notes that this last injunction indicates "an interesting reflection of the frequency with which the new communion service was supposed to be celebrated."[24]

MacCulloch finds evidence of widespread reluctance to participate in weekly communion in later years. He claims that Cranmer and the other architects of the English Reformation intended to institute weekly communion, but that people were reluctant to come weekly. MacCulloch suggests that part of this reluctance might be explained by the "fierce exhortations to self-examination" which formed part of the 1549 rite. The expense of buying enough bread and wine for the entire congregation may also have deterred church officials from pursuing weekly communion.[25]

The ideals of theologians and prayer books were just that—ideals. What we can know about the realities of daily parish life suggests that reception of communion continued to be infrequent. *Harrison's Description of England in Shakespeare's Youth* (1557) provides a contemporary description of a typical Sunday Anglican worship service "from the standpoint of a loyal Anglican with some Puritan, but no Separatist, tendencies."[26] He describes a lack of pastors for every parish. Printed homilies were read, with pastors preaching four actual sermons a year.[27] After describing the Scripture readings and prayers, he moves to communion: "This being done, we proceed unto the communion, if any communicants be to receive the eucharist; if not we read the decalogue, epistle and gospel, with the Nicene creed (of some in derision called the dry communion), and then proceed unto an homily or sermon, which hath a psalm before and after it, and finally unto the baptism of such infants

24 Diarmaid MacCulloch, *Thomas Cranmer: A Life* (New Haven: Yale University Press, 1996), 453.

25 "Cranmer and his colleagues had intended their communion service to be the centre-piece of the regular worship of the Church, but this was not happening; people did not want to make their communion on such a frequent basis," MacCulloch, *Thomas Cranmer*, 510. However, the only actual evidence that MacCulloch cites is the report of a Venetian diplomat in 1551, who "noticed the way that London households were sending along a single representative, often a servant, to communion services, and that some merchants were indeed making fun of the government's new requirements." 348.

26 Davies, *Worship and Theology in England*, vol. 1, 215, quoting Furnivall, F. James, et al., *Harrison's Description of England In Shakspere's Youth: Being the Second And Third Books of His Description of Britaine And England* (London: Pub. for the New Shakspere society, by N. Trübner & co., 1877–81) I, 32. The context and history of Harrison's *Description* is rather complicated. However, it is primary source material that formed part of Holinshed's *Chronicle*, from which Shakespeare drew much of his material for his historical plays. See https://sourcebooks.fordham.edu/mod/1577harrison-england.asp#Chapter%20I for a summary. The text of Harrison's *Description* can be found at: https://archive.org/details/harrisonsdescri00harrgoog.

27 Davies, *Worship and Theology in England*, vol. 1, 215.

as on every Sabaoth day (if occasion so require) are brought unto the churches; and thus is the forenoon bestowed."[28]

Based on the rubrics in the 1559 Book of Common Prayer and on the records of episcopal visitations and ecclesiastical directives, Davies suggests some other common features of liturgical life in the churches of Elizabethan England. As on the Continent, the congregants were expected to notify the church authorities if they wished to partake of Holy Communion. The pastors were also supposed to warn their people of the dangers of partaking in an unworthy manner.[29] We see here the continuing Reformation concern to teach and enforce "proper participation" in the Eucharist. Also, in keeping with the reforming principle that communion implied the presence of people who can commune (and not just the priest), the rubrics stipulated that there must be at least three other people to communicate along with the priest. In cathedrals or churches affiliated with colleges, weekly communion was the prescribed minimum for the deacons and priests.[30] But the rubrics also displayed pastoral wisdom in that they required ordinary parishioners to receive Communion just three times a year, with Easter Communion being one of the required occasions.[31]

This chapter will skip, rather artificially, over the years between the publication of the first Book of Common Prayer in 1549 to the accession of Mary Tudor in 1553. This is not because these years are unimportant, but from the perspective of studying communion frequency, there is a paucity of sources. These were years of advance and development for the new English Protestant church, but under the reign of Mary Tudor, a time of persecution and exile for many of the leading English and Scottish reformers. Many of them fled to the Continent, where they experienced the worship and societal changes that had occurred Zurich, Geneva, and Strasbourg, among other centers of reform. Their experiences there gave them a renewed vision for the continuing reform of the English church when they eventually returned.

---

28 Davies, *Worship and Theology in England*, vol. 1, 215. I have modernized the spelling. Especially interesting here is Harrison's reference to a service without communion being a "dry communion." This is a recurring accusatory phrase in discussions of communion frequency, but it is not clear to me where this phrase originated.

29 "Those who intended to communicate at the Lord's Supper or Holy Communion were requested to give their names to the curate, whose duty it was to warn notoriously wicked persons and forbid them to approach the Lord's table until they had openly declared their repentance and amendment, and to reject those unreconciled in a quarrel until penitent and prepared to return to amity," Davies, *Worship and Theology in England*, vol. 1, 216.

30 Davies, *Worship and Theology in England*, vol. 1, 216.

31 Davies, *Worship and Theology in England*, vol. 1, 217.

3.3   Reformation and Communion Frequency in Scotland (1556–1603)

This study follows the example of Brian Spinks, in highlighting the connections between developments in England and Scotland. Later polemics, and the political and ecclesiastical controversies of the early modern period, have tended to separate ideas, people, and movements that were intricately connected in their original contexts.

Along with the English Reformation, the Scottish Reformation also forms an essential background to the development of American Reformed churches. Both the theological and liturgical traditions of the Scottish Reformed churches profoundly influenced developments both in England and across the Atlantic in North America. As in England, the Scottish situation reveals the interdependence between historical circumstance and theology. Although the Scottish Reformation was driven by distinct theological goals and ideals, various historical realities influenced these theological views and liturgical practices, which were then perpetuated as traditions that were either venerated, or criticized, by later generations.

Although connected to reforming movements in England, the Scottish reform efforts had several distinctive characteristics. For example, John Knox and other Scottish Reformers were self-consciously trying to implement Genevan ecclesiastical policies and a Presbyterian form of church government, both of which were more controversial in England. In the many political struggles that embroiled both Scotland and England, the issue of the English church's status—as not fully "Reformed"—became a bargaining chip. Most notably, the minority of Scottish delegates at the Westminster Assembly (1643–53) exerted a disproportionate amount of influence, in large part because the English Presbyterians needed the support of the Scots, and their army, as they endeavored to establish a state-sponsored Presbyterian church.

This section will trace the development of the Scottish reformation, as seen in its foundational documents (3.3.1). Then, it will examine patterns of communion frequency in the early and later Scottish Reformed church (3.3.2). The high emphasis placed on preaching and the structures of catechetical instruction will be summarized (3.3.3), along with the system of church discipline that was eventually implemented (3.3.4). It covers the period from the official beginnings of the Reformed Church of Scotland as mandated and laid out in ecclesial documents (1556), to the ascension to the throne of James VI of Scotland to the English throne in 1603. James VI became James I of England. Because he united the kingdoms of Scotland and England, and because Scotland was solidly Reformed by this point, many in England hoped that it would now be easier to pursue the further reformation of the English church.[32] The beginning of his reign in 1603 is therefore a convenient historical place holder for what some scholars name the "Post-Reformation" period in British history. Although the histories of Scotland and England cannot be separated, they will be treated in somewhat insular fashions in the rest of this chapter. Later chapters will highlight the interdependent nature of their histories, especially in the areas of communion observance and communion frequency.

3.3.1 Scottish Ecclesial Documents and Communion Frequency

The progress of reformation in Scotland was, in some ways, slower than in England.[33] But once the reformation of the church finally took hold, it transformed the Scottish church to such an extent that it implemented many of the ecclesiastical structures of Geneva and the Swiss Reformation.[34] This is not surprising, given the overlapping networks of influence between Geneva, and the wider continental reformation, and Scotland. As in England and on the Continent, worship reform efforts in Scotland were fueled by a desire for the laity to participate fully in the worship of the church. The Reformers wanted to move the laity from visual reception observers of a weekly Eucharist to engaged communicants who understood and appreciated the profundity of the Word preached, eaten and drunk.

This emphasis appears in the Scots Confession (1560), Article XVIII, where the essential characteristics of the true church are delineated. These marks are the "true preaching of the Word of God," the "right administration of the Sacraments," and "ecclesiastical discipline uprightly administered."[35] The Scots Confession teaches the centrality of the Lord's Supper in the church and Christian life. In Article XXI, it affirms the importance of the sacraments by condemning those who devalue them. If the Supper is "rightly used," we are actually "joined" to Jesus Christ, and he becomes the "nourishment and food of our souls."[36] Following the trajectory laid out by Calvin, this union is described as being effected by the Holy Spirit, and the language used to describe this union is drawn from the Biblical description of the union of a man and woman in marriage (epitomized by Genesis 2:23).[37]

---

32 Spinks, "Anglicans and Dissenters," in Wainwright and Tucker, eds., *The Oxford History of Christian Worship*, 503–504.

33 Spinks, *Sacraments, Ceremonies and the Stuart Divines: Sacramental theology and liturgy in England and Scotland 1603-1662* (Aldershot: Ashgate Publishing Limited, 2002), 24.

34 "The Reformation in Scotland was among the most radical and thoroughgoing of the Calvinist reformations in Europe," Forrester, "The Reformed Tradition in Scotland," 473.

35 *The Creeds of Christendom*, vol. III, ed. Philip Schaff, rev. David S. Schaff (Harper and Row, 1931, reprint 1983, reprint, Grand Rapids: Baker Books, 1998), 461–462.

36 Schaff, *Creeds of Christendom*, vol. III, 468.

37 "So that we do confess, and undoubtedly believe, that the faithful, in the right use of the Lords Table, do so eat the body and drink the blood of the Lord Jesus, that he remains in them, and they in him:

This emphasis on the sacramental reality of communion with Christ was balanced by demands for catechesis and church discipline. Article XXII requires communicants to understand the "right use" of the sacrament and requires ministers to teach correctly about it. Improper use, by either communicant or teacher, nullifies the efficacy of the sacrament.[38] Thus, the Lord's Supper was to be taught purely, and understood truly, before anyone could partake safely. The ecclesiology and sacramental understanding of the Scots Confession demanded *more* frequency than during the medieval period, but also laid the groundwork for developments that would limit communion frequency in Protestant Scottish churches. The emphasis on correct teaching, proper participation, and the necessity of church discipline assumed an ever-increasing significance in the Scots Reformed tradition, which made frequent communion nearly impossible to achieve. The trajectory of this development is clearly observable in the First Book of Discipline.

While the Scots Confession does not prescribe anything about the frequency of communion, the First Book of Discipline (1561) is more specific. The First Book of Discipline brought order to the emerging Scottish Protestant church and attempted to regulate a large swath of ecclesiastical and social matters.[39] In the "ninth head," which discusses matters of "policy" in the church, the authors of the First Book distinguish what is "utterly necessary" for a church, and what is "profitable." It is essential for a church to preach the word, administer the sacraments correctly, to pray together, to instruct the ignorant and correct the wayward. But the authors also recognize that different churches should have latitude in how often they will observe these essentials.

Regarding communion, the Book of Discipline discusses the doctrine of the Lord's Supper in the "Second Head" (Of Sacraments) but discusses communion frequency in the "Ninth Head" (Concerning the Policie of the Kirk): "Four times in the year we think sufficient to the administration of the Lord's Table, which we desire to be distincted [sic], that the superstition of times may be avoided so far as

[margin: Necessary vs. profitable]

---

yea, they are so made flesh of his flesh, and bone of his bones." Schaff, *Creeds of Christendom*, vol. III, 469.

38 "Moreover, that the Sacraments be rightly used, it is required that the end and cause why the Sacraments were institute [sic], be understood and observed, as well of the minister as of the receivers: for if the opinion be changed in the receiver, the right use ceases; as is most evident in the rejection of the sacrifices: as also if the teacher plainly teach false doctrine, as were odious and abominable before God (albeit they were his own ordinance) because that wicked men use them to another end than God has ordained." Schaff, *Creeds of Christendom*, vol. III, 472.

39 Although some scholars say that the Book of Discipline was largely ignored, Cameron presents evidence to the contrary: "The extent to which the Book of Discipline was implemented has often been underestimated." He continues, "Indeed the evidence that is available points in the opposite direction." *The First Book of Discipline*, James K. Cameron, ed. (Edinburgh: The Saint Andrew Press, 1972), 70.

may be." It rejects the typical medieval practice of only taking communion at Easter, and then neglecting it the rest of the year. The chief concern is to dissuade people from simply going to communions because of "superstition."[40] It also stresses the importance of teaching correct doctrine about the sacrament and directs ministers to examine people more regularly about their spiritual state.[41]

The First Book of Discipline also exhorts every "master of household" to diligently instruct his family, children, and servants in true doctrine, so they can come to the Lord's Table. The authors of the First Book clearly teach that understanding right doctrine is essential to participation in the Lord's Supper, and any "master of household" who failed in their duty of instruction those under their care was to be disciplined and excommunicated.[42]

The First Book lays out a basic standard for participation in the Eucharist. If one cannot say the Lord's Prayer and the "articles of the belief" (meaning by this the Apostles' Creed), they cannot be admitted to the Supper. The First Book recommends that each "kirk" hold a yearly time of examination, where the minister and elders of the church examine everyone and assess parishioners about their knowledge of the Christian faith, as well as their competency to come to communion.[43] Those who refuse to participate in this process, and those who let their

---

40 The "Ninth Head" states further: "For your Honours are not ignorant how superstitiously the people run to that action [an observance of communion] at Pascha, even as if the time gave virtue to the Sacrament, and how the rest of the whole year, they are careless and negligent, as if it appertained not unto them but at that time only. We think therefore most expedient that the first Sunday of March be appointed for one time, the first Sunday of June for another, the first Sunday of September for the third, and the first Sunday of December for the fourth. We do not deny but that any several Kirk, for reasonable causes may change the time and may minister oftner, but we study to repress superstition." Cameron, ed., *The First Book of Discipline*, 183–84.

41 "All ministers must be admonished to be more careful to instruct the ignorant than ready to serve their appetite and to use more sharp examination then indulgence in admitting to their great Mysteries [that great Mystery] such as be ignorant of the use and virtue of the same. And therefore we think that the administration of the Table ought never to be without that examination passing before specially of them whose knowledge is suspect. We think that none are to be admitted to this Mystery who can not formally say the Lords prayer, the Articles of the Belief, and declare the sum of the Law." Cameron, ed., *The First Book of Discipline*, 184.

42 Cameron, ed., *The First Book of Discipline*, 185–86.

43 "For such as be so dull and so ignorant that they can neither try themselves, nor yet know the dignity and mystery of that action cannot eat and drink of that Table worthily. And therefore of necessity we judge that every year at the least public examination be had by the Ministers and Elders of the knowledge of every person within the kirk; to wit, that every Master and Mistress of household come themselves and their family so many as be come to maturity before the Minister and Elders and give confession of their faith. If they understand not, nor cannot rehearse the commandments of Gods law, know not how to pray, neither wherein their righteousness stands or consists they ought not to be admitted to the Lords table." Cameron, ed., *The First Book of Discipline*, 186.

children and servants persist in "willful ignorance," are to be dealt with through excommunication, and then handed over to the civil magistrate.[44]

In the minds of the authors of the First Book of Discipline, proper proclamation of doctrine should result in a moral life that honors God and does not disrupt the community. Understanding right doctrine and living a godly life are the necessary qualifications for participating in the Lord's Supper. This emphasis on the connection between communion and church discipline continued the trajectory of the Genevan reforms and was one of the chief characteristics of the Scottish reformation. As Margo Todd puts it: "Scotland's Reformation put the English puritan agenda to shame in its thoroughgoing reform."[45]

The First Book of Discipline deals with church discipline in the "Seventh Head" (Of Ecclesiastical Discipline). Ecclesiastical discipline is necessary for the "purity" of the church and it deals with "faults" which the civil magistrate either does not, or should not, punish.[46] The chapter outlines the process of church discipline. Faults and sins are to be dealt with in proportion to how public they are, and in relation to the attitude of the one who is at fault.[47] Those who do not repent should ultimately be excommunicated, and others are instructed to avoid social or religious interactions with them. The point of this rejection is to spur the sinner to repentance.[48] The patterns of repentance and public examination that developed will be treated below, but the First Book here clearly lays the groundwork for the tensions that would arise between the dual priorities of more frequent communion, and a rigorist understanding of ecclesiastical discipline.

Besides the Scots Confession and the First Book of Discipline, the Book of Common Order prescribed the shape of Reformed worship in Scotland. In many ways, this source is the most relevant since patterns of worship tend to be the most deeply ingrained in the lives of individuals and communities. While ecclesial documents set out a vision for the reforming churches of Scotland, the liturgical patterns and expectations of local communities were the locus where theological doctrines and ideals were fleshed out in daily life. The local parish and traditional patterns of worship also proved to be the most difficult to reform, which would

---

44 Cameron, ed., *The First Book of Discipline*, 186.
45 Additionally, "But given population distribution in early modern Scotland, and the direct impact of towns on their immediate landward, it is surely the case that the most significant portion of the Scottish population … experienced as remarkably successful a Reformation as anywhere in Western Europe, on a vastly larger scale than the Calvinist towns on the continent, and in a more profound, penetrating form than anywhere else in the British Isles." Todd, *The Culture of Protestantism in Early Modern Scotland* (New Haven and London: Yale University Press, 2002), 15.
46 Cameron, ed., *The First Book of Discipline*, 165.
47 Cameron, ed., *The First Book of Discipline*, 167–170.
48 Cameron, ed., *The First Book of Discipline*, 170.

help create the background and context for the communion frequency debates of the eighteenth and early nineteenth centuries.

The Book of Common Order is rooted in Calvin's Geneva. When Knox returned from Geneva, he brought with him the order of worship that had been used in the English church in Geneva. This liturgy was itself based on the Genevan liturgical model.[49] In 1562 the Scottish General Assembly authorized *The Forme of Prayers and Ministration of the Sacraments* for official use. According to Maxwell, it became known as the *Book of Common Order* after 1564.[50] The section on the Eucharist notes that communion is "commonly" held monthly but leaves the matter to the discretion of the churches. The introductory rubric remarks: "The day when the Lord's Supper is ministered, which commonly is used once a month, or so often as the congregation shall think expedient, the minister says as follows."[51] Maxwell points out that this rubric describes the communion frequency of the English congregation in Geneva.[52] It was an ideal which failed to take root in Scotland.[53]

This rubric was not changed in the editions of *Forme of Prayers* published in Scotland. What may have motivated Knox and the other Scottish Reformers to depart from the pattern of monthly communion, in favor of the quarterly communion recommended by the First Book of Discipline? Maxwell suggests that one reason may have been the desire of the Scottish Reformers to avoid "the superstition of times," as stated in the First Book of Discipline's "Ninth Head."[54] This seems

---

49 Maxwell, *A History of Worship in the Church of Scotland* (London: Oxford University Press, 1955), 48.

50 "After 1564 it gradually became known as the *Book of Common Order*, though it seems more commonly to have been spoken of as the Psalm Book. It continued in use until the Westminster *Directory* superseded it in 1645," Maxwell, *The Liturgical Portions of the Genevan Service Book*, 9.

51 Jonathan Gibson and Mark Earngey, eds., *Reformation Worship: Liturgies from the Past for the Present* (Greensboro: New Growth Press, 2018), 593. See also, Maxwell, *The Liturgical Portions of the Genevan Service Book*, 120.

52 "This rubric indicates that in the English Congregation at Geneva monthly Communion was the normal practice, as indeed it was the normal practice in all the Calvinistic Churches of the time (Calvin's own Church at Geneva excepted)." Maxwell, *The Liturgical Portions of the Genevan Service Book*, 201. Maxwell makes a broad statement here, regarding the "normal" practice of "all" the Calvinistic churches. In support of this, he only quotes three sources regarding the French Walloon church in Frankfurt, pastored by Valérand Pullain, which observed monthly communion.

53 "The rubric … was generally disregarded in Scotland. Despite the provisions of the first Book of Discipline, 1560, and the definite orders of the General Assembly of 1562, the tradition of yearly, or semi-yearly, Communion soon became highly valued as distinctively Scottish and Protestant, and so continued to this day in many parishes." *The Liturgy of the Church of Scotland Since the Reformation, Part II. The Book of Common Order*, Stephen A. Hurlbut, ed. (Charleston: The St. Alban's Press, 1950), 55. Why the tradition of yearly, or semi-annual, communion took hold in Scotland will be explored below.

54 Cameron, ed., *The First Book of Discipline*, 183.

reasonable, given that the Scottish Reformers avoided celebrating the Supper on any of the traditional Christian festal days, such as Christmas or Easter.[55] So, a desire to avoid celebrating communion on any of the formerly Catholic festivals may have encouraged the institution of communion four times a year. But this does not explain why communion in the Protestant Church of Scotland became an annual, or semi-annual, affair. Nor does it explain how this pattern of Protestant infrequent communion assumed the hallowed status of a revered tradition, with its own elaborate religious and communal rituals.

One factor which made frequent communion difficult to achieve was the emphasis the Church of Scotland placed on ecclesiastical discipline. This characterized the Scottish church from the beginning of the reforming movement. In addition to the evidence already surveyed from the First Book of Discipline, this emphasis is discernible in the first editions of the *Forme of Prayers*. It was published along with the Geneva Catechism and a short confession previously used by the English church in Geneva.[56] This emphasis on church discipline became an important feature of the Reformed Church in Scotland. This laid the groundwork for later conflicts and debates regarding communion frequency.

3.3.2 Rhythms of the Scottish Reformed Community

During the Reformation period, the frequency of communion was obviously not a matter of critical concern. Whatever the intentions of Knox and the other Scottish Reformers, the ideal of quarterly (let alone monthly) communion was seldom realized, and Scottish Reformed churches settled into a period where infrequent communion prevailed. This pattern developed despite one of the earliest General Assemblies (December, 1562) which prescribed quarterly communion in the towns, and twice a year in the countryside.[57]

---

55 Maxwell, *The Liturgical Portions of the Genevan Service Book 1556*, 204. See Forrester and Murray, eds., *Studies in the History of Worship in Scotland*, 37. However, Forrester writes: "There is evidence that John Knox insisted on frequent celebrations of the Lord's supper and its centrality in worship from the earliest days of the Scottish Reformation," "The Reformed Tradition in Scotland," 476. Here, he cites James S. McEwan, *The Faith of John Knox* (London: Lutterworth, 1961), 56–59. McEwan's main evidence comes from the fact that Knox prioritized celebrating the Lord's Supper, even before a church could be officially established. He contrasts this with Calvin, who counseled pastors to refrain from the Supper, until a church could be put in order. However, McEwan makes several broad claims and appears to have an agenda formed by the liturgical movement of the 1960s. More work should be done to explore his claims.

56 Wright, "The Scottish Reformation," 177.

57 http://www.british-history.ac.uk/report.aspx?compid=58926 [accessed October 14, 2013]. See also Maxwell, *The Liturgical Portions of the Genevan Service Book*, 204.

After recounting records of infrequent communion in Edinburgh, Glasgow, and Perth in the late 1500s, Burnet concludes: "These details show that neglect of the Sacrament was all too common, and even in the sixteenth century a yearly celebration was too easily regarded as a maximum."[58] Thus, infrequent communion came to be seen as a Scots-Reformed "tradition."[59] This simply perpetuated the medieval patterns of communion reception. In the matter of what became standard communion frequency the Scots-Reformed were less radical than English. But in the implementation of church discipline and rule of the church by elders and sessions, the Scots-Reformed were more radical than the English, who retained much of the structure and liturgical worship of the Catholic church.

Many scholars have offered explanations of why the Scottish Reformed church so quickly abandoned the ideals of monthly, or even quarterly, communion, as outlined in the *Forme of Prayers* and the First Book of Discipline. Some blame the tenacity of medieval Catholic tradition.[60] Others blame the Puritans.[61] While these various explanations might all capture aspects of the truth, one important factor is often overlooked. This is the same dynamic that made communion frequency difficult to achieve in Continental Reformed churches—the emphasis on catechesis and church discipline.

---

58 George B. Burnet, *The Holy Communion in the Reformed Church of Scotland 1560–1960* (Edinburgh and London: Oliver and Boyd, 1960), 14.

59 Maxwell, *The Liturgical Portions of the Genevan Service Book*, 204.

60 This is a common refrain in the literature. See e. g., Forrester, "Popular prejudices against, for instance, the frequent reception of communion died hard and triumphed over the Reformers' intentions and their theology of the Lord's Supper," "The Reformed Tradition in Scotland," 471. Earlier, Thomas Leishman, writing in 1891, claimed: "Everything tends to show that the prevailing custom of the laity at the time of the Reformation was to communicate only once a year, except in the case of the very devout, or at the approach of death. To this Popish practice the people of Scotland adhered with remarkable steadfastness. Quarterly communion was treated as a devout imagination. Edinburgh did begin with the medieval minimum of three communions, but had fallen back to two before Knox was in his grave, and no town ever seems to have thought of having more. In rural parishes annual communion was the rule, and the ecclesiastical records are full of cases in which years, sometimes many years in succession, passed without any celebration. Under presbyter and bishop alike this scandalous neglect prevailed." *Ritual of the Church of Scotland*, 342. This was vol. 5 of Robert Herbert Story, ed., *The Church of Scotland, Past and Present* (London: William Mackenzie, 1891), quoted in Hurlbut, *The Liturgy of the Church of Scotland*, 55–56. See also Burnet, *The Holy Communion*, 61, relying on William McMillan "Medieval Survivals in Scottish Worship," *Church Service Society Annual* 4 (1931–1932): 21–34.

61 "Under Puritan influences, which invaded Scotland from England, annual or semi-annual Communions became the rule—and indeed the practice of our Church in this respect has always been below its own standard; but repeated Acts of Assembly have enjoined or pointed to reformation in the matter." H.J. Wotherspoon and J.M. Kirkpatrick, *A Manual of Church Doctrine according to the Church of Scotland* (London: Oxford University Press, 1960, revised and enlarged by T.F. Torrance and Ronald Shelby Wright; originally published in 1919), 47.

Although historians lack complete documentary evidence, one effect of the Scottish Reformation was the quick spread and implementation of church government by elders, gathering in sessions. These became known as "kirk sessions."[62] These sessions were responsible for implementing the new Reformation emphases on Biblical preaching, proper administration of the sacraments, and church discipline. Although we have much more documentary evidence for what occurred in the towns, this still provides an accurate picture of parish life throughout much of post-Reformation Scotland. Indeed, the Scottish reform efforts were one of the most effective and thoroughgoing of the sixteenth century.[63]

As noted previously, the Scots followed one strand of the continental reformation when they emphasized church discipline as the "third mark" of the church. As local church sessions pursued the implementation of the reformation program, they created a climate in which frequent communion was almost impossible to achieve. This will be shown through a brief survey of how the early reforming efforts in Scotland impacted preaching, catechesis, and the processes of penance and church discipline.

3.3.3 The Role of Preaching and Catechesis

Writing in 1641, Alexander Henderson described the variety of communion frequency within Scottish Reformed churches and noted the emphasis on preparation and doctrinal knowledge. In some places in Scotland, communion was administered "upon one Sabbath, in other places upon two, or three Sabbaths, as it may be done most conveniently, which is determined by the Minister, and Eldership of the Church." The frequency depended on the "number of the Communicants" as well as the "Proficiency of the People in the way of Christ."[64] Henderson clearly affirms the Protestant priority of careful preparation, as he details the process of examination that precedes the actual communion. The "proficiency of the people" here refers to the expectation that only those who had a basic understanding of Christian doctrine, and especially of the Reformed view of the sacraments, should be admitted to the Lord's Supper. Additionally, unrepentant sinners were barred and excluded.[65]

---

62 "The Scottish Reformation's success in embedding itself in parish life is one of the most mysterious events in the sixteenth century: for that success is remarkable. Few records survive from before 1560 that allow us to peer into the daily life of Scottish parish churches, but as Reformed churches were established, they formed 'kirk sessions.'" Alex Ryrie, *The Age of Reformation*, 254.

63 Todd, *The Culture of Protestantism*, 15.

64 Alexander Henderson, *The Government and Order of the Church of Scotland*, (Edinburgh: s.n., 1641; Ann Arbor: Text Creation Partnership, 2011), 21, http://name.umdl.umich.edu/a43314.0001.001.

65 Henderson, *The Government and Order*, 20–21.

Henderson's description is complemented by other sources, and particularly the records of Kirk sessions. The Reformed liturgy in Scotland was dominated by preaching.[66] Todd contrasts this Word-centered worship with late medieval worship: "[It] was no longer centred on the dramatic, daily re-enactment of Christ's sacrifice in the mass; rather, communion became an annual or biennial affair, with long morning and afternoon sermons separated by catechism."[67] Those who took communion were also required to attend the preaching of the Word, as well as weekly catechism sessions.[68] This emphasis flowed naturally from the Reformed emphasis on the close connection between the Word preached and the Word sealed in the Eucharist.[69] Todd summarizes the "logo-centric" shape of Scots Reformed worship:

> For all the reformers' insistence on pairing word and sacrament as signs of a true church, communion in Reformed guise became an infrequent and intensely logo-centric event—preceded by doctrinal vetting and Saturday sermons of preparation, accompanied by two Sunday sermons and followed by a Monday sermon of thanksgiving.[70]

The heightened emotional intensity of the communion was stoked by preaching. Preaching sermons were delivered before the communion day, on the communion day, and shorter "exhortations" were given to each group who came forward to partake around the communion table.[71]

Preaching "book-ended" the Supper on both sides of the event: parishioners were exhorted to come "worthily" to the communion and were exhorted to live in a

---

66 "The Pastor is bound to teach the Word of God in season and out of season, and beside all occasional, and week day Sermons, which in Cities and Townes use to be at least two days every week, The Congregation doth assemble twice on the Lords day, and for this end notice is given of the time by the sound of a Bell." Alexander Henderson, *The Government and Order*, 15.

67 Todd, *The Culture of Protestantism*, 2.

68 Ian B. Cowan, *The Scottish Reformation: Church and Society in sixteenth century Scotland* (New York: St. Martin's Press, 1982), 149. See also Jane E.A. Dawson, "'The Face of Ane Perfyt Reformed Kirk': St Andrews and the Early Scottish Reformation," in James Kirk, ed., *Humanism and Reform: the Church in Europe, England, and Scotland, 1400–1643* (Oxford: Blackwell Publishers, 1991), 425–26.

69 "Protestantism is above all a religion of the book ... Particularly in the Calvinist version of the faith, the word, read, preached, sung, remembered and recited back at catechetical exercise or family sermon repetition—became the hallmark of communal worship and individual piety. The sermon came to be the central event of feast and fast, of regular Sunday worship and sacramental seasons." Todd, *The Culture of Protestantism*, 24. (One could almost say that the sermon became the main sacrament!)

70 Todd, *The Culture of Protestantism*, 24.

71 Todd, *The Culture of Protestantism*, 107–109. See also Henderson, *The Government and Order*, 24.

worthy manner afterwards. Church sessions took the primacy of preaching so seriously that they appointed special elders to search through the town to find anyone who might be skipping the sermon and fine them accordingly.[72] All this preaching built up the expectations of those who communed, which created an atmosphere of intense eucharistic experience. It is questionable whether this intensity could have been achieved, or sustained, without celebrating the sacrament infrequently.

Attendance at sermons, both on weekdays and on Sundays, was enforced by the church sessions. Traditional Scottish pastimes, such as dancing and picnics on Sunday afternoon, were replaced by times of catechism.[73] As Todd summarizes: "In parishes supplied with preachers, there were two sermons each Sunday, one in the morning, the other after noon, generally separated by catechetical teaching and exercises."[74] So, patterns of traditional festivity were replaced by patterns of ecclesiastical preaching and catechesis, which both ultimately enabled people to partake of the Lord's Supper. Participation in the sacrament, even more than listening to a sermon, defined the visible community of saints. Going through catechesis was the "liminal test" that granted full access to the community.

Todd argues that participation in communion "clearly served as a sort of puberty rite" and youths around the ages of fifteen and sixteen could participate only if they passed the session's catechetical examination.[75] So, full entrance into the church community was granted through a process of catechesis, and full participation in the continuing life of the church was maintained through catechesis as well.

Some pastors and church leaders implemented the reforms recommended by the First Book of Discipline and delayed the Lord's Supper so that people could be adequately catechized and prepared.[76] In the early 1600s "[m]inisters announced the upcoming communions from the pulpit at least a week or two in advance in urban settings, and from three weeks to three months in advance in rural areas, to allow sufficient time for preparation."[77] For individual parishioners, this "preparation" included two main parts: examination, followed by reconciliation. The process of examination involved the elders of the local "kirk" asking questions of every prospective communicant to assess their understanding of correct doctrine and

---

72 Todd, *The Culture of Protestantism*, 32–33.

73 Todd, *The Culture of Protestantism*, 24.

74 Todd, *The Culture of Protestantism*, 28. See also Henderson, *The Government and Order*, 17.

75 Todd, *The Culture of Protestantism*, 90–91.

76 Burnet, *The Holy Communion*, 48, 184–185.

77 Todd, *The Culture of Protestantism*, 91. Compare Henderson, "The Sabbath day next before the Communion shall be celebrated, public warning thereof is made by the Pastor, and of the doctrine of preparation, to be taught the last day of the week, or at least toward the end of the week; That the Communicants may be the better prepared, by the use of the means, both in private and public." *The Government and Order*, 22.

the moral uprightness of their lives.[78] If they passed the examination, they received a token, or ticket, which was necessary to gain admittance to the Supper.[79] The second part, reconciliation, included a "day of reconciliation," which was part of the prescribed schedule for a communion season. People were exhorted to make peace with each other, and were given time to do it, in the context of the community's preparation for observing communion.[80]

day of reconciliation

People also prepared through fasting: "Parishioners often came to the Saturday sermon fasting, or at least having fasted on designated days of the week before. Indeed, it was not at all unusual for annual spring communions to be preceded by several weeks of fasting—clearly reminiscent of pre-Reformation Lent."[81] This fasting included denying oneself food other than basic nourishment, and also abstinence from sex (as enjoined by the Westminster Directory).[82] It also meant attending a fast day sermon. Todd detects widespread support from the laity for these fast day sermons, and even support from local business leaders. Thus, apparently these fasting stringencies were important to the communities, even though they might involve economic loss.

This relates to the question of frequency, because obviously this sort of physical, sexual, and economic abstinence could not have been sustained for long periods of time. Perhaps *because* communion was often observed only once or twice a year, the communion experience could take on levels of intensity and spiritual focus that could not be achieved within a more frequent rhythm.[83] Indeed, this pattern is clearly discernible in the development of the communion "seasons," which began in the 1600s and flourished in the 1700s. Many parishes would come together for a series of "humiliation" days, with sermons preparing the people for communion. Then, large communions would take place, followed by a day of "thanksgiving" the next Monday, with more sermons. For many, these communion "seasons" were the apogee of their spiritual lives.

A key pattern emerges here that helps to summarize the evidence surveyed so far: in the Scots Reformed context, a theology of informed reception or catechetical aptitude reinforced the institutionalization of a pattern of infrequent communion.

---

78 Henderson, *The Government and Order*, 17–18.

79 Todd, *The Culture of Protestantism*, 96–98.

80 Todd, *The Culture of Protestantism*, 92.

81 Todd, *The Culture of Protestantism*, 93.

82 *A Directory for the publique worship of God, throughout the three kingdoms of England, Scotland, and Ireland together with an ordinance of Parliament for the taking away of the Book of common-prayer, … die Jovis, 13. Martii, 1644* (London: Printed for Evan Tyler, Alexander Fifield, Ralph Smith, and John Field …, 1644; Ann Arbor: Text Creation Partnership, 2011), 75, http://name.umdl.umich.edu/A36061.0001.001.

83 Todd, *The Culture of Protestantism*, 94.

Although the churches of post-Reformation Scotland led their people to the communion table more frequently than under Roman Catholic administration, the emphases on preaching, catechesis, and preparation excluded anything as frequent as weekly (or even monthly) communion, simply because of the practical mechanics and expectations of the catechetical process.

3.3.4 The Role of Church Discipline, Penance, and Reconciliation

The Scottish Reformed church took seriously its mandate to teach and enforce moral discipline and confessional orthodoxy in the church, as laid out in its founding ecclesial documents. This emphasis on correct doctrinal knowledge and moral rectitude mitigated against more frequent communion, because of the *time* needed to evaluate the doctrine and life of prospective communicants. Only those who understood communion correctly were allowed to partake.[84] As we have seen, the First Book of Discipline laid out a minimum standard of being able to recite the Lord's Prayer, the "Articles of the Beliefe," and the Ten Commandments.[85] However, the standard rose—in 1570 the Assembly mandated that children be examined by their ministers at ages nine, twelve, and fourteen. Other sessions passed similar injunctions, culminating in the general expectation that youths should come for their first communion around the ages of fifteen and sixteen.[86] Along with a regimen of catechizing for the youth, all the congregants were expected to participate in a "diet of examination" before communing:

> But catechising alone was not held to be sufficient. There was a public and special examination of old and young in the church, usually a week or more before the Communion. This "diet of examination" took the place of confession and absolution before Easter in the Old Church. It was an understood preliminary to every celebration for "such as are to be admitted to the table of the Lord Jesus." If it was found impossible to complete the examination of all the people before the appointed date, the Sacrament was delayed.[87]

The corollary to teaching correct doctrine was enforcing correct moral behavior. The Scots Reformed took the medieval system of penance and transformed it into

---

84 Burnet, *The Holy Communion*, 44–45.

85 Burnet, *The Holy Communion*, 45. See also Cameron, *The First Book of Discipline*, 184.

86 Burnet, *The Holy Communion*, 46.

87 Burnet, *The Holy Communion*, 48. Sometimes the examinations took place within the homes of families. However, in large parishes, the examinations were more public, with families reporting to designated locations (usually churches). Todd, *The Culture of Protestantism*, 91.

a thorough mechanism for dealing with individual, and social, sins.[88] The sessions, or elders, were responsible for the oversight of the community. Ministers and elders visited their parishioners throughout the year, often testing their knowledge of various catechisms (until the Westminster Assembly, 1643–1653, issued its Larger and Shorter Catechism, a translation of Calvin's catechism was employed).[89] Before communions, which were usually bi-annual, the sessions would typically divide a parish into "quarters," and elders would be assigned to "examine" the people in different quarters. This examination period could extend for several weeks.[90] Obviously, the sessions valued intellectual comprehension of correct doctrine and moral rectitude, rather than frequent communion.

Both kirk sessions and church members, for the most part, held a common understanding about their duties in regard to participation in communion. The sessions guarded the communion table closely, but the laity was sometimes just as determined to participate. The fact that sessions had to routinely appoint elders to guard the doors of the church, to prevent those without tokens from participating in communion, suggests how important communion was in this church culture. Thus, though communion was infrequent, participating in it, even by sneaking in or bringing a counterfeit token, was particularly important for the average parishioner.[91] However, the proper "door" to communion was through penance and church discipline. This revealed a depth of spiritual earnestness on the part of the average parishioner. Much of the laity were willing to submit to examination by the church elders, and to undergo the rites of penitence that were administered because of their own failings.

Penance was a ritual that was usually performed weekly. On Sunday mornings, those under the censure of the church had to sit on a special stool or bench near the front of the church building.[92] So, ironically, the Scots Reformed did observe

---

88 As Todd explains: "Traditional histories of the Scottish Reformation have too quickly claimed that the Reformers altogether discarded penance and the rites associated with it; in fact, the public confession of sin and demonstration of repentance not only remained in practice a rite of the kirk, it actually expanded to become arguably the central act of protestant worship in Scotland." *The Culture of Protestantism*, 128–29. See also Burnet, *The Holy Communion*, 52–63. Michael F. Graham details the slow spread of kirk sessions and highlights the role of presbyteries in implementing the ideals of the Scottish Reformed confessional documents. See "Social Discipline in Scotland, 1560–1610," in Raymond A. Mentzer, ed., *Sin and the Calvinists: Morals Control and the Consistory in the Reformed Tradition*, Sixteenth Century Essays & Studies, Volume XXXII (Kirksville, MO: Sixteenth Century Journal Publishers, Inc., 1994), 129–157.

89 Todd, *The Culture of Protestantism*, 74–75.

90 Todd, *The Culture of Protestantism*, 76–77.

91 Todd, *The Culture of Protestantism*, 116–117.

92 Todd, *The Culture of Protestantism*, 128–139. People had to sit on the stool of repentance during worship services on multiple days, depending on the severity of their sins.

weekly penance, if not weekly communion. Given the exacting nature of the work placed on the sessions—examining entire parishes and enforcing church discipline—more frequent communion does not seem possible within such a system. However, placing penance in the context of the Supper produced a profound theological statement. Although the "preparation sermon" on the Saturday before communion Sunday was given to all, it more particularly focused on the penitents, and on those who were about to be received back into the full communion of the church.[93] Todd summarizes the significance of this public reception of penitents before communion:

> Finally, however, ritual reincorporation of penitents at this juncture also served to underline visibly for the whole community the theological message of not only the Saturday sermons on sin and repentance, but also of the peculiarly Christian outcome of it all in ultimate forgiveness of the faithful.[94]

Because Scottish Reformed congregations sat around an actual table during the Lord's Supper, which erased social and gender hierarchies, this restoration of penitents was all the more meaningful. So, although communion may have been infrequent, it was surely a profound experience, with ecclesiological and sociological ramifications.[95]

3.4   Conclusion

Although the English Reformation achieved a degree of success sooner than in the Scottish Reformation, reform efforts in England had to constantly negotiate with the preferences, desires, and mandates of the English monarchs. Official attempts to reform worship and the liturgy, encapsulated in the Book of Common Prayer, mandated communion three times a year, but this was an ideal that was rarely met. As on the Continent, the focus was more on what was occurring in the Lord's Supper, in metaphysical and theological sense, rather than on issues of frequency.

In Scotland, although the pace of reform was slower, it eventually achieved more in the way of reproducing the Genevan models of worship and ecclesial governance. In addition to the program of catechesis, practices of penance, and pastoral care of the churches, the theological priorities and ecclesiological practices of the Scottish

---

93 Todd, *The Culture of Protestantism*, 95, 168.

94 Todd, *The Culture of Protestantism*, 96. Additionally: "It served as the final element of communion preparation by reifying a complex theological principle in a way that no amount of preaching could achieve. This was ecclesiology made flesh." 96.

95 Todd, *The Culture of Protestantism in Early Modern Scotland*, 108, 117.

Reformed made a high level of communion frequency almost impossible to attain. Because the post-Reformation church in Scotland placed such a high priority on church discipline, and on ensuring that everyone who came to communion understood the importance and seriousness of what they were engaged in, they created ecclesial structures and communal rhythms that institutionalized infrequent communion.

These dynamics would become sources of contention in the British Isles during the reigns of James I and his successors. The changing political and ecclesiastical situation in England would have profound implications for the Scottish church, and for Protestant communities in the New World. The communion frequency debates of the 1700s and 1800s were indelibly shaped by the emergence of what became known as the "Puritan" movement.

[handwritten margin note: Summary of this chapter's point.]

Chapter 4
Communion Frequency and Church Discipline in Post-Reformation England and Scotland (1603–1689)

4.1   Post-Reformation and the Question of Definitions

This study adopts the terminology of Bossy, Spurr, and others, in identifying the events of the seventeenth century as the "Post-Reformation." This term serves to highlight the contested nature of politics, religion, and social life after the events of the sixteenth century reform efforts.

Following the lead of Spurr in particular, it is helpful to summarize communion frequency in the "mainstream," or in most British parishes, rather than first focusing on authors and figures agitating for further reform (the "godly," or the "Puritans"). As Spurr points out "the mainstream was where radicalism began."[1] In the matter of communion frequency, both radical groups and mainstream parishes struggled with many of the same issues and manifest similar patterns. Additionally, while the issue of communion frequency became a more prominent issue after the reign of Elizabeth I (1558–1603), the religious structures that she established, and steadily maintained, form the necessary backdrop to understanding the later debates about communion frequency and how to properly prepare for, and participate in, communion. After a summary of the religious and ecclesiastical developments under Elizabeth I, this chapter will survey developments from the beginning of the reign of James I in 1603 until the Glorious Revolution in 1689 and the accession of William of Orange to the throne of England.

While previous scholarship viewed the beginning of Elizabeth's reign as the winding-down of the English Reformation, many scholars now discern a much longer and more complex process. In this view, Elizabeth's reign is merely a "midway point" of this larger historical picture.[2] This perspective is a profound shift in how

---

1   John Spurr, *The Post-Reformation: Religion, Politics and Society in Britain 1603–1714* (Essex: Pearson Education Limited, 2006), 5. As Spurr summarizes the contribution of Bossy the term "Post-Reformation" is "all about the way that people got used to the Reformation and started to live with it." Spurr, *The Post-Reformation*, 1. See also John Bossy, *Peace in the Post-Reformation* (Cambridge: Cambridge University Press, 1998).

2   As Peter Marshall summarizes: "The accession of Elizabeth in 1558 and her church settlement of the following year, were once regarded as the happy final destination of the English Reformation. It now seems barely a midway point on the journey. Historians have moved far from the perspective that enabled Dickens to view the religious tensions of Elizabeth's reign merely as 'residual problems.'" Marshall, "England," in Whitford, ed. *Reformation and Early Modern Europe*, 259.

historians view the English Reformation "away from the legislative framework and toward the complex social processes by which England acquired a Protestant culture."[3] Although scholars still attempt to understand the nature of Elizabeth's actual religious beliefs, there is a consensus that she believed that the 1559 settlement was a "terminus, rather than a way station to further reform."[4] The Elizabethan "Settlement" was an attempt to navigate between the extremes on both sides. In an environment rife with the threat of "popery," Elizabeth had to defend the English Protestant church. But she had no interest in giving in to the demands of those who wanted to push the reform efforts further.[5] Various groups believed that the reforming efforts had not gone far enough. Many of them were motivated by their experiences in continental reforming communities, or by the writings of continental Reformers. They desired to bring the English church into conformity with these models.[6]

The largest part of this group has been conveniently grouped under the label "Puritan." Much ink has been spilt over the origins and meaning of the term "Puritan."[7] This chapter will make no effort to add to the copious discussions of specialists.[8] This study will follow the lead of scholars like Bozeman and Bremer who retain the use of the term "Puritan" while also recognizing the concerns of other scholars who use "puritan" or another descriptor.[9] The use of "puritan" has become widespread because of the desire to emphasize the diversity of the movement, as well as the common ground between those who remained within the Established church and those who eventually left, or traveled along the fringes of the official church (whether by choice or because they were forced to by the authorities). Recognizing

---

3 Marshall, "England," 259.

4 Marshall, "England," 260.

5 "The Elizabethan Act of Uniformity and Prayer Book of 1559 were designed with an eye to reconciliation. Earlier versions of the liturgy were conflated and theological issues were left vaguely defined, rather as they were in the Thirty-nine Articles of 1563, the Church of England's basic doctrinal statement." Spurr, *The Post-Reformation*, 9.

6 Spurr, *The Post-Reformation*, 10.

7 Spurr comments, "As a product of controversy, the label 'puritan' would always enjoy a double life as a term of abuse and a descriptive label." *The Post-Reformation*, 23.

8 See the helpful overview and analysis of Randall J. Pederson, *Unity in Diversity: English Puritans and the Puritan Reformation, 1603–1689* (Leiden: Brill, 2014).

9 See Bryan Spinks, *Sacraments, Ceremonies and the Stuart Divines*, xii. Referencing Anthony Milton, *Catholic and Reformed. The Reformed and Protestant Churches in English Protestant Thought, 1600–1640* (Cambridge: Cambridge University Press, 1995), xii. Spinks points to the fact that recent scholarship has made the Anglican/Puritan terminology, "if not untenable, certainly undesirable and inaccurate. The word 'puritan' emerged as a term of abuse and was used quite indiscriminately by those who were content with the status quo against any who espoused further reform, or tighter discipline." See also Michael P. Winship, *Hot Protestants: A History of Puritanism in England and America* (New Haven: Yale University Press, 2018), who employs "puritan" throughout.

the complexity of the various movements and the range of beliefs and convictions of individuals is a worthy goal. However, as with the debate over "Reformation" versus "Reformations," stressing plurality and diversity can obscure the underlying unity of movements. Thus, while acknowledging the concerns of those who opt for "puritan," this study will retain "Puritan," and will also use "godly," which was one of the preferred labels used by members of this group when describing themselves.[10]

Whatever label is used, there is no doubt that various groups were united by fundamental beliefs about how the Church of England should be further "purified" or "reformed."[11] What were these beliefs, especially as they relate to the issue of communion frequency? Furthermore, how did these reformist beliefs impact the Scottish churches and, beyond them, the early American Reformed and Presbyterian churches? Returning to the research questions posed in chapter 1 (1.2), the focus will be on showing how patterns of communion frequency were related to wider patterns of political, pastoral, and ecclesial realities. It will also detail the Puritan focus on preparation for communion and the various factors in the Scottish church that made frequent communion impractical—despite general calls for more frequent communion.

Although the English Church under Elizabeth I was widely considered to be "Reformed," many of the features of its liturgical life and ecclesiastical structure were criticized as being remnants of medieval Catholicism. As a result of the intensity of the debate, and the heightened tensions because of the political power dynamics involved, the Puritans developed a self-conscious group identity—both in their own eyes, and especially in the eyes of their opponents.[12] Eventually (as of 1572), their dissatisfaction with the failure of further "reformation" in the English church led many of them to "separate" themselves from the official ecclesiastical structures of the English church. These groups became known as "Separatists."[13] Furthermore, because their efforts to fully "reform" the English church were frustrated, they focused their fervor on pursuing God within their own communities, or in their "prayer closets"—their individual private devotions. Instead of trying to "purify"

---

10 Spinks, "Anglicans and Dissenters," 501.

11 "It depicts accurately a substantive and often obsessive trait of the quest for further reformation: a hunger for purity. Purity in this context had reference to two distinct but linked concerns: primitivist and moral" ("primitivist" denoting the wish to return to the original 1st century church). Theodore Dwight Bozeman, *The Precisianist Strain: Disciplinary Religion & Antinomian Backlash in Puritanism to 1638* (Chapel Hill: University of North Carolina Press, 2004), 3. See also Francis J. Bremer, *Congregational Communion: Clerical Friendship in the Anglo-American Puritan Community, 1610 – 1692* (Boston: Northeastern University Press, 1994), and David D. Hall, *The Puritans: A Transatlantic History* (Princeton: Princeton University Press, 2019), who both retain the use of "Puritan," even while admitting the multi-valent meanings of the term.

12 Coffey and Lim, eds., *The Cambridge Companion to Puritanism*, 3.

13 Spinks, "Anglicans and Dissenters," 502.

the national church, they focused their attention on "purifying" their own spiritual lives, and their own local churches and communities.[14]

As these groups and this movement developed further, it led to a solidifying of boundaries between what became the "Anglican" church, and those groups or churches that defined themselves in opposition to the official, established, Church of England. However, those hard categories and boundaries developed over time. The situation was much more permeable and fluid during the reigns of Elizabeth and James I. Indeed, there were many within the established church that were calling for reforms and agitating for what would become identified as "Puritan" emphases. Furthermore, many of those advocating for further reforms left the Church of England only after they were effectively forced out, and many left reluctantly.[15]

Much has been written about Puritanism as a political, and as a religious, movement. However, not as much has been written about the Puritans and their views about the Lord's Supper. While the Supper was not the center of their theology, it was central to many of their concerns.[16] First, they carried on the concerns of the first generation of Reformers about restoring the sacrament to its "primitive" purity. Secondly, they desired to form a community of believers who understood the correct theology of the sacrament, and who were spiritually and morally qualified to participate. Thirdly, this concern to protect the "purity" of the Supper drove them into conflict with the established church and ecclesiastical authorities, because they desired greater control of access to communion, which became a larger issue with political ramifications, just as it had been in the continental reformation.

The ecclesiastical and theological tensions within both English and Scottish reforming movements traveled across the Atlantic and impacted early American Reformed and Protestant communion patterns. This influence took the forms of both people and print. Authors on both sides of the Atlantic wrote for, and to, each other. Printers in colonial America published works by English authors on communion practice and theology. This provides an essential part of the background to the communion debates of the 1700s and early 1800s. There were movements advocating more frequent communion in both England, Scotland, and the Americas. It was not just a "Reformed" or "Presbyterian" issue. On the contrary, it formed a central concern of the "Anglican revival" during the reign of James II.[17] There was

---

14 Coffey and Lim, eds., *The Cambridge Companion to Puritanism*, 4.

15 Coffey and Lim, eds., *The Cambridge Companion to Puritanism*, 5–6.

16 Arnold Hunt, "The Lord's Supper in Early Modern England." *Past & Present*, no. 161 (1998): 39–83; Accessed February 17, 2021. http://www.jstor.org/stable/651072.

17 See Brent S. Sirota, *The Christian Monitors: The Church of England and the Age of Benevolence, 1680–1730* (New Haven, CT: Yale University Press, 2014), 26–32, for a summary of the importance of frequent communion in the overall "Anglican revival" of the late 1600s, and especially in relation to the project of the moral and spiritual renewal of society.

also a parallel movement within the Roman Catholic church, though tracing the possible influences between these movements is beyond the scope of this project.[18] There are many tantalizing questions that deserve further research in this area.[19]

4.2   Communion Frequency in Post-Reformation England and Godly Communities

It is somewhat anachronistic to separate the Puritans too widely from the established church. The clergy and laity in both established parishes and godly communities wrestled with many of the same issues and challenges in their understanding and practice of the Lord's Supper. After surveying broad patterns of communion frequency in the seventeenth century, the focus will turn to specific authors and groups that represent the "godly" or Puritan concerns.

Spurr helpfully gathers evidence from a wide variety of local English parish records. It is difficult to make detailed conclusions about communion frequency. Historians must rely on self-reports of contemporary writers, and the financial records of local parishes. Expenditures on bread and wine for communions provide many clues, as well as other records. The evidence available suggests that both clergy and local parishioners struggled with the issue of participation and preparation for communion.

Despite the strong language in the Book of Common Prayer about the importance of the sacrament "the Lord's Supper was neither celebrated nor received frequently in the seventeenth century."[20] According to Spurr "[m]ost parish churches celebrated the sacrament three or four times a year, generally at Christmas, Whitsun

---

18 See Joseph Dougherty, *From Altar-Throne to Table: The Campaign for Frequent Holy Communion in the Catholic Church*, ATLA Monograph Series, no. 50 (Lanham, MD: The Scarecrow Press and American Theological Library Association, 2010.

19 So, for instance, there are parallels between the emphases of Puritan spirituality and certain movements within Roman Catholicism. As Hambrick-Stowe points out: "Puritans shared their zeal for 'heart religion', along with an Augustinian understanding of human nature and divine grace, with other believers of their period across Western Christendom. It was this era, for example, that saw the emergence of the Roman Catholic cult of the Sacred Heart of Jesus and the adaptation of spiritual disciplines originally developed within religious orders for the use of laity. The distinct contribution of Puritan practical divinity (along with that of their Reformed cousins on the continent), however, was its elimination of any distinction between the spirituality of clergy and laity," "Practical divinity and spirituality," in *The Cambridge Companion to Puritanism*, eds. Coffey and Lim, 197.

20 Spurr, *The Post-Reformation*, 282. For communion frequency in the Restoration in the Established (and emerging "Anglican") church, see Jeremy Gregory, *Restoration, Reformation and Reform, 1660–1828 Archbishops of Canterbury and their Diocese* (Oxford: Clarendon Press, 2000), 262–270.

and Easter."[21] Although this technically met the Prayer Book's standards (that everyone over the age of sixteen should receive the Supper three times a year), Spurr believes that most parishioners only received annually. At Easter, following centuries of tradition "a series of sacraments were celebrated to accommodate the whole parish."[22] Spurr bases his conclusions on contemporary witnesses, as well as local churchwardens' records and accounts about how much they spent on wine and bread for communions.[23] The more detailed records available for the early eighteenth century indicate that "most rural parishes celebrated communion three or four times a year at the great church festivals."[24] He contrasts this pattern with the Scottish church, where there was typically "an annual spring sacrament, held over several Sundays, at which all parishioners were obliged to receive."[25]

After noting that there remains much work to be done in this area, Spurr presents evidence from a few different parishes.[26] With each situation, there were a variety of factors that influenced communion attendance and reception. There is a noticeable difference in the patterns of reception in rural areas, compared to urban areas.[27] Based on the available evidence, it is clear that clergy did not believe their parishioners were coming to the sacrament often enough. Spurr concludes: "It is

---

21 Spurr, *The Post-Reformation*, 282.

22 Spurr, *The Post-Reformation*, 282.

23 Spurr, 282, lists these examples: "(...) in 1634–35 the typical urban parish of St Oswald in Durham spent between four and six shillings on bread and wine for each of the communions celebrated on 11 January, 1 June, 24 August, 19 October, and 23 November, but twenty-seven shillings on the Easter communion. So although there were six communions a year at St Oswald's, judging by the amount spent on bread and wine, over five times as many people received the sacrament at Easter as did at any other time of the year. At Clayworth, Nottinghamshire, in 1679, 18 parishioners received at Whitsun and 21 at Christmas, but there were 204 communicants at Easter. At Llanboidy, Carmarthenshire, in the early eighteenth century, 300 received at the Eastern communion, but only 40 attended the other communions." Spurr's sources here are, *Churchwardens' Accounts of Pittington and Other Dioceses in the County of Durham, 1580–1700*, vol. 84 (Edinburgh: Surtees Society, 1888), 187–88; *The Rector's Book, Clayworth*, H. Gill and E.L. Guilford, eds., (Nottingham, 1910), 43; G.H. Jenkins, *Literature, Religion and Society in Wales 1660–1730* (Cardiff, 1978), 71.

24 Spurr, *The Post-Reformation*, 282.

25 Spurr, *The Post-Reformation*, 282.

26 Spurr notes, "The patterns of lay reception in England have yet to be established." Spurr, *The Post-Reformation*, 282.

27 "Boulton used the Easter token books from the large suburban parish of St Saviour's, Southwark, to calculate that between the 1570s and the Civil War 80–98 per cent of potential communicants in the parish made an annual communion. However, in the London parish of St Botolph, Aldgate, attendance at the ordinary monthly communions in 1598 was about 50 while the nineteen Easter communion services saw 1,758 receive communion out of about 4,500 potential communicants." Spurr, *The Post-Reformation*, 283. Spurr here cites J.P. Boulton, "The Limits of Formal Religion: The Administration of Holy Communion in late Elizabethan and Early Stuart London," *London Journal* 10 (1984).

difficult to avoid the conclusion that the sacrament, even at Easter, was a minority interest in most seventeenth-century English and Welsh parishes."[28]

Part of the difficulty was the continuing tension between the twin Reformational ideals of both frequent *participation* and spiritual *purity*. Both "godly" pastors and clergy in the national English church emphasized the need for their congregants to prepare themselves before coming to the sacrament.[29] The various groups within the broader Puritan movement practiced different rhythms of communion. Despite their shared belief that the English church should be further "reformed," the Puritan movement split off into various sub-groups and sects. It "ultimately proved to be a uniquely fissiparous variety of Reformed Protestantism,"[30] and so it is difficult to generalize accurately about the movement. However, patterns do emerge.

The Puritans combined a deep appreciation for the holy mystery of communion with a serious trepidation of approaching the sacrament in an unworthy fashion.[31] Although they endeavored to provide Scriptural support for every aspect of their worship, this ideal did not produce uniformity of communion practice.[32] In his foundational study, Davies identifies three main groups in the Puritan movement: Independents, Baptists, and Presbyterians.[33] These groups were divided by both the frequency of communion and the method of participation, even though they were otherwise very similar.[34]

The Puritan Baptist groups practiced monthly communion.[35] Interestingly, a number of Baptist congregations "insisted upon the celebration of the Lord's Supper in the evening, thus following the original time of the institution by our Lord."[36]

---

28 Spurr, *The Post-Reformation*, 283. See also Spurr, "Religion in Restoration England," in Lionel K.J. Glassey, ed., *The Reigns of Charles II and James VII & II* (New York: St. Martin's Press, 1997), 112–114.

29 See Arnold Hunt, "The Lord's Supper in Early Modern England," 39–83 for more on the similar concerns of those who remained within the Church of England and Puritans on the issue of communion frequency. Further research can fruitfully explore these connections and contrasts.

30 Coffey and Lim, eds., *The Cambridge Companion to Puritanism*, 5.

31 The following overview is indebted to the work of Horton Davies, *The Worship of the English Puritans* (1948; repr., Morgan, PA: Soli Deo Gloria Publications, 1997).

32 "There is considerable diversity of modes of celebration of Communion amongst the Puritans, which implies that the guidance of the Scriptures was not as all-sufficient or as definite as the Puritans suggested." Davies, *The Worship of the English Puritans*, 204.

33 Davies, *The Worship of the English Puritans*, 204.

34 "Whilst for practical purposes the Independents and Baptists were united in liturgical practices (with the single exception of their celebration of the Sacrament of Baptism), they differed considerably both in the method of celebration of the Sacrament of Communion and in their views of the frequency with which it should be administered." Davies, *The Worship of the English Puritans*, 204–205.

35 "The Baptists, so the Broadmead Records inform us, held the Lord's Supper once every month. This was prepared for by a prayer-meeting held in the preceding week. Such was their custom during the Commonwealth." Davies, *The Worship of the English Puritans*, 205.

36 Davies, *The Worship of the English Puritans*, 205.

The English Congregationalists, or Independents, celebrated communion weekly. Davies posits that "[i]n all probability they inherited this custom from their predecessors, the Brownists."[37] This is supported by a quote from Robert Baillie's *A Dissuasive from the Errours of the Time* (1645), which argues against the Brownists and, by implication, against the Independents: "They teach, that the Lords [sic] Supper should be celebrated every Lords day: So preparation-Sermons before, and Sermons for Thanksgiving after the Lords Table, to them are needless."[38] Baillie clearly displays the typical concern of many Reformed theologians and pastors that frequent communion would displace proper preparation. Since Baillie was Scottish and was one of the representatives of the Scottish Reformed church at the Westminster Assembly, he was concerned that the Brownist sect's practice of weekly communion would displace what had become standard features of Scots Reformed liturgical practice—the preparation sermons beforehand, and the Thanksgiving sermons after a communion.

Other evidence of the English Independent practice of weekly communion comes from John Owen (1616–1683). His *A Brief Instruction in the Worship of God and Discipline of the Churches of the New Testament* (1667) is in the form of a catechism. Questions 39 and 40 deal with the Lord's Supper:

Q. 39 *Where and to whom is the ordinance of the Lord's supper to be administered?*
A. In the church, or assembly of the congregation, to all the members of it, rightly prepared and duly assembled, or to such of them as are so assembled.—1 Cor. Xi. 20-22, 28, 29, 33; Acts ii. 46.

Q. 40 *How often is that ordinance to be administered?*
A. Every first day of the week, or at least as often as opportunity and conveniency may be obtained.—1 Cor. Xi. 26; Acts xx. 7.[39]

---

37 Davies, *The Worship of the English Puritans*, 206.

38 Davies, *The Worship of the English Puritans*, 206, quoting from Baillie, 29.

39 *The Works of John Owen*, vol. XV, ed. William H. Goold (Johnstone & Hunter, 1850–53; reprint Edinburgh and Carlisle, PA: The Banner of Truth Trust, 1965; 1998), 512. Stephen Mayor comments on Owen's brevity in addressing the question of communion frequency, since it had been a somewhat contentious issue in the Reformed tradition: "The impression grows that a good deal of what Owen wrote about the Lord's Supper is rather formal and perfunctory, the expression of what was now a mature tradition." *The Lord's Supper in Early English Dissent* (1972; repr., Eugene: Wipf and Stock, 2016), 113. Owen makes another "perfunctory" reference to communion frequency when he addresses the role and responsibility of pastors in administering the sacraments. One of the things they are to "attend to" is "[t]he times and seasons of their administration unto the church's edification, especially that of the Lord's supper, whose frequency is enjoined. It is the duty of pastors to consider all the necessary circumstances of their administration, as unto time, place, frequency,

According to Crawford Gribben, the congregation that Owen pastored later in life practiced monthly communion. Gribben notes that this is contrary to Owen's earlier advocacy of weekly communion but does not find any written evidence about the reasons for the change.[40]

Additionally, the *Apologetical Narration* (1643), submitted by the Independents to the Westminster Assembly, as a defense of their principles and practices, describes a communion observance.[41] Davies concludes that, despite other variations in their communion practices "[t]here is, however, complete unanimity amongst the English Independents in the weekly celebration."[42] These ideals and emphases also impacted the Americas, as various groups left England and traveled to spaces where they could fully implement their liturgical and theological beliefs. However, in the New World, this supposed consensus about weekly communion did not hold.[43] The New England Independents typically came to the Lord's Table monthly. According to Davies: "It was certainly the practice of the New England Independents to have a monthly Communion. Cotton asserts 'The Lord's Supper we administer for the time, once a month at least'. This monthly celebration was still maintained at the end of the seventeenth century in New England."[44]

The English Presbyterians, on the other hand, adopted the Continental Reformed practice of quarterly communion.[45] Davies acknowledges that the Westminster

---

order, and decency." *The Lord's Supper in Early English Dissent*, 111, quoting Owen, *The True Nature of a Gospel Church*, in *Works*, XX, 438 ff.

40 Crawford Gribben, *John Owen and English Puritanism: Experiences of Defeat* (New York, NY: Oxford University Press, 2016), 240.

41 "Now for the way & practices of our Churches, we give this brief and general account. Our *publique worship* was made up of no other parts then the worship of all other reformed Churches doth consist of. As, publique and solemn prayers *for Kings and all in authority, &c.* the reading the Scriptures of the Old and New Testament; Exposition of them as occasion was; and constant preaching of the word; the administration of the two Sacraments, Baptism to infants, and the Lords Supper; singing of Psalms; collections for the poor, &c. every Lords day." *An apologeticall narration, humbly submitted to the Honourable Houses of Parliament. By Tho: Goodwin, Philip Nye, Sidrach Simpson, Jer: Burroughes, William Bridge,* (London: Printed for Robert Dawlman, M.DC.XLIII. [1643]; Ann Arbor: Text Creation Partnership, 2011), 8, http://name.umdl.umichap.edu/A85427.0001.001.

42 Davies, *The Worship of the English Puritans*, 207. He notes that it is, "less certain that it was the usual custom of the Independents to observe the Sacrament during the evening."

43 More research can be done to understand this process.

44 Davies, *The Worship of the English Puritans*, 206. Davies references Baillie, *A Dissuasive*, 29, John Cotton, *The Way of the Churches of Christ in New England*, 68, and then the *Diary of Samuel Sewall*, iii, 32. The practice of the New England Separatists will be surveyed in the next chapter.

45 "Independents had a weekly celebration of the Lord's Supper generally, but the interval between one Communion and the next was never longer than a month. It was, however, the general practice of the Presbyterians to have only four Communions during each year." Davies, *The Worship of the English Puritans*, 213.

Directory does not specifically prescribe a pattern of communion frequency, and he draws attention to the influence of the Scottish commissioners at the Assembly.[46] He claims that some English Presbyterians desired weekly communion.[47] Davies notes the connection between the infrequency of observance and the elaborate nature of the rituals of communion: "The very infrequency of Presbyterian celebration enabled the Communion to take a more elaborate form for them than the Independents."[48] Davies is speaking in generalities when he describes the communion practices of these various groups. Broad claims about groups and movements must be qualified by evidence from individual authors, as well as individual churches and communities. The works of selected authors will be examined below, and attention will be paid to discerning whether there are any common themes when they deal with questions of communion frequency and the qualifications that granted access to the Lord's Supper. However, the issue of communion frequency must first be situated within the larger context of preparation and purity.

4.3   Preparation and Purity in Godly Communities

Whatever else might be said about the groups that agitated for further reformation in the English church, they were all advocating for greater "purity."[49] Bremer argues that it was precisely the desire for greater church discipline, and thus purity in the church, that led the early Puritans to separate from the established church.[50] This concern for purity manifested itself in the Puritan emphasis on the need to prepare fully and properly before participating in the Lord's Supper.[51]

---

46 Davies, *The Worship of the English Puritans*, 213–14. The Westminster Assembly will be dealt with in more detail below, §4.4.4.

47 "There were, on the other hand, English Presbyterians who would have preferred a weekly celebration." Davies, *The Worship of the English Puritans*, 214. Here, Davies only cites the example of Richard Baxter. However, Baxter can only loosely be labeled as a "Presbyterian."

48 Davies, *The Worship of the English Puritans*, 214–15.

49 Bozeman, *The Precisianist Strain*, 4.

50 "Puritanism was concerned with the definition and pursuit of the Christian life. In the early decades of the movement it was not identified with a particular form of church government but rather with a concern that government provide church discipline. It was only the failure of the Anglican church structure to advance reform that led Puritans to consider and experiment with alternative means of church organization, or polity." *Shaping New Englands: Puritan Clergymen in Seventeenth-Century England and New England* (New York: Twayne Publishers, 1994), 58.

51 Puritan theologians also discussed "preparation" from the standpoint of conversion and salvation. That is beyond the scope of this thesis, though it is related. The Puritans were highly interested in the stages of conversion, and the stages of spiritual experience and piety. "Preparation" before conversion might parallel and connect to the ongoing process of sanctification, highlighted in self-examination and preparation before the Lord's Supper. See Francis J. Bremer, *Shaping New Englands*, 44–50.

John Geree (c. 1601–1649) illustrates this aspect of Puritanism in his classic portrait of a "Puritan," which carries additional weight because he was a Puritan himself.[52] Regarding the sacrament he writes:

> The sacrament of baptism he received in infancy, which he looked back to in age to answer his engagements, and claim his privileges. The Lord's Supper he accounted part of his soul's food: to which he labored to keep an appetite. He esteemed it an ordinance of nearest communion with Christ, and so requiring most exact preparation. His first care was in the examination of himself: yet as an act of office or charity, he had an eye on others.[53]

This was a common emphasis that united the various groups within the Puritan movement: proper preparation must precede participation in communion. The spiritual lives of those within Puritan churches and communities revolved around intensely spiritual personal and corporate events. Beyond the steady rhythms of daily prayers in the morning and evening, as well as catechism on Sunday, many families in the godly communities observed days of fasting. These were days of private prayer and fasting, for the purposes of either thanksgiving, or for penitence.[54]

Sometimes days of thanksgiving or humiliation were called by Parliament, or perhaps by ecclesiastical authorities, to mark occasions of special national concern. They were much less common than the "private" days that were held in individual communities, churches, or families.[55] Some Puritans also practiced fasting before receiving the Lord's Supper, or when their communities were being persecuted.[56] So, preparation for communion was part of a larger pursuit of intense spiritual devotion and heightened by the nature of the Puritan communities defining themselves in opposition to the wider community—especially the established ecclesiastical community.

---

52 "Geree draws an idealized picture. Although his work belongs to the character genre developed by Sir Thomas Overbury and John Earle, it is to some extent a self-portrait and a self-justification reflecting what we know of its author's life and opinions." John Geree, *The Character of an old English Puritan, or Non-Conformist* (London: A. Miller, 1646), in Lawrence A Sasek, ed., *Images of English Puritanism: A Collection of Contemporary Sources 1589–1646* (Baton Rouge and London: Louisiana State University Press, 1989), 207.

53 Sasek, *Images of English Puritanism*, 210.

54 Davies, *The Worship of the English Puritans*, 282.

55 "Such days of thanksgiving appear to have been a family festival to which neighbours were invited. There were also days of fasting and humiliation kept by Puritan families." Davies, *The Worship of the English Puritans*, 282. Lewis Bayly's best-selling *The Practice of Piety* (first extant edition is the second, appearing in 1612) describes the nature and function of a "public fast," *The Practice of Piety: Directing a Christian How to Walk, that He May Please God*, (Grand Rapids: Soli Deo Gloria Publications, 2019), 218–19.

56 Davies, *The Worship of the English Puritans*, 282–83.

Many authors and pastors wrote devotional works, specifically aimed at helping their readers and congregants pursue a more fervent spiritual life.[57] Hambrick-Stowe notes that "[t]hese popular texts became a means by which Puritan practical divinity was translated into regular spiritual practices by individuals, families and devotional groups."[58] Much of this spiritual fervor was focused on preparing adequately for communion. Holifield observes that "[t]he Puritan preachers spoke of the Lord's Supper primarily as a covenant seal and a source of assurance." Although they carried forward a generally Calvinistic understanding of what happened theologically in the sacrament, they focused more on the psychological aspects of communion.[59] This led to an intense emphasis on proper preparation for the Lord's Supper.

This stress on preparation also forced church leaders to preach, teach, and enforce high standards for admission to the Lord's Table. Although all Puritan ministers and leaders believed this in principle, there was a variety of actual practice. Some ministers held their congregants to a very high standard, while others (like William Perkins) accepted a general confession of faith and resolve to live a holy life.[60] Holifield notes that, even though some Puritan ministers held high standards, they "attempted to avoid impossible rigidity."[61] Despite their stress on proper participation, and spiritual purification, the Puritans believed it was better to come to the Supper than to stay away because of a fear of partaking in an unworthy manner.[62]

4.4 Case Studies: Puritans, Preparation, and Communion Frequency

When Puritans did achieve ecclesiastical and political control in various communities and colonies, they tried to fully implement their ideals for worship. In many instances, they "typically committed themselves to six full hours of public worship,

---

57 This was a phenomenon broader than just the Puritan, or even English, situation: "Puritan divinity arose during a period when devotional manuals abounded throughout Catholic and Protestant Europe thanks to new publishing technology." Coffey and Lim, eds., *The Cambridge Companion to Puritanism*, 196.

58 Charles Hambrick-Stowe, "Practical divinity and spirituality," 196. See also Owen C. Watkins, *The Puritan Experience: Studies in Spiritual Autobiography* (New York: Schocken Books, 1972), 9–12.

59 Holifield, *The Covenant Sealed*, 51, 53.

60 See Holifield, *The Covenant Sealed*, 56, for representative quotes from various Puritan ministers on this subject.

61 Holifield, *The Covenant Sealed*, 56.

62 "So they preached that communion was obligatory; abstention was sinful. Yet unworthy communion was equally sinful. The only alternative was repentance, holiness, and faithful attendance upon the sacrament, preceded by careful preparation." Holifield, *The Covenant Sealed*, 57.

three hours in the morning and three in the afternoon."[63] There were times when Puritan groups and leaders would devote extraordinary lengths of time to preaching and praying, especially during "fast days." Some of them brought together ministers from various churches and communities.[64] They certainly had enough time to practice frequent communion. Why did many Puritan communities not do so?

As Hambrick-Stowe notes, although most Puritans would probably assent to Calvin's theory of the spiritual efficacy of the Lord's Supper, they "opted for occasional rather than weekly celebration of the sacrament."[65] But he does not explain this any further. The following case studies explore the possibility that the Puritan priority of proper preparation, and the pursuit of a rigorous spirituality, overrode any desire for more frequent communion. Did the priority of communal sanctification, of catechesis, and—most importantly, of spiritual preparation—necessitate more time being spent to prepare both oneself, and to prepare the community?

This section explores the theme of the dual priorities of emphasizing the duty of participating in the Lord's Supper and the necessity of preparation. It summarizes the views of influential Puritan authors who wrote and preached about preparation for communion and communion frequency. It is important to understand this perspective because later generations, especially in the American Reformed churches, would reject this approach stridently, as they reconsidered the theological meaning of the Lord's Supper and the issue of frequency.

---

63 Hambrick-Stowe, "Practical divinity and spirituality," 199.

64 Benjamin Brook described one such occasion in London, hosted by the renowned Presbyterian pastor Stephen Marshall: "Mr. Marshall frequently united with his brethren in the observance of public fasts, when the services were usually protracted to a very great length. On one of these occasions, it is said, 'that Dr. Twisse having commenced the public service with a short prayer, Mr. Marshall prayed in a wonderful pathetic and prudent manner for two hours. Mr. Arrowsmith then preached an hour, then they sung a psalm after which Mr. Vines prayed nearly two hours; Mr. Palmer preached an hour and Mr. Seaman prayed nearly two hours. Mr. Henderson then spoke of the evils of the time and how they were to be remedied, and Dr. Twisse closed the service with a short prayer," *The Lives of the Puritans*, 3 vols., 1813, 248, quoted in Peter Lewis, *The Genius of Puritanism* (Haywards Heath: Carey Publications, 1975), 61.

65 "Puritans simultaneously lengthened the duration of worship and simplified its content, filling their services with four basic practices—psalm-singing, prayer, Bible reading and sermon preaching. Other practices included lay testimony, collection of an offering and the ordinances or sacraments of baptism and the Lord's Supper," Coffey and Lim, eds., *The Cambridge Companion to Puritanism*, 200.

4.4.1 Lewis Bayly (1575–1631)

A turn
to primary
sources

One of the most popular works of English practical theology was Lewis Bayly's manual *The Practice of Piety*.[66] It is a good example of "Reformed Anglicanism" in that Bayly (1575–1631) exemplifies a Puritan approach to intensely practical theology, even while remaining an ordained bishop in the Church of England.[67] Bayly's *Practice of Piety* originated as sermons. After his wife's death, he began shaping them into their final published form. The book went through many editions and was translated into several other European languages. In New England, it was even translated into the language of the native peoples of Massachusetts in 1665. John Bunyan, who wrote the even-more popular *Pilgrim's Progress*, was himself influenced by Bayly's *Practice of Piety*.[68] It can be safely assumed that Bayly's teachings on the Lord's Supper reached a large audience.

Bayly treats communion under the heading "Of the Practice of Piety in Holy Feasting." The Lord's Supper is the ultimate example of "holy feasting."[69] It is the "chiefest memorial of our redemption," and "every Christian should account this holy supper his chiefest and most joyful feast in this world." But because it is the "chiefest memorial," this requires serious preparation. If we participate in the sacrament properly, we can expect the "greatest assurance" of our own salvation. However, if we come in an "unworthy" fashion, we can expect "temporal judgements" in this life, and "eternal damnation" in the next. Accordingly, Bayly instructs his readers about how they can become a "due partaker of so holy a feast, and to be a worthy guest at so sacred a supper."[70]

The *Practice of Piety* deals with participating in the Lord's Supper in five chapters. The chapter titles themselves indicate Bayly's stress on the importance of prepa-

---

66 According to Hambrick-Stowe, it was "first published probably in 1611 (no first edition is extant; second edition in 1612) and quickly [went] through dozens of editions." "Practical divinity and spirituality," 196–197.

67 "Bayly's life itself illustrates the breadth of the Puritan movement, for he had a distinguished if tumultuous career in the Church of England. In 1616 he was consecrated as bishop of Bangor, a position he held, despite opposition (and some months in prison), until his death." Hambrick-Stowe, "Practical Divinity and Spirituality," 197.

68 Beeke and Pederson, *Meet the Puritans*, 73.

69 Bayly describes "Holy Feasting" as "a solemn thanksgiving, appointed by authority, to be rendered to God on some special day, for some extraordinary blessings or deliverances received." He cites the Passover and Purim as Old Testament examples, as well as the "fifth of November" (Guy Fawkes Day, the celebration of the failure of an attempt to assassinate James 1 in London in 1605). This is a good example of the phenomenon of national feast days, or sometimes "fast" days, that were proclaimed by the secular government, in response to political events; *The Practice of Piety*, 219.

70 Bayly, *The Practice of Piety*, 219.

ration, meditation, and approaching the sacrament in the appropriate manner.[71] He addresses communion frequency only tangentially. As with the other Puritan authors surveyed here, preparing properly for communion tends to be more prominent in their treatments than the issue of frequency.

Even though no one is worthy to approach the Lord's Supper, God accepts those who come with "due reverence," and this involves "three sorts of duties." There are duties that should be done before communion ("preparation"). Then there are duties that should be done during communion ("meditation"). Lastly, there are duties that should take place after communion ("action or practice").[72] Some may feel it is too dangerous to approach the Lord's Table, but Bayly warns that God will judge them just as harshly if they refuse to participate.[73] The sacrament is an important part of the Christian life, especially as it testifies to our union with Christ.[74]

There are a few passing references to communion frequency here, but that is certainly not the focus of his treatise.[75] One reference occurs when he discusses the "ends" (purposes) for which the Supper was established. It was created "[t]o keep Christians in a continual remembrance of" Christ's sacrifice. Accordingly "as oft as the sacrament is celebrated, so oft is he spiritually offered by the faithful."[76] When he connects communion to "assurance of eternal life," he indicates his ideal for frequency: "Oh, blessed are they who often eat of this sacrament; at least, once every month, taste anew of this renewing fruit, which Christ hath prepared for us at his table, to heal our infirmities, and to confirm our belief of life everlasting!"[77]

---

71 The chapter titles are: "21. The right manner of Holy Feasting, 22. Holy and Devout Meditations of the worthy and reverent receiving of the Lord's Supper, 23. An Humble Confession of Sins before the Holy Communion, 24. A Sweet Soliloquy to be said a little before the receiving of the Holy Sacrament, 25. A Prayer to be said after the receiving of the Holy Sacrament." Bayly, *The Practice of Piety*, xxx.

72 Bayly, *The Practice of Piety*, 220.

73 "But then thou wilt say, it were safer to abstain from coming at all to this holy communion: not so, for God has threatened to punish the willful neglect of his sacraments with eternal damnation both of body and soul (Numb.ix.13; Heb. ii.3; Matt. Xxvi.26; 1 Cor.xi.24.)." Bayly, *The Practice of Piety*, 223.

74 Bayly, *The Practice of Piety*, 228. He writes: "This union he shall best understand in his mind who doth most feel it in his heart. But of all other times this union is best felt, and most confirmed, when we duly receive the Lord's Supper: for then we shall sensibly feel our hearts knit unto Christ, and the desires of our souls drawn by faith and the Holy Ghost, as by the chords of love, nearer and nearer to his holiness." 229.

75 "And by the frequent use of this communion, Paul will have us to make a shew of the Lord's death till he come from heaven (1 Cor. Xi. 26; Acts iii. 21; i. 11)." Bayly, *The Practice of Piety*, 225.

76 Bayly, *The Practice of Piety*, 227.

77 Bayly, *The Practice of Piety*, 236, 237.

So, he urges monthly communion—at least, which implies he would support more frequent communion.

However, the stress in *The Practice of Piety* is on preparation. Although Bayly would surely resist this implication, his emphasis on preparation makes it seem that our experience of God's grace in communion depends on how well we prepare for it. Thus, the accent falls on man's agency, rather than God's. He urges his readers to come "prepared" to the Supper.[78] Proper preparation entails the "serious consideration of three things: the "worthiness of the sacrament," our "own unworthiness," and the "means whereby [we may] become a worthy receiver."[79] To help readers prepare, Bayly offers a model of confession, five pages in total, to pray before receiving communion.[80] To be a "worthy receiver," we must have "sound knowledge" of God, true faith, "unfeigned repentance," and "sincere charity" towards our neighbor.[81] Meditation before and during communion is also an important part of fully participating in the sacrament[82] He ends by detailing the "duties" that should be performed after communion, both by ourselves and also together with rest of the congregation.[83] The predominant theme is that, since the communicant has had such a profound experience of the sacrament, it should make a difference in their spiritual and practical life.[84] There is, however, one last mention of frequency: "Lastly, if ever thou hast found either joy or comfort in receiving the holy sacrament, let it appear by thy eager desire of receiving it *often* again."[85] It is precisely because

---

78 "O come, but come a guest prepared for the Lord's table; seeing they are blessed who are called to the Lamb's supper (Rev. xix. 9). O come, but come prepared, because the efficacy of the sacrament is received according to the proportion of the faith of the receiver." Bayly, *The Practice of Piety*, 223.

79 Bayly, *The Practice of Piety*, 223.

80 Bayly, *The Practice of Piety*, 238–243.

81 Bayly, *The Practice of Piety*, 243.

82 Bayly, *The Practice of Piety*, 245–255. As an example of the rich imagery Bayly employs to motivate his readers to meditate: "The bread of the Lord is given by the minister, but the bread which is the Lord is given by Christ himself. When thou takest the bread at the minister's hand to eat it, then rouse up thy soul to apprehend Christ by faith, and to apply his merits to heal thy miseries. Embrace him as sweetly with thy faith in the sacrament, as ever Simeon hugged him with his arms in his swaddling clothes." 252.

83 Bayly, *The Practice of Piety*, 255–262.

84 "And let this be the chief end to which both thy receiving and living tends,–that thou mayest be a holy Christian, zealous of good works, purged from sin, to live soberly, righteously, and godly in this present world; that thou mayest be acceptable to God, profitable to thy brethren, and comfortable unto thine own soul." Bayly, *The Practice of Piety*, 262.

85 Bayly, *The Practice of Piety*, 262, italics added. He continues: "For the body of Christ, as it was anointed with the oil of gladness above his fellows, so doth it yield a sweeter savour than all the ointments of the world; the fragrant smell of which allureth all souls who have once tasted its sweetness ever after to desire *oftener* to taste it again." italics added.

Bayly stresses the importance of receiving communion, that he exhorts his readers to both serious preparation, and more frequent communion.

4.4.2 Arthur Hildersham (1563–1632) and William Bradshaw (1570–1618)

Arthur Hildersham (1563–1632) and William Bradshaw (1570–1618) were contemporaries, and both lived through the years of turbulence that marked the beginnings of the English Puritan movement. Both struggled to pursue their calling as ministers and preachers, and Hildersham even spent some time in prison for his nonconformity.[86] They were friends, and Hildersham helped Bradshaw secure the patronage of wealthy benefactors. In 1609, Bradshaw published the first edition of his communicants' manual.[87] He also included another anonymous catechism on the same subject, which was written by Hildersham. The volume sold very well and was one of earliest examples of the "pre-communion handbooks" genre.[88] The Puritan leader John Cotton, a personal friend of Hildersham, commended Hildersham's catechism on the Lord's Supper highly.[89] This short survey of these two texts will focus on the relationship between purity, proper participation, preparation, and frequency.

---

86 Hildersham was one of the main signers and personalities behind the "Millenary Petition," to James I. This petition, supposedly signed by a "thousand" clergy with godly convictions, was submitted to the new monarch on his way from Scotland to assume the throne of England. The petition reiterated the concerns of previous Reformers with Puritan convictions and it was the occasion of the Hampton Court Conference in 1604. Hildersham was not invited to attend, and most of the proposals of the godly were rejected. See Bryan D. Spinks, *Sacraments, Ceremonies and the Stuart Divines*, 33–34.

87 The full title of the original was, *A Direction for the Weaker Sort of Christians, Shewing in What Manner They Ought to Fit and Prepare Themselves to the Worthy Receiving of the Sacrament of the Body and Blood of Christ.* It was later shortened to *A Preparation to the Receiving of the Sacrament of Christ's Body and Blood.* A critical edition has recently been published as *Preparing for the Lord's Supper*, Lesley A. Rowe, ed., (Grand Rapids: Reformation Heritage Books, 2019).

88 "It was one of the earliest examples of the specialist 'pre-communion handbooks,' a genre that reached its peak between 1660 and 1700. In fact, the Bradshaw/Hildersham book was in the top four early modern best-selling titles on the subject." *Preparing for the Lord's Supper*, xi, referencing Ian Green, *Print and Protestantism in Early Modern England* (Oxford: Oxford University Press, 2000), appendix 1, 591–672.

89 Cotton wrote: "Witness those Questions and Answers, wherein he [Hildersham] hath comprised the doctrine of the Lord's Supper … yet have they been of singular good use to many poor souls, for their worthy preparation to that Ordinance. And in very deed they do more fully furnish a Christian to that whole spiritual Duty, than any other, in any language (that I know) in so small a compass." John Cotton, "To the Godly Reader," in Arthur Hildersham, *Lectures upon the Fourth of John* (London, 1629), quoted in Rowe, ed., *Preparing for the Lord's Supper*, xi.

The subtitle to Part 1 of Bradshaw's text ("Showing What a Dangerous Sin It is to Receive This Sacrament Unworthily") clearly focuses on the issue of being "worthy" to partake. The key text is 1 Cor. 11:23-33. Bradshaw emphasizes the necessity of preparing fully for participation in communion. Since people prepare themselves for an ordinary feast, how much more should they prepare for this spiritual feast—especially when it is so "hurtful and dangerous" to not prepare?[90] He emphasizes the divine origin of communion, and maintains that people who come "so rudely and unprepared" forget the "high and sacred authority that has ordained" it.[91]

Since Jesus is "spiritually" and "effectually present" in the sacrament, preparation is important.[92] Those who come "worthily" experience true, spiritual nourishment in the Lord's Supper.[93] The mere frequency of communion is not sufficient. To receive the full spiritual blessing, one must be prepared, and it must be administered properly.[94] Because Bradshaw has such a high view of the sacrament, the issue of preparation was important to him.[95] It is not enough to have an intellectual understanding of the sacrament—we must feel its truth in our hearts.[96]

---

90 Rowe, *Preparing for the Lord's Supper*, 9.

91 Rowe, *Preparing for the Lord's Supper*, 14.

92 Bradshaw writes: "That albeit this sacrament is administered unto us now by the hands of weak and sinful men, yet they being the lawful ministers and substitutes of Christ, we are to receive it from their hands as from the hands of Christ Himself, who though He be not bodily yet is spiritually and will be as effectually present now as at the first institution and administration thereof." Rowe, *Preparing for the Lord's Supper*, 16–17.

93 He writes, "in this bread and wine we must look after bread and wine of another and higher nature, such whereby our souls are to be nourished and refreshed to everlasting life." Rowe, *Preparing for the Lord's Supper*, 25.

94 "Is not, then, this sacrament a mystery to be trembled at? Is it not a brutish sin, without any preparation, to rush upon the same?" Rowe, *Preparing for the Lord's Supper*, 21, 27.

95 "This sacrament, then, which seals so great a mystery as this is, cannot be profaned without great indignity to the mystery itself." Rowe, *Preparing for the Lord's Supper*, 31. He expresses a typically Reformed view of the efficacy of the sacrament: "it is by the ordinance of Christ (to the *worthy* receiver) a blessed instrument by means whereof Christ Jesus and His merits are applied and made effectual to their souls. Such is the union of the thing signified and the sign that in and through the eating of this bread and drinking this wine the soul of the *worthy* receiver does spiritually and by faith eat the body and drink the blood of Jesus Christ, and always finds such strength, comfort, and life therein as the body finds ordinarily in the eating of bread and drinking of wine." (emphasis added), Rowe, *Preparing for the Lord's Supper*, 31–32.

96 "For let our knowledge be never so great, yet if we be not often put in mind of it, if we be not taught how in such and such particular cases to apply it, if by the power of Christ's ordinance it be not beaten out of our head [and] into our heart, it will be as a dead letter unto us, yea, and most out of our head when we should most use it. For such was the particular knowledge of this sacrament in [the] church of Corinth. And so will be the knowledge of this or of any truth else if it be not revived and quickened in us by daily teaching and instruction." Rowe, *Preparing for the Lord's Supper*, 38–39.

Preparing to receive the sacrament is also important because the danger of being "guilty" of the body and blood of Christ is a real threat, according to 1 Cor. 11:27.[97] More specifically, to eat in an "unworthy" way is to come to the sacrament without a due regard for its spiritual value ("without any due reverence or respect of the mystery") and without proper preparation.[98] The more the "unworthy receiver" comes to partake of the sacrament, the more often they receive the "bane and poison of his own soul."[99] Bradshaw hastens to add that no one is worthy, in themselves. It is only the righteousness of Jesus Christ that makes us worthy to come to this sacrament.[100]

The second part of the pamphlet is dedicated to the topic of how to prepare properly for the sacrament of the Lord's Supper. Reminiscent of Bayly, Bradshaw concludes from 1 Cor. 11 that Paul teaches two "duties": the duty of examining ourselves before the sacrament, and the duty to not stop examining ourselves until we find evidence of grace, faith, and true repentance within us.[101] We must undertake a "diligent search and inquisition" into the condition of our "souls and consciences" to determine whether we are the "kind of persons as may be assured that the Lord will bid welcome to this Table." This must not be a cursory or superficial examination, but must be "most strict and accurate," like a metal worker testing the quality of their work.[102] This illustrates the deep and serious sacramental piety of the early Puritans.

He also exemplifies a typical Puritan understanding when he argues that those who are truly saved, and thus worthy to approach the sacrament, can "conclude infallibly that God does love and favor them," because of the presence of the "*saving graces.*"[103] The danger of receiving unworthily should not keep anyone from coming

---

97 To be "guilty" is to "offer some special disgrace and indignity unto the person and sufferings of Christ and (in a special manner) to sin against the great work of our redemption," and it really amounts to crucifying Jesus again. Rowe, *Preparing for the Lord's Supper*, 40–41.

98 Rowe, *Preparing for the Lord's Supper*, 42.

99 Rowe, *Preparing for the Lord's Supper*, 47.

100 "The best of men cannot be said (in themselves) to be worthy to receive this sacrament. Yet how unworthy soever we are in ourselves, if Christ deem us worthy and we be (in some measure) such persons as He has ordained this sacrament for, and if we do our uttermost to receive it in that manner, with such hearts and affections as He requires, we may be said (how unworthy soever otherwise we be) to be worthy receivers of this sacrament." Rowe, *Preparing for the Lord's Supper*, 42.

101 Rowe, *Preparing for the Lord's Supper*, 51.

102 Rowe, *Preparing for the Lord's Supper*, 52.

103 Rowe, *Preparing for the Lord's Supper*, 52.

to the Supper. On the contrary, because so much is at stake, we should endeavor that much more to make sure we are sufficiently prepared and ready to come.[104]

Arthur Hildersham's contribution is in two parts. The first is *A Brief Form of Examination* and is a basic catechism (i. e., it has a question-and-answer structure), designed to gauge a prospective communicant's knowledge of basic Christian doctrine. It addresses communion frequency briefly. The Lord's Supper should be received "[a]s oft as it may conveniently be administered in that church in which they have calling to live [sic = the church where they are members]."[105] Later, he argues that it is as necessary to come to the sacrament as it is to hear the Word preached, or to be baptized.[106] So, although Hildersham does not explicitly state what he believes about communion frequency, he clearly believes it is important to come to communion, whenever it is offered. Additionally, in Question 62, Hildersham reminds his readers that is a serious "sin" to "neglect" coming to the sacrament.[107]

The second part is titled *The Doctrine of Communicating Worthily in the Lord's Supper* and is another catechism. Hildersham also wrote and preached extensively on communion.[108] Spinks comments on the connection between these writings and Hildersham's focus on the sacrament: "The fact that these sermons were preached at communion services reflects the fact that regular celebration of the Lord's Supper was encouraged by many of the 'godly' ministers, in contrast to the thrice yearly, or in some cases, single annual celebration found in many Jacobean parishes."[109]

Throughout this work, Hildersham reiterates the necessity of spiritual preparation before communion, and the "extreme danger" or receiving the sacrament in an

---

104 "That the danger of receiving unworthily must not withhold us from receiving this sacrament but must make us so much the more studious to use the means of worthy receiving the same." Furthermore, commenting on 1 Cor. 11:28, "the more dangerous it is to receive unworthily, the more we must endeavor to be worthy receivers." Rowe, *Preparing for the Lord's Supper*, 75.

105 Rowe, *Preparing for the Lord's Supper*, 96.

106 "For it is [as] necessary to receive this sacrament when we may as it is to hear the Word preached when we may and as it is for them that are converted to the faith and for Christian parents … to seek and desire the sacrament of baptism upon the first opportunity that God shall offer them." Rowe, *Preparing for the Lord's Supper*, 135.

107 The last part of the answer to Question 62 states: "[Neglecting the sacrament] argues a profane and open contempt both of the commandment of our Savior Christ, who has charged us to come—and *to come often*—to this sacrament, and of those inestimable benefits which He offers us in it, and of the church and people of God, from whose fellowship we do thus divide and excommunicate ourselves." (italics added). Rowe, *Preparing for the Lord's Supper*, 136.

108 "In 1625 he was licensed to preach in the dioceses of London, Lincoln, Coventry and Lichfield. Hildersham's teachings centre mainly on the Lord's Supper, and are found in his *108 Lectures on the Fourth (Chapter) of John* (1609), *A Briefe Forme of Examination* (1619), *The Doctrine of Communicating Worthily in the Lord's Supper* (1619), and his *152 Lectures on Psalm 51*, preached at Ashby de la Zouch from 1626 to 1629." Spinks, *Sacraments, Ceremonies and the Stuart Divines*, 37.

109 Spinks, *Sacraments, Ceremonies and the Stuart Divines*, 37.

"unworthy" manner.[110] There is little here that is original. Rather, the importance of this source lies in its popularity, as well as in Hildersham's (and Bradshaw's) contributions to the overall English Puritan movement, since they were active in the early years of the movement's second main iteration, in the reign of James I. Hildersham's preoccupation with preparation, examination, and the danger of judgement is counter-balanced by his view of the spiritual benefits of receiving the Lord's Supper. Indeed, preparation and self-examination are important precisely because of the reality of communion with Christ that the faithful experience in the Supper.[111] He writes "everyone that comes worthily to this sacrament does indeed receive and apply Christ to himself for the nourishment and comfort of his soul."[112]

Along with these words of encouragement, Hildersham also establishes a rather high standard for prospective communicants. It reads: "No man can receive this sacrament worthily unless he has a true justifying faith and be undoubtedly assured that Christ with all His merits do belong unto himself."[113] Later, he claims that most people who come to the sacrament are hypocrites and will possibly be damned for coming unworthily.[114] Did this type of extreme statement help to lay the foundation of later Puritan struggles with the assurance of salvation? The history of the Puritans and Puritanism is filled with men and women struggling to understand the depths of their own depravity and uncertainty about whether they were saved. In many cases, this uncertainty kept them from coming to the sacrament and from participating in the Lord's Supper. Perhaps this is why Hildersham reassures his readers that they can come to the sacrament "worthily" if they truly desire to change and grow in grace, and if they are truly grieving for their sins and striving to resist them.[115]

4.4.3 Stephen Charnock (1628–1680)

Although Stephen Charnock (1628–1680) did not publish much during his own lifetime, he gained notoriety through the posthumous publication of his writings,

---

110 Hildersham's catechism totals one hundred questions. Of those, 1–19 directly address the issue of preparation, though the entire work is indirectly about this topic because Hildersham shares the typical Puritan assumption that proper preparation for the Supper requires correct doctrinal knowledge about what is happening (or not) in communion.

111 Rowe, *Preparing for the Lord's Supper*, 114–115. In particular, "Christ, and this benefit of his passion, is by this sacrament exhibited, given, and confirmed to us most fully and effectually."

112 Rowe, *Preparing for the Lord's Supper*, 120.

113 Rowe, *Preparing for the Lord's Supper*, 141.

114 "(…) the desire that most men have to this sacrament (as also their knowledge, faith, and repentance) is counterfeit and hypocritical, and consequently their coming to this sacrament [is] dangerous and damnable." Rowe, *Preparing for the Lord's Supper*, 148.

115 Rowe, *Preparing for the Lord's Supper*, 160, Question and Answer 92.

most notably *The Existence and Attributes of God*.[116] Although he is sometimes called a "Presbyterian," Wallace singles out Charnock as an example of the fluid boundaries between theological and ecclesiastical labels during this time period.[117] Charnock served as a chaplain for Oliver Cromwell's son, Henry, during Henry's time as governor of Ireland. This was part of an effort to send "godly" clergy into Ireland, to help reform the church there.[118] He returned to England in 1660 and, after the Restoration, spent fifteen years without a pastorate, traveling intermittently and preaching, possibly trying to elude the authorities. Charnock took on the task of co-pastoring a church in London in 1657 with Thomas Watson. He served there until his early death at age fifty-two. There is evidence that his published writings were also influential in New England.[119]

Charnock expounds 1 Corinthians 11 in *A Discourse on the End of the Lord's Supper*. He stands out from other Puritan writers because he deals with this topic more thoroughly, but also retains a stress on the priorities of both frequency *and* preparation/purity. He first deals with the issue of frequency as he provides an overview of the text. In a typical Puritan expository fashion, he breaks the text down into smaller phrases, or words. Dealing with 1 Corinthians 11:23-25, he explains:

Ὁσάκις, *as often.* The Lord's Supper ought to be often administered. The frequency is implied, though how often is not declared. Christ's death is to be every day fixed in our thoughts; and to help our weakness, there should be a frequent representation of it to our sense, i. e. in such a way as Christ hath instituted it, not as man may prescribe.[120]

---

116 He only published one sermon during his own lifetime, and even then, he only used the initials "S.C." although every other minister who published their sermons in the same collection used their full names. See James McCosh's introductory biography to *The Complete Works of Stephen Charnock, B.D.*, vol. I (Edinburgh: James Nichol, 1865), xxv-xxvi. Regarding Charnock's *Existence and Attributes of God*, J.I. Packer wrote that these discourses were, "one of the noblest productions of the Puritan epoch." *Encyclopedia of Christianity* 2:411, quoted in Beeke and Pederson, eds., *Meet the Puritans*, 145. In "Stephen Charnock on the Attributes of God," Joel R. Beeke and Mark Jones claim that "there is no doubt Charnock belongs to the upper echelon of Puritan theologians," in *A Puritan Theology: Doctrine for Life* (Grand Rapids: Reformation Heritage Books, 2012), 59–60.

117 Dewey D. Wallace, *Puritans and Predestination: Grace in English Protestant Theology 1525–1695*, (Chapel Hill: University of North Carolina Press, 1982), 159. See also Bremer, who notes that Charnock was "so firmly entrenched in the middle ground [between Presbyterians and Congregationalists] that contemporaries and historians alike found it difficult to agree on how to classify [him]." *Congregational Communion*, 188.

118 Bremer, *Congregational Communion*, 191.

119 See Holifield, *The Covenant Sealed*, 198–199 and 214 for Charnock's popularity in New England. Holifield shows how Increase Mather used Charnock's work, and the work of other English writers, as ammunition in his debate with Solomon Stoddard (see §5.4 below).

120 Stephen Charnock, *The Complete Works of Stephen Charnock, B.D.*, vol. IV (Edinburgh: James Nichol, 1865; reprint, Edinburgh: The Banner of Truth Trust, 1985), 393.

In his summary of 1 Cor. 11:26, he mentions "frequency" twice. Point four of his summary of the text is "[t]he frequency of it implied," and under "Doctrine," point two, he states "[t]he Lord's Supper ought frequently to be celebrated."[121] But self-examination is still necessary because the sacrament is not merely "an historical remembrance."[122]

While stressing the need for self-examination and preparation, Charnock returns to the issue of frequency throughout this sermon. He writes: "The Lord's Supper is to be frequently celebrated and participated of. *As often,* implying it ought often to be done."[123] However, it is impossible to determine a "fixed time" or precise pattern of frequency from this verse.[124] Although he grants that people have different life circumstances which might hinder them from communing, he also maintains that there is more "fruit" in one sacrament properly prepared for, than a "hundred" not prepared for.[125]

Turning to communion frequency in the New Testament, Charnock observes that it was "anciently often participated of." His use of the word "ancient" to describe the New Testament church is consonant with other Protestant and Reformed authors, especially among Puritan groups.[126] The weight of the evidence supports the conclusion that the first Christians held communion every Sunday, that is, every Lord's Day. The texts appealed to here are Acts 2:46 and Acts 10:7.[127] He notes that weekly communion was the practice of the early patristic church as well and sees a prophetic reference to this in Ezekiel 43:27.[128] Despite the example of the apostolic and patristic church, Charnock doubts whether weekly communion is a Biblical

---

121 Charnock, *Works*, vol. 4, 394.

122 Charnock, *Works*, vol. 4, 394.

123 Charnock, *Works*, vol. 4, 402.

124 "How often is not determined. There is no fixed time for the administration of this prescribed by any precept, no day commanded for it; but the celebration of it on the Lord's Day was the primitive practice." Charnock, *Works*, vol. 4, 403.

125 "Nor can there be a constant time for every particular person; because there are varieties in the cases of good men, who may, by some emergency, find themselves hindered one time, and not another." Charnock, *Works*, vol. 4, 403. Charnock stresses the need for preparation here: "Sometimes men's various callings administer to one more distractions than the calling of another, that they cannot rightly dispose themselves, nor spend so much time as is necessary to a due preparation; and there is more fruit by one sacrament, when men come with a suitable frame, than by a hundred slightly approached to." ibid.

126 See Theodore Dwight Bozeman, *To Live Ancient Lives: The Primitivist Dimension in Puritanism* (Chapel Hill, N.C., 1998).

127 Charnock, *Works*, vol. 4, 403–404.

128 "And this was afterwards kept up in the church in the time of Justin Martyr, and by some in the time of Austin, [Augustine] long after the other, which practice was perhaps grounded on Ezek. xliii. 27." Charnock, *Works*, vol. 4, 404. Charnock's interpretation of Ezekiel 43 is a bit forced but is standard Puritan exegesis.

necessity because the "law" was read in Jewish synagogues weekly, but the Passover was annual. Here, Charnock makes Passover the primary Old Testament reference point for the Eucharist and equates the "law" with a Protestant understanding of preaching.[129] This primary identification of the Lord's Supper with Passover will become a dominant theme in later Scottish communion frequency debates, but here Charnock does not develop it as much as later writers.

Why did communion become less frequent in later church history? Charnock proposes that frequency led to "coldness" and even "contempt" towards the sacrament: "The celebration [of the Lord's Supper] came to be more seldom, because the frequency of it begat a coldness in the affections of the people, and the commonness occasioned too much contempt of it. The esteem and reverence of this ordinance was dashed upon this rock."[130] Further, since "[g]reat preparations are necessary to great duties; affections must be exercised, which are wound up to a higher pitch by the novelty and rarity, and flag by the commonness of an excellent thing." Related to this, Charnock notes that fasting had become so "common" in his time that "true humiliation" was rare among those fasting.[131]

Although novelty might stimulate more spiritual fervor, he seems to finally decide that frequency should have priority over novelty: "Yet to be frequent in it is agreeable to the nature of the ordinance, and necessary for the wants of a Christian."[132] There are several reasons to come frequently to the Lord's Table. First, frequent communion will help us maintain a healthy spiritual balance.[133] If we focus on "fasting" too much, we will lose our appetite. Answering those who pointed to the Passover as a justification for annual communion, Charnock appeals instead to the daily sacrifices in the Jewish temple, which were examples of frequency.[134] He also insists that too much focus on our unworthiness can lead us to disobey God, if it keeps us away from communion for too long.[135]

---

129 "It is likely it is not absolutely necessary that it should be administered every Lord's day, when the word is preached. The passover, the Jewish sacrament, was but annual, though Moses, the law of Moses, was read every Sabbath in the synagogue." Charnock, *Works*, 404.

130 Charnock, *Works*, vol. 4, 404.

131 "The commonness of fasts in our days, and even at this time, hath driven true humiliation almost out of doors." Charnock, *Works*, vol. 4, 404.

132 Charnock, *Works*, vol. 4, 404.

133 "By too much fasting we often lose our stomachs." Charnock, *Works*, vol. 4, 404.

134 Charnock, *Works*, vol. 4, 404.

135 "It is not to be neglected out of a willful contempt, or a pretence of humility. Disobedience is not a part of humility, but the fruit of pride against God; and though a sense of unworthiness may be so great as to hinder a free and cheerful approach, and deter for a time, yet there ought to be endeavors to get rid of these clouds. We must not rest in lazy and idle complaints. That is no true sense of our own unworthiness which hinders us from a necessary duty." Charnock, *Works*, vol. 4, 404.

His final judgment on the wisdom of frequent communion is: "Frequent it should be. The too much deferring doth more hurt than the frequent communicating. The oftener we carefully and believingly communicate, the more disposed we shall be for it." Furthermore "[i]f we abstain from it for reverence, we may rather come for reverence; for if it be worthily received, it increaseth our reverence of God, and affection to him. That is the best reverence of God which owns his authority."[136] In other words, it is better to obey the Scriptural injunctions to come to the Lord's Supper, rather than focusing on our feelings of not being worthy.

There are weighty reasons to not neglect the sacrament of communion. The primary reason is because Jesus Christ himself instituted and commanded it.[137] Also, closely tied to this is the consideration that, just as we respect the dying wishes of a friend, how much more should we respect the dying wishes of our Savior?[138] Thirdly, the "ends of it declare the unworthiness of neglecting it."[139] What are these ends? They are: to help us remember Christ, to seal the covenant, to renew our covenant with God, and to be a means of communion with God.[140]

Furthermore, the "benefits of this ordinance require frequency."[141] There are five specific benefits of the Lord's Supper. It weakens sin in us (1).[142] It also nourishes the soul (2) and increases the faith and grace in our lives (3).[143] This third benefit is directly related to frequency. The more often we come to the sacrament, the more often our faith can be increased: "Faith is increased thereby; as the oftener the word is heard, so the oftener sacraments are used, the more doth faith thrive."[144] Even more, it increases our "sense and assurance of [God's] love" (4) and in the Supper

---

136 Charnock, *Works*, vol. 4, 404.

137 Charnock, *Works*, vol. 4, 404–405.

138 Charnock, *Works*, vol. 4, 405.

139 Charnock, *Works*, vol. 4, 405–408.

140 He displays his high regard for the spiritual communion we have with Christ in the Supper when he writes: "God gives us to feast our souls on earth, so that we do in a manner eat and drink with him in this love banquet. Take, eat, manifests a communion; Christ is really presented to us, and faith really takes him, closes with him, lodgeth him in the soul, makes him an indweller; and the soul hath a spiritual communion with him in his life and death, as if we did really eat his flesh and drink his blood presented to us in the elements." Charnock, *Works*, vol. 4, 408.

141 Charnock, *Works*, vol. 4, 408.

142 Charnock, *Works*, vol. 4, 408–409. Regarding how it weakens sin, he writes: "The word declares the evil of sin, and the sacrament shews it in the person of our Saviour; sin is known by the word to be deadly, and it is seen to be so in the supper." 408.

143 Charnock, *Works*, vol. 4, 409–410.

144 Charnock, *Works*, vol. 4, 410. He makes several statements relating to frequency here: "The ordinance, therefore, is of frequent use for the building up and bringing forth more lively and juicy fruits." 409; "If we come with weak grace and strong breathings, we may return with strong grace and full satisfaction. Do not little sparks need frequent and gentle blasts to blow them up?" 410; "If we would maintain the fire, it must not be by removing the fuel." 410.

"union with Christ is promoted" (5).[145] He asks: "Can we too *often* clasp about him; can the union be often renewed, and become too close and strait?"[146]

Charnock then moves on to two points of practical application. The first is: "How much is the neglect, if not contempt, of this institution to be bewailed! How sad a thing is it, that many for many years have turned their backs upon breasts of milk!"[147] Some may have legitimate reasons for not coming to communion, but they should not neglect it habitually.[148] Jesus Christ, as the one who instituted the sacrament, should be obeyed and trusted, even if we don't feel worthy.[149] If we neglect communion, we are really showing disrespect to Christ.[150] If some neglect the sacrament because they feel that the communion elements are just ordinary bread and wine, they should remember that the elements are "consecrated" and bear the "stamp of Christ" himself.[151] For those who might be stuck on the issue of their "unworthiness," Charnock forcefully states "[i]f you are not fit for this ordinance, you are not fit for heaven."[152]

The second practical application of this text is Charnock's "exhortation" to observe the Lord's Supper, and to do it "frequently."[153] The sacrament brings us into spiritual contact with the "living Savior."[154] Additionally, the sacrament is one of the "steps" that God has ordained to lead us up into fellowship with him.[155] Christ is our "friend," and should we not "often be in those ways where we may meet with our best friend?"[156]

---

145 Charnock, *Works*, vol. 4, 410–411.

146 Charnock, *Works*, vol. 4, 411.

147 Charnock, *Works*, vol. 4, 411.

148 Charnock, *Works*, vol. 4, "Though it may not always be frequented, yet it is not always to be omitted." 411.

149 "Christ is a better judge of the weakness of our hearts, our proneness to forgetfulness, the difficulty to preserve faith as well as obtain it. And he instituted it as an act of kindness as well as authority, that it might be observed, not neglected by us." Charnock, *Works*, vol. 4, 412.

150 He writes, "How can such [who habitually neglect communion] free themselves from unworthy reflections upon Christ?" and "We must either quite discard our faith, or discard our neglect." Charnock, *Works*, vol. 4, 412.

151 "It is true, it is common bread, it is common wine in itself; but it is consecrated bread, and consecrated wine in its use. It hath the stamp of Christ upon it." Charnock, *Works*, vol. 4, 413.

152 Charnock, *Works*, vol. 4, 413.

153 Charnock, *Works*, vol. 4, 414.

154 "Though a dying Saviour is remembered, yet a living Saviour is sought for in it; and shall not we be as ready to seek a living Christ in the sacrament, as the women were to seek a dead Christ in the sepulcher? Mat. xxviii. 1." Charnock, *Works*, vol. 4, 414.

155 "The way to ascend to the top of a pinnacle is not to run from the steps which lead to it." Charnock, *Works*, vol. 4, 414.

156 Charnock, *Works*, vol. 4, 416.

A set of rhetorical questions relates more directly to the issue of communion frequency. He asks: "Have you no graces that need strengthening?"[157] Since we come "often" to our daily meals of natural food, why would we not come more frequently to our spiritual meal?[158] If we want our faith to be strong, we need our faith to be strengthened frequently.[159] To come to the Supper in faith "exercises" our faith, and increases our spiritual vitality.[160] More seriously, when we don't come to the Supper, we are "gratifying" Satan.[161]

Charnock's treatment of the issue of communion frequency manages to hold together the twin priorities of frequency and preparation in a way that is rather unique among those who wrote on this topic, and among Puritan writers in particular. Charnock clearly values and urges his readers to come more frequently to the sacrament of communion, while also retaining the standard Reformed and Puritan stress on the necessity of serious soul-searching and preparation beforehand. His emphasis on the dangers of coming in an unworthy manner are carefully balanced by pastoral exhortations to rely on God's mercy and trust that the righteousness of Christ, received by faith, is what makes us truly worthy. Charnock urges his readers to come to the Supper as frequently as possible, and to take seriously their need to prepare themselves for the blessings that come from communion. Charnock's emphasis on frequency, as compared to the other representative Puritan authors surveyed here, highlights the diversity of opinion and practice that characterized the Puritan movement. While all Puritans continued the Reformed stress on purity and preparation, authors like Charnock also emphasized the desirability of frequency, continuing the trajectory laid out by Calvin, Bucer, and others.

---

157 Charnock, *Works*, vol. 4, 416.

158 "Who would come but seldom to his stated meals? He that would fast one day would scarce fast two, but by force. We are yet in a journey, and we need strength to go forward; we are beset with diseases, and we need medicines to cure us; we are often faint, and we need cordials to revive us. Are our souls so fully established, our affections so ready at our call, as not to need sensible objects sometimes to a greater activity; so doth a spiritual faith. Can you, then too often embrace the cross, drink down the blood of Christ, and put your hands into his wounds?" Charnock, *Works*, vol. 4, 416.

159 "It is certain, that as we would have faith, we must attend upon converting ordinances, so if we would have strength of faith, we must frequent strengthening institutions." Charnock, *Works*, vol. 4, 416.

160 "It is by a frequent exercise of faith, according to the methods of Christ, that believers would be as lions (as Chrysostom saith) breathing fire terrible to the devils themselves." Charnock, *Works*, vol. 4, 416.

161 "If the frequent attendance be a means to strengthen grace, the neglects are a means to weaken; and the devil rejoices in the decays of grace, next to preventing any grace at all." Charnock, *Works*, vol. 4, 417.

4.4.4 Westminster Assembly: Frequency and Church Discipline (1643–1653)

There are two main issues to be examined in relation to what the Westminster Assembly eventually presented in its official documents about communion. The first issue is that of communion frequency; the other is the question of who could be allowed to commune, and who had the authority to make that decision. The issue of who could participate in the Lord's Supper was hotly debated during the Westminster Assembly. In their optimism to finally achieve a fully "reformed" church, some Puritans pushed for the legal right to bar people from communion through ecclesiastical discipline. This exposed a fault line between various parties and different understandings of what communion was.[162] The legal right to "suspend" or "sequester" unrepentant or flagrant sinners from the Supper was urged by many Puritans at Westminster.[163] Others argued stridently against this. This debate occurred in a wider context: Puritan ministers had increasingly resorted to *not* holding communion services, because they could not guard the "purity" of the sacrament.[164] But not everyone agreed with this rigid standard. Prominent among the critics was the controversialist William Prynne (1600–1669).[165] Prynne was a

---

162 "The controversy demonstrated once again the centrality of the covenant doctrine in Puritan sacramental theology, just as it uncovered the ambiguity in the definition of the Lord's Supper as a covenant seal." Holifield, *The Covenant Sealed*, 110. See also Chad B. van Dixhoorn, "Unity and Diversity at the Westminster Assembly (1643–1649): A Commemorative Essay," *The Journal of Presbyterian History*, (Summer, 2001): 105–106, 109.

163 This was already an issue at the level of the local parish: "In the parish churches, puritan ministers were hamstrung over the reformation they could legally bring about on their own. They could finally cut out the offensive parts of the Book of Common Prayer without fear, but they had no control over discipline, and that meant that they had no control over what was for many puritans the heart of church reform, the Lord's Supper. The 'pure waters' of the Lord's Supper, as one minister put it, had to be protected 'from the pollution of the common feet of the wild beasts.' That protection parish ministers could not provide, and increasingly, out of desperation, in the 1640s they were shutting down the Lord's Supper completely." Winship, *Hot Protestants*, 119.

164 Winship, *Hot Protestants*, 119.

165 Prynne argued that sitting under the preaching of the Word in an "unworthy" manner was just as dangerous as coming to the Lord's Supper unprepared, and that ministers had no right to exclude someone from the sacrament, unless they were also excommunicated from the church. He also worried about giving presbyteries too much power. See *Foure serious Questions of Grand Importance, Concerning Excommunication, and Suspension from the Sacrament; propounded to the Reverend Assembly, and all Moderate Christians, to prevent Schismes, and settle Unity among us, in these divided Times; by a Lover both of Peace and Truth* (London, 1644). In response to critics, Prynne also wrote *A Vindication of foure Serious Questions of Grand Importance Concerning Excommunication and Suspension from the Sacrament of the Lords Supper* (London, 1645).

lawyer of Puritan convictions who wrote a series of controversial works.[166] This conflict has been labeled the "Erastian Controversy," although the exact influence and applicability of the label could be questioned. The main issue was whether churches should, or could, have the legal right to bar and exclude people from the Lord's Supper.[167] Prynne believed that the reformation of the church would be impeded by the imposition of ecclesiastical discipline.[168] Scottish leaders and representatives at the Assembly like Samuel Rutherford and George Gillespie took up Prynne's challenge and defended the proposals to allow church discipline and suspension.[169]

This debate occurred in the wider context of what type of church would be instituted, or tolerated, by the government.[170] Many of the Westminster divines wanted to create a national English Presbyterian church, even though they disagreed among themselves about what this national church should look like. Should they adopt the "four office" view of Scotland and Geneva, with pastors, teachers, deacons, and lay elders, or should it be more loosely organized and possibly include a modified form of episcopacy? Or should they even grant autonomy to the local churches, as the "Independents" or, as they styled themselves, "Congregationalists" wanted?[171]

---

166 Because of his attacks on plays (a favorite pastime of King Charles) and his later attacks on bishops, Prynne twice suffered the punishment of having his ears cropped (sliced off). See Winship, *Hot Protestants*, 92, 101. It is no coincidence that the persecuted protagonist of Nathaniel Hawthorne's *The Scarlet Letter* (1850) is named Hester Prynne, although the irony there is profound, since Hawthorne is critiquing Puritanism.

167 Apparently, Prynne and other opponents of "sequestration" drew inspiration from the work of Thomas Erastus in Heidelberg. At least some of these "Erastians were themselves zealous reformers, convinced that suspension of the ungodly from the sacrament impeded the moral reformation of society," which was a similar argument that Erastus had himself used when he opposed the adoption of a presbyterian church government in Heidelberg. See Holifield, *The Covenant Sealed*, 111. Erastus and Erastianism have both been misunderstood and caricatured in historiography and polemics. See Charles Gunnoe, *Thomas Erastus and the Palatinate: A Renaissance Physician in the Second Reformation*, Brill's Series in Church History, vol. 48 (Leiden: Brill, 2011).

168 "He believed, rather, that 'speedy reformation' of the Church and society would never result from that 'strict discipline, which really reforms very few, or none.' In Prynne's opinion, common admission to the sacrament, in a Church carefully administered by government officials who would ensure that communicants lead lives of decency and decorum, was the only means to oversee and protect the moral welfare of England." Holifield, *The Covenant Sealed*, 111.

169 See "To the Reader" in George Gillespie, *Aarons Rod Blossoming, Or, The Divine Ordinance of Church Government Vindicated* (London, 1646), and also Samuel Rutherford, *The Divine Right of Church Government and Excommunication* (London, 1646).

170 See John Spurr, *The Post-Reformation*, 101–108 for a summary of the context and various parties involved at the Westminster Assembly.

171 These churches tended to be small, and there were not many of them. The taxonomy of these churches is complicated. Spurr summarizes: "However small and disparate these congregations were, they had a common identity as 'Independent' and 'separatist' churches in the mid-1640s, not

When the Westminster Assembly finally delivered a proposal for a national Presbyterian church in 1645, the issue of access to the Lord's Supper proved to be an obstacle. Parliament did not want to grant churches total control over access to the sacrament. The Assembly's proposal would give ecclesiastical power to the elders of the local Presbyterian churches (either locally or in wider regional assemblies) to bar people from the sacrament. But the civil authorities wanted to give people the chance to appeal their cases to a committee of laymen under the supervision of Parliament.[172] This highlights, again, the importance of the Eucharist in a country like England, where participation in the church (entered through baptism, and maintained through continued participation in communion) was a political and civic issue—not just a religious issue.

The legacy of the debate about "sequestration" and controlling access to the Lord's Table is also important because of the question of whether it was a "converting" ordinance or not. In his reply to an anonymous pamphlet attacking his position, William Prynne introduced the concept that the Lord's Supper was a "converting" (i. e., leading to conversion) ordinance. According to Prynne's contemporary, William Morice, this became the main point at issue in the debates about access to the sacrament.[173] Additionally, it influenced later discussions in England and the Americas.[174] Prynne also advocated more frequent communion. In 1656, after the Westminster Assembly had ended, he published a fiery tract, condemning the

---

least because they all had a common interest in opposing the plans of the Westminster Assembly. A comprehensive and coercive national church would have no room for gathered churches. Thus a broad 'Independent' coalition was formed which embraced many of the sects and gathered churches, the sober clerical 'Independents', much of the New Model Army, and a phalanx of Erastian and Independent MPs ..." *The Post-Reformation*, 104–105.

172 Spurr, *The Post-Reformation*, 105.

173 Morice was Charles II's secretary of state and a lay theologian. In his view, "Whether the sacrament be a converting Ordinance, is the pole where upon the sphere of this whole dispute doth hang and turn, we cannot move any way but we meet with a new meridian tending unto and centered in this pole ... and if we can therefore elevate this pole to such a degree, as to prove the sacrament to be a converting ordinance, then those which are yet unconverted may lawfully have access, thereby to attain conversion." William Morice, *Coena quasi Koine: or the Common Right to the Lords Supper Asserted, Wherein That Question is Fully Stated* (London, 1660), 310, quoted in Holifield, *The Covenant Sealed*, 113.

174 "Prynne's innovation was a stroke of genius that not only altered the contours of the admission controversy but also informed English and American sacramental discussion for well over a century." Holifield, *The Covenant Sealed*, 113. Additionally, "Rather than describe the Lord's Supper merely as an allurement to piety [as Erastus had done], Prynne called it a 'converting ordinance,' thus coining an effective slogan to demolish the bar to the sacrament." Holifield, *The Covenant Sealed*, 114.

factionalism and division of the English churches.[175] One of his chief concerns was to argue for the frequency of communion.

Moving to the other issue now, the Assembly had left the matter of communion frequency somewhat vague. Here, as in many points, the Westminster Directory's origins as a compromise document are evident. The Directory does not specify an exact understanding of frequency, but simply recommends communion to be held "frequently." The question of "how often" is left to the ministers and rulers of each local congregation to decide.[176] However, it clarifies that the "[t]he Ignorant and the Scandalous are not fit to receive this Sacrament of the Lords Supper," clearly taking a stand in the issue of "sequestration" and exclusion from communion, and upholding the position of Rutherford and Gillespie, who had opposed Prynne on the issue of access to communion.[177] The example provided for the pastoral "exhortation" that should be given before the Supper balances the dual priorities of warning people about the dangers of approaching in an unworthy manner, while also encouraging those weak in faith to come without fear.[178]

Regarding preparation for the Supper, the Directory specifies that if it cannot be "frequently administered," then there should be an announcement on the Sunday before the next observance of communion, so that people will have time for "due preparation." Furthermore, that time, or some other time before the Supper, should be set aside for teaching the people about the process of preparation, participation, and how to use "all means sanctified by God" so that they can "come better prepared" to the "heavenly Feast."[179]

To summarize, the Westminster divines seem to state their preference for "frequent" communion in terms that sound close to a weekly rhythm. However, if that is not feasible, then they stress the importance of proper preparation and participation. One wonders what mechanism for proper instruction and preparation they

---

175 Prynne, *A Seasonable Vindication of the frequent Administration of the Holy Communion, to all Visible Church-members, Regenerate or Unregenerate* (London, 1656).

176 "The Communion, or Supper of the Lord is frequently to be celebrated: but how often, may be considered and determined by the Ministers and other Church-Governours of each Congregation, as they shall find most convenient for the comfort and edification of the people committed to their charge." *A Directory for the publique worship of God*, 48, http://name.umdl.umich.edu/A36061. 0001.001.

177 Holifield, *The Covenant Sealed*, 114–116.

178 *A Directory*, 50.

179 "Where this Sacrament cannot with conveniency be frequently administered, it is requisite that public warning be given the Sabbath day before the administration thereof: and that either then, or on some day of that week, something concerning that Ordinance, and the due preparation thereunto, and participation thereof be taught, that by the diligent use of all means sanctified of God to that end, both in public and private, all may come better prepared to that heavenly Feast." *A Directory*, 48–49.

envisaged if it were feasible to have communion "frequently"? Perhaps the answer is to again situate the Directory within its historical context, where different parties represented at the Assembly were already practicing different rhythms of communion frequency.[180] It is probable that this section on the Lord's Supper summarizes the concerns of all represented, leaving room for interpretation and adaptation.[181]

When the communion frequency debates erupted in Scotland and the Americas in the 1700s and 1800s, the Westminster Directory is not referred to often, either in support of more frequent communion, or to argue for what became the status quo of infrequent celebration in Scotland. Others have pointed out how the Westminster Directory was received with some reserve in Scotland, and that the General Assembly did not intend for it to replace Scottish liturgical customs.[182] The English Puritans influenced the Scottish Reformed church, as much as the Scots influenced the English.[183] Although communion frequency was not the most important issue for the divines gathered at Westminster, they perpetuated the Genevan and Puritan pattern of stressing the importance of preparation and purity in receiving the Lord's Supper, and left the matter of frequency vague and under the final determination of local churches.

---

180 "Independents had a weekly celebration of the Lord's Supper, but the interval between one Communion and the next was never longer than one month. It was, however, the general practice of the Presbyterians to have only four Communions during the year. The Parliamentary Directory laid down no definite rule as to the frequency of celebration, but in the debate it was proposed to require at least a quarterly Communion ... The infrequency of Communion amongst the English Presbyterians was probably due to the examples of their Scottish brethren ... Communion in Scotland was often more infrequent than this, for there was a popular feeling that the Lord's Supper, like the Passover, ought to be celebrated once yearly." Davies, *The Worship of the English Puritans*, 213–14.

181 See Old, *Holy Communion in the Piety of the Reformed Church*, 358, for another, complimentary, interpretation: "The dilemma was simply that if the Puritans insisted on a frequent celebration, the celebrations would become more routine. If they wanted a more intense celebration they would have to be less frequent. This would allow for preparatory services with special preaching to help communicants prepare for the sacrament as well as allow the elders to exercise true sacramental discipline." This dynamic did characterize later debates within the Scottish church and the Americas, although Old does not offer any evidence for his assertions here about the Puritans.

182 Donaldson, "Covenant to Revolution," in Forrester and Murray, eds., *Studies in the History of Worship in Scotland*, 52–64.

183 George W. Sprott, *The Worship of the Church of Scotland, During the Covenanting Period 1638–1661* (William Blackwood and Sons: Edinburgh and London, 1893; reprint, Lexington: Forgotten Books, 2012), 19–31.

4.4.5 Thomas Doolittle (1630?–1707)

Thomas Doolittle attended grammar school in Kidderminster and heard Richard Baxter (1615–1691) preach in his youth. Baxter's preaching was instrumental in his conversion. Doolittle called Baxter his "father in Christ."[184] Although ordained as a Presbyterian, Doolittle served in a Church of England parish in St. Alphege, London Wall. In 1662, he was ejected from his pastorate because of Nonconformity. This began an itinerant life of starting Nonconformist academies and preaching wherever he could, often in defiance of the law and sometimes risking arrest. Despite these challenges, Doolittle had great influence on many students in the various schools that he started. Some of the most notable were Matthew Henry, John Kerr, and Edmund Calamy, who all became influential nonconformist leaders, writers, and pastors. Doolittle's death marked the end of an era, since he was the last to die of the London ministers who were ejected because of their nonconformity.

Of his multiple publications, his *A Treatise Concerning the Lord's Supper* (1665) was extremely popular.[185] In particular, in the New England colonies, "Many Hundreds" of his manual were sold there.[186] Doolittle wrote to urge his readers to take seriously their obligation to participate in communion. He provides a particularly clear example of the twin Puritan priorities of both frequent participation and thorough preparation. His passionate appeals to his readers to both come more frequently to the Supper, and to prepare themselves through extensive meditation, prayer, and self-examination, reveal a paradox at the heart of Puritan sacramental and pastoral theology. How is it possible to come more frequently, given the amount of time recommended to spend preparing for the Lord's Supper?

The question of "assurance" provides the overarching theme for Doolittle's treatise, which was a common Puritan theme and chief concern of the movement.[187] The Word of God provides assurance, but so does the Lord's Supper. When people

---

184 Beeke and Pederson, *Meet the Puritans*, 180. The rest of this biography is indebted to Beeke and Pederson.

185 "It was so popular that it went through at least twenty-eight English editions, twenty-two Scottish editions, and twenty-six New England editions, as well as translations into German and Welsh." Beeke and Pederson, *Meet the Puritans*, 183.

186 Holifield, *The Covenant Sealed*, 198, quoting Increase and Cotton Mather, "A Defence of the Evangelical Churches," in John Quick, *The Young Mans claim unto the Sacrament of the Lords Supper* (Boston, 1700), 62.

187 "To get assurance of the love of God and eternal life, should be thy great work and business in this world, else how canst thou die with comfort." Thomas Doolittle, *A Treatise Concerning the Lord's Supper; with Three Dialogues For the More Full Information of the Weak in the Nature and Use of This Sacrament*, (no place of publication: Ravenbrook Publishers, 2016; reprint, Aberdeen: George and Robert King, 1844; originally published 1665), 4.

do not come to the Supper, they are neglecting a means of gaining assurance.[188] Doolittle's goal is to "prevent" the "two great evils" of not coming often enough to, and not preparing enough for, communion.[189]

The main text is 1 Cor. 11:23-25 and communion frequency is mentioned several times.[190] However, the themes of preparation and the dangers of coming unworthily dominate the treatise.[191] It is a Christian's duty to come to communion, and it is our duty to come "often."[192] Those who "neglect" the Supper are neglecting a source of spiritual strength:

> Do you know what it is that you have lost by neglecting it? And might it not have been much better with you in your spiritual condition, if you had frequently attended upon God therein? ... Oh! you cannot tell what you have lost by omitting it, what grace you have lost, what comforts and joys you have lost, that others have found in the frequent and conscientious use of this ever to be praised ordinance.[193]

"Doubts" and hesitations about being worthy to receive are a constant theme in personal narratives about receiving communion in this period. Thus, writers like Doolittle and others had to deal with these questions. In part, it was a product of the Puritan's emphasis on the necessity of a true conversion. So, the "doubts of weak" Christians who are hesitant to come to the Supper had to be assuaged. Here, Doolittle sounds two notes at the same time. On the one hand, he is pastorally sensitive and reassures his readers that the simple desire to be "willing" is proof that one

---

188 "And, indeed, the long absence of some believers from, and the careless hasting of all ungodly to, the Supper of the Lord, is much to be lamented." Doolittle, *A Treatise Concerning the Lord's Supper*, 4.

189 Doolittle, *A Treatise Concerning the Lord's Supper*, 5.

190 Frequency is also treated in the imaginary dialogues at the end of Doolittle's treatise. Dialogue I ("A short Dialogue, between a Minister and a private Christian that desires to partake of the Lord's supper") mentions communion frequency, using language similar to Chapter 6. The "Minister" asks, "Is it the duty of believers often to partake of the Lord's supper?" and the "Christian" replies, "1. Christ's command; 1 Cor. xi.26. 2. The apostle's practice; Acts ii.42; xx.7. 3. Their own necessity, being often dull; John xx. 9, and often doubting; Matt. Xxvii. 17, (....)." Doolittle, *A Treatise Concerning the Lord's Supper*, 165.

191 Doolittle, *A Treatise Concerning the Lord's Supper*, 13.

192 Doolittle, *A Treatise Concerning the Lord's Supper*, 15.

193 Doolittle, *A Treatise Concerning the Lord's Supper*, 34.

has actually "received" Christ.[194] On the other hand, Doolittle is uncompromising about the necessity of deep soul-searching before receiving the Lord's Supper.

Regarding the issue of frequency, Doolittle believes that 1 Cor. 11 teaches receiving communion "often," although no exact rhythm of frequency can be deduced from the text: "Baptism is but once to be administered, but the Lord's Supper is often to be received, the frequency is not determined, often it must be, how often is not expressed. If you had opportunity every Lord's day, and you redeemed and improved it, your soul may thrive and grow the more in grace and holiness: meals that are for nourishment must be often."[195] Our spiritual needs are similar to our physical needs. We do not need to be told how often to eat natural food and drink, yet we have innate needs that we sense deeply because they keep us alive. In the same way, we need to sharpen our spiritual senses, increasing our spiritual hunger, which should drive us to more frequent communion.[196] Our sense of spiritual weakness and our failings should drive us to come to the sacrament.[197]

But, frequency by itself is not sufficient. It must be preceded by serious preparation.

In his words, we must "be painful and serious in making preparation for it."[198] Since the people of Israel had to prepare before participating in the Passover, how much more should Christians prepare before the Supper?[199] How much time should be spent? Doolittle envisions "days" of preparation beforehand.[200] We must only come to the Supper "after painful and serious preparation: no preparation, no

---

194 Doolittle, *A Treatise Concerning the Lord's Supper*, 37. See also, 40: "Are you therefore willing to forsake every known sin? willing to perform every known duty? willing to bear every burden he shall lay upon you? willing to be what he would have you to be? Then you are one of his people, and you may be sure he died for you in particular."

195 Doolittle, *A Treatise Concerning the Lord's Supper*, 42.

196 "You often eat, and you often drink for the nourishment of nature, and yet it is not told you how often you must eat, how often you must drink, but the sense and feeling of the want of your food, will direct you unto this: so if you have but a sense and feeling of the want of this ordinance, and the things that are there to be conferred upon believers, that would guide you to a frequent iteration of this ordinance." Doolittle, *A Treatise Concerning the Lord's Supper*, 42.

197 "Thus if you seriously consider your own frequent wants, and often reflect upon your often need of this ordinance, you will see sufficient reason for your often participation of so frequently needful an ordinance." Doolittle, *A Treatise Concerning the Lord's Supper*, 46.

198 Doolittle, *A Treatise Concerning the Lord's Supper*, 47.

199 Doolittle, *A Treatise Concerning the Lord's Supper*, 47–51.

200 "It is not sufficient to spend an hour of the night before, or in the morning you are to approach unto it; but *some days before* to have it in your thoughts, that you may consider the greatness of the work you are to go about." Doolittle, *A Treatise Concerning the Lord's Supper*, 52, italics added.

participation."[201] Preparation is so important, because the sacrament is so special.[202] To be sure, our preparation does not merit God's blessings; rather, God works through the entire process, which includes our preparation.[203] Proper preparation is important because it leads to great blessings. If we sow abundantly, we shall reap an abundant spiritual harvest.[204] Although Doolittle stridently warns his readers to prepare thoughtfully and thoroughly, this is grounded in the larger context of God's desire to bless His people through this sacrament.[205]

Doolittle's treatise is a classic example of Puritan eucharistic piety, and his popular work influenced many. It combines both the urgency to participate more frequently in communion, as well as an intense call to prepare extensively, participate thoroughly, and to live in such a way that one is always ready to come to the Lord's Supper. Although he believes that Scripture teaches the necessity, and the spiritual value of, frequent communion, this emphasis is almost drowned out by his resounding call for preparation, soul-searching, and self-examination before each communion. This level of spiritual maturity, and effort, was challenging. Of course, Doolittle believed he was simply proclaiming the clear teachings of Scripture. Later generations would find these demands unrealistic, which would contribute to the decline of the Puritan's spiritual vision. Before that happened, however, Doolittle would influence many readers, especially in the American colonies.

4.4.6 Matthew Henry (1662–1714)

Matthew Henry serves as a convenient link between this chapter and the next.[206] Although Henry was an English preacher, pastor, and writer, his *The Communicant's Companion; or Instructions and Helps for the right receiving of the Lord's Supper*

---

201 Doolittle, *A Treatise Concerning the Lord's Supper*, 52.

202 He writes, "the more excellent and noble any thing is, the more heinous is the abuse thereof." Doolittle, *A Treatise Concerning the Lord's Supper*, 54.

203 As he states, "(...) for though God doth not bestow the great things in the sacrament for our preparation, yet he will not give them without our preparation." Doolittle, *A Treatise Concerning the Lord's Supper*, 56.

204 Doolittle, *A Treatise Concerning the Lord's Supper*, 59–60.

205 "God makes great preparation for us in this ordinance: therefore we should make great preparations when we come to partake of it." Doolittle, *A Treatise Concerning the Lord's Supper*, 61.

206 On Henry, see Allan Harman, *Matthew Henry: His Life and Influence* (Fearn, UK: Christian Focus Publications, 2012) and Hughes Oliphant Old, "Henry, Matthew," *Dictionary of Major Biblical Interpreters*, ed. Donald McKim (Downers Grove, IL and Nottingham, UK: InterVarsity Press, 2007), 520–524. More recent scholarship includes Jong Hun Joo, *Matthew Henry: Pastoral Liturgy in Challenging Times* (Eugene, OR: Pickwick/ Wipf and Stock Publishers, 2014), and Joo, "Communion with God as Word-Centered Piety: Exploring the Pastoral Concern and Thought of Matthew Henry (1662–1714)," *TTJ* 16.1 (2013): 73–85.

was popular in New England. Originally published in 1704, it was reprinted in New England in 1716 and 1723, by Fleet and Crump.[207] In England, the *Communicant's Companion* "underwent a respectable eight printings within its first twenty years."[208] Other sources give us additional information about Henry's actual communion practice. In his biography of his father Philip, Matthew Henry states that his father observed monthly communion in his church.[209] A biographer of Matthew Henry notes that he followed his father Philip's practice.[210] Henry provides yet another example of combining a deep eucharistic piety with a strong emphasis on proper preparation and self-examination, alongside of exhortations to frequent communion.

The issue of communion frequency surfaces several times in the *Communicant's Companion*. In a clever maneuver, excuses for not participating in communion are turned around and used to show how they are actually a reason why one should come to communion: "Instead of making your unreadiness an argument against coming to this ordinance, make the necessity of your coming to this ordinance an argument against your unreadiness."[211] For Henry, communion is a means of grace that God has appointed for the good of his people. If we neglect it, we are starving our souls and damaging ourselves spiritually.[212] To those who fear they are "unworthy" and that they might "eat and drink judgment on themselves," Henry responds, "[w]hat is said for the conviction and terror of hypocrites and presumptuous sinners, notwithstanding our care to distinguish the precious and the vile, they misapply to themselves: and so the heart of the righteous is made sad, which should not be made sad."[213] Those that most fear the judgment of God are in the least amount of danger of falling under that judgment.[214] To stay away from

---

207 Holifield, *The Covenant Sealed*, 198.

208 Holifield, *The Covenant Sealed*, 127.

209 "Usually once a month he administered the ordinance of the Lord's Supper." Matthew Henry, *An Account of the Life and Death of Mr. Philip Henry, Minister of the Gospel, Near Whitchurch in Shropshire,* (1712; repr., Edinburgh: Banner of Truth Trust, 1974), 134.

210 According to John Bickerton Williams, Matthew Henry "attended to the ordinance of the Lord's Supper with the members of the church on the first Sabbath in every month." *Memoirs of the Life, Character, and Writings of the Rev. Matthew Henry,* 3rd edition (London: Joseph Ogle Robinson, 1829), 169.

211 Matthew Henry, *The Communicant's Companion. By the Rev. Matthew Henry. With An Introductory Essay; By the Rev. John Brown,* Edinburgh (Boston: Crocker and Brewster, 1828).

212 He writes, "(…) though we are tied to ordinances, God is not; but if you have opportunities for it, and yet neglect it, and when it is to be administered, turn your back upon it, you serve your souls as you would not serve your bodies; for you deny them their necessary food, and the soul that is starved is as certainly murdered as the body that is stabbed, and his blood shall be required at thy hands." Henry, *The Communicant's Companion,* 72.

213 Henry, *The Communicant's Companion,* 73.

214 Henry, *The Communicant's Companion,* 76.

communion because our faith is weak is the same as staying away from the doctor because we are sick, or not eating because we are hungry.[215]

We are to be "frequent and constant" in our participation in the ordinance of the Lord's Table. According to the words of Jesus' institution of the Supper "the solemnity is oft to be repeated." Although baptism is administered only once, the Lord's Supper is "the table in Christ's family, at which we are to eat bread continually."[216] Because it is a family meal, all members of God's family should be present at the family meal.[217] Henry makes a creative comparison, and contrast, with the Passover. In the Old Testament, the Passover was mandated as an annual observance, but it had much harsher penalties for those who did not participate. In the New Covenant, although we have more liberty to determine the frequency of the Lord's Supper, its superiority over the Passover points to the propriety of much greater frequency.[218] In his only suggestion about the specific frequency of communion, Henry obliquely refers to the desirability of monthly communion.[219]

In a trope that Doolittle also employed, Henry contrasts how often we sin with how often we should desire to come to communion.[220] Because we often fall short of God's expectations and often break his law, we should come often to the sacrament.[221] In a refreshing departure from the characteristic Puritan emphasis on extensive preparation before communion, Henry encourages his readers to come to

---

215 "This ordinance was appointed chiefly for the relief of such as you are; for the strengthening of faith, the inflaming of holy love, and the confirming of good resolutions; in God's name therefore use it for those purposes; pine not away in thy weakness while God has ordained thee strength; perish not for hunger, while there is bread enough in thy father's house, and to spare; die not for thirst, while there is a well of water by thee." Henry, *The Communicant's Companion*, 76–77.

216 Henry, *The Communicant's Companion*, 77.

217 "Where there is the truth of grace, this ordinance ought to be improved, which, by virtue of divine appointment, has a moral influence upon our growth in grace. The great Master of the family would have none of his family missing at meal-time." Henry, *The Communicant's Companion*, 77–78.

218 "If a deliverance out of Egypt merited an annual commemoration, surely our redemption by Christ merits a more frequent one, especially since we need not go up to Jerusalem to do it." Henry, *The Communicant's Companion*, 77.

219 "If this tree of life, which bears more than twelve manner of fruits, yieldeth her fruit to us every month, I know not why we should neglect it any month." Henry, *The Communicant's Companion*, 77.

220 He writes, "While we are often sinning, we have need to be often receiving the seal of our pardon," and, "While we are often in temptation, we have need to be often renewing our covenants with God, and fetching strength from heaven for our spiritual conflicts. Frequent fresh recruits and fresh supplies, are necessary for those that are so closely besieged, and are so vigorously attacked by a potent adversary." Henry, *The Communicant's Companion*, 78. Compare Doolittle's use of a similar rhetorical question in *A Treatise Concerning the Lord's Supper*, 42, 43, 45.

221 "Much of our communion with God is kept up by the renewing of our covenant with him, and the frequent interchanging of solemn assurances"; and furthermore, "[i]t is a token of Christ's favour to us, and must not be slighted, that he not only admits, but invites us oft to repeat this solemnity, and

the Lord's Supper, even if they have not had sufficient time to prepare thoroughly.[222] He focuses more on God's willingness to receive us and on our opportunity to receive God's grace in communion, regardless of our level of preparation.[223] The prospect of communion should motivate people to repent of their sins, so they can participate in the Supper.[224]

Henry exhorts his readers to come to the Lord's Supper as often as they can, whenever it is observed.[225] Although he believes in frequent—at least monthly—communion, he also reminds his readers that God is not "bound" by his own ordinances and can bless his people even if they are not able to come to the sacrament.[226] These words are especially meaningful when read in the context of Matthew Henry's life and ministry. His father Philip was ejected from the ministry in 1662.[227] Both father and son were part of the non-conformist Puritan movement and Matthew Henry had to preach in private houses. For the non-conformists, with their strict beliefs about the nature of the church, qualifications for ministers and laity, and participation in the Lord's Table, it was not always possible to come to communion as often as they might desire. Meetings were watched, broken up by the officers of the government, and ministers often had to flee or risk arrest.[228] In this context, Henry displays pastoral acumen in assuring his readers that God is still sovereign and can bless his people, even if they are prevented from gathering and worshiping him as they believed they should.

The sections of *The Constant Communicant* on the topic of self-examination before the Lord's Supper situate Henry firmly within the Puritan tradition. While he stresses the importance of coming to the Supper frequently, he also emphasizes the importance of preparation and self-examination. Henry is a bit more pastoral

---

is ready again to seal to us, if we be but ready to seal to him." Henry, *The Communicant's Companion*, 78–79.

222 "If indeed thou canst not allow so much time for solemn secret worship in preparation for this ordinance, and reflection upon it, as others do, and as thou thyself sometime hast done, and wouldst do, yet let not that keep thee from the ordinance; thy heart may be in heaven, when they hands are about the world; and a serious Christian may, through God's assistance, do a great deal of work in a little time." Henry, *The Communicant's Companion*, 79–80.

223 "The less time we have for preparation, the more close and intent we should be in the ordinance itself, and so make up the loss. A welcome guest never comes unseasonably to one that always keeps a good house." Henry, *The Communicant's Companion*, 80.

224 Henry, *The Communicant's Companion*, 81–82.

225 "Those that, by the grace of God, do still keep up a love for this ordinance, should contrive their affairs so, as if possible, not to mis any of their stated opportunities for it." Henry, *The Communicant's Companion*, 82.

226 Henry, *The Communicant's Companion*, 82.

227 Beeke and Pederson, eds., *Meet the Puritans*, 323.

228 Bremer, *Congregational Communion*, 227–230.

than the other authors surveyed here, in that he emphasizes the fact that believers are inherently qualified to come to communion. Unlike Doolittle, he does not stress "painful" preparation, or at least not to the same extent. As a popular commentator on the Bible, and as a popular author, Henry's perspective formed the eucharistic opinions and practices of many others. The themes of frequency, and the demands of preparation and purity, would be carried into the New World and would play a prominent role in the later communion frequency debates of the 1700s and early 1800s Scotland, and in the Americas.

4.4.7 Conclusion

What emerges from this survey is the fact that there was a pattern of unity-in-diversity among the Puritans: some emphasized the need for preparation over frequency (e. g. Bayly, Hildersham & Bradshaw), others balanced the two (Doolittle, Westminster Assembly) whereas still others highlighted the need for frequent communion more than urging long and intense preparation (Charnock, Henry, and Prynne). As with the sixteenth-century Reformers, the Puritans were not a homogenous body. Additionally, there were many areas of overlap and convergence between Puritans/Dissenters and those who remained within the Church of England. It is anachronistic to characterize the Puritans as simply focused on the preaching of the Word, when the Lord's Supper was central to their theology, and to their spiritual experiences. They stressed the importance of proper preparation precisely because they believed communion was a way that God blessed his people, and that people could experience levels of intimacy in it rarely found elsewhere. However, because of this emphasis on preparation and self-examination, communion frequency fell most naturally into a monthly rhythm. Although some Puritan congregations did practice weekly communion, it is doubtful that such an intense regimen could have been sustained over a long period of time. Indeed, we will see that later generations of Puritans drifted into patterns of infrequent communion.

4.5   Scottish Reformed Communion Frequency

While the English Puritans agitated for the further reformation of the English church, the Scottish Protestant church navigated its own variegated history. The liturgical practices that emerged within the Scottish Reformed churches set the stage for later debates. But it is not enough to simply examine the liturgical and theological understanding of the Scottish Reformed church. Practical and basic economic factors also played a role in affecting communion frequency. The overall picture is nuanced and complicated. The inter-related web of concerns, traditions, and beliefs all contributed to the intensity of the communion frequency debates that erupted later. When the various factors are categorized, two main sets emerge. First, there are theological and liturgical factors (see 4.5.1): an emphasis on hearing the Word preached before communicating, practices of penance, catechesis, and ideals for the pastoral care of churches. Next, there are cultural, economic, political and practical factors (see 4.5.2): the pre-Reformation tradition of infrequent communion, poverty (the cost of wine and bread, cost of the large community dinner at the pastor's house on the Monday following a communion Sunday), political disruption, lack of clergy, ministerial neglect, and the logistical challenges of large communions.

Obviously, these categories blend into each other in many ways. However, for the purposes of overview and analysis, it is helpful to focus on distinguishing the sets of beliefs, practices, and practical realities that helped make infrequent communion the norm in early modern Scotland. The rest of this section will outline some of the practical, cultural, and economic factors that helped to institutionalize infrequent communion (4.5.2), but first we will turn to theological concerns and liturgical practices (4.5.1). This survey will incorporate evidence from the post-Reformation era to the 1700s, which became the context for the frequency debates that continued into the 1800s and beyond.

4.5.1 Infrequent Communion: Theological and Liturgical Factors

Previous sections (see 3.3) detailed the importance of preaching, catechesis, and the processes of examination and penance. All those emphases continued in the 1700s. Some unique features developed in the context of the Scottish Reformed celebration of communion. An important part of communion observance was the "Preparation" sermon, given on the Saturday before a communion. Though it may have had Catholic roots, this "Preparation" sermon slowly grew in popularity, and Burnet claims it was "almost universal in the seventeenth and eighteenth" centuries.[229] Additionally, the "distribution of tokens as a rule after this service was a strong inducement to attend."[230] Practically, this became a time of heightened spiritual fervor which would be difficult to sustain more regularly.

Another distinctive feature of Reformed worship in Scotland was gathering the congregation around a long table for communion, or around a group of tables in the church. Of course, this was motivated by a desire to reproduce, as closely

---

229 Burnet, *The Holy Communion*, 51. Burnet sees a parallel in the short communion guide that was published under Archbishop John Hamilton in 1559, entitled "Ane Godlie Exhortation." It included an example of an exhortation that Catholic clergy were to deliver to their people before they received communion. Burnet, *The Holy Communion*, 50.

230 Burnet, *The Holy Communion*, 51.

as possible, the New Testament Lord's Supper.[231] But this liturgical practice had obvious practical ramifications as well. This practice made it inevitable that communion would be infrequent, simply because of the time needed to move congregants through successive turns at the table, to hear the "table addresses" for each group, and the other liturgical practices that developed around this tradition. On the other hand, while communion may have been infrequent, the Scots Reformed developed liturgical practices that made it intensely meaningful and sitting around a table was a powerful statement of the unity of the church—a visual symbol of the unity enacted by the Lord's Table. The intensity of eucharistic celebration multiplied exponentially with the advent of the communion season, a Scots Reformed sacramental expression that forms an essential part of the context for the frequency debates of the 1700s and beyond (4.5.3).

4.5.2 Political, Economic, and Practical Factors

Political disturbances also affected communion frequency. In the 1600s, two parties warred over questions of loyalty to the English King Charles II. This first major schism in the Scottish Protestant church profoundly disrupted communion frequency. The "Resolutioners" were broadly royalists, while the "Remonstrants," or "Protesters" viewed the Scottish Kirk as corrupt because of compromises made to the King and so began holding their own church meetings and their own General Assembly. They viewed themselves as the true guardians of the Reformation legacy. This political disunity manifested itself in infrequent communion, because warring parties would not sit down at the same table in their local churches, and held communions within their own factions: "But the breach meant something more damaging still—the discontinuing of the Holy Communion in many towns and rural parishes for years on end."[232] The Scottish church was regularly disrupted by political upheavals, and in these situations, partaking of the sacrament was a political act, not just an ecclesiastical ceremony. When the Kirk was divided against itself, infrequent communion was one result.

Economic factors also played a role in making frequent communion simply too expensive. For much of its history, Scotland was an extremely poor nation, and so many parishes could not afford the bread, wine, or serving utensils for the Lord's Table.[233] According to Burnet "[i]n the early seventeenth century many ministers

---

231 Burnet, *The Holy Communion*, 23. See also Maxwell, *A History of Worship in the Church of Scotland*, 65–66.
232 Burnet, *The Holy Communion*, 119–120.
233 Burnet, *The Holy Communion*, 212.

had still to provide the elements at their own expense, which was a direct temptation to infrequent celebration."[234]

Another practical factor was a lack of clergy in early modern Scotland: "In 1643 the six Sessions of Edinburgh, considering that the neglect of the Lord's Supper was still due to the inadequate supply of ministers and catechists as in the Reformation era, petitioned the Burgh Council for increased financial assistance."[235] However, James Kirk has challenged the received notion that early Reformed Scotland suffered from a lack of qualified ministers.[236] It is beyond the scope of this project to evaluate his research, but at the least, it indicates that there were other causes for the standardization of infrequent communion besides a lack of ministers.

Sometimes, ministers simply neglected the sacrament. The frequency of communion could be quite subjective. The Scottish Presbyterian system had given the responsibility of scheduling communion to the minister and the church session, with "the proposal usually emanating from the "thoughts" of the minister that another celebration was timely, which were passed on to his session. As a rule the session readily concurred."[237] With not much else to determine communion frequency besides the "thoughts" of the minister, it is not surprising that some parishes fell into a pattern of infrequency. But this responsibility was repeatedly abused, as highlighted by many instances where parishes would go for years without any communion.[238] This provoked an understandable reaction, and no doubt fueled some of the desire for more frequent communion.

Additionally, although theological convictions certainly played a role in establishing infrequent communion, sometimes it was just the weather or the fickle attendance of the local nobility: "Even after the date of a Communion had been announced it was sometimes changed. The parish of Anwoth in Rutherford's ministry provides two quite common excuses—inclemency of weather, and deference to 'the gentry.'"[239] A Kirk register from 1689 relates that communion was delayed because the local "laird" was sick and could not attend.[240]

The logistical challenges of large communions also affected frequency patterns. In the 1700s, the custom of large, annual communion celebrations became entrenched,

---

234 Burnet, *The Holy Communion*, 195.

235 Burnet, *The Holy Communion*, 184, 194. See also Maxwell, *The Liturgical Portions of the Genevan Service Book*, 204 and Donaldson, "Reformation to Covenant," in Forrester and Murray, eds., *Studies in the History of Worship in Scotland*, 37.

236 James Kirk, *Patterns of Reform: Continuity and Change in the Reformation Kirk* (Edinburgh: T&T Clark, 1989), 134–135.

237 Burnet, *The Holy Communion*, 165.

238 See Nigel Yates, *Preaching, Word and Sacrament: Scottish Church Interiors 1560–1860* (London and New York: T&T Clark, 2009), 21, for examples of dramatically infrequent communion.

239 Burnet, *The Holy Communion*, 165.

240 Burnet, *The Holy Communion*, 165–66.

where many parishes would gather to celebrate over a period of days. Such a gathering took time and impacted the communities economically and logistically. The communions lasted about two weeks, and so this could simply not be repeated more frequently.[241] As Schmidt remarks, the focus on "festivity" mitigated against "frequency."[242] Because these large gatherings and their influence on communion frequency became a flashpoint in the trans-Atlantic communion frequency debates, it is necessary to explore them further.

4.5.3 Scottish Communion Seasons and Sacramental Festivity

The origins and history of the Scottish communion seasons are important because they were one of the contested practices in the frequency debates. In a study of the eucharistic spirituality which characterized the communion seasons in both Scotland and colonial America, Bracken Long aptly summarizes some features of the emerging communion seasons:

> Ironically the steadily declining lack of Communion observances in Scotland contributed to the rise of the sacramental occasions … From May to October, worshipers and revelers from around the Scottish countryside would make their way from kirk to kirk, celebrating the harvest and renewing ties with family and friends. Some would regard this as their annual time of spiritual renewal; others would attend as many holy fairs as they could, seeking social delights more than spiritual ones.[243]

The communion season was not just a single communion service. Rather, it was a five-day process of preparation, examination, preaching, the communion services, and then a day of thanksgiving on the Monday immediately after the Sunday communion.[244] These communion seasons were necessarily infrequent, because of the time involved and the monetary expense required for these large, spiritually demanding gatherings.

---

241 Todd, *The Culture of Protestantism in Early Modern Scotland*, 85.

242 Leigh Eric Schmidt, *Holy Fairs: Scotland and the Making of American Revivalism* (Grand Rapids: Wm. B. Eerdmans Publishing Co., 1989; 2nd ed. 2001), 183–192.

243 Kimberly Bracken Long, *The Eucharistic Theology of the American Holy Fairs* (Louisville: Westminster John Knox Press, 2011), 139. The communion seasons originally grew of the context of Scottish settlers in the Ulster region of Ireland—what became known as the "Scots-Irish." See Marilyn J. Westerkamp, *Triumph of the Laity: Scots-Irish Piety and the Great Awakening, 1625–1760* (New York: Oxford University Press, 1988), 15–42.

244 Yates, *Preaching, Word and Sacrament*, 46, citing Douglas Ansdell, *People of the Great Faith: The Highland Church 1690–1900* (Stornoway, 1998), 114–15.

The communion seasons directly impacted communion frequency, especially as the Scots began to migrate to the Americas, taking their sacramental traditions with them. Schmidt outlines the main features of the communion seasons, which flourished in the late 1600s and early 1700s:

> What separated the festal communions from earlier sacraments were such characteristics as outdoor preaching, great concourses of people from an extensive region, long vigils of prayer, powerful experiences of conversion and confirmation, a number of popular ministers cooperating for extended services over three days or more, a seasonal focus on summer, and unusually large numbers of communicants at successive tables.[245]

There was popular support for mass communions throughout Scotland, despite official attempts to do away with them.[246] Burnet attempts to explain their popularity: "First and perhaps foremost, they provided for so many not only high occasions in their religion, but high occasions in their ordinary lives which had so little variety or diversion. The longer the intervals between these irregular 'works,' the more keenly the people looked forward to them."[247] The communion seasons institutionalized a rhythm of infrequent communion that culminated in intense experiences shared by large numbers of people.

This "grass-roots" sacramental movement forms the background and context of the "frequency debates" of the late 1700s and early 1800s. The traditions surrounding communion seasons were also transplanted to the Americas, as Schmidt has shown, and formed the context for the birth of American "revivalism." It is vital to understand the contours of the Scottish communion seasons, and their importance in the communion frequency debates that ensued later. In Scotland, the issue of frequency was inextricably connected to the entire cultural rhythm of the "sacramental seasons." Biblical exegesis was not enough—at issue was a Presbyterian tradition, combined with popular experiences and expectations of what "communion" should look, sound, and feel like.

---

245 Schmidt, *Holy Fairs*, 24. Yates comments: "It is, however, a myth that communion was celebrated in the churchyards because of lack of space in the churches. Communicants, did however, wait in the churchyard for their turn to receive communion and tents were frequently erected to shelter the ministers who preached to them. At some services there might be as many as 30 sittings for communion and the service could take all Sunday. Communion services normally lasted at least an hour, sometimes two, and occasionally even four." He clarifies that groups who seceded from the Church of Scotland did hold open-air communions, and that there are a few examples from the Covenanter period of open-air communion, though these examples have been "highly mythologized." *Preaching, Word and Sacrament*, 45–46.

246 Burnet, *The Holy Communion*, 224.

247 Burnet, *The Holy Communion*, 224, 127.

The 1700s marked a turning point in the movement for more frequent communion in Scotland. Local synods recommended more frequent communion, primarily to discourage people gathering for the extended, and sometimes chaotic, mass-communions or "communion fairs." They also encouraged "Winter Communions," since the colder weather would put a damper on "sacramental fairs." However, these efforts and recommendations were largely ignored.[248] The General Assembly was no more successful than these local synods:

> The highest governing body of the church regularly issued acts urging more frequent communion in hopes of promoting "the glory of God, and edification of souls" as well as in hopes of taming the "disorders" of the summer and early fall communions. In 1701, 1711, 1712, and 1724 the General Assembly encouraged more frequent communions and particularly wanted to see the sacrament celebrated "throughout the several months of the year."[249]

Despite these official recommendations, the General Assembly and regional synods did not have any way to implement these suggestions. It will be helpful to briefly survey the acts of General Assembly that dealt with communion frequency at the national level, since these decisions are often in the background of the published sources.

The 1645 General Assembly, meeting in January in Edinburgh, was noteworthy because it received the Westminster Confession of Faith and Directory for Worship (along with certain qualifications) as the standards for doctrine and worship in Scotland. The report of a committee dealing with questions of worship addressed issues created by the celebration of multi-parish communions. It stipulates that if a minister travels to another parish to help celebrate communion there, he must make sure to provide someone to fill his post in his own parish "lest, otherwise, while he is about to minister comfort to others his own flock be left destitute of preaching." This was a standard expectation which would be violated during the height of the communion season movement, and a standard which subsequent Assemblies tried to enforce. The committee also mandated that if someone travels to another parish to receive communion, they must have a "testimonial" from their own pastor. Furthermore, pastors are not to refuse "testimonials" to those who wish to receive communion elsewhere, so long as these members are "without scandal."[250]

---

248 Schmidt, *Holy Fairs*, 185.

249 Schmidt, *Holy Fairs*, 186.

250 "Acts: 1645," in *Acts of the General Assembly of the Church of Scotland 1638–1842* (= *Acts* hereafter), ed. Church Law Society (Edinburgh: Edinburgh Printing & Publishing Co, 1843), 111–135. *British*

In 1701, the General Assembly in Edinburgh addressed the issue of communion frequency in Session 20, on March 8:

> The General Assembly recommends to Presbyteries to take care that the Sacrament of the Lord's Supper be more frequently administered within their bounds, and that the number of ministers to serve thereat be restricted, so that neighbouring churches be not thereby cast desolate on the Lord's Day.[251]

This refers to the practice of holding communion seasons in a town, during which hundreds, or perhaps thousands, of people from the surrounding towns would converge, and multiple preachers would be needed for the days-long ceremonies. Session 6 of the 1711 General Assembly in Edinburgh continued the agenda of 1701:

> The General Assembly, considering that in some places the Sacrament of the Lord's Supper is administered only in the summer season, wherethrough people are deprived of the benefit of that holy ordinance during the rest of the year; do therefore recommend to Presbyteries to do what they can to get it so ordered, that the Sacrament of the Lord's Supper may be administered in their bounds through the several months of the year.[252]

John Willison referred to this Act of Assembly as he argued for more frequent communion in his immensely popular *Sacramental Catechism* (1720). He remarks that this act was specifically aimed at the practice of some parishes which filled the summer months with communion celebrations, straining the ministers and depriving people of the opportunity to commune during the rest of the year.[253]

The General Assembly took up the issue of communion frequency again in 1712, again in Edinburgh. Session 11, on May 13, passed an "Act appointing the more frequent Celebration of the Sacrament of the Lord's Supper." It references previous acts calling for more frequent communion and challenges the regional gatherings of ministers in each presbytery to implement these acts. Furthermore, it instructs the presbyteries to inquire whether individual ministers are following the recommendations of the General Assembly. If it is discovered that any minister

---

History Online, accessed June 9, 2020, http://www.british-history.ac.uk/church-scotland-records/acts/1638-1842/pp111-135.

251 "Acts: 1701," in *Acts*, 301–311. *British History Online*, accessed June 9, 2020, http://www.british-history.ac.uk/church-scotland-records/acts/1638-1842/pp301-311.

252 "Acts: 1711," in *Acts*, 450–459. *British History Online*, accessed June 9, 2020, http://www.british-history.ac.uk/church-scotland-records/acts/1638-1842/pp450-459.

253 Willison, *A Sacramental Catechism: Or, A Familiar Instructor for Young Communicants* (Glasgow: David Niven, 1794), ix–x.

neglects to hold the sacrament for an entire year, the presbyteries are charged to hold him accountable and to record their decisions so that larger ecclesial bodies may be informed of the situation.[254]

In 1720, a committee of the Presbytery of Edinburgh "recommended that outdoor sermons should be discontinued, and that the Sacrament should be celebrated in one or more of the churches in the Presbytery each month of the year."[255] The General Assembly tried again to encourage more frequent communion in its 1724 meeting in Edinburgh. Session 6, on May 20, notes that the 1711 Act to promote more frequent communion "has not had its full effect," and so the Assembly "do hereby revive and renew the said Act; and do appoint Presbyteries to do all they can to have the Sacrament of the Lord's Supper more frequently administered in their bounds throughout the several months of the year."[256] It also encouraged local presbyteries to deal with the "disorders" that were occurring during communion celebrations and repeats the necessity to make sure all pulpits are filled, even if ministers travel to another parish to help serve communion.[257] In 1751, the General Assembly again recommended more frequent communion, but had to compromise with requiring annual communion in each parish.[258] Burnet comments: "No further

---

254 "The General Assembly, considering that the Assemblies of this National Church have, by several acts, appointed the frequent celebration of the holy Sacrament of the Lord's Supper in all the congregations of this Church; and judging that the due observation of these acts will greatly tend to the glory of God, and edification of souls; therefore, they do hereby enjoin all Presbyteries to inquire if the said acts be duly observed by all the brethren; and in case any minister shall neglect to celebrate the Sacrament of the Lord's Supper in his parish for a whole year, the Assembly appoints the Presbytery in which the said parish lies to call for an account of the reasons of his omission of that great and solemn duty and ordinance, and to approve or disapprove the same as they shall see cause, and to record their diligence in this matter." "Acts: 1712," in *Acts*, 459–478. *British History Online*, accessed June 9, 2020, http://www.british-history.ac.uk/church-scotland-records/acts/1638-1842/pp459-478.

255 Burnet, *The Holy Communion*, 215–216.

256 "Acts: 1724," in *Acts*, 566–570. *British History Online*, accessed June 9, 2020, http://www.british-history.ac.uk/church-scotland-records/acts/1638-1842/pp566-570.

257 "Acts: 1724," in *Acts*, 566–570. *British History Online*, accessed June 9, 2020, http://www.british-history.ac.uk/church-scotland-records/acts/1638-1842/pp566-570.

258 The session on May 20, 1751, was entitled, "Act anent the more frequent Celebration of the Sacrament of the Lord's Supper." It reads, in part: "The General Assembly renews the 11th Act of Assembly, 1712, appointing the more frequent celebration of our Lord's Supper; and in order to the better observance of the said Act, every Presbytery, at their privy censures, before the winter Synod, are hereby appointed to inquire at each of their brethren, whether they have administered that sacrament, once at least, the preceding year, and in case any of them have not done it, their excuses shall be marked in the minutes, and what the Presbytery has done in approbation or disapprobation thereof, and report the same in writing to the Synod." 'Acts: 1751', in *Acts*, 704–706. *British History Online*, accessed November 12, 2020, http://www.british-history.ac.uk/church-scotland-records/acts/1638-1842/pp704-706.

Acts of Assembly relating to the Communion were passed during the century after 1751, so we may assume either that the Assembly in virtual despair gave up making rules and just let things take their course; or that it tacitly resolved to be content *sine die* that a yearly Communion had become established in most parishes."[259]

Schmidt summarizes the growth of the frequency controversy and points out that, though ecclesial bodies like regional presbyteries and the national General Assembly tried to encourage more frequent communion, the real battle was fought among the ministers who published pamphlets and treatises advancing their own views on communion frequency.[260] It is these debates to which we will turn now.

4.6   Conclusion

The developments in post-Reformation England and Scotland clearly demonstrate that communion frequency was affected by a host of factors. It was never a case of simply reading the Bible, determining what it said about communion, and then putting it into practice. The religious communities and authors surveyed thus far allow us to posit some tentative answers to two of the sub-questions guiding this research (1.2). We have seen how patterns of communion frequency in both Scotland and England were shaped and impacted by historical, political, and ecclesiastical considerations. Also, it has been demonstrated that the desire for church discipline and proper participation were key concerns in both the Church of Scotland, and in Dissenting/Puritan groups in England. These priorities put the stress on mechanisms like church discipline, catechesis, and examination by elders in Scotland, and on spiritual practices such as self-examination and preparation in England. These mechanisms took a good deal of time and worked against any desires for more frequent communion. This is especially apparent in Scotland where infrequent communion became established as an important tradition, despite the repeated directives from ecclesial bodies to pursue more frequent communion in local parishes. This period also saw the emergence and development of the Scottish communion season, which would play an important role in the later communion frequency debates of the 1700s-1800s, and in the early American revivals.

---

259 Burnet, *The Holy Communion*, 215. Schmidt comments: "Even as late as 1795, an advocate of frequency said he knew of only one Presbyterian church in Scotland that had succeeded in going to quarterly communions." *Holy Fairs*, 186, referencing *An Address to the Christian People, under the Inspection of the Reformed Presbytery, Concerning the More Frequent Dispensing of the Lord's Supper* (Glasgow: n.p., 1795), 55.

260 Schmidt, *Holy Fairs*, 187.

Chapter 5
Communion, Preparation, and Ecclesial Identity in American Reformed Churches (1620–1758)

5.1　The Allure of Purity in the New World

This chapter aims at tracing the dynamic between practices of preparation, barriers to communion, and communion frequency in the godly communities of New England, especially in relationship to developments in Old England, and at identifying some of the historical, social, and political factors that influenced both communion frequency and preparation for communion in the New World. The issue of how the Lord's Supper created and defined the boundaries of the religious group assumed central importance in the godly communities of the New World, because they were finally able to create churches that were "pure." A perceived lack of purity in (among other things) the way the Lord's Supper was organized in Old England had been the primary reason for their departure. Thus, they were now finally able to set a better example. However, debates and conflicts would soon erupt about the viability of these pure churches and about the way they arranged participation in the sacraments of baptism and communion.

This chapter begins in 1620, with the establishment of the Plymouth Bay colony, and ends with the death of Jonathan Edwards, in 1758. Edwards was a friend and correspondent with John Erskine, one of the main voices in the Scottish communion frequency debates, which form the main area of analysis of the latter part of this research project in Chapter 6. This chapter begins with connecting the concerns and motivations of those who came to establish new religious communities in the New World (5.1). It then describes the main features and patterns of communion frequency and membership in the community in the early colonies of New England (5.2). After highlighting the theme of preparation for communion in colonial churches (5.3) it surveys the controversy between Solomon Stoddard (5.4) and Edward Taylor (5.5) about standards for admitting people to communion. The selected writings of two representative New England Puritan pastors, Samuel Willard (5.6) and Cotton Mather (5.7) will be examined, focusing on their treatment of preparation and participation in communion. Several communion sermons of Jonathan Edwards will be analyzed (5.8) with special attention to his statements on frequency and proper preparation. Finally, the influence of the Scots-Irish and their communion traditions will be connected to the wide-spread movements of revival in the American colonies (5.9).

5.2   Frequency and Sacramental Boundaries in Colonial Puritanism

Worship patterns in the Americas were dependent on the European and British traditions of the colonists, but also quickly developed in ways that reflected the context of the colonial period. Communion practices can be surveyed geographically, as well as theologically, because in the early years of New World colonization, communities tended to be quite homogenous. For instance, English Separatists established the Plymouth Bay colony in 1620. However, the settlers who founded the Salem Colony, north of Plymouth Bay, in 1628, did not consider themselves as "Separatists." Their convictions about worship and ecclesiology drove them to immigrate and, though they shared many of the same beliefs as the established church, they looked forward to worshiping God as they believed the Bible required in the New World.[1] The other major colony in New England was the Massachusetts Bay Colony, which swelled in numbers in the 1630s due to a large wave of immigration.[2] Those who emigrated to New England saw themselves as examples for Old England.[3] Ministers on both sides of the Atlantic shared news, letters, prayers, books, and encouragement. They saw themselves as also part of the wider movement of Reformed churches and raised money for the support of refugees from the Continent.[4] Therefore, it is best to adopt a trans-Atlantic perspective when surveying the Puritans and early colonists in the New World.

Previous sections have focused on Reformed and Presbyterian communion practices and polemics in England and Scotland. However, this research focus can give the impression that Reformed churches, godly communities, Puritans, and Presbyterians were all hermetically sealed off from other religious communities. Obviously, that is not the case. As noted previously (4.2), the available evidence suggests that, in the post-Reformation period, English congregants in the Established church communed with about the same frequency as those in godly, or Puritan communities. Even when groups like the Independents (or Congregationalists)

---

1 Karen Westerfield Tucker, "North America," in *The Oxford History of Christian Worship*, 588. So also, Bremer: "The settlement of Bible Commonwealths was intended not only to preserve the immigrants' freedom to worship God as they pleased but also to inspire those left behind. This aim was in contrast to that of the Plimoth [sic] Plantation, established in 1620 by Separatists who had sought their own religious freedom with no expectation that they would influence others." Bremer, *Shaping New Englands*, 9.

2 Tucker, "North America," 589.

3 "[T]he thrust of the Puritan movement was to transform the English-speaking world. The settlement of Massachusetts and the other colonies was in part an effort to implement the reform agenda that had been frustrated in England. But the clerical leaders of the migration also hoped that the new England would inspire and assist those who remained behind to continue the struggle to transform the old one." Bremer, *Shaping New Englands*, xi, and especially 9–13.

4 See Francis J. Bremer, *Congregational Communion*.

observed weekly communions, the exhortations and complaints of pastors and authors reveal similar instances of frustration with their flocks.

However intricately connected they remained to Old England, the New England Puritans pursued their own path in many ways, as they sought to establish churches and towns in accordance with the Word of God. The two earliest accounts of Lord's Supper observance in New England are Thomas Lechford's *Plain Dealing: or, News from New England* (1642) and John Cotton's *The Way of the Churches of Christ in New England* (1645). These accounts come from opposite sides of the doctrinal and liturgical divide. Lechford was an Anglican and a lawyer, who lived for a time in the Massachusetts Bay colony.[5] He was somewhat critical of the New England Puritan movement, while John Cotton was a Puritan celebrity. Cotton, who had immigrated to the Massachusetts Bay Colony, was trying to defend and explain the Congregational system of church polity there, with the hope of influencing the deliberations then taking place at the Westminster Assembly.[6] Lechford describes a monthly observance of the Lord's Supper in Boston, which was the center of the Massachusetts Bay Colony. He describes a process where "notice" about the Supper was given a "fortnight" before the observance, and where only the "Church" was allowed to remain in the meeting house during the Supper itself. These were the members who had been able to provide an oral testimony to the effects of God's grace in their lives. The number of people who could receive the Supper were a "great deal less" than those that could not receive communion. Additionally, the minister and elders sat around the "Table," while everyone else sat in their seats.[7]

In Lechford's description, two aspects stand out. One is the selective nature of participation in communion. The New England Puritans demanded much from those who desired to receive communion and who believed they were worthy to do so. Secondly, the practice of the ministers and elders sitting at the communion table by themselves presented a vivid reminder that the clergy were set apart from the people. This is starkly different than the Scots practice of everyone in the church receiving the Supper around the same table, along with the minister and elders, or at least in closer proximity. The communion table was closely guarded

---

5 Lechford had made the mistake of helping to represent William Prynne in court, and thus had incurred the wrath of Archbishop Laud. As a result, he was banished to New England. He struggled to make a living there, and repeatedly clashed with the civil and religious authorities there. See J. Hammond Trumbull's introduction to Thomas Lechford, *Plain Dealing, or, News From New England* (London, 1642; reprint, Boston: J.K. Wiggin and Wm. Parsons Lunt, 1867), ix–xl.

6 Bremer, *Shaping New Englands*, 63–64.

7 "Once a month is a Sacrament of the Lords Supper, whereof notice is given usually a fortnight before, and then all others departing save the Church, which is a great deal less in number then those that go away, they receive the Sacrament, the Ministers and ruling Elders sitting at the Table, the rest in their seats, or upon forms: All cannot see the Minister consecrating, unless they stand up, and make a narrow shift." Lechford, *Plain Dealing, or, News From New England*, 45–46.

as well.[8] Lechford relates that anyone in Boston could come in and simply watch the ceremony, even if they were not full members of the "Church," but that those from another church in the countryside who wished to participate had to first come and present themselves to an elder, who would then announce their name to the congregation.[9]

Cotton's description and explanation of Puritan worship in New England agrees with Lechford's, at least in the broad outlines. In typical Puritan fashion, he relates that the Lord's Supper is offered to those who "neither want [lack] knowledge nor grace to examine and judge themselves before the Lord."[10] Additionally, those who "lie under any offence publicly known" must "first remove the offence" before they can come to the sacrament.[11] He confirms Lechford's claim that members of other churches were only allowed to participate in the Supper if they had letters of recommendation from their own church.[12] But in a subsequent tract, Cotton challenges Lechford's claim that people are forced to leave the building during communion, and says that anyone is free to watch any part of the service.[13] Regarding frequency, Cotton states: "The Lord's Supper we administer for the time, once a month at least, and for the gesture, to the people sitting; according as Christ administered it to his Disciples sitting."[14] Evident here is Cotton's appeal to the example of Christ and the early, apostolic church. Cotton's use of the phrase "for the time," creates the impression that he, and the New England churches, were open to other options in communion frequency. Although Lechford and Cotton are our earliest sources on American Puritan worship, both emphasized certain features for their own purposes. An accurate picture is probably found somewhere in the middle between their two accounts.[15]

---

8 "In early American Congregationalism, only the regenerate of the local congregation and those outsiders with written verification of their spiritual status or with local approval were welcomed to the second seal—and renewal—of the covenant, the Lord's supper." Tucker, "North America," 592.

9 Lechford, *Plain Dealing, or, News From New England*, 46–47.

10 John Cotton, *The Way of the Churches of Christ in New England* (London, 1645), 67.

11 Cotton, *The Way of the Churches*, 67–68.

12 Cotton, *The Way of the Churches*, 68.

13 "It is not true that we hold out any at all, English or Indian, out of our Christian Congregations. All without exception are allowed to be present, at our public Prayers and Psalms, at our reading of Scriptures, and the preaching and expounding of the same, and also at the admitting of Members and dispensing of seals and censures." Cotton, *The Way of Congregational Churches Cleared* (London: 1648), quoted in Adams, *Meeting House to Camp Meeting*, 32.

14 Cotton, *The Way of the Churches*, 68.

15 According to Adams "while Lechford tried to maximize offensive practices of a [sic] New England he wished to discredit by association with the most extreme Separatist ways, Cotton tried … to minimize especially such practices that would be unpalatable to English Puritans who remained within the Anglican church." *Meeting House to Camp Meeting*, 32.

Thomas Weld(e) (1595–1661) wrote a similar description and explanation of New England church practice and communion observance: "For the administration of the Supper, because Christ bids us do it often, we commonly have it monthly, though we tie not ourselves to any set time, but alter it as often as good reason appears, and for better remembrance of the duty, and preparation thereunto, the Elders give notice the Lords day afore, and stirs them to an holy preparation for so holy a duty."[16]

Another early witness to beliefs about communion frequency in New England is Thomas Hooker's *A Survey of the Summe of Church Discipline* (1648). In this massive treatise, Hooker argues for the biblical superiority of Congregationalism, particularly as manifested in New England, and responds to the criticisms of Presbyterians like Charles Herle and Samuel Rutherford.[17] His "Manner of Administration Peculiar to the Supper" includes these references to frequency:

> First, it is a Sacrament of our nourishment, and our growing up in the Lord Jesus, and therefore it is appointed by him to be frequently used, as being one of the standing dishes which the Lord Christ hath provided for the daily diet and the household provision of his faithful ones, who are his family, 1 Cor. 11.26, 34. *as often as ye eat this bread, &c.*

Hooker then moves on to argue for the need of a "double consecration," of both the bread and the wine, which was a typical concern for the Congregational theologians.[18] Beyond the mention of "frequently used," Hooker does not clarify his ideals about communion frequency.

An additional source dealing with communion frequency in the colonial period is a letter from Richard Mather (1596–1669), a Puritan minister in Boston. In 1655, the governor of the Massachusetts Bay Colony asked Richard Mather about communion frequency and whether it should be celebrated every Sunday. In a letter to another pastor, Mather summarizes his response. He first acknowledges that "there ought to be a frequent use of that Ordinance" and he would not "condemn any church that shall observe it every Sabbath." But he denies that it would be a sin

---

16 Thomas Weld, *A brief narration of the practices of the churches in New-England* (London: Printed by Matth. Simmons for John Rothwell, 1645; Ann Arbor: Text Creation Partnership, 2011), 8, http://name.umdl.umich.edu/A96168.0001.001.

17 Hooker was designated by the colonial clergy to respond to Presbyterian criticisms from authors in England and Scotland, and his *Survey* was the result. See Bremer, *Shaping New Englands*, 65.

18 Thomas Hooker, *A Survey of the Summe of Church Discipline. Wherein the Way of the Congregationall Churches of Christ in New-England, is Warranted and Cleared, by Scripture and Argument, and all Exceptions of weight made against it by sundry Learned Divines* (London: John Bellamy, 1648), Part 3, Cha 2, 32–33. On the unique stress the Congregationalists placed upon the "double consecration," see Davies, *The Worship of the English Puritans*, 208–209.

to not observe the sacrament every week.[19] He deals with how to interpret texts like Acts 20:7 and Acts 2:42 and admits that though these texts may describe instances of the apostolic church celebrating the Lord's Supper, they do not clearly state that it should always be observed every Sunday.[20] He considers Acts 2:46, where the early disciples worship daily in the temple and "break bread" from house to house, and Mather asserts that if this supports weekly communion, it also proves daily communion.

Mather acknowledges that authorities like Calvin and William Ames stated their preference for frequent communion, but also clarified that there might be good reasons to have it less frequently. He also cites writers like Bullinger and (Wolfgang) Musculus who believed the Bible did not prescribe any set frequency for the Lord's Supper.[21] He also argues that determining the best rhythm for communion is part of the greater "liberty" for the scheduling and observing of "ceremonies" of worship in the New Covenant era.[22] Mather's short letter is notable as one of the few Puritan sources uncovered in the course of research that interacts closely with sources and texts that address communion frequency.

Thomas Shepherd (1605–49) was another prominent New England pastor and author. His *First Principles of the Oracles of God* (1658) presents a basic systematic theology in the form of a catechism. In the section on the sacraments, Shepherd recommends frequent communion. The Lord's Supper is the "Sacrament of our growth in Christ, being new-born, because it is food given to nourish us, having received life." Regarding frequency "it is to be administered and received often that we may grow." However, Shepherd also stresses the need for preparation when he writes that "children and fools, and wicked, ought not to partake of the Sacrament, because they cannot examine themselves, and so renew their Faith."[23]

Hambrick-Stowe summarizes the patterns of communion frequency in Puritan New England. The Lord's Supper was offered after the sermon and prayer "in the morning (ideally once a month but actually anywhere from six to twelve times

---

19 "But if this degree of frequency be of necessity, so that if it be not so it will be sin, this is more then yet I do apprehend, nor do I remember any word of G.[od] or of the apostles, that doth so require." *Collections of the Massachusetts Historical Society* [*MHSC* hereafter] 4th ser., vol. 8 (Boston: Wiggin and Lunt, 1868), 72, https://archive.org/details/collectionsmass27socigoog/page/n96/mode/2up.

20 Mather, *MHSC*: 72–73, https://archive.org/details/collectionsmass27socigoog/page/n96/mode/2up.

21 Mather, *MHSC*: 74, https://archive.org/details/collectionsmass27socigoog/page/n98/mode/2up.

22 Mather, *MHSC*: 74–75, https://archive.org/details/collectionsmass27socigoog/page/n98/mode/2up.

23 Thomas Shepherd, *The First Principles of the Oracles of God* (London: Printed for John Rothwel, 1655; Ann Arbor: Text Creation Partnership, 2011), 16, http://name.umdl.umich.edu/A59663.0001.001.

annually) and Baptism in the afternoon as occasion required."[24] The sacraments were marked off from other means of grace like prayer, or preaching, because they occurred on specific Sundays and were "restricted to members of the church covenant."[25] Hambrick-Stowe also summarizes the contours of communion preparation and participation: "The minister would announce the scheduled celebration two weeks in advance, to remind members to prepare themselves for the Sacrament. Thus, whether all worshipers engaged in extensive preparatory exercises, if administered monthly, the Sacrament was either mentioned or administered on three weeks out of four or five."[26]

The diary of Samuel Sewall (1652–1730) a prominent figure in the Massachusetts Bay colony who served as a judge, printer, and businessman, also provides insight as to how communion was viewed in Puritan New England. In 1677, when Sewall was twenty-five, one of his early entries in his diary describes his apprehensions about joining a church and participating in the Supper. He "could hardly sit down to the Lord's Table." Although he wanted to leave the church, he was afraid that leaving might make him even less "fit" to participate next time. Deciding whether to participate in the Lord's Supper provoked a crisis of faith for Sewall: "But I never experienced more unbelief." He was afraid that God might strike him dead because of his lack of faith. Still, he desired to "glimpse" Christ in the Supper, though he did not attain this. Yet, he hoped to be able to participate next time, and to "do better."[27] For the New England Puritans, the Lord's Supper could be, and was intended to

---

24 Charles E. Hambrick-Stowe, *The Practice of Piety: Puritan Devotional Disciplines in Seventeenth-Century New England* (Chapel Hill: The University of North Carolina Press, 1982; repr., 1985), 123.

25 Hambrick-Stowe, *The Practice of Piety*, 123.

26 Hambrick-Stowe, *The Practice of Piety*, 125. So, also, Holifield: "Nevertheless, whether a church administered the sacrament weekly, as occasionally happened, or observed communion only one day each month, the Lord's Supper was an exalted symbol of New England piety." *The Covenant Sealed*, 160.

27 "And I could hardly sit down to the Lord's Table. But I feared that if I went away I might be less fit next time, and thought that it would be well to withdraw, wherefore I stayed. But I never experienced more unbelief. I feared at least that I did not believe that there was such a one as Jesus Xt., and yet was afraid that because I came to the ordinance without belief, that for the abuse of Xt. I should be stricken dead; yet I had some earnest desires that Xt. would, before the ordinance were done, though it were when he was just going away, give me some glimpse of himself; but I perceived none. Yet I seemed then to desire the coming of the next Sacrament day, that I might do better, and was stirred up hereby dreadfully to seek God who many times before had touched my heart by Mr. Thacher's praying and preaching more than now. The Lord pardon my former grieving of his Spirit, and circumcise my heart to love him with all my heart and soul." Davies, *The Worship of the American Puritans*, 198, quoting *The Diary of Samuel Sewall*, M. Halsey Thomas, ed., (New York: Farrar, Straus & Giroux, 1973), I, 40.

be, a profoundly moving and meaningful experience.[28] Normally stoic figures like Increase Mather reportedly wept at the communion table, and Samuel Sewall also records being moved to tears during communion.[29]

The issue of participation in communion was complicated by the New England churches' strict understanding of themselves as communities of "visible saints." They challenged people to give a testimony of how they had come to realize their profound depravity, their need for grace, and their assurance that they were indeed part of the "elect."[30] Many people could not give this testimony, and so they could not receive communion. Therefore, to understand patterns of communion frequency in the Puritan colonies, it is necessary to also survey their attitudes towards the process of preparation before the sacrament. Because of the high standards erected around both membership in the church, and also participation in communion, patterns of frequency must be examined within the broader framework of ecclesiology and the rhythms of Puritan devotional life.

5.3   Communion and Preparation in the Colonial Period

Discussions about communion frequency in the Reformed tradition and Reformed churches usually involved the delicate balance of pursuing an ideal of more frequent communion than had been the norm in the medieval period, but also focusing on the necessity of training people and preparing them to approach the Lord's Supper with the appropriate attitudes of repentance and confession of sins. The need for serious and strenuous preparation and self-examination was stressed adamantly by many of the Puritans. As we have seen, they were motivated by the desire to complete the unfinished reformation of the English church. When they were repeatedly frustrated, persecuted, and deprived of their pulpits and their livings, many of them set sail for the New World.

Two things must be recognized about many of the godly who emigrated to the American colonies. First, they tended to be the "hottest" of the "hot" Protestants—as

---

28 "Through the words of institution, the eucharistic prayer, and the symbolism of the bread and wine the people were led once again through the stages of the redemptive drama revealed in the work of Christ. The Lord's Supper was occasion for renewed repentance followed by the experience of union with Christ." Hambrick-Stowe, *The Practice of Piety*, 126.

29 Horton Davies, *The Worship of the American Puritans*, 208.

30 Davies, drawing on Morgan, says this demand for testimony regarding conversion was an invention of the New England Puritans, which they then exported back to Old England. See Davies, *The Worship of the American Puritans*, 199, and Edmund S. Morgan, *Visible Saints: The History of a Puritan Idea* (New York: New York University Press, 1963; repr., Ithaca, N.Y.: Cornell University Press, 1965), 33, 63–66.

the Puritans were called in Old England.[31] They were so convinced of their views about the nature of true reformation that they were willing to risk it all and start a new life in dangerous and uncertain conditions. Therefore, they were concerned to guard and protect the "holy" community that they had come to create. As John Winthrop famously said, they were setting out to create a "city on a hill." They would do just about anything to make sure that light did not go out and was not dimmed.[32]

Another aspect of the overall vision and ambition of these godly immigrants was their belief that establishing a holy community in New England would also be good for *Old* England.[33] They believed that if they could establish a truly "Biblical" community and live out the "beauty of holiness" before a watching world, then the world would sit up and take note. This was their chance to demonstrate how following God's precepts in life and worship would be blessed by God. Accordingly, every turn of fortune or fate provoked serious soul-searching on the part of the godly in the New World. Bad crops or attacks from the indigenous people were interpreted as judgments from God, which demanded days of fasting, humiliation, and communal repentance. So, the stakes were raised in the New World.

Many in Old England were cautious and leery of what they heard about developments in the colonies. Although John Cotton eventually migrated to New England and joined the Boston colony, he was originally very skeptical of some of the innovative practices that took root in the New World.[34] New England Puritans advanced the logic of "congregationalism" further than they had in England. Congregationalists believed that only a local church could be a "church."[35] They rejected ideas like the "Church of England." Furthermore, Anglican churches in England could not be "true" churches. This created tension in the matter of communion practices. When the Puritan immigrants traveling with John Winthrop came from England in 1630, they were not automatically accepted by the existing Congregationalist churches in Salem. Samuel Skelton, the minister in Salem, would not allow them to participate in the Lord's Supper, and their children could not be baptized.[36]

---

31 The phrase comes from the pamphleteer Percival Wilburn, writing in 1581: "The hotter sort of Protestants are called Puritans." *A Checke or Reproofe of M. Howlet's Untimely Screeching* (1581), quoted in Patrick Collinson, *The Elizabethan Puritan Movement* (Oxford: Clarendon Press, 1967; paperback, 1990), 27.

32 See Michael P. Winship, *Hot Protestants*, 79–81; John Winthrop, "A Modell of Christian Charity," *MHSC*, 3rd ser., 7 (1838), pgs. 46, 47.

33 Bremer, Introduction," *Shaping New Englands*, xi.

34 Winship, *Hot Protestants*, chap. 8.

35 Winship, *Hot Protestants*, 86–87.

36 Winship, *Hot Protestants*, 86.

The pressing issue that caused so much strife (on both sides of the Atlantic) was how to determine the precise boundaries of the visible covenant. As they set out to define the godly community, how could they tell if someone was "in" or "out"? Being "out" would, of course, also mean that they would not have access to the Lord's Supper. Preparation was expected to be part of daily life in Puritan communities. The colonists in New England carried on the spiritual regime of the Puritans in Old England: "Individuals engaged in self-examination on a regular basis, and families gathered to confess their sins, pray for forgiveness, and thank God for the blessings that he had bestowed upon them."[37]

Preparation was especially expected, and in some cases required, before admission to the Lord's Table. The pastor Thomas Shepherd (1605–1649) routinely spent an entire day, or longer, in preparation for the Lord's Supper.[38] Jonathan Mitchel (1624–1668), a prominent pastor of the Congregational Church in Cambridge, Massachusetts, had high standards for his congregants, and for himself. According to Cotton Mather (Richard Mather's grandson who also pastored in Boston and became one of New England's most influential intellectuals), every two months Mitchel would spend an entire day in fasting in preparation before the sacrament.[39] Mitchel also expected prospective communicants to be able to give some "relation of the work of conversion, such as hath been ordinarily used in most of our churches, or somewhat equivalent thereto" before they could be admitted to full "communion," or membership in the church, or to "admission to the Lord's Table." However, if they were unable to recount their conversion experience, Mitchel also wrote a somewhat extensive list of three ways in which prospective communicants could demonstrate that they were sufficiently prepared for the Lord's Supper. They could answer questions about their conversion, make a "serious, solemn and savoury profession or confession" of their faith, or they might be "eminently known to excel in gifts and grace."[40]

Standards for admission to the sacrament were intertwined with expectations for membership in the Puritan churches of New England. Membership in the colonial Congregational churches came to depend on the ability to recount one's experience of God's grace, and provide evidence of true conversion.[41] According to

---

37 Bremer, *Shaping New Englands*, 56.

38 Holified, *The Covenant Sealed*, 164, referencing Shepherd's *Meditations*, 49, 58 and Shepherd's "Diary," August 24, November 13, February 12, April 23, 1643.

39 Davies, *The Worship of the American Puritans*, 200–201, citing Cotton Mather, *Magnalia Christi Americana*, 2 vols. (London, 1702; rpt. Hartford, Conn., 1820), II, Bk. iv, 74–75.

40 Davies, *The Worship of the American Puritans*, 199–200, citing Cotton Mather, *Magnalia Christi Americana*, 2 vols. (London, 1702; rpt. Hartford, Conn., 1820), II, Bk. iv, 83.

41 See Winship, *Hot Protestants*, 89, for John Cotton's approval, and perhaps his original influence, in instituting this procedure.

the *Platform of Discipline* (1649), their charter of ecclesiastical self-identification, only those who made a "personal & publick confession," of how God had worked in their spiritual lives could be baptized, and then admitted to communion.[42] At ecclesiastical gatherings in 1657 and 1662, the New England pastors reaffirmed that only those who could testify to God's grace working in their lives could receive the Lord's Supper and vote in church business matters.[43] However, not everyone could provide this verbal testimony.

Contemporary records indicate a general hesitancy to take the steps necessary to participate in the sacrament.[44] Hall writes:

> Whatever the exact percentages, almost every congregation contained a clump of persons who attended regularly, were deemed Christian in how they behaved, had their children baptised (early or late), but who never came forward to describe themselves as converted.[45]

Hall maintains that it is not accurate to describe these people as "lax." On the contrary, they were probably overly scrupulous and concerned about their spiritual worthiness to receive the Lord's Supper. They had heard, quite clearly, the dire warnings of the preachers when they stressed the dangers of coming unprepared and unworthily to the Supper, echoing Paul's warnings in 1 Corinthians 11. Solomon Stoddard, the prominent pastor of Northampton in the frontier regions of Connecticut, and the grandfather of Jonathan Edwards, wrote that some people were "scared out of Religion."[46] Winship estimates that the "ordeal" of giving a personal narrative of conversion excluded as much as fifty percent of population of the Massachusetts Bay colony from both membership in the church, and from participation in communion.[47]

---

42 Richard Mather, *A Platform of church discipline gathered out of the Word of God* (Cambridge, MA: S.G. at Cambridge in New England, 1649; Ann Arbor: Text Creation Partnership 2011), 17–18, http://name.umdl.umichap.edu/A55001.0001.001.

43 Hall, "New England, 1660–1730," Coffey and Lim, eds., *The Cambridge Companion to Puritanism*, 146. He cites the testimony of Benjamin Wadsworth (Boston, 1724), the Connecticut General Assembly of 1676, and Solomon Stoddard, who "estimated in 1708 that the ratio for the churches in general was four halfway to each full member."

44 Hall notes that contemporary sermons and church records indicate a "reluctance among baptized adults to complete their membership in the Lord's Supper." "New England, 1660–1730," in Coffey and Lim, eds., *The Cambridge Companion to Puritanism* (Cambridge: Cambridge University Press, 2008), 147.

45 Hall, in Coffey and Lim, eds., *The Cambridge Companion to Puritanism*, 148.

46 Hall, in Coffey and Lim, eds., *The Cambridge Companion to Puritanism*, 148, quoting Solomon Stoddard, *The Inexcusableness of Neglecting the Worship of God* (Boston, 1708), 22–23.

47 Winship, *Hot Protestants*, 90.

But it was not only church members who worried about their worthiness to approach the Lord's Table. Even such a prominent pastor and theologian like Thomas Shepherd could struggle with assurance about his worthiness. His journal entries reveal a deep struggle whether or not he really believed in Christ, because the sacrament is only "for them that believe."[48] He also struggled with doubts about the reality of Christ's spiritual presence in the Supper.[49] Shepherd honestly recorded his sense of his own sinfulness during the Supper: "When the sacrament came, my heart not feeling the presence of the Lord, I began to mourn inwardly for my sins as standing between God and my soul."[50]

The high standards for church membership and participation in the sacrament deterred many from both membership and from coming to communion. Although they were unable to give a "testimony" of their conversion, they still wanted their children to be part of the church. The decision of the 1662 Synod, or the "Half-Way Covenant" was an imperfect solution.[51] It allowed the children of baptized parents who could not receive the Supper to be baptized themselves. In essence, there were two levels of church membership: baptism and then participation in communion. Parents could have their children baptized, but the parents were still barred from the Supper—they were only "halfway" into the covenant.[52]

The next section will survey selected works from a few prominent American Puritan writers, highlighting their stated opinions about participation in communion, as well as communion frequency. As they wrestled with the issues of how to judge membership in the church and wider community, they provide further examples of ecclesial and spiritual ideals eclipsing ideals for communion frequency. The views of these writers help to answer the question of how the desire for church discipline and preparation has impacted patterns of communion frequency (see 1.2).

5.4   Solomon Stoddard (1643–1729)

The "Half-Way covenant" was a precarious arrangement. In the 1670s prominent church leaders like Solomon Stoddard questioned the tight restrictions that had been placed on participation in communion. Stoddard drew on various English

---

48 Journal entry for January 23, 1642, quoted in Davies, *The Worship of the American Puritans*, 196.
49 Journal entry for April 10, 1643, quoted in Davies, *The Worship of the American Puritans*, 196–97.
50 Journal entry for July 10, 1643, quoted in Davies, *The Worship of the American Puritans*, 197.
51 On the Half-Way Covenant, see Morgan, *Visible Saints*, chap. 5; David D. Hall, *The Faithful Shepherd: A History of the New England Ministry in the Seventeenth Century* (Chapel Hill: University of North Carolina Press, 1972), 199–207; Bremer, *The Puritan Experiment: New England Society from Bradford to Edwards*, rev. ed. (Hanover and London: University Press of New England, 1976; 1995), 161–67.
52 Tucker, "North America," 592.

writers and began teaching that the Supper was a "converting ordinance."[53] That is, it could help those who were not truly regenerate to fully repent. This challenged the existing practice in New England Puritan churches. By the 1700s, any baptized adult who was not living a scandalous life could participate in communion in some congregations. But preparation was still expected beforehand. By the time Stoddard began pastoring on what was then the "frontier," only half of his congregation was officially part of the church. In response to this, Stoddard advocated lowering the standards for inclusion in communion.[54] Increase Mather (son of Richard and father of Cotton), one of the most respected clergymen in New England, took Stoddard to task for this and initiated an intense rivalry that lasted many years. Edward Taylor entered the controversy as well, and his response will be surveyed below. What were Stoddard's main arguments, and how did they relate to the issue of communion frequency?

Stoddard published his first book in 1687—*The Safety of Appearing at the Day of Judgement, In the Righteousness of Christ: Opened and Applied*, which questioned important Puritan beliefs about the Lord's Supper, or at least confused them and left Stoddard open to attack. In chapter VII, Stoddard discusses the sacraments. He focuses on how they reassure us of God's goodwill towards us—"this shews that it lies much upon the heart of God to strengthen our Faith in this particular, that it is safe appearing before God in Christ's Righteousness." Furthermore, God "desires to give [us] all manner of assurance, and would leave no room for doubting."[55] Stoddard's emphasis here is on what the sacrament does to the faith of the recipient. His more troubling assertions come in chapter XI.

The topic of his chapter is the "discouragements" that Christians face, and how to deal with them. Stoddard commends attending the preaching of the Word and coming to the sacrament. He stresses the subjective, faith-confirming aspects of the sacrament: "Attend the Sacrament of the Lords Supper: the great design of this Ordinance is for the strengthning [sic] of Faith, therein is offered to us special communion with a crucified Saviour." He also states: "[T]hey are afraid that they shall eat and drink judgment to themselves: but God no where requires a faith of

---

53 Tucker, "North America," 593. See also E. Brooks Holifield, "The Intellectual Sources of Stoddard-eanism," *The New England Quarterly* (Sep., 1972): 373–392.

54 According to Grabo, "by 1677 Stoddard began to reject its conclusions [the Half-Way Covenant] and to plead for opening the Lord's Supper to all who asked for it." *Edward Taylor's Treatise Concerning the Lord's Supper*, Norman S. Grabo, ed., (Michigan State University Press, 1966), xx. Francis J. Bremer clarifies that Stoddard was not simply advocating "open communion," which had been practiced at various times in a couple of colonial churches. Rather, Stoddard was maintaining that communion could serve as a "converting ordinance." Stoddard's own church in Northampton rejected this claim in 1690, even as it allowed "open communion." See Bremer, *The Puritan Experiment*, 214.

55 Stoddard, *The Safety of Appearing* (Boston: Samuel Green, for Samuel Phillips, 1687; Ann Arbor: Text Creation Partnership, 2011), 146, http://name.umdl.umich.edu/N00357.0001.001.

assurance in those that partake of that Ordinance: this Ordinance is a special help to those that are in the dark with a good conscience."[56] Stoddard is lowering the bar of self-examination and of being able to give a testimony about having saving faith.

After some private exchanges with Edward Taylor, who stridently opposed Stoddard's teaching that the sacrament was a "converting" ordinance, Stoddard clearly stated his tenets in *The Doctrine of Instituted Churches* (1700). Stoddard challenged various aspects of the congregational church structures in New England. This affected his views about admittance to the Lord's Supper. He asserted that those who were qualified to join the church were therefore qualified to participate in communion.[57] He also challenged the demand that only "visible saints" could come to communion.[58] Since it was so difficult to know whether one was really sanctified, there would always be levels of doubt about one's "worthiness" to approach the Lord's Table.[59]

Stoddard extended his argument further in 1708, with *The Inexcusableness of Neglecting the Worship of God Under a Pretence of being in an Unconverted Condition*. When he discusses the Eucharist he maintains that "sanctifying holiness" is not necessary to qualify one to come to communion. If one can be "in covenant" with God, through the church, then one is qualified for the Lord's Table. One does not have to be "regenerate" because all Jews could partake of the Passover. As long as one is not "scandalous" one may come to communion.[60] Here Stoddard undermines the New England Puritan ecclesiology and their understanding of the sacraments. The first generation of immigrants had come to the New World to establish pure churches and a pure observance of the Lord's Supper. In his efforts to encourage

---

56 Stoddard, *The Safety of Appearing*, 338–339, http://name.umdl.umich.edu/N00357.0001.001.

57 "Those Adult Persons that are fit to be admitted into the Church, are to be admitted to the Lords Supper. All Adult Persons that are fit to be admitted into the Church, ordinarily have all those qualifications requisite to the participation of the Lords Supper." *The doctrine of instituted churches explained and proved from the word of God by Solomon Stoddard …* (London: Printed for Ralph Smith …, 1700; Ann Arbor: Text Creation Partnership, 2011), 19, http://name.umdl.umich.edu/A61661.0001.001.

58 "Such Adult Persons as are worthy to be admitted into the Church, or being in the Church are worthy to be continued without censure, are to be admitted to the Lords Supper; it is utterly unreasonable to deny the Adult Members of the Church, the Lords Supper, and yet not lay them under censure; If they are guilty of any such offence as to be denied the Lords Supper, why are they not censured? If they are not worthy to be censured, why are they kept from the Lords Supper?" *The doctrine of instituted churches*, 20, http://name.umdl.umich.edu/A61661.0001.001.

59 Grabo, ed., *Edward Taylor's Treatise Concerning the Lord's Supper*, xxvii.

60 *The inexcusableness of neglecting the worship of God, under a pretence of being in an unconverted condition. Shewed in a sermon preached at Northampton, the 17th. Decemb. 1707. being the time of the sitting of the Inferiour Court. / By Solomon Stoddard, Pastor of Northampton. ; Imprimatur, J. Dudley* (Boston in N.E.: Printed by B. Green. Sold by Samuel Phillips, at the brick shop., 1708; Ann Arbor: Text Creation Partnership, 2011), 11–12, http://name.umdl.umich.edu/N01152.0001.001.

and enable more people to come to communion, Stoddard prepared the way for developments that would dismantle this project.

Although Stoddard does not mention any specific understanding of an ideal for communion frequency, he certainly desired to convince more people to come and participate. In a sermon published in 1717, focused on moving young people to conversion, Stoddard questions the spiritual vitality of the youth of New England. Although they "come universally to hear the word of God" in sermons, Stoddard doubts how diligently they pursue the other "secret duties of Religion." This is chiefly because of their reluctance to come to the Lord's Supper, when "scare [sic] five or six of them in a Town" actually participate in communion.[61] He laments that so many young people either "neglect" the Supper, or do not prepare themselves to receive it.[62]

Stoddard's legacy is complex, and he must be understood in the context of the continuing tensions in the Puritan communities, as they wrestled with the implications of a system they had established. The ideal of pure churches and pure sacramental celebrations proved much harder to achieve than had been expected. Stoddard was motivated by the noble desire of enabling more people to come to the Eucharist. But his stance provoked vocal responses.

5.5 Edward Taylor (c. 1645–1729)

The most formidable opponent Stoddard faced was the poet-pastor Edward Taylor, who also labored in Northampton, Connecticut. At the time, Northampton was the "frontier." Taylor is now remembered primarily for his poetic meditations on the Lord's Supper, which he wrote as an aide for his own spiritual preparation before administering the Supper. But Taylor also wrote a series of substantive replies to Stoddard's theology of participation in communion. These replies appeared in the form of sermons, in years 1701–1703. Although they were not published during Edward's lifetime, they are a substantial response to Stoddard.[63]

---

61 *Three sermons lately preached at Boston. I. Shewing the vertue of Christs blood to cleanse from sin. II. That natural men are under the government of self-love. III. That the Gospel is the means of conversion. : To which a fourth is added, to stir up young men and maidens to praise the name of the Lord.* / By Solomon Stoddard A.M. Pastor of Northampton (Boston, 1717; reprint, Gale, Sabin Americana Print Editions 1500–1926), 106.

62 Stoddard, *Three sermons lately preached*, 108.

63 According to Grabo, these sermons were the "most important opposition Stoddard encountered, and deserve high praise, for they leave all the other books of the controversy far behind in rational inventiveness, rhetorical turns, logical subtlety, complexity, and depth of insight." *Edward Taylor's Treatise*, xix.

Taylor continues the Puritan emphasis on the necessity of serious preparation before participating in communion. In a series of sermons based on the text of Matthew 22:12, Taylor focuses on the image of the wedding garment and expounds on the necessity of coming with the right "clothes" to the Table. Taylor argues that the wedding feast in the parable corresponds to the Lord's Supper. He stresses the importance of participating in the sacrament, as well as the importance of preparing properly before coming to this "wedding feast": "It will be a contempt of the highest honor and favor to neglect or make light of the invitation. But yet if thou comest unprepared thou comest unbeseeming the nature of the feast."[64] Since we would prepare ourselves if we were invited to feast by a civil ruler, how much more should we prepare ourselves when we are invited to a banquet with the King of Kings?[65] Our level of preparation should reflect the importance of the occasion to which we are invited in the sacrament of communion.[66] Taylor rebukes those who neglect to come to the Lord's Supper, and distinguishes various types of neglect. Both those who do not come at all, and those who do not prepare beforehand, are both guilty of neglect.[67] Taylor argues that those who do not prepare themselves are really resisting the invitation to the wedding feast.[68]

For Taylor, a key part of coming to the wedding feast with the correct "wedding garment" in Jesus' parable is equated with coming prepared to, and by properly celebrating, the Lord's Table.[69] He reiterates the imperative of preparation in emotional and moving language.[70] Preparing for the "gospel wedding feast" [i. e., the Lord's Supper] is "the best work you can be employed in … it is God-glorifying work, it's Christ-magnifying work, it is grace-advancing work, it's soul-ennobling work, it's sin-mortifying work."[71] Taylor also addresses the issue of not coming to the

---

64 Grabo, ed., *Edward Taylor's Treatise*, 19. In Taylor's original text, he writes "wedden" instead of "wedding." I have modernized his text throughout this section.

65 *Edward Taylor's Treatise*, 19–20.

66 Taylor notes the "glory and honor put upon all such as come preparedly to celebrate this gospel marriage feast." and "this is the honor and glory that God confers on all such as rightly attend this wedding. They are invited guests, they come preparedly. They are adorned with the highest ornaments of the gospel; they are admitted into the Bridegroom's presence; the richest dainties of gospel provision are made for their entertainment." Grabo, ed., *Edward Taylor's Treatise*, 20.

67 Grabo, ed., *Edward Taylor's Treatise*, 20–21.

68 Grabo, ed., *Edward Taylor's Treatise*, 21–22.

69 Grabo, ed., *Edward Taylor's Treatise*, 22–23.

70 "Not to prepare is a contempt of the invitation and of the wedding; it is to fall short of the end of the invitation to you, which is nextly your preparation. Wherefore consider of this. It is to abide in a sordid and filthy, naked and sinful state. It is to abide without the wedding garment, which is a right beautiful garment. It is therefore to abide graceless and damnable, and what shame is this? Oh! strive to avoid this shame by preparing for this wedding supper." Grabo, ed., *Edward Taylor's Treatise*, 23.

71 Grabo, ed., *Edward Taylor's Treatise*, 23–24.

Supper. For Taylor, serious preparation should enable us to come to the Supper, and not "neglect" it.[72] Because participating in the Supper is commanded by God, not coming is culpable: "Consider that you greatly damnify yourselves in not coming to this gospel feast."[73]

Although Taylor does not mention him by name until later in this series of sermons, Stoddard is a clear target when Taylor denies that the sacrament is a "converting" ordinance. It strengthens the faith, and the grace present in those partake, but it does not create faith or grace.[74] Taylor repeats this point throughout the sermons, from various angles, as he mounts a full-scale rebuttal of Stoddard and others who believe the Lord's Supper was a converting ordinance.[75] When he does name Stoddard, he groups him with Erastus, William Prynne, and other "anti-disciplinarians" that "suck in" the errors of Erastus. Taylor clearly sees a connection between one's views on church discipline and whether the Supper is a converting ordinance. Taylor responds to Stoddard in exhaustive detail, though he only quotes Stoddard infrequently. Rather, the bulk of Taylor's treatise is an extended exegesis of the text of Matthew 22:12, which keeps returning—almost to the point of redundancy—to the assertion that the Lord's Supper is not a converting ordinance. He also adds many exhortations as to how to properly prepare, approach, and partake of the sacrament. His belief about the restrictions that should surround the Supper reflects, and is kept in balance by, his deep belief in the spiritual power and efficacy of partaking of it, while robed in the "wedding garment" of saving faith in Jesus Christ.[76]

---

72 "Come and celebrate this supper. You are called to it. You ought therefore to come. Being prepared and so fit to honor the King by your approach, see that you come to this feast. Oh! you ought not to neglect such a call; you will never be able to answer such a neglect, and you must be called to an account for it." Grabo, ed., *Edward Taylor's Treatise*, 24.

73 Grabo, ed., *Edward Taylor's Treatise*, 25.

74 "Hence it appears that the gospel wedding feast or the Lord's Supper is no converting ordinance; it's not a grace begetting ordinance. That it never was ordained of God to give the first grace, but that it is only a grace strengthening ordinance." Grabo, ed., *Edward Taylor's Treatise*, ed., 41.

75 Grabo, ed., *Edward Taylor's Treatise*, 64, 66.

76 He ends his treatise with: "The feast will nourish thee. Thou wilt grow by it. It's wholesome food for such as have a principle concoctive of it. And all those that have the wedding garment are such as have this principle. It's a principle of spiritual life, and this is conveyed into the soul with the wedding garment. Hence this food will nourish thee … Christ provided what will be suitable to their state, and hence it will nourish and cherish, and therefore thou wilt find it make for thy spiritual proficiency and growth in grace. This is for thy comfort." Grabo, ed., *Edward Taylor's Treatise*, 221.

5.6   Samuel Willard (1640–1707)

The Sacramental Meditations (1711) of Samuel Willard provide a good example of the dilemma of frequency or preparation. Willard served as a vice-president of Harvard College and a teacher at Boston's Third, or South, Church.[77] Willard's *Sacramental Meditations* are a series of expositions of the chief points of theology, which usually conclude with an application to the Lord's Supper. The emphasis is on helping readers prepare themselves spiritually to receive and benefit from communion.

At the end of his book, in the last two meditations, Willard confronts the issue of whether to participate in communion in an interesting format, namely by interviewing himself. Although these dialogues with himself are hypothetical, they surely reveal how many wrestled with the issues of communion and participation in colonial Boston. Willard's treatment reveals the dynamics of acknowledging the

demand and duty of coming to communion, while also doubting one's worthiness to come. The subtitle of the last two meditations is "Discouragements Revisited." Meditation XLIII focuses on doubts about having an "Interest in Christ" and Meditation XLIV on doubts fueled by the "Sense of Former Unprofitableness." In Meditation XLIII he delves into the "dilemma" he feels between participation and preparation. He feels the weight of his "covenantal" obligation to participate in the "ordinance" of communion but is afraid to come. As he states, "I am afraid to tarry away and I am afraid to go."[78] He decides that, if he were sure it was his duty to come, that he would do so.

In this connection, Willard also considers the question of whether the sacrament is a "converting" ordinance or not. If it were a "converting" ordinance, like the "Preaching of the Word," then he would be sure to come. He would not worry excessively about his worthiness to come, because it would be a duty for all to come, just as it is a duty for all to sit under the preaching of the Word.[79] However, if he believed that the sacrament was only for the nourishing and strengthening of those

---

77 Davies, *The Worship of the American Puritans*, 185.

78 Samuel Willard, *Some Brief Sacramental Meditations, Preparatory for Communion at the Great Ordinance of the Supper* (Boston: B. Green, 1711), 234. He explains: "I dare not stay behind because Christ himself hath said, *Do this in Remembrance of me*; and made it a Sacred Ceremony for the showing forth of his Death till he cometh. And if I absent my self, I shall Scandalize the Profession that I have made: and if I Go, that awful word terrifies me, *He that eats and drinks unworthily, eats and drinks Judgment to himself*: and if I may be a true believer and yet come under this guilt, how much more then, if I am still out of Christ, and have never received him by a Saving Faith?"

79 Willard, *Sacramental Meditations*, 234.

who have true faith, then he would be more anxious about coming in an unfit manner.[80] He indicates that this is his actual position.

He argues that the officers of the church have a special obligation to make sure that only those who are worthy come to participate in the Lord's Table, through a process of "Observation or Trial."[81] Willard clearly has in mind a process of examination by the elders, and of some sort of ecclesiastical discipline for those who are living in "Notorious Pollution."[82] Willard compares the prohibition in the Law against someone with leprosy participating in the Passover, and claims it is similar to someone in the New Covenant era who comes to the Lord's Supper, but is still an "utter Stranger to Regeneration and Sanctification."[83] He stresses the need for self-examination and for keeping watch over the state of our souls, to ensure that we do not "pollute" the sacrament.[84] He reminds his readers that, when someone comes to communion in an obviously unconverted state, this action "despiseth the Lord of Glory, and tramples upon the blood of the Covenant."[85]

Willard then states the crux of the New England Puritan dilemma, regarding participation in communion: "How then shall I dare to come to this Ordinance until I am fully assured of mine interest in Christ by a thorough Conversion?"[86] He asks "[s]hall I come or shall I tarry away?"[87] He risks coming as a "Hypocrite" and bringing judgment on himself. Yet, if stays away, he risks neglecting the ordained means of grace.[88] Furthermore, if he stays away until he gains "full Assurance," would that not slow down the process of gaining assurance? What if he dies without attaining assurance?[89]

---

80 "But if it is not by appointment, a Converting Ordinance, but for the *Nourishment* of Grace in the Converted, (of which I am persuaded) I then conclude, that though I Sin in that I remain unworthy, and do not restlessly Seek after the Grace to make me fit, and by this discover that I vilely undervalue this Ordinance; yet I should Sin more in coming, when I am assured that I am in my Sins." Willard, *Sacramental Meditations*, 234–35.

81 Willard, *Sacramental Meditations*, 235.

82 Willard, *Sacramental Meditations*, 235.

83 Willard, *Sacramental Meditations*, 236.

84 Willard, *Sacramental Meditations*, 236.

85 Willard, *Sacramental Meditations*, 238.

86 Willard, *Sacramental Meditations*, 238. He continues: "For if I am not Converted, I sin in coming" but he realizes he might be "deceived," and even though he believes he sees evidence of the Spirit's work in his life, he is in "suspense" over whether these works are really "Counterfeit."

87 Willard, *Sacramental Meditations*, 238.

88 "Or shall I fly away, and therein if I am one of his, neglect a precious Medium of Communion with him, and hinder my self of that Fellowship with him which is to be had in this Ordinance, and thereby signify an undervaluing esteem of it, and thus add to grieve his holy Spirit?" Willard, *Sacramental Meditations*, 239.

89 "Shall I tarry till I have gotten a full Assurance before I come; and will not my thus absenting my self be a great hindrance to my gaining of it? Is not God Sovereign? doth [sic] he not keep many of his

As Willard counsels himself, and his readers, he focuses on the grace of God, who receives those who are "weak in Faith as well as the strong."[90] Moments of doubt and weakness are the most important times for us to come to the Lord's Supper.[91] Coming to communion is a vital means of strengthening faith in Christ and union with him: "If ever I have loved him, it becomes me to maintain that love, and not to impair it by alienation from his Communion."[92] Despite his doubts and misgivings about not being worthy, Willard ends with hopefulness and an attitude of relying on God's promises of grace to those who honestly admit their need of it.[93]

In Meditation XLIV Willard asks a series of questions that center on the possibility that he came to the sacrament in the wrong way, which may be why he did not feel the sense of communion that he hoped for in the sacrament. These questions once again reveal the Puritan dilemma caused by the dual emphasis on proper preparation and frequent participation.[94] He asks "[s]hall I measure my Duty by the Success?"[95] In other words, he reminds himself that it is his duty to come to the Lord's Supper, regardless of what spiritual experiences he may, or may not, have during communion.

As in the previous meditation, Willard ends with hope and faith. Much like Job, he resolves "though he hide his Face, I will wait for him."[96] Furthermore, "I know that the Command is my warrant; and for me to neglect will be my Sin: and I believe that the blessing is his Prerogative to give."[97] Thus, although Willard wrestles with

---

own Children in darkness, doubts, and fears all their days? If I absent till then, it is possible that I may live & dye without this Ordinance." Willard, *Sacramental Meditations*, 239.

90 Willard, *Sacramental Meditations*, 239.

91 "Never hath a Soul more need of getting near to Christ, than when Satan and a misgiving heart offer most strongly to persuade it to call in question its interest in him." Willard, *Sacramental Meditations*, 240.

92 Willard, *Sacramental Meditations*, 240.

93 "My faith and love are so weak, and the contrary Corruption in me is so strong, that it grieves me, it shakes me, it gives mine Adversary the advantage to frighten me: but yet I know that there is an Evidence which encourageth the drooping Soul to wait on the Lord." Willard, *Sacramental Meditations*, 241.

94 "Though I have used the Means, yet I may have erred in the Manner of my Attendance upon them," and, "Possibly I went for Comfort, when I wanted Abasement: I was too proud in my Preparations, and for that reason he with-held the Manifestations of himself to me; and in this very withdrawing he left a sensible touch on me, which was a fruit and witness of his being still with me after the best manner." Willard, *Sacramental Meditations*, 246–47.

95 Willard, *Sacramental Meditations*, 247.

96 Willard, *Sacramental Meditations*, 247.

97 Willard, *Sacramental Meditations*, 248. And finally, he ends: "I come to thee, that thou wilt graciously remove all that is impedimental to my free and full communion with thee: I cannot do it for my Self, but I look to thee who art able to do it in and for me." Willard, *Sacramental Meditations*, 248.

his own unworthiness to come to the Eucharist, he ends by reaffirming his faith in God's command to come, and the belief that his faith in God's goodness will enable him to come in a worthy manner. In these *Meditations*, Willard provides a window into the inner world of a New England Puritan, wrestling with the themes of being worthy to come to communion, trying to prepare himself to receive, and ultimately trusting in God to enable him to come, and to make him worthy.

5.7 Cotton Mather (1663–1728)

As one of the last, and perhaps one of the most influential, transmitters of the Puritan tradition in the New World, Cotton Mather's legacy is complex. He viewed his own time as one of degeneration and departure from the ideals of the first generation of Puritan immigrants. In his voluminous writings, he strove to capture, preserve, and pass on the intense devotion to God and to the pursuit of purity that had characterized so many of those who had journeyed to the colonies. However, he did not simply transmit everything uncritically. Mather wrote for his own time, and modified his theological inheritance for his own purposes.

For instance, in the introduction to his life of Jonathan Mitchel, published in 1697, Cotton Mather distanced himself from Mitchel's, and his own father Increase's, insistence that one should be able to recount their conversion experience before being able to join a church. But Cotton Mather also warned against the other extreme of "*Laxness* in Admission to the Lord's *Holy Table*."[98] Mather also directly attacks those who believe the Lord's Supper was a "converting ordinance" in this introduction. If it was, then should not the "heathen" come to communion, so they can be converted?[99] He holds up Mitchel as a model pastor for how he examined people before communion.[100] Mather reminds his readers that maintaining and protecting the "purity" of the Lord's Table was one main motivation for those who came to the "Wilderness" of New England. He exhorts his readers not to abandon

---

98 Cotton Mather, *Ecclesiastes: The Life of the Reverend & Excellent Jonathan Mitchel* (Boston, 1697; Ann Arbor: Text Creation Partnership, 2011), Epistle Dedicatory, 7, http://name.umdl.umich.edu/N00651.0001.001.

99 "But above all, their Notion is to be Rejected, as a *Church corrupting Principle*, who Assert that the *Sacrament* is a *Converting Ordinance*. *Papists, Erastians*, and some others, whom I forbear to mention have so taught; but their *Heterodoxy* has been abundantly Refuted ... If the Sacrament were appointed to be *Converting Ordinance*, then the most *Scandalous* in the World, yea, *Heathen* people ought to it Administered unto them, for we may not withhold from them the Means appointed for their *Conversion*." Mather, *Ecclesiastes*, 10.

100 Mather, *Ecclesiastes*, 7–8.

this legacy.[101] However, it was difficult to balance the dueling priorities of examining people before communion, and encouraging them to come more frequently.

By 1714/15 Cotton Mather and other New England ministers had to exhort their congregations about the importance of coming to the Lord's Supper. No doubt many parishioners had taken the dire warnings about the dangers of unworthy partaking to heart, and hesitated to approach the sacrament. Mather's *A Monitor for Communicants* was subtitled "An Essay to Excite and Assist Religious Approaches to the Table of the Lord."[102] At the end of his pamphlet, Mather includes "A Testimony," written by a number of New England minsters who had gathered in Dedham, in 1714, to address the issue of "children of the covenant" who were not coming to the sacrament ("neglecting" it) because of their feelings of being unfit and unprepared.[103] This neglect was a serious matter for these pastors, and leads logically to provoking the "wrath of God."[104] Furthermore, this neglect is "diametrically opposite to the required glorifying of God's Name, and Advancement of his Kingdom, and doing of his Will."[105] To help remedy this chronic neglect, they recommend Cotton Mather's *A Monitor for Communicants* as a very "solid and orthodox" work, that will help to remove the objection that people feel "unfit" to come to the Table of the Lord.[106] Additionally, they believe Mather's tract will contribute to the "desired Reformation of the aforesaid Neglect of the LORD'S SUPPER" and they solemnly

---

101 "*To use all Lawful means to keep Church Communion pure, is a Duty incumbent upon all Churches, and most eminently on Churches in New England. It is known to the World, that Church Reformation, and Purity as to all Administrations therein, was the Thing designed by our Fathers, when they followed the Lord into this Wilderness: And therefore Degeneracy in that Respect would be a Greater Evil in us, than in any People.*" Mather, *Ecclesiastes*, 16.

102 Cotton Mather, *A Monitor for Communicants. An Essay To Excite and Assist Religious Approaches to the Table of the Lord. Offered by an Assembly of the New-English Pastors, unto their own Flocks, and unto all the Churches in these American Colonies; with A Solemn Testimony to that Cause of God, and Religion, in them* (Boston: S Kneeland, 1750; originally published in 1715).

103 According to the pamphlet, the context was that "very many of the Children of the Covenant do contentedly persevere in a most scandalous and criminal Neglect of that holy Ordinance; most absurdly justifying their Delinquency therein by an Allegation of their unfitness and unpreparedness for it, which it self [sic] is an heinous Iniquity." Mather, *A Monitor*, 14–15. The other ministers who signed the document were Zechariah Whitman, Peter Thacher, John Norton, John Danforth, Joseph Belcher, and Nathanael Eeles." Mather, *A Monitor*, 16.

104 "And for as much as by this Means the spiritual and eternal Estates of Men are under no small Disadvantages, and the visible Covenant-People of GOD dreadfully exposed unto unchurching & discovenanting Dispensations, under the provoked Wrath of Heaven," Mather, *A Monitor*, 15.

105 Mather, *A Monitor*, 15.

106 Mather, *A Monitor*, 15.

charge all their readers to repent of their neglect and to come to Lord's Supper as they should.[107]

In Mather's *Monitor* itself, he stresses the value and necessity of coming to the Lord's Table, in a "worthy" manner.[108] Coming to the Lord's Table in a "worthy" fashion is important for spiritual health: "Worthy Approaches to the Table of the Lord, are excellent Actions; and they have a Tendency to make excellent Christians."[109] Mather provides a long list of the spiritual advantages of coming to the Table in a "worthy Manner." Among other blessings, it can confirm faith, and provide a remedy for "distempers" in our souls and minds.[110] He forcefully asks, "Oh! Why will you deny, to your selves, these great Consolations of God?"[111] He knew the response would be a reference to the feeling of being "unworthy" and to the fear of being "judged" by God for communing in an unworthy manner.[112] This is the answer that Mather represents as being a common excuse, and it is probable that many people in New England did indeed labor under these feelings of spiritual unworthiness and fear of judgement.

Mather responds by turning this excuse back on those who gave it. He asks whether they have tried to prepare themselves to come, or if they are just making excuses. It is a sin to come in an unworthy way, but also a sin to simply make excuses about not being worthy.[113] Mather encourages his readers to come to the Lord's Supper if they have faith, even if they are not sure about the sincerity of their faith. If there is no glaring hypocrisy in their lives, any amount of faith qualifies them to come, which is their "duty."[114]

---

107 "And in the Name of the LORD JESUS CHRIST, We solemnly Charge such of our People as are guilty of the scandalous neglect of the sacred Supper of the Lord, to endeavour to repent and reform, as they will Answer to their great Judge at the Last Day." Mather, *A Monitor*, 16.

108 "It is much to be desired; and how sweet unto our Soul, would be the Desire accomplished! That the TABLE of the LORD may be more generally, and after the most worthy Manner approach'd unto!" Mather, *A Monitor*, 1. The emphasis here is on encouraging people to come to communion whenever it is offered, and to not make excuses for neglecting it.

109 Mather, *A Monitor*, 1.

110 Mather, *A Monitor*, 2. He continues, "It would comfort you under your Temptations, and with comfortable Seals thereof bring home the everlasting Love of God unto you. It would admit you to intimate Interviews with Heaven, and advance you to heavenly Satisfaction and Assurance, be a sweet Emblem of your coming to sit with your Saviour in his heavenly Places."

111 Mather, *A Monitor*, 2.

112 Mather, *A Monitor*, 2-3.

113 "Have you done, all that you can do, that you may not come Unworthily? If you have not, then you stay away Unworthily. 'Tis a Sin, to come Unworthily. But, Sirs, 'tis also a Sin to stay away Unworthily." Mather, *A Monitor*, 3.

114 "Tho' you are not fully sure, of your Sincerity, yet you may come, and may do it in Faith, inasmuch as you have no Evidence remaining, to proclaim and pronounce a predominant Hypocrisy: You

Mather details how his readers should prepare themselves to come to the sacrament. After they cry out to God, to ask for his help, admitting their inability to make themselves worthy, Mather distinguishes two aspects of preparation: habitual and actual.[115] "Habitual" preparation is our daily state of mind, or soul, and could also be described as meditation. Mather encourages his readers to mediate on important spiritual truths such as God's covenant of grace and our appropriate response to it, Jesus' sacrifice for our sins, and to be sensitive to the "working" of grace in our souls.[116] All this is the "habitual" preparation that should precede coming to the Lord's Supper. Mather is describing the state of mind, and pattern of life, that should characterize one who is ready to come to the sacrament in a "worthy" manner.

Beyond this "habitual" preparation is the "actual" preparation, which should take up as much time as is necessary to bring our souls "in an heavenly Temper."[117] In the actual preparation, one should first review and evaluate their "habitual" preparation, to ensure it is thoroughly enough.[118] Then, following the injunction of 1 Cor. 11:28, one should enter into a time of rigorous self-examination.[119] Mather first presents a list of questions to use for spiritual self-interrogation, and then offers further directions about the process of self-examination and preparation. He directs his readers to focus on doing the necessary work of preparation *now*, rather than worrying about their past failings.[120] He reminds his readers that the "Church is a Hospital," where they need to come for healing. But this pastoral sensitivity to human frailty is quickly overshadowed by a renewed emphasis on the work of preparation and a detailed description of how to participate fully in every aspect of the communion service.

Mather describes this process of sacramental meditation as the "worthy Manner of coming unto the Table of the Lord."[121] He limits himself to two main directives. First, during the communion service, we should meditate on the spiritual mean-

---

have now no evident Bar to your doing of your Duty; and so you may and must go on with your Duty." Mather, *A Monitor*, 3.

115 Mather, *A Monitor*, 5–7.

116 Mather, in a typically Puritan fashion, attempts to balance the need for holy desires without demanding perfection: "Tho' you may be discouraged by the Defects which may still attend the Work of Grace in your Souls, yet you must feel the working of holy Desires in your Souls, to have that Work effectually carried on." Mather, *A Monitor*, 7.

117 Mather, *A Monitor*, 8. He writes, "A time is to be set apart for it, a little before your coming. You must not begrudge Time for such a weighty and awful Affair." Mather, *A Monitor*, 7.

118 "You best prove that you have done the Things that accompany Salvation, by doing of them." Mather, *A Monitor*, 8.

119 Mather, *A Monitor*, 8–11.

120 Mather, *A Monitor*, 11.

121 Mather, *A Monitor*, 12.

ings behind the sacramental actions and symbols.[122] Here, Mather follows a long tradition of exhortations in sacramental manuals, without adding anything new or original. Mather clearly desires his readers to have a deeply moving experience during communion.[123] Mather's second directive is to make every moment count during the communion experience. This continues the theme of self-examination, but here the focus is on the future. Mather basically encourages his readers to make spiritual resolutions and to set goals for their further sanctification, fueled and motivated by their communion experience. His assumption is that the experience of the Lord's Supper will help the one person making spiritual resolutions to keep them, or at least make progress in them.[124]

Although Mather does not specifically discuss the issue of communion frequency in this work, he exemplifies the tension that existed in the Puritan churches of New England. On the one hand, Mather exhorts his readers to undertake the difficult and serious business of preparation and soul-searching before coming to communion. On the other, he directly addresses the problem of habitual neglect of the sacrament in New England churches. Thus, Mather is seeking to correct a problem which was created, in part, by the Puritan emphasis on the need to prepare properly before the Lord's Supper.

In 1726, Cotton Mather published the much more extensive *Ratio disciplinae fratrum Nov.-anglorum*. It addresses larger questions than just communion, but it still provides valuable information about Mather's ideals and New England Puritan practice. The main motives of his work are to explain and defend the organization, structure, and worship of the Congregational churches in New England.[125] When

---

122 "You must behold the Sacramental Elements, and the Sacramental Actions; and affect your Hearts with suitable and Heart-melt[ing?] Meditations upon them." Mather, *A Monitor*, 12.

123 As one example among several meditations Mather suggests: "When the Bread is taken by the Pastor; and so anon, when the Wine is taken, Your Tho[ught] must be on that Subject; I see, I see, how t[he] Son of God has taken our Nature; how the Wor[d] was made flesh. When the Bread is blessed; Your Thought[s] are to be: Thus was my Jesus consecrated, an[d] set apart for the Work of a Redeemer. And anon, when the Wine has Thanks given upon i[t,] Your Thoughts are to be Oh! What Thank[s] what Thanks do I owe for my Jesus!" Mather, *A Monitor*, 12.

124 He writes: "You may find intervening Spaces, while you are about this Work of the Lord, for [t]o prosecute many special Designs of Godliness, which would here have then most effectual Prosecution. There are intervening Pauses, where[o]f 'tis a Pity a Moment should be lost." Mather, *A Monitor*, 14.

125 "THOSE *English Colonies* in *America,* which are distinguished by the Name of NEW-ENGLAND, were formed upon the Glorious Design, of erecting CHURCHES, wherein the *Reformation* should be carried on, unto farther Degrees of Scriptural and Primitive *Purity*; than would be allowed by the *Times* in *Europe*, not yet wholly recovered out of the *Antichristian Apostacy* [= Roman Catholicism, GS]." *Ratio disciplinae fratrum Nov-Anglorum. A faithful account of the discipline professed and practised; in the churches of New-England. : With interspersed and instructive reflections on the discipline of the primitive churches. : [Seven lines from Ezekiel]* (Boston:: Printed for S. Gerrish in

Mather describes the colonial communion practices, he provides insight into the actual practices of preparation that formed the eucharistic context of Puritan New England:

> When the LORD's SUPPER is to be administered, the *Pastor* gives Notice of it a Week before hand. And when the *Lord's Day* for it arrives, he usually accommodates the solemn Occasion before him, with a Sermon upon some agreeable *Doctrine of the Gospel.* In most Places there are held *private Meetings* of the Christians, on some Day of the Week, *Preparatory* to the Communion; and it is a frequent thing for the Pastor to be present at some or other of them; or else perhaps to hold a *Public Lecture.*[126]

This vignette fits comfortably with the Puritan emphasis on preparation and an intellectual understanding of the Lord's Supper. Mather carried on the tradition of stressing the importance of purity and preparation, even as he helped to cultivate a vibrant eucharistic theology.

5.8 Jonathan Edwards (1705–1758)

Jonathan Edwards, the grandson of Solomon Stoddard, succeeded him as the Congregationalist pastor in Northampton, Massachusetts. As a leader in the Great Awakening, he also shared many of the typical Puritan views about the nature of preparation and participation in the Lord's Supper. A brief survey of some of Edwards' sermons reveals his strong belief in the spiritual blessings that come from partaking of the sacrament, counter-balanced by the necessity to prepare beforehand through self-examination. This survey will begin with Edwards' sermon on 1 Cor. 10:16, and then briefly summarize relevant portions of other sermons that address either the themes of frequency or preparation.

In Sermon 1 (no date given), Edwards expounds on 1 Cor. 10:16, and explains the various types of communion that we have in the Lord's Supper. We have communion with Christ, communion with other Christians throughout the world, and communion with the "church triumphant in heaven."[127] He writes "[w]e have in this sacrament the sum of the gospel in sensible signs."[128] Because of the deep realities of what occurs spiritually in communion, Edwards rebukes those who "neglect"

Cornhill., 1726; Ann Arbor: Text Creation Partnership, 2011), 1, http://name.umdl.umich.edu/N02341.0001.001.

126 Mather, *Ratio disciplinae fratrum Nov-Anglorum*, 96.
127 Edwards, *Sermons on the Lord's Supper*, Don Kistler, ed. (Orlando: The Northampton Press, 2007), 7–10.
128 Edwards, *Sermons on the Lord's Supper*, 17.

it and do not participate when it is offered. They are "guilty of casting a visible contempt upon the body and blood of Christ."[129] Edwards contrasts his context with the early church where "there was not in the primitive times of the church such a neglect of this ordinance amongst professing Christians as is nowadays."[130] Christians have "very express and positive commands" to attend the sacrament. If they "live in neglect of it," how can they expect God to bless them?[131]

A common excuse for not coming to the Supper is that people "aren't prepared to come, and [they claim] it is not their duty to come when they are not prepared."[132] Those who make this excuse are not being serious about their religious duties in general.[133] For those who are serious, the answer is to focus on preparing themselves, so that they can come to the Supper.[134] Edwards sternly warns "your unpreparedness won't lighten your punishment for your neglect of your duty."[135]

There is a process to follow to prepare before coming to the Supper. We must "carefully and strictly examine ourselves whether we are in any way of sin."[136] This is a serious business because "[i]f we allowedly live in any way of wickedness and yet come to the Lord's Supper, it will dreadfully aggravate our guilt."[137] Appealing to 1 Cor. 11:28, and Paul's warnings about self-examination, Edwards proposes: "We should, before every sacrament make a set business of examining ourselves."[138] Other ways to prepare thoroughly include: making sure we are "in charity with our brethren," meditating on the meaning of the "ordinance" of the Lord's Supper, prayer for God's "presence and blessing … so that we may see Christ at His Table," making sure the "holy, pure, and solemn ordinance" is not "defiled." For Edwards, and for most Puritans, it is important to prohibit people from coming to the Supper if they are living in open defiance of God's standards—what Edwards describes as being "openly scandalous."[139] Additionally, participating in the sacrament should motivate us to more seriously pursue a life of holiness afterwards.[140]

---

129 Edwards, *Sermons on the Lord's Supper*, 20.
130 Edwards, *Sermons on the Lord's Supper*, 22.
131 Edwards, *Sermons on the Lord's Supper*, 22.
132 Edwards, *Sermons on the Lord's Supper*, 22.
133 "Their concern for their souls is not great enough to bring them here as appears by their neglect of other appointed duties." Edwards, *Sermons on the Lord's Supper*, 23.
134 Edwards, *Sermons on the Lord's Supper*, 23.
135 Edwards, *Sermons on the Lord's Supper*, 24. Additionally, "Your punishment for abstaining won't be the less for your willfully unfitting yourself."
136 Edwards, *Sermons on the Lord's Supper*, 25–26.
137 Edwards, *Sermons on the Lord's Supper*, 26.
138 Edwards, *Sermons on the Lord's Supper*, 26.
139 Edwards, *Sermons on the Lord's Supper*, 28–29.
140 Edwards, *Sermons on the Lord's Supper*, 29–30.

In Sermon 2, preached in 1732, on 1 Cor. 11:26, Edwards explains more about what it means to be "fit," or worthy to partake of the Lord's Table. The main qualification for coming is *not* feeling qualified to come. In other words, if we feel a deep sense of our unworthiness to come, then we should definitely come.[141] The more we see our sinfulness, the more we should also see our need to be strengthened spiritually through the sacrament.[142] The sermon ends with a reminder of the importance of coming, of forsaking sins, and of rejoicing at the opportunity to participate in the "holy and sacred" event.[143]

Sermon 3, on Luke 22:19 (1734), contains a hint of Edwards' view about communion frequency. One of the reasons presented for participating in communion is that it is "necessary for our good that we should often remember the Lord Jesus Christ." Additionally, "[w]e need frequently to remember Christ to excite in us acts of faith in Him" and "[w]e need often to remember Christ to excite us to imitate Him."[144] Another reason to commune is that, "Christ is now absent from us as to His humble Person. We should therefore frequently remember Him … We need such helps to remember Christ, for we are very apt to forget Him."[145]

Sermon 4, on 1 Cor. 10:17, preached in January 1750/51, contains material that relates directly to the issue of whether communion is a "converting" ordinance or not. In this matter, Edwards parted ways with his grandfather Solomon Stoddard. Edwards clearly believes that the Supper is only for those who can claim some sort of experiential relationship with Jesus Christ.[146] It is a family meal. Therefore, he rejects the idea that one can become part of the family through this meal. One must be part of the family first.[147] The sermon ends with both an invitation to attend the Lord's Supper as a "feast of love," and a call to "examine ourselves as to our walk."[148]

---

141 "But if you are sensible of your need of Christ and His salvation … you are one who is evangelically fit. 'Tis true, you are unworthy to come to the Lord's Supper, or the least mercy in the world; but if your unworthiness is what you acknowledge and lament and deplore, you are one who is evangelically fit." Edwards, *Sermons on the Lord's Supper*, 48.

142 "Again, if you say that you are sinful, that you see so much sin and corruption in yourself, so much the more you need to come and receive Christ's body and blood." Edwards, *Sermons on the Lord's Supper*, 49.

143 Edwards, *Sermons on the Lord's Supper*, 50–53.

144 Edwards, *Sermons on the Lord's Supper*, 65.

145 Edwards, *Sermons on the Lord's Supper*, 66.

146 "Hence such as know that they have no such union with Christ and His people ought not to come to this ordinance." Edwards, *Sermons on the Lord's Supper*, 76.

147 "The very notion of a church sitting down together at the Lord's Table is God's family sitting down at this table as His children. Therefore, the design is not to make men children of God. They aren't admitted into the family so that they may be received into the family." Edwards, *Sermons on the Lord's Supper*, 77.

148 Edwards, *Sermons on the Lord's Supper*, 78.

Sermon 5, on 1 Cor. 10:16 (1745), explains various aspects of what "communion" means and stresses the familiar themes of guarding the purity of the sacrament, examining ourselves regularly, and taking care that we do not approach the Supper in an "unworthy" manner. The distinguishing mark of being "unworthy" is not examining ourselves.[149]

Sermon 6, on 1 Cor. 11:28-29 (1756), dwells at length on the topic of self-examination before partaking of the Supper, since that is the main thrust of the sermon text. This is also one of the few places in this selection of sermons where the issue of communion frequency is directly addressed. The New Testament church observed the Lord's Supper "very often," perhaps even daily (based on Acts 2:46 and Acts 20:7).[150] But, based on Paul's rebuke to the Corinthians in 1 Cor. 11:28-29, Edwards concludes that this frequency basically bred contempt. The Corinthians quickly fell into various abuses of the sacrament, and Edwards posits that these abuses were facilitated by the frequency of communion in Corinth.[151]

He also elaborates on what it means to be "unfit" to receive communion.[152] It is not a matter of whether we deserve it, because no one deserves God's grace. It is a matter of whether we admit our sins, hide nothing, and are earnestly trying to live according to God's standards. The basic problem is that those who are unworthy are harboring sin in some form or fashion. Edwards presents a detailed list of ways in which to examine oneself before coming to the Lord's Table. If his hearers really took this to heart and tried to follow his suggestions before every communion, that would take strenuous effort. Edwards here exemplifies the Puritan emphases on preparation and examination that mitigated against any desires or ideals for more frequent communion: "Let this doctrine warn all persons carefully to examine themselves before they come to the Lord's Supper so that they don't seal their own damnation."[153]

---

149 Edwards, *Sermons on the Lord's Supper*, 94–95.

150 "They were wont to have the sacrament of the Lord's Supper in the primitive church very often, by all accounts of ecclesiastical history; and it seems by the account of holy Scripture that they were at first wont to celebrate this ordinance daily." Edwards, *Sermons on the Lord's Supper*, 98.

151 "And it coming so frequently the Corinthians, it seems, were wont to improve it for a profane use, that is, for the same end as they did their meals in their own houses, to satisfy their hunger and thirst and to nourish their bodies." Edwards, *Sermons on the Lord's Supper*, 98.

152 "They who come with this unfitness or in this unworthy manner, all the while living in known sins or having never truly resolved against living in such sins, and harboring a spirit of hatred and ill will to their brethren, or aiming at nothing else but only some by-end perfectly depart from the design of the ordinance. They eat and drink judgement to themselves, that is to say, their eating and drinking does but the more expose them to eternal damnation and seals that damnation." Edwards, *Sermons on the Lord's Supper*, 106.

153 Edwards, *Sermons on the Lord's Supper*, 108.

In summary, although in these sermons Edwards often exhorts his hearers in the strongest possible terms to come to the sacrament and not "neglect" it, the emphasis is on preparation and self-examination. These, and similar concerns, eventually led Edwards to believe that some sort of profession of faith should be made before coming to communion. This directly challenged Stoddard's legacy regarding open communion. This was the last straw in an often troubled and contentious relationship between Edwards and his congregation. Conflicts of personality and simmering tensions exploded, and the church voted to dismiss Edwards from his job.[154] This conflict did not involve questions of frequency, but it does illustrate the tangled web that often surrounds questions of church practice and theological disagreements. As Calvin had discovered, theological ideals often conflict and must be tempered by pastoral and political realities. Just as Calvin had once been driven into exile because of his uncompromising stance on church discipline, so Edwards was forced to leave because of his convictions about the qualifications for coming to communion.

Throughout his life, Edwards corresponded with other church leaders abroad and maintained a keen interest in international political events. A letter to the Scottish pastor John Erskine (1721–1803) is one of the few instances where Edwards directly discusses communion frequency. Erskine, as we will see in the next chapter, wrote one of the most influential pleas for more frequent communion in the early 1700s. He published his *An Attempt to Promote the Frequent Dispensing of the Lord's Supper* in 1749, and his friend Thomas Randall (1710–1780) published a similar pamphlet in the same year. Erskine and Randall read each other's works, borrowed from each other, and recommended the other's works to their readers. Erskine acted as a book supplier to Edwards, and others, with the goal of providing good theological literature to other pastors.[155] Erskine also facilitated the publication of many of Edwards' works in Britain.[156]

---

154 For this "qualifications Controversy," see George M. Marsden, *Jonathan Edwards: A Life* (New Haven: Yale University Press, 2003), pgs. 341–374; Alan D. Strange, "Jonathan Edwards and the Communion Controversy in Northampton," *MJT* 14 (2003): 57–97; Ricky F. Njoto, "The Lord's Supper in the Hands of a Sensitive Preacher: The Bible in Edwards' Sermons on 1 Corinthians 10," *Jonathan Edwards Studies*, vol. 9, no. 2 (2019): 28–59.

155 Of the 301 books owned by Edwards at his death, as many as one-third may have been gifts from John Erskine. See Jonathan M. Yeager, *Enlightened Evangelicalism: The Life and Thought of John Erskine* (Oxford: Oxford University Press, 2011), 147. Additionally, "Although widely appreciated as a clergyman, Erskine's primary contribution to evangelicalism was not as a minister, but as a disseminator of information, primarily through the sending and propagating of religious ideas through books." Yeager, 11; see also 147–150 for the friendship between Edwards and Erskine.

156 "Erskine propagated books not only because he loved ideas, but also because he determined that this was the best way that he could contribute to the evangelical revival [both in Britain, and abroad]." Yeager, *Enlightened Evangelicalism*, 12.

Edwards had read, or was familiar, with the efforts of Erskine and Randall to promote more frequent communion in Scotland. On November 15, 1750, eight years before his death, Edwards wrote Erskine. Erskine had sent Edwards a copy of Randall's work, and Edwards gratefully acknowledged the present and affirmed his support of their efforts:

> We ought not only to praise God for every thing that appears favourable to the interests of religion, and to pray earnestly for a general revival, but also to use means that are proper in order to it; and one proper means must be allowed to be, a due administration of Christ's ordinances: one instance of which is that, which you and Mr. Randal have been striving for; *viz.* a restoring the primitive practice of frequent communicating.[157]

Edwards' interaction with John Erskine is a prime example of the trans-Atlantic network that continued in the eighteenth and nineteenth centuries. Just as the first Puritans who came to New England hoped to influence and be an example to Old England, so the efforts of Scottish pastors and theologians to influence changes in communion frequency, or to preserve the traditional patterns of observance, would affect Reformed communities on both sides of the Atlantic in years to come. This network of influences will be explored and developed in the next chapter when the debates about communion frequency began in earnest in the middle of 1700s and early 1800s. That chapter will focus on pastors and theologians who debated the issue of communion frequency in Scotland, which was the provenance of most of the writers, and where the issue of frequency was more urgent because of various cultural and ecclesiastical traditions that had developed there.

5.9 Scots-Irish Influence in Early America and the Seedbed of Revivalism

This survey has so far focused narrowly on the Puritan communities of New England. These were the first waves of immigrants who carried on the Reformed tradition in the New World. They are also foundational because they self-consciously tried to implement reforms that they identified with the "best" Reformed churches on the continent. This, for the New England Puritans, formed an intellectual and spiritual connection with the traditions of church discipline stemming from Bucer, Calvin, and Knox, among others. But the New England Puritans were not the only Protestants to come to the Americas. The first representatives of the Reformed

---

157 *The Works of Jonathan Edwards, With a Memoir by Sereno E. Dwight*, Edward Hickman, ed. (Edinburgh and Carlisle, PA: The Banner of Truth Trust, 1834, repub., 1974, repr., 1995), cxxiii. https://www.ccel.org/ccel/edwards/works1.i.xviii.html.

tradition to come to the New World were indeed the English Dissenters and Puritans. The next wave of Reformed immigrants was the Scotch-Irish. These were Scottish Presbyterians who had first migrated to Ulster, and then came to the Americas.[158] Their first presbytery was formed in Philadelphia in 1706. Before that time, Presbyterian immigrants were scattered and dispersed throughout the colonies.[159]

This is where the relevance and influence of the Scottish Reformed church is most clearly seen in the formation of American Presbyterianism, and in the developing societies of the colonies.[160] These Scottish immigrants brought the tradition of annual, or semi-annual, communion seasons with them. This rhythm of communion frequency set them apart from the Congregational churches, that traced their roots back to their Separatist and Puritan founders.[161] Although the Congregational churches practiced monthly, or sometimes weekly, communion, their high standards for conversion, church membership, and inclusion in the sacrament meant that more Presbyterians participated in the Lord's Supper—even though they observed it less frequently.[162]

The surviving documentary evidence for early Presbyterian communion practices shows clear continuity with the Scottish traditions already surveyed. Accounts of sacramental observances at Londonderry, New Hampshire in 1732 and 1734, at Booth Bay in Maine (April, 1767), and in Western Pennsylvania (c. 1770) recount the typical pattern of annual or semi-annual communion, examination by the elders before communion, multiple ministers assisting in the work, days of preparation, fasting, and preaching beforehand, a thanksgiving service on the Monday after the

---

158 Robert Milton Winter, "American Churches and the Holy Communion: A comparative study in sacramental theology, practice, and piety in the Episcopal, Presbyterian, Methodist, and German Reformed traditions, 1607–1875," PhD diss., (Union Theological Seminary, 1988), 352–54. See also Westerkamp, *Triumph of the Laity: Scots-Irish Piety and the Great Awakening, 1625–1760* (New York: Oxford University Press, 1988).

159 Bradley Longfield, *Presbyterians in American Culture*, 1–2. Some scholars argue that the relative isolation and marginalization of the early Presbyterian communities in the colonies served to accentuate their cultural and religious distinctives, to help preserve their communal identities. See Longfield, *Presbyterians in American Culture*, 4–5; Ned C. Landsman, *Scotland and Its First American Colony, 1683–1765* (Princeton, NJ: Princeton University Press, 1985), 132–34; Westerkamp, *Triumph of the Laity*, 137–38.

160 "Next to the English, the Scots-Irish formed the most numerous group of settlers in the colonies." Winter, "American Churches and the Holy Communion," 354.

161 Winter, "American Churches and the Holy Communion," 355.

162 As Leonard J. Trinterud observes "in one branch of Puritanism the Sacrament was a holy festival, often held out of doors because of the number who participated. In the other branch the Sacrament was a solemn ordinance, observed by half a dozen or ten who were the true church." *The Forming of an American Tradition: A Re-examination of Colonial Presbyterianism* (Philadelphia: Westminster, 1949), 18–19.

communion Sunday, communicants sitting at long tables, and the use of communion tokens.[163] Besides the weight of Scottish tradition, there were also practical concerns about the weather, traveling conditions, and the time taken off from the regular labors of farming demanded by these large communion gatherings. So, at Booth Bay, communion was held twice a year, in April and October. This coincided with natural breaks in the agricultural cycle and afforded better weather for traveling.[164]

According to observers, these communion seasons had many beneficial features. They provided an opportunity for communities to visit with each other, and strengthened social bonds. The extended time of services—spread out over multiple days—increased the spiritual impact of the communions, resulting in many conversions. On a very practical note, these communion seasons also resulted in many marriages.[165] Despite the critiques of communion-frequency reformers, these sacramental occasions fulfilled the spiritual and social needs of the communicants. Because of the infrequency of the communion, and the emotional buildup of special services, sermons, and the large crowds that gathered, these mass communions brought the intensity of Scottish Presbyterian eucharistic piety into the New World.[166] The Scotch-Irish revival tradition led to powerful evangelism and large gatherings, with intense and emotional conversion experiences.

The (first) Great Awakening (ca. 1726–1741) was a continuation of the Irish and Scottish revival tradition and it "arose out of distress over the vast amount of irreligion and the spiritual coldness and unconcern of church members."[167] Holifield notes that the "awakenings" also caused separation between churches, and that these divisions centered on "matters of ritual practice."[168] The movement was anchored

---

163 Winter, "American Churches and the Holy Communion," 360–374.

164 Winter, "American Churches and the Holy Communion," 362, f.n. 170. See Thomas C. Pears and Elizabeth Freeman Reed, "Sessional Records of the Presbyterian Church of Booth Bay, Maine, 1767—1778." *Journal of the Department of History (The Presbyterian Historical Society) of the Presbyterian Church in the U.S.A.* 16, no. 5 (1935): 203–40. Accessed January 30, 2021. http://www.jstor.org/stable/23323779.

165 Winter, "American Churches and the Holy Communion," 373–74.

166 Julius Melton, *Presbyterian Worship in America: Changing Patterns Since 1787* (Louisville: WMJK/Pickwick Publications, 1967/1984; reprint, Eugene: Wipf and Stock Publishers, 2001), 16. See also Longfield, *Presbyterians and American Culture*, 7, 10.

167 Melton, *Presbyterian Worship in America*, 16; Longfield, *Presbyterians and American Culture*, 7–8. See also Frank Lambert, *Inventing the Great Awakening* (Princeton: Princeton University Press, 1999); Thomas S. Kidd, *The Great Awakening: The Roots of Evangelical Christianity in Colonial America* (New Haven and London: Yale University Press, 2007).

168 "During the revivals of the 1740s the discontent created still further separation. The divisions during the great awakening were essentially over matters of ritual practice: who should preach, how sermons should be delivered, who should receive baptism, who should be admitted to the Lord's Supper, how much decorum should mark worship? And those questions were so intense that

firmly in the Scottish revival context, and also possibly influenced by Dutch currents. Gilbert Tennent (1703–1764) was an associate of Theodore Frelinghuysen, a Dutch Reformed priest ministering in New Jersey. Additionally, Gilbert's father William (1673–1746) had started a "Log College" to train ministers in the Scottish model of theological education.[169] Gilbert Tennent and other graduates of the Log College continued this Scots Reformed revival in the American context.[170] The influence on the Scotch-Irish tradition of communion seasons on the growth of American revival movements is well documented.[171] Less known are the sacramental aspects of the preachers, and preaching, of revival.[172]

Preachers like the Tennents and Samuel Davies (1723–1761) sparked popular revival movements, but also maintained a focus on the Lord's Supper. William Tennent urged his hearers to come to the sacrament and "Eat like a person sensible that the king in whose presence thou art, is thy best and greatest friend."[173] Davies exhorted his hearers to realize that the sacrament was also a covenantal "contract" waiting for their consent, and so they should "rise and crowd round the table of the Lord, and there annex our solemn seals, and acknowledge it as

---

between 1745 and 1770 nearly 100 congregations broke from the established churches and formed separate communities: dividing towns, severing relationships, and expanding religious—and ritual—diversity on an unprecedented scale." E. Brooks Holifield, "Peace, Conflict, and Ritual in Puritan Congregations." *The Journal of Interdisciplinary History*, vol. 23, no. 3 (Winter, 1993): 568.

169 Longfield, *Presbyterians and American Culture*, 8.

170 "By 1728 Tennent's preaching was inspiring 'spiritual awakenings' rooted in congregations that had a distinctly Scottish flavor. These were mirrored by awakenings in the surrounding areas led by his brother and other Log College graduates. The Scottish revival tradition generally emphasized that genuine conversions took months to negotiate, with careful instruction in doctrine, under the close watch of a skilled preacher." Longfield, *Presbyterians and American Culture*, 8. This would be one major difference between the first "Great" Awakening and the Second Awakening. In the next large-scale revival movement, the emphasis was placed on more immediate conversion experiences. Worship practices and preaching were all shaped by the goal of motivating sinners to "convert" at the revival meetings, rather than go through a process of soul-searching, as had been characteristic of the Puritan movements.

171 For example, Schmidt, *Holy Fairs* and Westerkamp, *The Triumph of the Laity*.

172 "The Log College men were known for their sacramental preaching, and together published a book of sacramental sermons." Winter, "American Churches and the Holy Communion," 394, referencing Gilbert Tennent, et. al., *Sermons on Sacramental Occasions by Divers Ministers* (Boston: J. Draper, 1739). Bracken Long demonstrates that "the American sacramental occasions exhibited a eucharistic theology that was solidly Reformed yet included a mystical strain, expressed within the context of frontier revivalism." *The Eucharistic Theology of the American Holy Fairs*, 2. See also James B. Bennett, "'Love to Christ'"—Gilbert Tennent, Presbyterian Reunion, and a Sacramental Sermon," *American Presbyterians* (Summer 1993): 77–89.

173 Winter, "American Churches and the Holy Communion," 394, citing William Tennent, "Sermon on 1 Corinthians 11:26," ed. by Thomas C. Pears, *Journal of the Presbyterian Historical Society* 19 (June 1940): 76–84.

our deed and act." If they did not come to the Table, they were rejecting God.[174] Gilbert Tennent reminded readers that feeling unworthy does not disqualify one from attending communion. Neglecting the sacrament shows "ingratitude toward Christ's dying love."[175] But this did not translate into Stoddard's position of viewing the Supper as a converting ordinance. On the contrary, the New Side preachers strongly stressed the purity of the Table and endeavored to keep those who were not repentant from coming. They combined an evangelistic fervor with a desire to bring people to communion, while also fencing the Table.[176] Thus, Presbyterian churches at this time continued to examine prospective communicants and distribute communion tokens, although not with the same rigor as Presbyterians in Scotland.[177] For most of the preachers associated with the Awakening, evangelistic fervor was complementary to a high regard for the Lord's Supper.

5.10 Conclusion

Not everyone who came to the New World came for religious reasons. But for those who did, they had the unprecedented opportunity to construct churches and communities that followed God's mandates in the Scriptures—at least, as they understood them. Despite these high ideals, early American colonies that identified themselves as part of the Reformed tradition, and which were striving to bring the Reformation to its completion, were quickly divided over issues of church membership, baptism, and standards of access to the Lord's Supper. When the Scots-Irish came to the Americas in large numbers, they brought with them their traditions of enthusiastic, deeply spiritual, and evangelistic communion seasons.

---

174 Winter, "American Churches and the Holy Communion," 389, citing Samuel Davies, *Sermons on Important Subjects*, 5 vols. (Baltimore: Mason L. Weems, 1816), 2:139.

175 Winter, "American Churches and the Holy Communion," 390, citing Gilbert Tennent, *The Duty of Self-Examination Considered in a Sermon on 1 Corinthians 11:28 ... Before the Celebration of the Lord's Supper* (Boston: n., 1739), 132, 136, 142–44. See Braken Long, *The Eucharistic Theology of the American Holy Fairs*, chap. 5, for a summary of Gilbert Tennent's sacramental preaching. She notes that "[w]hether in the fields of New Jersey or the streets of Philadelphia, Gilbert Tennent always maintained that the celebration of the Lord's Supper was crucial to the life of faith, that proper preparation was necessary for participation in the sacrament, and that unparalleled comfort and joy are found when the believer meets Christ in communion." 87.

176 "The obligation to fence the Tables was taken with special seriousness by members of the New Side party, though by modern standards the Old Side was far from lax in its practice ... In contrast to the Old Side preachers, the New School evangelists strove to bring every worshiper present to the Lord's Table." Winter, "American Churches and the Holy Communion," 389.

177 Winter, "American Churches and the Holy Communion," 390–393.

These communion seasons formed the site of many of the first large revivals in the American colonies.

Although the Puritans and Scots who came to the New World stressed the importance of preparation and self-examination, this was because they valued the Supper so highly. They believed that God would bless them as they partook of the sacrament, in proportion to their efforts at preparation. Indeed, many pastors and laity had deeply spiritual experiences during communion services. Combined with evangelistic preaching, large crowds, and the revival movement that coalesced into the Great Awakening, communion services played an important role in the formation and development of the young American churches. These churches would continue to be influenced by their English Puritan and Scots-Irish traditions in the mid-1700s and 1800s, as authors on both sides of the Atlantic debated the merits of more frequent communion.

Chapter 6
Scottish Reformed Communion Frequency Debates:
A Trans-Atlantic Perspective (1716–1840)

This overview will seek to answer the final research sub-question (1.2): "What were the key exegetical and polemical strategies of these debates? What can contemporary churches learn from them, as leaders today seek to make wise choices in the matter of communion frequency?" Therefore, it will examine the *main points of argumentation*, and the *typical polemical strategies*, in debates over communion frequency in the Scottish Reformed context of the 1700–1800s. Furthermore, the *historical backgrounds* and *contexts* of both liturgical practices and eucharistic theology will be highlighted. This overview adopts a trans-Atlantic perspective because, although the Scottish communion frequency debates began in Scotland, they spilled over into the Americas through publications and through immigration. These debates were the confluence of many of the themes that have been traced throughout this study. Accordingly, this survey begins with the publication of John Willison's *Sacramental Directory* (1716) and ends with the J.W. Alexander's "The Sacrament of the Lord's Supper" (1840). Although it is somewhat artificial to separate developments in Scotland from those in England, in the 1700s, authors who argued for more frequent communion in the English context tended to be members of the Established church, which increasingly moved away from its Reformed roots, into what can be accurately called a more "Anglican" direction.[1] The similarities and contrasts between Scotland and England in the 1700s and 1800s deserve more research, but that is beyond the scope of this book.[2]

6.1   Theological Voices and Texts

In analyzing the writings of those who argued for or against more frequent communion, the historical situations and contexts of these theological voices will be briefly

---

1 On the importance of frequent communion in the developing Anglican church of the late 1600s and 1700s see, Jeremy Gregory, *Restoration, Reformation, and Reform, 1660–1828*, 264 and Sirota, *The Christian Monitors*, 26–32, 62–63.

2 For a preliminary study see my "Weekly Communion: A Criterion of Catholicity? A Short Survey of Historical Claims in Reformed Debates," in *Reforming the Catholic Tradition: The Whole Word for the Whole Church*, Joseph Minnich, ed. (Leesburg: The Davenant Institute, 2019), 153–197.

summarized. The emphasis will be on discerning the common lines of argumentation and polemical strategies utilized in the frequency debates. Thus, in each case we will ask: What lines of argumentation or polemical strategy does this author use in either promoting or countering more frequent communion? These authors have been chosen because they were the major voices in the frequency debates. Although other sources exist, the authors surveyed here either quote, refer to, or explicitly attack each other much of the time, which manifests their relevance in their own time. Furthermore, some of them continued to be quoted in the American context, reprinted for popular audiences, or even appealed to in contemporary frequency polemics. During the research for this project, only a few sources came to light which defend the Scots Reformed *status quo* of less frequent communion. As is perhaps typical of movements agitating for change, those advocating for change were more vocal and published more material. The following authors will be surveyed in chronological order on the pro-frequency side: John Willison, John Erskine, Thomas Randall, John Mason, and John Brown of Haddington. Defending the Scottish tradition of communion seasons and infrequent communion were John Thomson, John Anderson, and Alexander Duncan. They will be considered after John Mason since they reply directly to his work. After summaries of each of these writers, their arguments and polemical emphases will be compared, contrasted, and analyzed in a concluding section.

6.1.1 John Willison (1680–1750)

John Willison was one of the most popular and influential Scots Presbyterian writers of the 1700s. He served as a pastor in Brechin, and then later in Dundee. His *Sacramental Directory* (1716), *Sacramental Meditations* (1747), *Sacramental Catechism* (1720) and *Young Communicant's Catechism* (1734) were immensely popular (on both sides of the Atlantic), and so shaped the sacramental imagination of an entire generation of Reformed communicants.[3] Willison's works were part of an immense body of sacramental devotional literature that emerged in the late 1600s and extended into the 1800s.[4] He was also one of the ministers, along with George

---

3 Schmidt, *Holy Fairs*, 46. See also Bracken Long, *The Eucharistic Theology of the American Holy Fairs*, 105–109, and Ian MacLeod, "The Sacramental Theology and Practice of the Reverend John Willison (1680–1750)," PhD diss., (University of Glasgow, 1994), chap. 1 for a biographical overview.
4 Schmidt notes that there were, "at least eight American editions of his *Sacramental Meditations* to 1821 and ten American editions of his *Young Communicant's Catechism* to 1839." *Holy Fairs*, 232, note 67. Schmidt shows how important "devotional reading" was in the process of sacramental preparation that all true believers were to undertake before communion: "The devotionals clearly supplemented and supported the spiritual disciplines of self-examination, personal covenanting, and secret [private] prayer, but they especially reinforced the tradition of retired meditation upon the sufferings of Christ." Schmidt, *Holy Fairs*, 142. See also Bracken Long, *The Eucharistic Theology of the American Holy*

Whitefield (1714–1770), who preached at the largest documented revival in Scottish history, at Cambuslang, in 1742.[5] This was a prime example of the emotional and spiritual power of the Scottish communion season. It is estimated that at least 30,000 people were in attendance and 3,000 communion tokens were distributed at the massive communion service.[6] In his pastoral ministry, Willison was hindered by various circumstances from pursuing his ideals for frequent communion, and he does not prescribe any frequency in his writings as the Biblical norm.[7] But he believed that what had become the standard Scottish practice of annual, or even bi-annual, communion was substandard and problematic.

Willison's *Sacramental Catechism* will be surveyed here, as a succinct statement of his views. Willison explains and justifies the writing of his catechism in a preface. On this subject of the Lord's Supper, he states that "too much cannot be written or preached, seeing it is the epitome of the whole Christian religion, both as to doctrine and practice."[8] Willison recounts the spiritual fervor many Scots experienced during communion seasons, and exhorts his readers to reject "formalism" in their communion observance:

> Sacrament days in Scotland have been solemn and sealing days, yea of heaven to many; at such occasions many have had their trysts, and Bethel meetings with God, which they will never forget. O let us all then beware of formality creeping in among us in our preparations for, and partaking of this solemn ordinance; for then God will withdraw himself from our assemblies, and our solemn feasts will be melancholy and heartless.[9]

Although Willison later advocates more frequent communion, he reminds his readers of the necessity to participate in an *intentional* way: "O communicants, however frequently you approach the Lord's table, yet still make conscience of secret, serious, and solemn preparation for it; press always for a token of Christ's

---

Fairs, chap. 6, for Willison's influence, and MacLeod, "The Sacramental Theology and Practice of the Reverend John Willison (1680–1750)".

5 Bracken Long, *The Eucharistic Theology of the American Holy Fairs*, 107–109.

6 Burnet, *The Holy Communion*, 244.

7 In his first pastorate at Brechin, he had to contend with a rival Episcopalian minster, who scheduled his own communion services to conflict and compete with Willison's, MacLeod, 21, 216–17. Later, at Dundee, he was able to move to holding communions twice a year, which was more frequent than the average practice. MacLeod, 221, summarizes: "As a realist, Willison saw infrequency as a continuing problem which had beset the Reformed Church from the beginning, and he recognized that change would be slow, and, 'by degrees'. Quarterly observance, therefore, was a realistic target at which to aim, and he welcomed whatever moves any parish made towards realizing it."

8 John Willison, *A Sacramental Catechism: Or, A Familiar Instructor for Young Communicants* (Glasgow: David Niven, 1794), iii.

9 Willison, *A Sacramental Catechism*, v–vi.

love at his table."[10] He gives various reasons for writing his catechism, and one of them stresses *due preparation*: "I aim to reprove and reform those who rush upon this ordinance in an ignorant or careless manner, without due preparation; by shewing who only have a right to this table, what is the nature and importance of the work of communicating, with the sin and danger of doing it unworthily."[11] Here Willison exemplifies the tension that he, and other proponents for more frequent communion, had to maintain—even while they argued for greater frequency, they also stressed preparation and spiritual examination.

Willison's work also highlights the *seriousness* with which many Scots conducted this spiritual preparation and examination, as he lays out a series of "marks of grace" that prospective communicants should look for in their own hearts. He aims to help "troubled and exercised souls" prepare for communion, even though they are "oft filled with doubts and fears, lest they be unworthy communicants."[12] In other words, Willison's *Sacramental Catechism* functions as a spiritual diagnostic tool, to guide those wishing to commune through the maze of their own spiritual states.

As Willison continues to summarize the main points of his tome, he presents his last purpose for writing, which is to argue for the propriety of more frequent communion. Willison admonishes "those who satisfy themselves with communicating once in a year or two years," and argues that the "unfrequent celebration and participation of this blessed feast" is an evil that plagues the Scots Reformed churches. Willison appeals to his readers not to neglect the "dying words" of Christ (a rhetorical flourish that appears often in pro-frequency polemics). Willison argues that more frequent communion would soften hearts, fortify us against sin, and increase our love for Jesus Christ.[13] He asks pointedly: "Is it possible for us to meet with Christ, and taste of his sweetness and fulness in this ordinance, and not long for another meeting?"[14]

Willison then turns to answer one of the standard objections to more frequent communion:

> Let none think, that the frequency of the administration would expose to contempt; for I am sure no worthy communicant will undervalue this ordinance, because of a frequent repetition, but rather prize it the more. Did the primitive Christians bring it to contempt

---

10 Willison, *A Sacramental Catechism*, vi.

11 Willison, *A Sacramental Catechism*, vii.

12 Willison, *A Sacramental Catechism*, vii.

13 "Is not the frequent use of this ordinance, in the way Christ hath appointed, an excellent help, to soften our hearts, renew our repentance, strengthen our faith, inflame our love, increase our thankfulness, animate our resolutions against sin, and encourage us to holy duties, and shall we willingly neglect it?" Willison, *A Sacramental Catechism*, viii.

14 Willison, *A Sacramental Catechism*, vii–viii.

by partaking every Lord's day? Nay, was not their esteem of it much higher than those who dispense, or receive it only once in two years? I wish, the words of our dying Savior, and the acts of our General Assembly, relative to this matter, were more adverted to, by one and all of us.[15]

Indeed, several Scottish ecclesial statements had recommended more frequent communion, or at least tried to encourage churches to follow the directives of the Westminster Directory and Book of Common Order.[16] Many—if not most—churches in Scotland, however, were falling short of these ideals. Willison finds three main causes for communion infrequency: laziness, economic and cost considerations, and the multiplicity of sermons and preachers at the prolonged sacramental seasons. These reasons will be recycled in other pro-frequency sources. It is important to note that when Willison advocates "frequent communion," he is confronting readers who most likely attended communion annually, or less. Willison is "glad to hear, that in some parishes, ministers have begun to celebrate this ordinance twice in the year," which is a reminder that "frequent communion" meant something quite specific in this context.[17] In Willison's context, then, "frequent communion" is anything more than once a year.

In the actual text of his *Catechism*, Willison addresses the issue of frequency briefly, but his treatment is important since it reveals the main points of his argumentation. He states that, while baptism is the sacrament of initiation, the Lord's Supper is "for nutrition" and should be received often.[18] He offers three reasons to partake often:

A. We are obliged to it: 1. By our Saviour's words at the first institution, 1 Cor. Xi. 25, 26. 'As often as ye do 'this;' which have the virtue of a command to frequency in communicating.

2dly, By the example of the apostles and primitive Christians, whose practice it was to communicate frequently, nay, for ordinary, every Lord's day, Acts ii.42, 46. Acts xx.7.

3dly, Our souls necessities do call for frequency in partaking; for we are oft ready to forget Christ, and therefore we oft need this ordinance to bring him to our remembrance. We

---

15 Willison, *A Sacramental Catechism*, viii. Later in this preface, Willison refers and quotes to the acts of General Assemblies in 1701, 1712, and 1711, which had all urged more frequent communion. The statements of these Assemblies are treated in §4.5.3.

16 Willison, *A Sacramental Catechism*, viii–ix.

17 Willison, *A Sacramental Catechism*, x.

18 Willison, *A Sacramental Catechism*, 84.

are oft subject to spiritual deadness, weakness of faith, and decays of grace; and therefore have frequent need of this ordinance, for strength and quickening.[19]

In answering the question whether we are to follow this apostolic example, Willison answers that, though the first Christians undoubtedly partook with greater fervency, we have the same spiritual needs as they did, and we have the "same obligations of love and gratitude to him."[20] Willison also answers the question as to whether frequency would breed "formality." He responds that "formality" can accompany any of our religious duties, and yet we persist in those. His second answer stresses the need for spiritual preparation:

> *2dly*, This fault [formality in observing the Supper] is in no ways chargeable upon the holy ordinance and institution of Christ, but upon the corruption and carelessness of our hearts; which we ought diligently to watch and strive against; endeavouring in Christ's strength, as often as we partake, so often to prepare for it, with all due care and solemnity.[21]

There is a danger that frequency will breed formality, but any religious duty can be observed with "formality." This danger should not deter us from the duty, and from appropriate preparation and pursuit of spiritual fervency. The concern over "formality" resurfaces as one of the chief points of disagreement in later frequency debates. In summary, Willison argues from the Bible, Scottish church history, and practical and pastoral theology. This rhetorical structure of arguments resurfaces in other sources in the early Scots Reformed communion frequency debates. It is noteworthy, however, that Willison, who wrote so many popular works on spiritual preparation for communion, also argued for greater frequency.

6.1.2 John Erskine (1721–1803)

Another important Scots Reformed voice in this debate is John Erskine's *An Attempt to Promote the Frequent Dispensing of the Lord's Supper*, originally published in 1749. Erskine sought to present a biblical, theological, and practical case here for more frequent communion in the Scottish Reformed church. Erskine was a leader of the Evangelical party of the Scottish church and he maintained a large network of correspondents throughout Europe and in the Americas.[22] He bought

---

19 Willison, *A Sacramental Catechism*, 85.
20 Willison, *A Sacramental Catechism*, 85.
21 Willison, *A Sacramental Catechism*, 85.
22 For Erskine's role in the Evangelical party, as opposed to the Moderates, in the Church of Scotland, see Yeager, *Enlightened Evangelicalism*, 5–8.

and sent many books to his network of friends, in an effort to propagate sound doctrine. One of his chief correspondents and friends in the New World was Jonathan Edwards. Erskine personally sent Edwards a large collection of books, and their correspondence highlights the trans-Atlantic nature of the communion frequency debate.[23]

In 1748, John Erskine was a young minister in the town of Kirkintilloch, which was part of the synod of Glasgow and Ayr.[24] This ecclesial body, meeting in October, 1748, drafted an overture concerned with the frequency of communion and attendant practices in the Scottish Reformed church. Strong opposition ensued, which prompted Erskine to write his treatise, defending the synod's overture.[25] The committee's report targeted the typical Scottish practice of observing communion because it hindered greater frequency.[26] In opposition to this pattern of infrequency followed by "holy fair" intensity, the committee recommended celebrating the Lord's supper "at least four times a year, in every parish." They hoped this would bring the Scottish Reformed church closer to the "word of God, to the apostolic practice recorded therein, to the practice of the primitive church, and that of all other Protestant churches, as well as to several overtures and acts of assembly of this church in former times."[27] Noteworthy here is the emphasis on conformity to both Scripture and apostolic/primitive practice, as well as an ecumenical concern for conformity to the practice of "other Protestant churches."

The Overture did not make an immediate impact on the Church of Scotland. More influential were the series of pamphlets, on both sides of the issue, that

---

23 See §5.8, for the friendship between Erskine and Edwards, and for Erskine's role as theological disseminator.

24 Kenneth J. Stewart, "Accelerating the Rhythm: Two Eighteenth Century Scottish Presbyterians on the Frequency of the Lord's Supper," in Ian Clary and Steve Weaver, eds., *The Pure Flame of Devotion: The History of Christian Spirituality: Essays in Honor of Michael A. G. Haykin on his Sixtieth Birthday* (Joshua Press, 2013), 303.

25 As Erskine summarizes the overture: "That it would have an evident tendency to the reviving and promoting of true religion, that the Lord's Supper should be more frequently administered among us, than what generally obtains, that holy ordinance being celebrated only once a year in each parish, (excepting in a few places) and, in some parishes, but once in two years." *An Attempt to Promote the Frequent Dispensing of the Lord's Supper* (Kilmarnock: J. Wilson, 1783), 3. The *Attempt* was later included in a collection of Erskine's writings, *Theological Dissertations* (London: Printed by Edward and Charles Dilly), 1765.

26 "That, if this be allowed, we must add, that the manner in which this holy ordinance is commonly administered among us, greatly obstructs the more frequent administration of it; and particularly the number of sermons on such occasions, and the many parishes thereby laid vacant on the Lord's Day, are accompanied with several great inconveniences, if not also too often with scandalous profanations of that holy Day." Erskine, *An Attempt*, 3–4.

27 Erskine, *An Attempt*, 4.

ensued.[28] Erskine wrote his *Attempt* in the wake of the Synod of Glasgow and Ayr, to help advance the cause of holding more frequent communions. He maintains that the synod's "overture" in favor of more frequent communion entails two primary considerations. The first question asks "[i]s the design of the dispensing of the Lord's Supper in every congregation, at least four times a year, in itself good?" Secondly, "are the means proposed for gaining that end, the most proper, and least exceptionable?"[29] The main points of Erskine's *Attempt* will be surveyed, since it is one of the most thorough and influential defenses of frequent communion in the Scots Reformed tradition.[30]

Erskine divides his pamphlet into three sections. In Section 1, he summarizes the synod's overture, the reactions to it, and explains his rationale for writing the treatise. He first examines the theological nature of the sacrament, moving freely from systematic theology to practical and pastoral theology. He then examines Biblical data regarding communion frequency, focusing on the New Testament. In Section 2, he turns to a historical survey of the early church and patristic church. He then appeals to the "practice of the purest reformed churches" and the Scottish Reformed church "in her best times." In Section 3, he anticipates the objections of his readers, and provides answers to seven of these possible objections. Section 4 contains Erskine's concluding observations on the synod, long quotes from John Willison and Thomas Randall, as well as responses to further objections to the overture, based on the practical difficulties of implementing the synod's recommendations.

In Section 1, Erskine asks a key question: "If the Lord's Supper is an ordinance of so comforting and improving a nature, as almost all acknowledge it, should we not account the frequent enjoyment of it a privilege?"[31] He then poses a rhetorical question: "Ask your own hearts, O Christians, are you in any danger of remembering these things too much?"[32] Interestingly, Erskine downplays baptism (because infant baptism does not involve the volition of the infant) and argues that communion provides Christians with their sense of identity: "The Lord's Supper is a visible badge of our Christian profession."[33]

---

28 MacLeod, "The Sacramental Theology and Practice of the Reverend John Willison," 234–35.

29 Erskine, *An Attempt*, 5.

30 For other surveys and discussions of Erskine, and his views on communion frequency, see, Hughes, "Holy Communion in the Church of Scotland in the Nineteenth Century," PhD diss., (University of Glasgow, 1987), 15–18; MacLeod, "The Sacramental Theology and Practice of the Reverend John Willison," 236–240; Yeager, Enlightened Evangelicalism, 106–110; Stewart, "Accelerating the Rhythm," 299–320 = chap. 7 in Stewart, *In Search of Ancient Roots: The Christian Past and the Evangelical Identity Crisis* (Downer's Grove: IVP Academic, 2017).

31 Erskine, *An Attempt*, 6.

32 Erskine, *An Attempt*, 7.

33 Erskine, *An Attempt*, 8. There is no doubt that Erskine has a high view of the Supper: "The Lord's Supper is also intended as a seal and confirmation of the fulness and freedom of the offers of grace in

The main texts Erskine uses to argue for frequent communion come from the New Testament, which is a pattern followed by other writers in favor of frequency. 1 Cor. 11:25 and 11:26 are the "only passages that look like an injunction of any precise degree of frequency in partaking of the Lord's Supper. It is "probable their practice [of the early church] was founded on a New Testament precept, plain to them, though to us dark and obscure."[34] This sounds suspiciously like an argument from silence, and is a similar tactic used by some Roman Catholic apologists, who appeal to the unwritten tradition of the church. For Erskine, it is inconsistent for theologians to appeal to "apostolic example" when discussing the change from the seventh-day Sabbath to the first-day Lord's Day, and then to dismiss the apostles' communion frequency practices.

Another important text is the Emmaus Road narrative: "Less than a week after [the institution of communion at the "last supper"], even the very day of our Lord's resurrection, being the first day of the week, and the Christian Sabbath, the Lord's Supper is again dispensed by Jesus himself."[35] There are eucharistic implications in Luke 24: "Jesus could have discovered himself to them how and when he pleased. Sure then, he who does nothing in vain had some wise reason for chusing [sic] to do it in these, rather than in other circumstances. And what reason so probable, as to put a distinguishing respect on the sacrament of the supper, by making it the first means of manifesting himself to these disciples?"[36] Others, like the early English advocate of Presbyterianism Thomas Cartwright, maintained that it was not the "breaking of bread" which manifested Jesus to the disciples, but the special "manner of asking a blessing before meat." Erskine thinks this is dodging the plain meaning of the text.[37] He also blames Roman Catholic appropriations of this passage to argue for communion in just one species for the failure of Protestants to understand it correctly.[38]

Texts in Acts are also an important battleground for Erskine, and others who argued for more frequent communion. The "breaking of bread" in Acts 2:42 and 2:46 are both eucharistic and display a pattern of frequent gathering and worshipping in the early church.[39] Erskine concludes that the first Christians would worship daily at

---

the everlasting gospel. For as really as the minister offers the bread and wine to the communicants, so really God the Father offers Christ, the bread of life, to every one of us for the nourishment of our souls." Erskine, *An Attempt*, 9.

34 Erskine, *An Attempt*, 15.
35 Erskine, *An Attempt*, 16.
36 Erskine, *An Attempt*, 16.
37 Erskine, *An Attempt*, 17.
38 Erskine, *An Attempt*, 17.
39 Regarding Acts 2:42, Erskine argues: "The words *esan proskarterountes*, which we render *continued stedfastly*, properly denote *constancy*, or *perseverance in an exercise*, or *waiting continually upon any thing*, as appears from the use of the same word, Acts i.14. vi.4. viii. 13. and x.7. Rom. xii.12. and

the Temple, but then would retire to a house, where they would celebrate the Lord's Supper: "In the temple, to convert infidels; in the private house, to strengthen and confirm believers." But this is not limited to just weekly communion. Erskine thinks this verse shows that the early Christians in Jerusalem partook of the sacrament daily.[40] Acts 20:7 suggests that the "first day of the week," was a day of worship for the early church. Erskine highlights the fact that Paul stayed in Troas for seven days, even though he was hurrying to reach Jerusalem. Although Paul could have called for a general meeting of the Christians in Troas, he chose to wait until the first day of the week, when the church would gather. A central part of this gathering, according to Acts 20:7, was "breaking bread." For Erskine, this means celebrating communion, and he remarks: "It adds probability to this, that Chrysostom terms the Sabbath *the day of bread*."[41] From Paul's censure in 1 Cor. 11:20-21 that the Corinthians were not eating the Lord's Supper when they came together in one place, Erskine draws the implication that the Corinthians were intending to come together in one place, *in order* to eat the Lord's Supper.[42]

Section 2 of the treatise deals with evidence from church history. Like many Protestants, Erskine regarded the early church as a model to follow.[43] Based on

---

xiii.6. And therefore whatever is meant by breaking of bread, it is plain they were as constant in that, as in attending on the apostle's doctrine, and public prayer. All then we have to enquire is, if the expression relates to the Lord's Supper, or to a common meal." Erskine, *An Attempt*, 18. Commenting on Acts 2:46, Erskine appeals to the Greek grammar to show that the English translation of the verse is misleading. Erskine provides the passage in English: "And they, continuing daily with one accord in the temple, and breaking bread in a house, did participate the food with gladness and singleness of heart." However, Erskine argues for an alternate translation: "*Kath' emeran*, in the first clause of the verse, signifies *daily*, or *from day to day*: and hence it was imagined, *kat' oikon* must signify, *in every house*, or *from house to house*: whereas it is evident, from the use of the preposition *kata*, when applied to place, that it denotes some precise determinate place [a list of verses follow] and never relates to more places than one, except the substantive to which it is joined be in the plural number, as in Luke xiii 22. Acts v. 15. viii. 1,3. and xx. 20 or be connected with an adjective denoting universality, as Acts xv. 36." Erskine, *An Attempt*, 20–21. Erskine also references further evidence from a Roman inscription with similar Greek grammar and from the Arabic and Syriac versions of this verse.

40 Erskine, *An Attempt*, 22.
41 Erskine, *An Attempt*, 22–23.
42 Erskine, *An Attempt*, 23.
43 Erskine draws evidence for weekly, Lord's Day, communion (and sometimes daily) from Pliny's letter to Trajan, Justin Martyr, Tertullian, Minutius Felix, Cyprian, Victorinus of Petau, Basil of Caesarea, Ambrose, Jerome and Augustine. "The practice of those, who lived in the very infancy of the church, must deserve peculiar regard. Their thorough acquaintance with the style in which the New Testament was writ, the customs to which it alludes, and with many other peculiarities which are now almost buried in obscurity; but especially their conversing with the apostles, or their immediate disciples, must give them great advantages for understanding the religion of Jesus. And as many of them sealed their doctrine with their blood, we cannot reasonably entertain the

the testimony of various patristic sources, he claims that the church "of the first four centuries" exemplifies a pattern of frequent communion. In fact, the church in those times did not just celebrate communion on every Sunday, but sometimes more often than that.[44] But over time the church declined from the early church's more "primitive purity," which was a standard Protestant polemic refrain.[45] As part of this polemic, the "church of Rome" is to be blamed for introducing and establishing infrequent communion.[46] In opposition to this, Erskine appeals to the "practice of the purest reformed churches" in the matter of communion frequency. He cites the "Bohemians," who celebrate four times a year, and refers to a national synod of French Protestants which met in 1664. Although their practice was currently quarterly communion, the synod desired greater frequency. The Lutherans commune every Sunday and the Anglicans are obligated to commune at least three times a year. Apparently, some Scots worried that the greater communion frequency would bring them closer to "prelacy," but Erskine turns the question around—if the Church of England is obeying Christ more faithfully in this matter, is that a reason to disobey?[47] Erskine closes the section with a survey of the communion practices of the Scottish Reformed church "in her best times" and highlights various ecclesial documents from the Reformed Church of Scotland that sought more frequent communion.[48]

In Section 3, Erskine anticipates several objections and responds to them. Some of the objections are weightier than others, but all of them reveal some of the key issues in debates about communion frequency. For example, some argued that the early Christians had frequent communion because they were much more spiritual than people in later times. In more degenerate times, frequent communion would be dangerous. The response is that people are weaker when they do not take advantage of this means of grace more frequently. The church in Corinth was by no means perfect, but Paul does not tell them to observe communion less frequently.[49] Another objection appeals to the Jewish Passover. Since it was yearly, the Lord's Supper should follow this pattern. Erskine replies that although the Passover was annual, the Jews also participated in daily sacrifices as well, which

---

least suspicion, that they would dare knowingly to alter the least circumstance in the last, the dying command of their dear Master." Erskine, *An Attempt*, 24–27.

44 "These passages are more than sufficient to prove, that during the first four centuries, the sacrament of the Lord's supper was dispensed even oftener than once a-week, and that it was a constant branch of the sanctification of the Sabbath." Erskine, *An Attempt*, 27.

45 Erskine, *An Attempt*, 27–33.

46 Erskine, *An Attempt*, 32–33.

47 Erskine, *An Attempt*, 33–34.

48 Erskine, *An Attempt*, 37–48.

49 Erskine, *An Attempt*, 48–49.

also prefigured Christ.[50] The most important objection, though, was the fear that celebrating the Supper frequently would "lessen the solemnity of the ordinance, and bring it into contempt." Since this is repeated so often in frequency debates, Erskine's four rejoinders are worth noting:

1. Since God commanded frequent communion, then He foresaw any possible attendant dangers. This does not negate our duty to obey His commands.[51]

2. Early church history and experience during the Reformation, the time of the "covenanters," and current practice in New England show that frequent communion and reverence can coexist.[52]

3. Scripture also warns about the dangers of not praying with proper reverence, and of hearing the Word preached. Should we then participate less in these other means of grace?[53]

4. Erskine's fourth response is really a restatement of his previous point, except that he includes "meditation" and "self-examination" as other "religious exercises" that are engaged in, frequently, with great profit.[54]

Another objection centers on the degree of preparation appropriate to the Lord's Supper. As the closest approach to God that we can attain on this earth, it requires a great deal of awe, reverence, and "solemn preparation." Erskine asks whether proper reverence necessarily entails "a fast-day, with three sermons, and a preparation day, with two sermons, before every time the sacrament is dispensed"?[55] Moreover, there were more days of thanksgiving and joy in the Old Testament, compared to days of fasting and humiliation.[56] To those who believe that frequent communion is an innovation and "all innovations are dangerous," they should remember that it is an innovation in the same way that Luther's doctrine of justification by faith was an innovation. These only appear as innovations because the truth was

---

50 Erskine, *An Attempt*, 49.
51 Erskine, *An Attempt*, 50.
52 Erskine, *An Attempt*, 51–52.
53 Erskine, *An Attempt*, 52.
54 Erskine, *An Attempt*, 53.
55 Erskine, *An Attempt*, 54. Though some appeal to the many "preparations" and purifications the Jews had to undergo, in order to justify these rigors of preparation for communion, Erskine appeals to the differences between "legal and evangelical dispensation." We have the "spirit of adoption" and thus are not bound by the "bondage" of the Law." Erskine, *An Attempt*, 55.
56 "And here I cannot but take occasion to remark, that the day of atonement was the *only anniversary day of fasting*, humiliation and confession of fins which God enjoined the Israelites. All their other annual holidays, except these which they themselves appointed, after their return from the Babylonish captivity, were days of joy and thanksgiving. If then the Jews had more thanksgivings than fasts, why should not the Christians? Is not our cause of joy greater?" Erskine, *An Attempt*, 55.

lost.[57] Regarding the argument that the majority of Scots are opposed to frequent communion, Erskine counters that we should follow the Word of God, and not the opinions of men.[58] The 1700s saw a series of "secessions" from the Church of Scotland, revolving around issues of upholding the Solemn League and Covenant. Communion practices, and participation in communion, were focal points of conflict.[59] But authors like Erskine believed they were standing on the sure foundation of God's Word, and so they were willing to push forward in their reform efforts.

Section 4 closes the treatise. Erskine quotes John Willison and Thomas Randall at length, and then responds to various questions about the practicality of implementing the synod's overture regarding more frequent communion. Randall's *Letter* had not yet been published, but he had sent it to Erskine and Erskine states that reading it prompted his own thinking on the subject. He quotes liberally from it, and commends it to his readers as well worth their examination.[60] What these objections chiefly reveal is the complex nature of the various Scots Reformed communion traditions that had developed. To move towards greater frequency impinged upon an entire network of liturgical practices that would have to change. It was almost as if Erskine was arguing for another "reformation," but it was a reformation of Protestant liturgical customs. Erskine's *Attempt* stands as one of the most influential of the Scottish Reformed sources in the communion debates of the 1700s. Because of his prominence in Scotland, his connections throughout Europe and the Americas, and his work as a bridge-builder in trying to build a trans-Atlantic Evangelical coalition, his arguments were quoted often by later writers, and they contributed to the growth of the frequent communion movement in Scotland and abroad.

6.1.3 Thomas Randall (1710–1780)

Thomas Randall wrote *A Letter to a Minister from his Friend, Concerning Frequent Communion* at roughly the same time as John Erskine published his treatise arguing for weekly communion. Randall served for forty-two years as the minister of Inchture, and his great grandson, Randall Thomas Davidson, became the Archbishop of

---

57 "The truest and purest antiquity is on our side: whereas our present practice is a plain defection from the primitive pattern." Erskine, *An Attempt*, 56.
58 Erskine claims there was a silent majority who approved of the Overture for more frequent communion, and then appeals to Calvin, Baxter, an anonymous "minister in the shire of Ayr," John Willison's *Sacramental Catechism*, and Jonathan Edwards, as proponents of frequent communion. Erskine, *An Attempt*, 56–59.
59 See Burnet, *The Holy Communion*, chap. 10.
60 Erskine, *An Attempt*, 71.

Canterbury in 1903, in an interesting twist of history.[61] The key point of Randall's essay is summarized in the "Advertisement" at the very end, in which he attempts to correct several typographical errors in the original printing. As he summarizes his key argument: "The Principle which all along is gone upon, is, That in using Means for Promoting Christ's Religion, the greatest Success and Blessing is to be expected upon such as are of Christ's Appointment; and the Right or Wrong of what is said in this Letter turns entirely on this Hinge."[62] Randall's concern is that, since the Lord's Supper is a divinely-appointed means of grace, therefore it should be celebrated more frequently.

Randall begins his essay with a quote from the Preface to the Book of Common Order, which previews his main points of argumentation. The Preface refers to the Word of God, the witness of "antiquity," and the example of the "best reformed Churches." Similarly to Erskine, Randall adopts this basic rhetorical structure, and so his treatise follows the same general pattern. He does not add much that is original and follows the same general lines of argument as Erskine. As stated previously, he and Erskine had read each other's manuscripts, and quoted from each other—Randall more so than Erskine.

Yet, following the pattern of presenting Biblical arguments first, Randall makes a couple of original claims. The first contribution involves an appeal to special revelation. He asks, "[w]hat hath Christ himself, who made the Institution, said about it? or what Directions hath the Holy Spirit given, who revealed the Mind of Christ to his Church after he was ascended?"[63] In other words, Jesus did not teach directly on everything, but revealed some things to the apostles through the Spirit.[64] Because of this move, Randall can elevate the communion practices of the Apostolic church to the divinely-revealed will of Jesus. As he then states, "one of the first Things the Spirit led the Apostles and the Believers in Christ to, was a frequent, if not daily Remembrance of the Lord in his Supper."[65]

---

61 *Miscellanea Genealogica et Heraldica*, ed. W. Bruce Bannerman, vol. 5, third series, (London: Mitchell Hughes and Clarke, 1904), 317–318. Interestingly, Randall had studied and received ordination in the Netherlands. See Hughes, "Holy Communion in the Church of Scotland in the Nineteenth Century," 15, citing A.L. Drummond, *The Kirk and the Continent* (Edinburgh: Saint Andrew Press, 1956), 140.

62 Thomas Randall, *A Letter to A Minister from his Friend*, 89. For another survey of Randall's *Letter* see Stewart, *In Search of Ancient Roots*, chap. 7.

63 Randall, *A Letter*, 4.

64 He here quotes 1 Cor. 14:37.

65 Randall, *A Letter*, 7. This theological claim is similar to one sometimes made by Roman Catholic and even some Anglican apologists, as they argue for aspects of their theological traditions that are not as obviously supported by Biblical texts, but were supposedly delivered by Jesus during the forty days after his resurrection and before his ascension.

A similar strategy is used when he deals with 1 Cor. 11. To lend weight to Paul's testimony, Randall states that Paul had a special revelation on this topic (connecting a series of New Testament texts—1 Cor. 11:23, Gal. 1:11-17, Acts 22). Jesus must have given Paul specific directions about the frequency of communion in the early church. In this hypothetical special revelation, Jesus approved the practice of the apostolic church, which Randall maintains was weekly communion, if not oftener.[66] Randall claims that Acts 2 gives us an apostolic model of continuing "steadfastly" in preaching, in prayers, and in "breaking of bread," which he interprets as communion. If then, the church has preaching and prayers every week, why do we not also celebrate communion weekly?[67] This becomes one of Randall's most used tropes—prayers, preaching, and communion are all means of grace—why then make use of some of the means of grace more frequently than others?

After Scripture, the testimony of church history is important. Randall repeats the standard claims about the purity of the early church and cites various patristic sources. His attitude about his own times is noteworthy. Randall writes with typical Protestant zeal about the "light" of the Reformation dawning in the darkness and bringing deliverance from the "Antichristian Egypt" of the Roman church.[68] He also seems to believe that he is living in the "Glory of the latter Days," when he expects the light of the Reformation to spread throughout the world.[69] Part of this increase of light, Randall argues, would be an increase in frequent communion. But Randall realizes that the Reformation is not complete, because the Reformers did not all attain the ideal of weekly communion. So, we must "go beyond" the Reformation at this point.[70] This provides a key insight into understanding the psychology of authors advocating for more frequent communion. They viewed themselves as the next generation of reformers—they had a mission to fulfill. They believed that God, the Scriptures, and the most faithful witnesses from church history were on their side. This was no idle debate. It was a matter of urgency and faithfulness to God's Word.

Earlier (2.9), the stream of the Swiss Reformation stressing the importance of church discipline was summarized. How did Randall's vision fit into that tradition? For Randall, frequent communion would also improve church discipline. More frequent communion would demand more frequent self-examination, which would

---

66 Randall, *A Letter*, 10–11.

67 Randall, *A Letter*, 8.

68 Randall, *A Letter*, 28. Although Randall claims to set forth the Reformers' "knowledge" of frequent communion, his citations of only one reformer, Calvin, fail to achieve his goal. This tells us less about what the Reformers actually believed about frequent communion and more about the stature of Calvin as a theological authority in the Scottish reformed church in the 1700s.

69 Randall, *A Letter*, 29.

70 Randall, *A Letter*, 29.

lead to a healthier spiritual state and help facilitate greater Christian unity[71] Participation in the Lord's Supper could be a means to separate the wheat from the chaff in churches. When Paul exhorted the Corinthians to "purge out the old leaven," he did not tell them stop observing the Supper frequently. Churches should both practice effective church discipline and hold the Supper frequently.

Later generations would accuse Reformed churches of being unbalanced, and stressing preaching to the detriment of the sacraments. In response, Randall argues that the undue emphasis on "preaching" during communions has led many people to think that listening to a "table address" was the main point of communion. It also tended to favor those ministers who could preach fervently, leading to an unhealthy emphasis on the pastor's preaching abilities. Simplifying the service, and eliminating much of the communion-preaching, would give people space to reflect, meditate, and remember the Lord Jesus.

Another "advantage" of frequent communion is that it would take an argument "out of the Mouths of our Enemies," who criticize the sacramental "occasions" as having no ground or warrant in Scripture. Randall posits that if the Reformed churches focused on celebrating the Supper properly, critics of Christianity would be less able to capitalize on the abuses attendant on these gatherings (as Scottish poet Robert Burns so famously did in his 1785 poem, "The Holy Fair").[72]

Randall offers an important qualifier: these advantages will not be automatic effects—we must still pursue communion intentionally, lest we fall into formality.[73] However, the possibility of doing something (frequent communion) poorly should not dissuade us from attempting it at all. Randall concludes his pamphlet with various observations and exhortations.[74] He ends with a postmillennial exhortation about the progress of God's kingdom in the world and sees more frequent communion as part of this process.[75] Again, the emphasis is on Randall as Reformer, pushing ahead in calling the Scottish church back to the Scriptures, and the practice of the early church, and the ecclesial standards of the Scottish Reformed church. Although he does not add much that is new or original, his *Letter* was influential in its own right, and was quoted by later authors, though not to the same extent as Erskine's. Together, Erskine and Randall can be considered as the instigators of the Scottish communion frequency debates and their works influenced later authors who argued for more frequent communion.

---

71 Randall, *A Letter*, 41–43. This section is somewhat obscure, but Randall is referencing divisions and slights that occurred because of the typical way the Supper was observed in Scotland at the time. He seems to be saying that, if ministers stayed in their own parishes, these divisions would be decreased.

72 Randall, *A Letter*, 45–46. For Burns' critique, see Schmidt, *Holy Fairs*, 169–183.

73 Randall, *A Letter*, 46–47.

74 Randall, *A Letter*, 72–86.

75 Randall, *A Letter*, 81–82.

6.1.4 John Mitchell Mason (1770–1829)

The debate between John Mason of New York and his critics, John Thomson, John Anderson, and Alexander Duncan, will be surveyed because the debate takes up and continues the same themes that were developed in the Scottish Presbyterian church, and shows how they developed in the American context. Schmidt states that the "interlocutors were numerous" in the frequency debate, but that the exchange between John Mason and his critics stands out and exemplifies the main themes in these debates.[76] Mason was the son of a Scottish Presbyterian minister, but was born in America. However, since he was educated at Edinburgh, he clearly had deep connections to the Scots Reformed church.[77] No doubt, Mason saw himself as a new "reformer," carrying on the work of the Reformation, while Thomson, Anderson and Duncan defended traditional Scots Reformed eucharistic piety against Mason's critique.

The movement towards more frequent communion received a significant impetus from the publication of Mason's *Letters on Frequent Communion* in 1798. Mason was an influential pastor of a church in New York that was part of the Associate Reformed Presbytery—a group that had split off from the Church of Scotland.[78] At least within his own church, he was able to implement a controversial ban on the days of fasting, preparation, and thanksgiving that had been a part of the Scottish sacramental tradition.[79] Mason's book also influenced the wider Presbyterian church in America:

> The Old School pastor and author William B. Sprague called its publication an "important service" which Mason "rendered to the Church." And James W. Alexander drew inspiration from it when, in 1840, he wrote for Old School consumption an article advocating greater frequency and simplicity in celebrating the sacrament.[80]

---

76 Schmidt, *Holy Fairs*, 187.

77 On Mason's life and influence, see Stewart, *In Search of Ancient Roots*, 116, and Hughes, "Holy Communion in the Church of Scotland in the Nineteenth Century," 22–23.

78 On the "Secession" and formation of the "Associate" Presbytery to which Mason belonged, see Burnet, *The Holy Communion*, 231–241. John Brown of Haddington (6.1.8), was also a prominent member of the Associate Reformed denomination.

79 Melton, *Presbyterian Worship in America*, 39–40, citing Theodore F. Savage, *The Presbyterian Church in New York City* (New York: Presbytery of New York, 1949), 43.

80 Melton, *Presbyterian Worship in America*, 39–40, quoting Sprague, *Annals of the American Pulpit; or Commemorative Notices of Distinguished American Clergymen* (New York: Robert Carter & Brothers, 1859), vol. IV, 2–3. Alexander and his article are treated below (6.1.9).

Mason wrote nine letters in his *Letters on Frequent Communion*.[81] The first letter introduces the series. Letter 2 argues for the necessity of frequent communion. Letters 3–8 deal with objections to frequent communion. Letter 3 answers the charge of "innovation." Letter 4 deals with the charge that frequency will lead to "irreverence" and a "want of preparation." Letters 5–7 argue against the traditional Scots Reformed fast days and days of thanksgiving surrounding communion. Letter 8 considers popular arguments for the sacramental fasts and thanksgivings. Letter 9 ends the series by setting forth the "benefits" of frequent communion.

Overall, the letters are full of excessive rhetorical flourishes, and do not have the same substantive theological or historical depth as other voices surveyed here. They also rely on Erskine's *Attempt* in many places. However, they stirred up a strong response.

Mason saw himself as a reformer, who was pushing churches in the Scottish Reformation to be fully Biblical, and to abandon man-made traditions that had taken root.[82] Mason contends that, in the current communion practice of Scots Presbyterians, there is not the "frequency nor simplicity which were the delight and the ornament of primitive churches."[83] By the criterion of "simplicity," Mason attacks the fast days and thanksgiving days that had become part of standard Scots Reformed practice. There is no middle ground here. Frequent communion is an "indispensable Duty."[84] Mason uses the rhetorical trope that communion is the "dying command of our Lord Jesus Christ," and implies that if we do not obey his dying wishes, we are inexcusable. Although Jesus' dying words (quoted from Paul's summary in 1 Cor. 11) do not actually give precise instructions on how frequently we are to observe the Supper, this inexactitude should not beguile anyone into "carelessness."[85] For Mason, the words "as often" clearly indicate frequency.[86] Following Jesus' instructions for communion is an indicator not just of whether we obey, but how much we love him.[87]

---

81 Mason's *Letters* were published in various formats, with some editorial changes along the way. He first published them anonymously, because of their controversial nature. John Mason, *Letters on Frequent Communion, Addressed Particularly to the Members of the Associate-Reformed Church in North-America* (New-York: T. & J. Swords, 1798); *Letters on Frequent Communion* (Edinburgh: J. Ritchie, 1798); *Letters on Frequent Communion, in The Writings of the Late John M. Mason, D.D.* (New York: Ebenezer Mason, 1832); *Letters on Frequent Communion, in The Complete Works of John M. Mason, D.D.* (New York: Baker and Scribner, 1849).

82 Mason, *Letters on Frequent Communion*, 10.

83 Mason, *Letters on Frequent Communion*, 12.

84 Mason, *Letters on Frequent Communion*, 15.

85 Mason, *Letters on Frequent Communion*, 15–16.

86 Mason, *Letters on Frequent Communion*, 16.

87 Mason, *Letters on Frequent Communion*, 18.

In Letter 3, Mason confronts the charge of "innovation." Other reformers were also accused of innovation, so this accusation is really a badge of honor. The same three-pronged rhetorical structure utilized by Erskine and Randall also appears in these *Letters*. Mason appeals to Scripture, then to examples from church history, to finally cite various Protestant authorities and the examples of the "best Reformed churches." When he deals with Scripture to prove the necessity of frequency, Mason interacts with only two New Testament texts—Acts 20:7 and 1 Cor. 11:20. This is rather odd for a reformer endeavoring to bring the church back to the teachings of Scripture. In his treatment of Acts 20:7, Mason seems to advance beyond the arguments of Erskine and Randall. While they argued simply for more *frequent* communion on the basis of this text, Mason is arguing for *weekly* communion.

The next point in the three-pronged rhetorical structure is church history. By his own admission, Mason relies on the previous work of John Erskine and Joseph Bingham's *Origines Ecclesiasticae* (Book 15, Ch. 11). Frequent communion characterized the young and healthy church, while the onset of decay and corruption was signaled by declining frequency, reaching a low ebb in the late medieval period.[88] All this, of course, serves the polemical purpose of showing the necessity of the Reformation.[89]

Mason then moves to the last rhetorical commonplace of most Scots Reformed pro-frequency polemics—the example of the "purest Reformed churches," a trope that we saw in the Preface to the Book of Common Order. These churches include the constitution of the Dutch church (1581), the Reformed Churches of France, and the Church of Scotland, at least according to First Book of Discipline and the Westminster Directory.[90]

In Letter 4, Mason turns to answering the objection that frequent communion will breed irreverence and a lack of preparation. Irreverence is a danger in any religious duty, but that should not prevent us from observing the Sabbath, reading the Scriptures, family religion, or prayer. What about preparing for communion? Mason is not advocating carelessness when approaching communion and posits that long seasons without communion do not stimulate preparation, but rather encourage worldliness and spiritual sloth. Additionally, a drop of true humility, combined with frequency, is worth more than an ocean of preparation for infrequent reception.[91] The anti-frequency line of reasoning would conclude that "the Lord requires more holiness from us in sacramental, than in other services; i. e. allows us

---

88 Mason, *Letters on Frequent Communion*, 37–38.

89 Mason, *Letters on Frequent Communion*, 42–43.

90 Mason, *Letters on Frequent Communion*, 45–46. Mason is also dependent on Erskine for these examples.

91 He retorts: "It is the most perverse of all perversions to *displace* a duty by *preparing* for it." Mason, *Letters on Frequent Communion*, 51.

to be less holy in the latter, than in the former."[92] Is God more holy in communion, than during the other times in which we approach him? Mason quotes Lev. 10:3 and Heb. 10:19, 22 to the effect that God requires us to be holy whenever we approach him. To press the point even further—since infrequency aids "preparation" and "reverence," then why not have communion as infrequently as possible?[93]

Letter 5 considers the customary days of fasting and thanksgiving which had come to define the Scots Reformed communion services. The days of fasting and thanksgiving are not compatible with obeying Jesus' intent with regard to communion frequency.[94] The communion seasons are: (1) not warranted by the Bible, (2) contrary to judgment of most of the Church, and (3) attended by various evils.[95] The last possible ground of support for the days of fasting is that the Christian church has always approved of fasting before "special duties." Mason does not deny the importance of fasting, but he asks for a divine linkage (in Scripture) between fasting (as preparation) and the Lord's Supper. If we must fast before communion, then why not fast before all other religious duties (such as baptism, prayer, the Sabbath, family worship, and before prayer at meals)?[96] The "levelling" effect of Mason's sacramentology manifests itself here. Can he really mean to suggest that we have communion with Christ in the same way during a prayer before a meal as we do in the Eucharist?

In his eagerness to relegate the sacrament to a more "ordinary" position, a position which would not require "extraordinary" preparation, including fasting days, Mason once again seems to deny any special grace available in the Supper. As he puts it:

---

92 Mason, *Letters on Frequent Communion*, 52.

93 Mason, *Letters on Frequent Communion*, 54–55.

94 Mason, *Letters on Frequent Communion*, 56.

95 One important analogy from the Old Testament used in the frequency debates centers on the "great day of expiation," which included a solemn fast in Israel. Advocates of infrequency asked how much more, then, should we fast before the Eucharist, which fulfills the Day of Atonement? Mason points out the lack of a positive command in the New Testament, and lists five additional reasons: (1) the Jewish fast was "peculiar to the old dispensation," (2) the old/Jewish dispensation "ceased with the law of Moses," (3) the Scots Reformed fast days are preparation for communion, whereas the Jewish fast accompanied the Day of Atonement, (4) the Lord's Supper does not properly fulfill the Day of Atonement, but Passover, nor was the Passover preceded by fasting. Additionally, Mason challenges those who find warrant for a "Monday thanksgiving" day in the "holy convocation" after Passover to be consistent and find a modern-day application for the seven days of unleavened bread which followed the Passover. John Thompson will happily accept this challenge, as will be seen in the next section. Lastly, Mason presses the logic of drawing too close a correlation between the Day of Atonement and the Lord's Supper. By this logic, we should only observe communion once a year. Mason pushes further and asks why could we not also have daily communion (or even twice daily), based on the precedent of the Old Testament daily sacrifice? Mason, *Letters on Frequent Communion*, 60–61.

96 Mason, *Letters on Frequent Communion*, 62.

I would, therefore, beg the Christian to point out a single blessing to be supplicated or expected at the holy communion, which he does not, or at least ought not, to supplicate and expect in *every* approach to God through the faith of Jesus.[97]

As we will see, this "leveling" of the Lord's Supper also occurs in other writers in the frequency debates, so it is worth noting this tendency in Mason's polemics.

Letters 6–8 continue Mason's attack on days of public fasting and thanksgiving. The Scots Reformed did indeed generate a novel liturgical pattern, and even its advocates did not try to find much support in church history. But Mason strikes an extremist tone when he attempts to capture the Reformation spirit and claim that anything "added" to the manner of celebrating the sacraments, besides what has come to us from Christ and the apostles is "an *abuse*, a *profanation*, an *accursed invention*."[98] By this standard he would condemn the practice of other Reformed churches which did not commune around tables, as was the Scots Reformed custom. In his last letter, Letter 9, Mason sets forth the "benefits of Scriptural [frequent] communion." He presents six statements of these benefits. These statements all revolve around the poles of being more faithful to the Bible's teachings and bringing spiritual benefits. One creative claim is that more frequent communion would improve the spiritual vitality of churches and would drive out hypocrites and "unworthy members."[99]

In summary, although Mason's *Letters* were popular and influential, his actual exegesis is not on the same level as John Erskine, or even Thomas Randall. He only deals with two New Testament texts and makes passing references to the Old Testament. His historical appeals are a bit weightier, but do not go in much detail. Mason's prowess is surely in his rhetorical flourishes. He was a master of the barbed attack and the stinging rhetorical question. In the final analysis, Mason seems to have written the right tract at the right time. There was a growing movement for frequent communion, and Mason caught the wave at just the right moment.

6.1.5 John Thomson (1799)

John Thomson was a Scottish minister residing in Glasgow. Although he was an elderly man who had lost some of his ability to write, he felt compelled to respond to the *Letters* of John Mason.[100] Thomson regards Mason as a young man who is too brilliant and eloquent for his own good. Thomson's response reads like a

---

97 Mason, *Letters on Frequent Communion*, 66.
98 Mason, *Letters on Frequent Communion*, 74.
99 Mason, *Letters on Frequent Communion*, 118.
100 Thomson, *Letters addressed to the Rev. John Mason.* Further biographical details about Thompson are elusive. He is important as a source because he (1) responds to Mason, who is an important

crotchety old grandfather, trying to beat some sense into a young upstart. Although Thomson rightly chides Mason for his over-blown rhetoric, Thomson's rhetoric is just as pretentious and sometimes reads like a long *ad hominem* attack, punctuated by moments of theological reasoning.[101]

Interestingly, Thomson consistently appeals to the Old Testament in support of his claims. Erskine, Randall, and Mason tend to bring in Old Testament texts only tangentially (to prove a minor point, or when they rebut arguments for preparatory fasting days, arguments which relied on the Old Testament). Thomson, however, goes straight to the Old Testament as he defends the days of preparation and "solemnity" that he feels should surround the observance of the Lord's Supper. As we will see, the hermeneutical and typological priority of the Old Testament is shared by others like John Anderson, and Alexander Duncan, who argued against Mason's proposals about weekly communion. Although Thomson claims it is difficult to follow Mason's line of reasoning, because of his "flowery descants of flowing eloquence," he fills much of his pamphlet with his own flowery and eloquent condemnations of Mason's rhetorical flourishes. Accordingly, there is much rhetoric in both Mason and Thomson, but this summary will focus on Thomson's actual rebuttal, rather than his personal attacks on Mason.

The issue is complicated by the fact that Mason was associated with a group that splintered from the Church of Scotland (the "seceders"), and Thomson insinuates that other people in the "Secession" had put Mason up to writing his *Letters on Frequent Communion*. Thomson claims to see intrigue and conspiracy and suggests that others have used Mason for their own nefarious purposes. In Thomson's view, Mason is assaulting the cherished traditions of the Church of Scotland, and this assault is magnified by the tensions of the "Secession."[102] Thomson only penned four letters, in response to Mason's nine, and they are considerably shorter—no doubt owing to Thomson's age and difficulty in writing. Cutting through the rhetoric, Thomson offers several specific responses to Mason in Letter 1.

First, Mason is mistaken to assume that the stress on "preparation" for communion results from ignorance and superstition. "Solemnity" is just as important as

---

source and (2) because there are fewer sources that defend the Scottish communion *status quo*. Thus, his pamphlet is a useful representative of the anti-frequency side of the debate.

101 To pick only one sample of Thomson's rhetoric: "Never were there stronger evidences of a rooted prejudice than what appears in your Letters. If you were one, Sir, who might be supposed to be endowed with slender intellects, or a very limited capacity, it might extenuate, though not excuse you, especially in the self-confident manner in which you express yourself and treat your subject." Thomson, *Letters Addressed to the Rev. John Mason*, 27–28.

102 Thomson, *Letters Addressed to the Rev. John Mason*, 3–4 and 40–41. On the "Secession," see Burnet, *The Holy Communion in the Reformed Church of Scotland*, 234–238.

frequency, if not more so.[103] In fact, frequency will decrease reverence. Moreover, the warnings of 1 Cor. 11:27 about the dangers of communing "worthily" must not be brushed aside.[104] Even though he is arguing against frequency, Thomson does not want anything in his response to lessen the importance of the Lord's Supper.[105] Furthermore, the Scots Reformed sacramental customs are sanctioned by the Scriptures.[106]

In Letter 2, Thomson wants a "golden mean" between neglect of the sacrament (which he also condemns), and the "extravagance" which Mason argues for.[107] Because he emphasizes frequency so much, Mason neglects the "exercises" and "preparations" that enable people to communicate effectively.[108] All the spiritual benefits Mason sees in communion derive from the "preached gospel" and Mason exalts the Supper at the expense of preaching.[109] This is a common theme and concern in communion frequency debates. His arguments will be surveyed in some detail, in order to demonstrate the exegetical strategies of those defending infrequent communion.

Thomson offers an interpretation to Acts 20:7 and 1 Cor. 11:20, the only two New Testament texts that Mason appealed to. Regarding Acts 20:7, Thomson basically accuses Mason of arguing from silence. Just because the early disciples met on the first day of the week and "broke bread" does not mean that they had communion every time they gathered on the first day.[110] Furthermore, Mason admits that the first disciples communed on other days of the week, which weakens his appeal to Acts 20:7.[111] Concerning 1 Cor. 11:20, the "irregularities" Paul rebukes could not have occurred except when the Corinthians came together as the church, but did these "irregularities" occur every single time they gathered as the church? In other words, "irregularities" when they communed does not prove they communed every time they gathered.

The apostolic church communed more frequently because, first, they were experiencing persecutions and needed more "comfort"; and second, they expected the imminent return of Christ, which may have "excited them to frequency."[112]

---

103 Thomson, *Letters Addressed to the Rev. John Mason*, 8.
104 Thomson, *Letters Addressed to the Rev. John Mason*, 11.
105 Thomson, *Letters Addressed to the Rev. John Mason*, 13.
106 Thomson, *Letters Addressed to the Rev. John Mason*, 14. He does not list any Scripture texts in this introductory letter, but does deal with various texts in his later letters.
107 Thomson, *Letters Addressed to the Rev. John Mason*, 16.
108 Thomson, *Letters Addressed to the Rev. John Mason*, 17.
109 Thomson, *Letters Addressed to the Rev. John Mason*, 18.
110 Thomson, *Letters Addressed to the Rev. John Mason*, 19.
111 Thomson, *Letters Addressed to the Rev. John Mason*, 20.
112 Thomson, *Letters Addressed to the Rev. John Mason*, 22.

Thomson appeals to Matt. 9:15, suggesting that Jesus was "with" the early church in a more meaningful way, but that afterwards, the church would "fast." In an interesting move, Thomson dismisses Mason's appeals to church history because he believes the early church quickly fell away from purity. He finds support for this in the letters to the seven churches in Revelation. Thomson also points out that "papists" appeal to the "thorny copse of antiquity" to prove their claims, so he judges antiquity to be a dangerous grounding for any Christian practice.[113]

In Thomson's sacramental theology, God has established various ordinances for the salvation, edification, and comfort of his people. In these ordinances, the sacrificial death and atonement of Jesus Christ are the "sum and substance." Some of the divine ordinances and institutions are for the conversion of sinners and the daily spiritual nourishment of the saints. In a sense, we should "commemorate" the Lord's death every single day. (Thomson appears to refer to basic spiritual disciplines like prayer and meditation on Scripture, but he does not elaborate.)

Other divine ordinances "belong more properly, though not exclusively, to the Christian Sabbath, and to the preaching of the gospel, which is a stated feast." Thomson states that "to preach the gospel is to preach a crucified Christ." Thus, it can be said that every Sabbath when the gospel is preached, the church "commemorates" the death of Jesus and his love for sinners.[114]

Thomson then turns to the Old Testament, where he finds two types of religious ordinances. Thomson discerns "ordinary or daily religious services of the Jewish church," and also "extraordinary" ordinances and institutions. These "extraordinary" ordinances had the same purpose and design as the "ordinary" and "daily" services—to foreshadow the salvific work of Jesus Christ.[115] Thomson's key point is that these "extraordinary" services were infrequent, and that only two of them correspond with the sacraments in the New Testament: Circumcision = Baptism, and Passover = Lord's Supper. With the Passover, there was a great deal of God-ordained "solemnity" during the observance of Passover, so there should also be large doses of solemnity during communion.

Regarding fast days in preparation for communion, Thomson finds Biblical warrant for preparatory fast days in the "four days which may be called preparatory to the killing of the paschal lamb."[116] These days prior to Passover required special religious "exercises not common to other days." The Jews had to gather "bitter herbs" during the days of preparation before Passover, which typifies "that painful contrition and anguish of spirit which New Testament believers experience, while

113 Thomson, *Letters Addressed to the Rev. John Mason*, 23–24.
114 Thomson, *Letters Addressed to the Rev. John Mason*, 25.
115 Thomson, *Letters Addressed to the Rev. John Mason*, 26.
116 Thomson, *Letters Addressed to the Rev. John Mason*, 27.

they look upon him [Christ] in the gospel Passover [sic]."[117] Additionally, Thomson appeals to the six "feast days" after the Passover in order to find Biblical warrant for special days of religious services surrounding the Lord's Supper.

In Letter 3, Thompson repeats much of the same material, but an important difference between him and Mason emerges. Indeed, this is a major difference between writers advocating frequent communion and those defending the Scottish *status quo*. Thomson believes that true "examination" (as commanded by Paul) will be sorrowful. Thomson doubts that anyone can truly "examine" themselves without "being penetrated with most intense sorrow, while, at the same time, he, by faith, contemplates the wounded Saviour, pierced by his sins."[118] Thomson clarifies that he does "approve of frequency of this communion," but he denies that this is positively and expressly commanded in Scripture.[119] This surprises at first. How can Thomson say he favors frequent communion? The point to remember is that people in Scotland could "communicate" up to eight times a year, by traveling or visiting other churches and participating in their communions.

In Letter 4 Thomson scores a rhetorical point when he attacks Mason's lack of Scriptural argument. Instead of debating about church history, Thomson prefers to rely on "scriptural antiquity."[120] Mason's citation of authors and preachers who also advocate frequent communion is irrelevant because the "greater number of respectable ministers" follow the established Scots Reformed practices of infrequency and sacramental fasting and thanksgiving.[121] Thomson admits that there have been problems and "irregularities" at the large sacramental "seasons" and multi-parish gatherings, but points to the large gatherings around the ministries of John the Baptist and Jesus. The spiritual blessings outweigh any negative consequences in these gatherings.

Schmidt summarizes the result of the written debate between John Mason and John Thompson, in the context of the growing movement towards communion frequency: "Mason's book itself, though indebted to earlier formulations, marked something of a turning-point: it was among the fullest, most influential treatises on the subject, a text that was said to have 'made a great sensation among Scottish people everywhere' and one that helped further solidify the official line of thought on the issue."[122] Thompson's response did not garner as much attention, but other

---

117 Thomson, *Letters Addressed to the Rev. John Mason*, 27.
118 Thomson, *Letters Addressed to the Rev. John Mason*, 34.
119 Thomson, *Letters Addressed to the Rev. John Mason*, 37.
120 Thomson, *Letters Addressed to the Rev. John Mason*, 39.
121 Thomson, *Letters Addressed to the Rev. John Mason*, 40.
122 Schmidt, *Holy Fairs*, 190, quoting from Jacob van Vetchen, *Memoirs of John M. Mason, D.D., S.T.P. with Portions of his Correspondence* (New York: Robert Carter and Brothers, 1865), 68–69.

respondents to Mason like John Anderson (treated below, 6.1.6), were heavily indebted to him.

Both Mason and Thomson are given to rhetorical excess and when they do turn to Scriptural exegesis, their conclusions seem forced and sometimes far-fetched. Thomson's refusal to deal with church history is remarkable. He claims the high ground of the Bible and disdains to get involved in the details of the past. This biblicism might have served him well in the confrontation with Mason, but more awareness of how the Scottish communion seasons evolved in the context of history may have tempered his claims about their Biblical foundations. Thomson offered a spirited resistance to Mason but could not stop the growth of the frequent communion movement.[123]

6.1.6 John Anderson (c. 1748–1830)

John Anderson was another theological combatant in the scuffle stirred up by John Mason. He wrote a response to Mason in 1800 that was heavily dependent on Thomson (who he quotes at length in his footnotes).[124] Although brief, his pamphlet is important to survey, if only because the voices for communion frequency outnumbered the voices defending traditional Scots Reformed practice and Anderson defended the practices that Mason and other pro-frequency voices attacked. As it often happens in movements for change, those lobbying for change have the most to say, while those defending the *status quo* were more reluctant to enter the fray. This summary will not repeat arguments that he borrows from Thomson but will focus on Anderson's own contributions. Contextually, Anderson was a minister in a group that had splintered off from the main body of the Scottish Presbyterian church. He began his ministry in Scotland, and then traveled to Pennsylvania, which had

---

123 Schmidt comments: "But more important than Mason's specific tract was the weight of opposition to the traditional practices: the number of works for frequency simply dwarfed the number for festivity … If after 1800 the process of moving from festivity to frequency still often remained slow, it was nonetheless all but inexorable … As the logic of frequency triumphed, semiannual and quarterly communions gradually came to supplant the annual festivities of the summer season." *Holy Fairs*, 190.

124 John Anderson, *Communion Seasons Defended: A Scriptural Response to John M. Mason's "Letters on Frequent Communion"* ed. Sean McDonald (2013). Originally published as, "Of Humiliation-days before, and Thanksgiving-days after, the Administration of the Lord's Supper," in Anderson's, *Vindicae Cantus Dominici. In two parts: I. A discourse of the duty of singing the book of Psalms in solemn worship. II. A vindication of the doctrine taught in the preceding discourse. With an appendix: containing essays and observations on various subjects* (Philadelphia: David Hogan, 1800), 301–321. The larger work was a defense of singing only Biblical psalms in worship, and the appendix contained miscellaneous essays on themes related to worship in Reformed churches. The original text can be found at: https://archive.org/details/vcantusd00ande/page/n17.

many other conservative Scots immigrants.[125] As with Thomson, he saw himself as defending the traditional Scots Reformed sacramental practices against dangerous innovations. Like John Mason, he is important as a link between Scotland and the Americas and demonstrates how Scottish frequency debates spanned the Atlantic.

[handwritten margin note: Atlantic Spread of the debate]

Anderson begins his pamphlet with the same quotation from Witsius that Mason appealed to in his *Letters*.[126] However, Mason appealed to Witsius when Witsius describes the frequent communion of the early church, and the subsequent decline in spiritual zeal. Mason had acknowledged that Witsius does not advocate for frequent communion in his present context. Anderson seizes on the quote because it encapsulates his own concerns about frequent communion:

> Since our Lord hath not precisely determined the time of communicating; but by the expression *as often*, hath only recommended the frequent practice of it in general; it seems requisite, especially amidst a great prevalence of corruption, that a medium should be observed; lest, by too great a frequency, this sacred provision should be disesteemed, or the table of the Lord slighted and neglected.[127]

This encapsulates two key elements of the "careful frequency" position: that the Bible does not give clear instruction about frequency, specifically, but commands frequency in general; and that, when people are spiritually immature or corrupt, we should be careful that they do not profane the Table of the Lord. The term "careful frequency" highlights the fact that those arguing against proponents of weekly communion were not necessarily opposed to more frequent communion. In some cases, they admit that people do not come to communion often enough. However, they are more concerned that people do not come carelessly, and they want to maintain the "solemnity" of the Lord's Supper, which they believe is incompatible with communion that is too frequent.

---

125 On Anderson, see James Price, "Letters of Rev. John Anderson, D.D., and Matthew Henderson," *Journal of the Presbyterian Historical Society* (September, 1902), pgs. 341–343. See also James P. Miller, *Biographical Sketches and Sermons of Some of the First Ministers of the Associate Church in America* (Albany: Hoffman and White, 1839), 359–366. For the complex history of various groups in the Scottish church see William Lyons Fisk, *The Scottish High Church Tradition in America: An Essay in Scotch-Irish Ethnoreligious History* (Lanham, MD: University Press of America, 1995).

126 "The admirable Witsius, after a short detail of the original frequency of communicating, and of its decline with the 'increase of numbers and the decrease of zeal,' exclaims, 'Alas! how far are we at this day from the sanctity and zeal of the ancients!'" Mason, *Letters on Frequent Communion*, 42–43, quoting Witsius, *De Oeconomia Foederum* (1677), 4.17.33. Mason acknowledges that Witsius is apprehensive that greater frequency would lead some to not value the sacrament properly, but he maintains that is not a legitimate concern in the 1800s.

127 Anderson, *Communion Seasons Defended*, 5, quoting Herman Witsius, *De Oeconomia Foederum*, 4.17.33.

Anderson lays out his case in six short sections. First, he argues that the Lord's Supper is a uniquely solemn spiritual occasion. Secondly, he states the necessity of preparing for the Lord's Supper. Thirdly, he argues for the propriety of fasting in preparation for the Lord's Supper. In his fourth section, he attempts to refute the allegation that communion seasons are superstitious. Fifthly, he deals with the "practical suitability" of the communion seasons. In the last section, he presents his own eucharistic theology and exegetes various texts relating to frequency.

As with Thomson, Anderson believes the Supper has a "unique solemnity."[128] This becomes his interpretive grid through which to evaluate considerations about frequency. If a practice highlights and contributes to the solemnity of communion, that makes it a good thing. If it detracts from solemnity (as frequency does, in his view) then that negates any other value that frequency might bring to the observance of the sacrament. In this connection, Anderson continues the trajectory laid out by Thomson of focusing on Old Testament texts. This is a consistent pattern in Scottish authors who argue against frequent communion. The numerous solemn days of the Old Testament are the background against which we should interpret, and celebrate, the Lord's Supper.[129]

As a corollary to the solemnity of the Supper, Anderson stresses the necessity and "duty" of preparing for it, relying on 1 Cor. 11:28. 2 Chronicles 30:18-20 is also cited, in which some of the Jews were punished by God for eating the Passover without following the process for purification.[130] This is a stark typological warning about the necessity of eating the Lord's Supper in the proper way and demonstrates the flexible hermeneutic at work in Anderson's argumentation. What happened to the Old Covenant people is a model for us to follow, or to avoid. How then should we prepare for communion in the New Covenant? Through "an exercise of solemn prayer, meditation, and self-examination, necessary before communicating; the neglect of which even in real Christians, may cause very heavy corrections."[131] Anderson denies that proper preparation results in a "legal spirit," and rather maintains that we see so much spiritual pride precisely *because* so many do not engage in these spiritual "exercises."

One of the key points of contention in frequency debates is the question of how much time should be spent preparing beforehand.[132] For advocates of infrequency,

---

128 Anderson, *Communion Seasons Defended*, 7.
129 "The Old Testament church had more solemn days, such as that on which the children of Israel stood before the Lord in Horeb. And there were to be such days under the New Testament dispensation also." Anderson, *Communion Seasons Defended*, 8.
130 Anderson, *Communion Seasons Defended*, 9.
131 Anderson, *Communion Seasons Defended*, 9.
132 "Such preparation for the Lord's Supper being necessary, a competent portion of time for it must also be necessary." Anderson, *Communion Seasons Defended*, 9.

the emphasis on proper preparation, as they define it, necessitates a longer interval between communions. Mason had argued that true preparation is not a "multitude of outward performances" or "various exercises of public worship."[133] Anderson attempts a *reductio* in response—if what Mason says is true, would this not do away with the necessity for all of the other means of grace? If such a small dose of real repentance is of so much spiritual value, do we really need "prayers" and the "hearing of the Word"? Additionally, Mason's statement undermines the necessity of frequent communion itself. Why do we need frequent communion if we have "one hour, one minute of genuine humiliation"?[134] Anderson correctly notes the tendency of Mason's overemphasis on frequency to tend in the direction of devaluing the importance of the sacrament.[135] For Anderson, a "gracious contrition for sin" seems to be the chief attribute of being prepared to partake of communion.[136] Additionally, it is inconceivable to him that this contrition can be attained without devoting considerable time to spiritual reflection and prayer. Therefore, because of this key eucharistic emphasis, communion must necessarily be infrequent.

Preparation should also involve fasting, which was another aspect of the Scottish communion traditions that were attacked by advocates of frequency. Anderson dismisses the contention of those who advocate fasting only when there is some extraordinary circumstance or extreme time of trial.[137] There are two reasons for fasting: when we are under a conviction of sin, or when we have a "duty" to perform, in which we need special spiritual help and support.[138] The obvious implication is that the Lord's Supper involves both conditions. But fasting is not merely abstinence from food. It is the "solemn exercise of self-examination and self-judging, which the apostle enjoins as previously necessary to communicating. It is the exercise of searching and trying our ways and turning to the Lord."[139] Anderson anticipates an objection—if we should fast before the Lord's Supper, why not also fast before a baptism? This is more than a passing objection. Advocates of frequency often brought baptism into the discussion, and point out the disparity between levels of "preparation" and intensity of participation.[140] To Anderson, the two sacraments cannot be compared in this way and "there are no such express directions about

---

133 Anderson, *Communion Seasons Defended*, quoting Mason, *Letters on Frequent Communion* (Edinburgh: J. Ritchie, 1798), 50, 51. See §6.1.4 for Mason on the nature of "true" preparation.
134 Anderson, *Communion Seasons Defended*, 10, 11.
135 See §6.1.4.
136 Anderson, *Communion Seasons Defended*, 11.
137 He refers to Ezra 9:5; Acts 10:30; James 4:9, 10; Matt. 17:21.
138 Anderson, *Communion Seasons Defended*, 12.
139 Anderson, *Communion Seasons Defended*, 12, 13.
140 See §6.2 below, for a concluding overview and comparative analysis.

preparation for circumcision or baptism, as about the Passover and the Lord's Supper."[141]

The next stage in the argument concerns a defense of the Scottish "communion seasons."[142] Since these highlight the solemnity of the sacrament, and since they allow people to prepare thoroughly, they are salutary and helpful, even though they are not expressly commanded by God in Scripture. Accordingly, we have liberty to observe days of "humiliation" and "thanksgiving," as long they are all focused on what is explicitly commanded, which is the Lord's Supper itself.[143]

When Anderson turns to Scriptural exegesis, he presents a more positive statement of his theology of the Lord's Supper. First, he considers the meaning of the word "often" in the New Testament. Scripture does not explicitly state how "often" we should partake of the Lord's Supper. This is a key point in the "careful frequency" theological framework. According to 1 Cor. 11:26 (one of the favorite verses of the pro-frequency camp), the Supper should be observed "often," but it does not prove that it should be observed "in all states of the church, either every Lord's Day, or even every month."[144] To counter the pro-frequency interpretation of "often" in 1 Cor. 11, Anderson points to Heb. 9:25 and 2 Cor. 11:23.[145] These verses clearly describe events that did *not* happen every week. Although there are differences in the Greek between 1 Cor. 11:26 and these passages, it does seem that Paul (and the writer to the Hebrews) can describe something as occurring "often," without necessarily indicating weekly frequency.[146]

Anderson next offers his interpretation of Acts 20:7 and 1 Cor. 11, both key texts for the pro-frequency camp. He relates his own travels to Philadelphia, where he visited a church which happened to celebrate the Supper on that day. He asks if he would be justified in concluding that this church celebrates the Supper every

---

141 Anderson, *Communion Seasons Defended*, 14.

142 Anderson, *Communion Seasons Defended*, 15.

143 Anderson argues that observance of communion seasons is not superstitious for someone, if we only regard: "(1) the opportunity that providence affords him for such an exercise, (2) the suitableness of it to his case, and (3) its consistency and connection with other duties; nor is he at all chargeable with formality, merely on account of that frequent recurrence." Anderson, *Communion Seasons Defended*, 15.

144 Anderson, *Communion Seasons Defended*, 19.

145 "In Hebrews 9:25 the word 'often' is used with respect to the high priest's entering into the holy place every year. When Paul says that he was 'in deaths oft' (2 Corinthians 11:23), one may doubt whether he was so every week, or even every month." Anderson, *Communion Seasons Defended*, 19.

146 Heb. 9:25 and 2 Cor. 11:23 use πολλάκις, which can mean, "many times," "often," "frequently," while Paul uses ὁσάκις in 1 Cor. 11:26, which can mean, "as often as." Clearly, there is an overlap in semantic range. See entries in Walter Bauer, *A Greek-English Lexicon of the New Testament and Other Early Christian Literature*, trans. and rev. by W.F. Arndt, F.W. Gingrich, and F.W. Danker (Chicago: University of Chicago Press, 1979).

Sunday? So then, for Anderson, we do not possess enough information to say that the church in Troas observed the Supper on every first day of the week (Acts 20:6-7).[147]

Regarding 1 Cor. 11, Anderson disagrees that the phrase "come together in the church" necessarily refers to an official worship service. To claim this is the same as claiming that every time the New Testament mentions "breaking bread," this must refer to the Lord's Supper as well.[148] Anderson does not examine any textual evidence to confirm his claim here, except in a reference note to Luke 24. He notes that some have read the "breaking of bread" by Jesus in the Emmaus Road narrative with eucharistic overtones, but dismisses this as an absurd notion, since it is not "probable that these two disciples, as yet, knew anything of the institution of the Lord's Supper."[149] Anderson maintains that the wording of "come together in the church," or "in one place," can also refer to simply gathering to hear the Word or to pray, and refers to Acts 10:27 and 13:44 in support of these usages. He then seizes the rhetorical and theological high ground with a quote from Calvin, commenting on 1 Cor. 11:17. As Anderson quotes Calvin "[t]his, in my judgment, does not respect abuses in the Lord's Supper only, but other evils, such as the apostle mentions in the two following verses."[150]

One of the main focal points in these Scottish communion frequency debates is whether the Lord's Supper is a "feast" or a "fast"? Anderson strongly maintains that it is *not* a feast.[151] To require the Lord's Supper as a part of every Lord's Day worship service would be to revert to Old Testament patterns of "feast days." We see here that, to Anderson, "feast" is an irrevocably Old Covenant term, and closely aligned to Roman Catholic "feast" days. He operates with a definition of "feast" which is dominated by Old Testament considerations, read through an anti-Roman Catholic filter. This differs from the use of the term "feast," as used by the pro-frequency camp.[152]

Another common topic in frequency debates is the relative priority of the Word over the Sacrament. Because of the priority of the preached Word (the "testa- ment"), people must be carefully instructed through the Word, before they partake of the Supper (which is the "seal" of the testament). Anderson also claims that

---

147 Anderson, *Communion Seasons Defended*, 20–21.

148 Anderson, *Communion Seasons Defended*, 21.

149 Anderson, *Communion Seasons Defended*, 30.

150 Anderson, *Communion Seasons Defended*, 22. Anderson, and the editor of the most recent edition of this work, do not provide a reference for this quote from Calvin. However, it agrees substantively with Calvin's *Commentary on the Epistles of Paul to the Corinthians*, vol. 1 (Edinburgh: Calvin Translation Society, 1848; reprint, Grand Rapids: Baker Books, 2005), 364.

151 Anderson, *Communion Seasons Defended*, 19.

152 See §6.2.2 for specific examples.

pro-frequency writers link the benefits of communion too closely to the actual "outward" act of partaking. On the contrary, he compares communion to baptism, and argues that spiritual benefits continue far beyond the actual time of baptism, or communing.[153]

Anderson also argues that more frequent communion would undermine the special "solemnity" of the Lord's Supper. In response to pro-frequency authors who question why we are not suspicious of frequency in other religious duties (like prayer, Scripture reading, meditation), Anderson draws a distinction between the Supper and the other ordinances. Since the Lord's Supper is a "sensible" (sensory) ordinance it should be infrequent, so that our senses are not dulled. For Anderson, it is a serious question whether Christians can observe the Supper frequently, and not lose the "sensible impression of the outward sign," because of the weakness of our human nature.[154]

For Anderson to caution against frequent communion does not mean that he opposes it completely. In fact, he claims that he does not intend to "discourage any attempt towards bringing about a greater frequency of the Scriptural practice of communicating."[155] He acknowledges that Calvin desired frequent communion and laments the "lukewarmness" of many church members in their attitudes towards the Supper. However, we must "beware of whatever tends to lessen our impression of the solemnity of this ordinance." Anderson seeks to strike a balance between neglecting the ordinance and a lack of preparation for it. He believes that a healthy spirituality, and healthy churches, would seek communion more frequently than at present, but also believes that "no church is authorized to determine positively how often in the month, or in the year, we are to communicate."[156]

Anderson is an important voice in these debates because he articulates the "careful frequency position" succinctly. Although he relies on Thomson in the overarching structure of his argument, he does provide a few additional points of argumentation for the Scottish communion seasons. His focus is on the Old Testament, as was Thomson's. Because of the "early corruptions" in the early church, he cautions readers about appealing to early church history as normative. Scriptural "warrant" is the only norm.[157] This stance fits within the wider pattern of careful frequency authors not engaging in historical arguments. As a Scottish minister who emigrated to

---

153 "The benefit of baptism, once received, is continued to the end of life; so the benefit of the Lord's Supper does not pass away with the transient act of receiving, but is abiding and operative afterwards." Anderson, *Communion Seasons Defended*, 20.

154 Anderson, *Communion Seasons Defended*, 23.

155 Anderson, *Communion Seasons Defended*, 23.

156 Anderson, *Communion Seasons Defended*, 24.

157 "With regard to the example of Christians after the apostolic age, recorded in human writings; the early corruptions that seem to have obtained, especially in the administration of the sacraments,

Pennsylvania, he serves as a link connecting Scots Reformed communion practices and patterns in the Americas.

6.1.7 Alexander Duncan (1777–1844)

Alexander Duncan, a Scottish minister, penned another strident response to John Mitchell Mason.[158] In 1807, he published *A Disquisition on the Observance of the Lord's Supper with a View to the Defence* [sic] *of the Presbyterian Plan of Administrating That Ordinance.* It included "A Short Review of Mr. Mason's Letters on Communion" as an appendix. He notes that he received a copy of Anderson's work after his own had gone to press, but provides several quotes from Anderson, in the hopes that more readers in Britain will become familiar with it.[159] In general, as we have seen before, there are more sources arguing for more frequent communion, because they are arguing for the purpose of changing the *status quo*. There are fewer defenses of the *status quo*, so it is important to include a short summary of Duncan's treatise. At two hundred and twenty-three pages, it is the longest, and most substantive, of the "careful frequency" sources uncovered during the course of research.

Duncan has two main goals. First, he endeavors to demonstrate the Biblical basis for large, multi-parish gatherings to celebrate the Lord's Supper, arguing that this is a superior way to observe the sacrament. Second, he critiques advocates of weekly communion. He goes further than other writers surveyed thus far and argues that large multi-parish eucharistic gatherings are the best expression of Presbyterian principles.

There are five sections in Duncan's treatise. Section one deals extensively with Biblical teachings on the nature of the Lord's Supper and focuses on explicating the Old Testament background. Section two applies the conclusions from section one and argues that "occasional observance" of communion accords best with the theological nature and function of the Supper. Section three further explains the desirability of infrequent communion, especially as it relates to the solemnity of the Supper. Section four responds to objections and deals with church historical arguments used to argue for frequent communion. Section five details Duncan's argument for the continued observance of special days of preparation and solemn

---

admonish us to be cautious of imitating them in any one thing in which we cannot see that they had Scriptural warrant." Anderson, *Communion Seasons Defended*, 24.

158 As with John Thompson, further biographical details about Alexander Duncan have been elusive.
159 Duncan, *A Disquisition*, vii. He also quotes John Thompson several times throughout his essay. He is responding to Mason, and so quotes his work, but does not directly argue against Erskine, Randall, or John Brown of Haddington.

celebration of the Lord's Supper on an infrequent basis. Finally, an appendix considers and responds to Mason's *Letters on Frequent Communion* in more detail. This survey will summarize the main points of Duncan's sections, but will also group material together in a way that shows the overall coherence of Duncan's argumentation.

In his Preface, Duncan makes a claim that becomes one of the main themes of his essay. He equates advocacy of frequent communion with "Independent principles," which undermine the Presbyterian system. Thus, as he responds to arguments for frequent communion throughout the rest of his work, he is also defending Presbyterian ecclesiology.[160] He admits that the Independent customs of communion observance are appealing and have a *prima facie* plausibility.[161] But there are dangers as well. One danger is that the less spiritual will be satisfied by perfunctory frequent communion, and encouraged in their worldliness, instead of challenged to spend more time in "religious services" that prepared them for the Lord's Table.[162] Here Duncan makes the standard argument that greater frequency will result in less spiritual intensity and seriousness.

In section one, Duncan lays down his foundational claims. Though Duncan is arguing against frequent communion, this does not mean that he devalues the sacrament. On the contrary, he urges the importance of the Lord's Supper as a "peculiar ordinance of salvation" that has a "special purpose … beyond what the preaching of the word could accomplish." It is not a "sign for bare contemplation. The observance of it lies in dispensing and receiving."[163] Additionally, "the ordinance of the Supper, by sealing this covenant, must be an eminent mean of spiritual nutrition. There is no grace it is not calculated to strengthen and improve."[164] As a meal of

---

160 "The late vigorous dissemination of Independent principles, followed up by a practical exhibition of the Independent plan to an extent hitherto unknown in North Britain [= Scotland], may sufficiently apologize for calling the attention of the public to the subject of the following sheets." *A Disquisition on the Observance of the Lord's Supper with a View to the Defence of the Presbyterian Plan of Administrating That Ordinance* (Edinburgh: Thomas Turnball, 1805; reprint, Carlisle: George Kline, 1807), v.

161 He grants that the "mode of observing the ordinance of communion has an imposing appearance, and is apt to throw serious Christians off by the value of the ordinance, by primitive usage, and other considerations apparently unconnected with the Independent scheme." *A Disquisition*, v.

162 Duncan, *A Disquisition*, v–vi.

163 Duncan, *A Disquisition*, 21.

164 Duncan, *A Disquisition*, 28.

"communion" it is a feast of Jesus with his friends.[165] To observe the Lord's Supper is to "glory in the cross of Christ" and it is also a "celebration" of the death of Christ.[166] It is not merely a mournful looking back upon the death of Jesus; it is also a triumphant declaration of Jesus' resurrection.[167] The Supper is also a fitting time to make personal vows to God, and to renew our commitment to him.[168]

It is important to remember that careful frequency authors were not trying to minimize the sacrament. Rather, they saw themselves as giving it the respect it deserved. Duncan explicitly rejects the views of Zwingli, and affirms the view of Calvin that the Supper is "an ordinance in which Christ crucified is really, though only spiritually, present in, or by the symbols employed."[169] Since the Supper is "the grand ordinance of spiritual nutrition, [it] ought to be frequent during the life of a saint."[170] However, "frequent" does not necessarily entail "weekly" communion.

Section two presents Duncan's "conclusions" from his claims in section one. Duncan's stress on the Old Testament characterizes his treatise, and he goes further here than other "careful frequency" authors. He stresses the fact that the Supper fulfills and replaces the Passover, to the exclusion of the other Old Testament feasts.[171] Only the Passover actually "typified" Christ and so it was the only "sacramental" feast of the Old Covenant.[172] Duncan shares this emphasis with other "careful frequency" advocates like John Thompson and John Anderson. Stressing the primary symbolic and typological importance of the Passover appears to strengthen their case that the Lord's Supper is a solemn event and should be accompanied by appropriate levels of preparation and solemn observance. Additionally, since the Passover was observed annually, this primary correlation between the Supper and

---

165 "Now of all ordinances, the Supper, from the very relation it bears to the first kind of fellowship, is the most calculated to promote this divine and blissful communion … Here Jesus holds a feast with his professed friends." In the Supper, "they *commune with him*; while he, on the other hand *communes with them* by the words of institution, or by the operation of his Spirit calling to remembrance." Duncan, *A Disquisition*, 30.

166 Duncan, *A Disquisition*, 36.

167 "Communicants, by the observance of this ordinance, stand forth to public view, ranged under the standard of the cross, the armies of heaven who follow the Lamb in his vesture of blood." Duncan, *A Disquisition*, 38.

168 Duncan, *A Disquisition*, 38–39.

169 Duncan, *A Disquisition*, 52.

170 Duncan, *A Disquisition*, 40.

171 Duncan, *A Disquisition*, 9–11.

172 The other major feasts of the Old Testament, Pentecost and the Feast of Tabernacles, "did not, like the passover, typify Christ in some particular view of his character and work, so that ordinances bearing on the verification in the fulness of time, and thus answering to them, could be appointed," and "It was, from its peculiar nature and references, of the three annual solemnities, the only sacramental feast, and corresponding to it there is but one sacred feast in the Christian Church, the Lord's Supper." Duncan, *A Disquisition*, 12, 14.

Passover provides additional support for infrequent communion.[173] Duncan states all of this either explicitly or implicitly throughout his pamphlet.[174]

Weekly communion would "reduce it to a level with the usual dispensation of grace, as in no respect more solemn," and to remove any "marks of speciality" from the sacrament.[175] Since the Passover was not part of the "stated," or regularly occurring worship, of the Old Covenant, and since Jesus did not specify anything different, then he concludes that the Supper should not be part of the "stated" worship of the Christian church (we will consider below how Duncan dealt with the New Testament proof texts for frequent communion appealed to by his opponents).[176] If the Supper is observed regularly, as a part of weekly worship, then it will lose its "impressive effect."[177]

Duncan also makes a broader claim about the use and appropriateness of "symbols." He maintains that the use of "symbols" was "an accommodation to an imperfect state of the church" in the Old Covenant era.[178] In the New Covenant era, when the church is more mature, there is less need for symbols: "The ordinance of the Supper is thus, as far as the use of symbols is concerned, somewhat like a relic of God's ancient method of training up his church."[179] The mature church should focus primarily on the "simple preaching of the gospel," rather than ceremonies and symbols.[180] God does not want "his people constantly under the sensible pledges of his favour" because this would eventually make communion mere routine, and would rob it of its "striking and strongly confirming effect."[181] Further, if frequency is the goal, then Duncan asks why not pursue more than weekly communion? Why not hold communion "twice, thrice, four times a-week"?[182] Weekly communions cannot sustain the "solemnity" required by a proper observance of the Lord's Table. Those who practice weekly communion shorten the worship service, which lessens

---

173 "If the Supper was appointed instead of the Passover, as the correspondent ordinance in the present economy, then, *mutatis mutandis*, its nature and use, or the purposes it was intended to serve, must be the same with those of the ancient sacrament." Duncan, *A Disquisition*, 14.

174 Duncan, *A Disquisition*, 51.

175 Duncan, *A Disquisition*, 42.

176 Duncan, *A Disquisition*, 42.

177 Duncan, *A Disquisition*, 42–43.

178 Duncan, *A Disquisition*, 44.

179 Duncan, *A Disquisition*, 44.

180 "Instead of all the other symbols and carnal ordinances of the law, we were to enjoy the simple preaching of the gospel, the plenary and unveiled dispensation of spiritual privilege." Duncan, *A Disquisition*, 44.

181 Duncan, *A Disquisition*, 45.

182 Duncan, *A Disquisition*, 63.

its spiritual profundity.[183] Additionally, Duncan repeats the standard concern that "familiarity breeds contempt."[184]

Sections three and four deal with church history and the evidence of the New Testament. Here, Duncan also repeatedly stresses the important function of the Lord's Table in symbolizing the visible unity of the Christian church. But the Lord's Supper does not only symbolize this unity—it also helps to create and confirm the visible unity of the church. In this sense, it is both a powerful sociological symbol, as well as a religious symbolic rite.[185] In this *ecumenical* consideration we encounter Duncan's strongest argument for his view. Weekly communion restricts the opportunities for members of different churches to gather and manifest the "unity" and "fellowship" that all Christians have with each other. Although weekly communion might strengthen the unity of individuals in a particular church, Duncan sees great benefit in the tradition of multi-parish extended communions, which brought people together from many different towns and churches.

Although he considers historical evidence more than Thomson and Anderson, Duncan is suspicious of claims to church history. Instead of appeals to historical "facts," he appeals to "principles." For Duncan, the primary task is to determine the Biblical teaching on the nature and purpose of the Lord's Supper, and to judge history, and everything else, by that standard.[186]

Regarding the early, apostolic church, he wonders whether the apostolic church's practice was "hostile to the presbyterian method" of large, occasional communion observance. However, the immaturity of the early church counts against making dogmatic appeals to it.[187]

While interpreting various texts in the New Testament that relate to communion frequency, he states three general conclusions in the first part of section four: first

---

183 Duncan, *A Disquisition*, 71.

184 He worries that, "according to human infirmity great familiarity with solemn institutions will ever tend gradually to remove the impression God designed they should make, and with it much of the peculiar effect they were framed to produce." Duncan, *A Disquisition*, 72.

185 Duncan, *A Disquisition*, 60.

186 He acknowledges the rhetorical effectiveness of appeals to history, but asks, "But who knows not that we are to judge of facts by principles, and that many practices which boast of high antiquity are far from deserving approbation or perpetuity? Let the nature and design of the Lord's Supper first be determined, and let every usage antient or modern be tried by this standard." Duncan, *A Disquisition*, 80.

187 Duncan, *A Disquisition*, 81–82. Duncan posits that Jesus probably delivered the pattern of Presbyterian government and worship during the forty days he spent with his disciples after his resurrection. Ironically, this same argument from silence is used by Catholic and Anglican apologists to justify the institutions and practices of their respective communions, and Thomas Randall used it to argue *for* frequent communion! See §6.1.3, for Randall's use of this argument.

"[w]e have no express injunction of frequency,"[188] secondly "[t]here is no evidence from the New Testament, that the Lord's Supper was observed every first day of the week," and thirdly "[c]ertain intimations, unfriendly to the idea of weekly communion occur."[189] Let us briefly review these arguments in turn.

The first claim Duncan interacts with is the often-repeated appeal to the "dying words of Christ," which are "usually brought forward in triumph" by pro-frequency writers. Although the words of Jesus at the institution of the Lord's Supper are important, they cannot be used in favor of any pattern of communion frequency that would "remove the idea of solemnity" or "prevent the manifestation of unity" in the sacrament. Duncan then turns to 1 Cor. 11:26, which is a favorite text for pro-frequency authors. He maintains that the Greek word ὁσάκις [hosakis] does not mean merely "as often as," as is commonly stated, but means something like "whensoever."[190] Regarding the use of ὁσάκις in 1 Cor. 11:26 "[t]he frequency of the exercise is neither implied, affirmed, nor denied in it."[191] Paul's point is not to mandate frequent communion by the use of ὁσάκις, but rather to simply warn the Corinthians of the danger of mismanaging the Supper "whenever" they observe it, because of their pattern of abuses.[192]

Duncan's second major argument is: "There is no evidence from the New Testament, that the Lord's Supper was observed every first day of the week."[193] The main point of contention is the meaning of the phrase "breaking bread." Proponents of frequent communion tend to interpret "breaking of bread" in the New Testament as instances of communion. However, "[i]t cannot be reckoned fair or candid, to bring forward every passage where the breaking of bread is mentioned, as if this ordinance were always meant," since this was merely the standard Jewish expression for partaking of a meal.[194]

Third, as to the "certain intimations" that are "unfriendly" to the idea of weekly communion in the New Testament, Duncan surveys 1 Cor. 10, 1 Cor. 11:20, and

---

188 He maintains, "the frequency of observance is left to be inferred from the importance of the ordinance, and to be regulated by the most proper plan of accomplishing all its ends." Duncan, *A Disquisition*, 86.

189 Duncan, *A Disquisition*, 94.

190 "The word 'HOSAKIS "as often as," would require much criticism to elicit the idea of frequency, yet it has often been held out to the people on account of the sound of the English rendering as complete proof [of frequent communion]." Duncan, *A Disquisition*, 87.

191 Duncan, *A Disquisition*, 87.

192 "The apostle had heard of great abuses in the observance of the Supper. He wrote to correct these, not to excite to frequent communing. For the purpose of correction and admonition, he lays out the form of the institution to serve as a model, and to impress with a sense of the solemnity of the ordinance." Duncan, *A Disquisition*, 88.

193 Duncan, *A Disquisition*, 92.

194 Duncan, *A Disquisition*, 92.

various texts from Acts which he believes support the pattern of many Christians in a geographical area coming together to observe the Lord's Supper.[195] From the evidence of early church history, Duncan concludes that there was no uniformity of practice, and that the various attempts at regulating communion practices were not always ideal.[196] He argues that the very terms used by the early church to describe communion, *koinonia* and *synaxis*, implied a "gathering together" that manifested the "fellowship" of the church.[197] In this connection, he rejects several lines of evidence normally appealed to by advocates of weekly communion.

He warns his readers of accepting everything the church fathers wrote or did, because of the early rise of "gross errors and dreadful abuses" regarding the Lord's Supper.[198] The antiquity of a practice or belief does not prove its validity.[199] Rather, we must judge the practices of the early church by the principles of the apostolic church and, ultimately, by Scripture.[200] The early church may have started observing communion weekly, and even daily, based on their high estimation of the spiritual value of the Supper, while also losing sight of what Duncan believes is the primary design of the Lord's Supper—manifesting the visible unity of multiple churches within a geographical area.[201]

Turning to the sixteenth century Reformers, he agrees with Calvin that annual communion is inspired by the devil, but also states that "[t]he reformed have learned, and from Calvin too ... to call no man master on earth."[202] Thus, even if Calvin advocated for weekly communion, that does not automatically justify the practice. Additionally, Duncan speculates that the "zeal" of the first generation of

---

195 Duncan, *A Disquisition*, 94–112. He summarizes: "We conclude therefore, that the members of different congregations, as many as could, joined together at certain times in the ordinance of the Supper to testify their unity in the profession of Christ and for this end the ordinance was dispensed now at one place of meeting, now at another, in routine, sometimes in Corinth itself, then at Cenchrea the port-town, where there was confessedly [a] church, however small, and the members of which seem to be included among the Corinthians to whom the epistle is addressed." Duncan, *A Disquisition*, 113.

196 "From these accounts we can only gather that uniformity of practice did not obtain even in the age that succeeded the apostolic; and that afterwards different regulations were made by councils and bishops with a view to uniformity, but not always the best." Duncan, *A Disquisition*, 114.

197 Duncan, *A Disquisition*, 114.

198 "We must not judge from every expression, of the sentiments of the Fathers; and neither must we from every notice or illusion, reason to the general plan of observance, or form schemes of the universal practice in primitive times." Duncan, *A Disquisition*, 116.

199 "Of rectitude and propriety, antiquity has long been acknowledged to be no infallible test." Duncan, *A Disquisition*, 117.

200 Duncan, *A Disquisition*, 117–118.

201 Duncan, *A Disquisition*, 118.

202 Duncan, *A Disquisition*, 120.

Reformers may have carried them too far in this area.[203] Calvin's "spiritual" view of the Sabbath is also problematic, as another instance of Calvin reacting too much to the practices of the late medieval church.[204]

The Genevan practice of quarterly communion must also be taken into account as well as Calvin's concern that too frequent observance might lead to people not taking communion seriously enough.[205] Duncan concludes that: "However strange it may appear, what is styled by the advocates of weekly observance infrequent communion, has ever on reflection been considered as upon the whole most favourable even to the interests of religion."[206] Duncan finally argues that the rise of the "independent scheme," along with its observance of weekly communion, has brought further issues to light—issues that Calvin did not have to deal with. These new developments have highlighted other reasons to not pursue weekly communion.

In the final section—section five—Duncan launches a defense of the Scottish tradition of fast days, thanksgiving days, and preparation days before receiving communion. Advocates of weekly communion routinely attacked these days and the attendant customs, but Duncan is convinced of their spiritual and practical value. He admits that they have never been proposed as "essential" to the proper observance of the Lord's Supper, but they are still valuable.[207]

He then responds to objections against the days of thanksgiving and preparation. He presupposes that "humiliation" and "thanksgiving" are the dominant themes in observing the Lord's Supper, and therefore proposes that enough time should be chosen and marked out for people to prepare adequately before receiving communion.[208] The basic assumption of advocates for weekly communion is that the Supper is not a fitting occasion for fasting.[209]

Regarding fasting in preparation for communion, Duncan's arguments are a bit tedious and complicated. The main point is that, although the days of fasting, thanksgiving, and preparation are not mandated by Scripture, they are not contrary

---

203 Duncan, *A Disquisition*, 120.

204 Duncan, *A Disquisition*, 120.

205 He quotes a passage from Calvin that was generally neglected by advocates of weekly communion: "To celebrate the Supper once every month, would indeed be more agreeable to me, provided more frequent dispensation did not produce negligence." Duncan, *A Disquisition*, 123. See §2.9.2, for the same quote from Calvin, in a more contemporary source.

206 Duncan, *A Disquisition*, 123.

207 Duncan, *A Disquisition*, 124–25.

208 "If humiliation and thanksgiving be judged proper, some time must be allotted for them; and such days must be chosen as shall best suit the relation in which these exercises stand to the Supper." Duncan, *A Disquisition*, 134.

209 Duncan, *A Disquisition*, 137.

to Scripture and are salutary and beneficial.[210] Because the Supper is so important and meaningful, the more we prepare ourselves, the more deeply we will be affected and moved by our reception of communion.[211] Here is a strong emphasis on the quality of the recipient's faith—not on what God does to recipients through the Supper.

The solemnity of the Lord's Supper is another prime reason why the "preparatory exercises are seasonable and proper."[212] Although preparation can take place in private, Duncan cites the fact that God commanded public preparatory services in the Old Testament, and—again—the great spiritual utility of preparation services.[213] Because one of the main purposes of the Lord's Supper is to manifest the unity of the visible church, large, public gatherings accomplish this admirably, and so they are of great value. Duncan argues that weekly communion can never attain the same level of spiritual unity and communion made visible, both to fellow Christians, and to the watching world.[214]

Duncan's last major argument is that: "The mode of observing the Supper among us, is farther justified by the present state of the church, and the character of the age in which we live."[215] Although Duncan doubts much of the rhetoric used about the supposed "purity" of the early, or "primitive" church, he argues that the current state of the church falls far short of the apostolic times. Therefore, less frequent communion is more appropriate in times of spiritual degeneration.[216] If people do not have the time or interest to devote to spiritual preparation now, either once or twice a year, why should we assume they will be ready to come to communion more frequently?[217] Duncan ends his treatise with several practical points related to how the preparatory days can best be observed and regulated.[218]

---

210 "The object is not to prove such a call for fasting and thanksgiving as would render these exercises indispensably necessary to the due administration of the sacrament; but solely to shew, from the nature and design of the ordinance, that there is a propriety and expediency sufficient to vindicate their appointment." Duncan, *A Disquisition*, 148.

211 "The more extensive and deeply affected the views of sin under which they approach the table of the Lord, the more eager will be the actings of faith on the crucified Saviour, and the more abundant the consolation of atonement." Duncan, *A Disquisition*, 153.

212 Duncan, *A Disquisition*, 159.

213 Duncan, *A Disquisition*, 164–165.

214 Duncan, *A Disquisition*, 165–169.

215 Duncan, *A Disquisition*, 184.

216 Duncan, *A Disquisition*, 187.

217 Duncan, *A Disquisition*, 188.

218 "The authority of appointing such days of public worship as are connected with the Supper, belongs to the office-bearers of the church." Duncan, *A Disquisition*, 191; "When the days are appointed, they ought to be kept." 192; "It is proper that an uniformity of worship, particularly of the mode of celebrating the Supper, should obtain in a religious body." 194.

In conclusion, Duncan presents a thoughtful and detailed justification and defense of the Scottish pattern of infrequent communion, along with the traditions surrounding the preparatory days. His defense is much more cogent than John Thompson's, and on the same level as John Anderson's. He does identify and isolate many central issues of exegesis and historical interpretation. For instance, how should we weigh the evidence of history? What are the controlling typological models by which we understand the Lord's Supper, Passover, and the entire system of Old Testament feasts? How should we interpret the key New Testament texts? One of Duncan's key principles is that the Lord's Supper manifests the spiritual unity of Christians. He interprets everything else in light of this. His faithfulness to his foundational beliefs is commendable. He presents a defense of the Scottish system of sacramental festivity and continues the line of development laid out by the English Puritans in his stress on the absolute necessity to prepare spiritually before receiving the Lord's Supper.

6.1.8 John Brown of Haddington (1722–1787)

John Brown of Haddington's life is the stuff of legend. Rising from poverty, this orphaned child grew into one of the Scotland's most respected and beloved preachers and authors. His inauspicious beginnings and his rapid acquisition of languages such as Latin and Greek prompted urban legends and spiteful slander. As a result, any summary of John Brown's life must navigate through a tantalizing mix of historical truth and hagiographical embellishment.

He was born in 1722, near Abernathy, in Scotland. An early experience of seeing the Lord's Supper administered, and hearing the pastor preach about Christ, made a deep impression on him. His parents died when he was eleven, and he lived with various families. While tending sheep for an elderly man, John managed to teach himself Greek, Latin, and Hebrew. This was viewed with suspicion and some even accused him of being taught by the devil. Brown eventually received ministerial training in the new seminary started by members of the Associate Synod—the same denomination that Mason was a part of. After his ordination, he served as the minister in Haddington for thirty-six years, until his death in 1787. During those years, he taught numerous ministerial students and wrote several popular books. His catechism was especially popular in Presbyterian households in Northern Ireland.[219]

John Brown stands solidly in the stream of frequency debates surveyed thus far. His *An Apology for the More Frequent Administration of the Lord's Supper* was pub-

---

219 John Macleod, *Scottish Theology in Relation to Church History Since the Reformation* (Edinburgh: Banner of Truth, 2015; originally published in 1943), 193.

lished posthumously in 1804.[220] It is one of the more lucid treatments of communion frequency, containing many counter-arguments original to Brown.[221] According to the publisher's preface, Brown was the first minister in his association of churches to introduce bi-annual communion, though he desired greater frequency. The *Apology* was found in Brown's papers after his death, apparently edited and ready for publication. Although his pamphlet was published in 1804, Brown deals with many of the same themes that have been traced so far. He does not quote any of the other authors surveyed here. Brown arranges his pamphlet into sections, and they will be summarized here to show the flow and progression of thought in his arguments. Sections 1–7 deal with New Testament texts and church history, sections 8–11 present theological arguments, and section 11 answers objections. This last section is especially helpful, because the objections Brown considers provide insight into the common concerns about frequent communion at that time.

Pro-frequency authors appeal often to church history to buttress their case. Among these authors, Brown stands out because of his extensive use of historical argumentation. He maintains that communion was usually held every Sunday in the early church. This is proved by 1 Cor. 11: 25-26.[222] The phrase "as oft" proves that Paul approves of the frequency that then prevailed. If we claim to follow the example of the apostles in changing the day of worship and in having a system of church government with synods and presbyteries, then why do we not follow their example in frequent communion?[223] This pattern continued for the first 300 years of church history. In a footnote Brown appeals to various church fathers.[224] Protestant reformers are also called as witnesses: "All the Protestant Divines that I have read on this point, –declare themselves zealous for the more frequent administration of this ordinance."[225] He then quotes from Calvin, John Owen, Luther, and refers in passing to Doolittle, Campbell, Willison, Henry and "a multitude of others."

---

220 For a brief biography, see "John Brown of Haddington or Learning Greek Without a Teacher," in A.T. Robertson, *The Minister and His Greek New Testament* (1923; reprint, Vestavia Hills, AL: Solid Ground Christian Books, 2008), 103–108.

221 John Brown, *An Apology for the More Frequent Administration of the Lord's Supper; with Answers to the Objections Urged Against It* (Edinburgh: J. Ritchie, 1804). Interestingly, Brown does not address the issue of communion frequency in his popular work of systematic theology, *Compendium View of Natural and Revealed Religion*, originally published in 1782, but republished as *The Systematic Theology of John Brown of Haddington*, Introduced by Joel R. Beeke and Randall J. Pederson (Ross-shire: Christian Focus Publications; Grand Rapids: Reformation Heritage Books, 2002).

222 Brown's text mistakenly reads 1 Cor. "ii"; however, this seems to me simply to be a printer's error because he actually quotes 1 Cor. 11. He also references Luke 24:30, 31, 35; Acts 2:41, 46; Acts 20:7; 2 Cor. 11:20, 21.

223 Brown, *An Apology*, 5–6.

224 Brown, *An Apology*, 6–7 and 14–15.

225 Brown, *An Apology*, 7.

Brown then makes the standard appeal to other Protestant churches, as expressed in their ecclesial standards. He claims that "all" of them have opposed annual, or bi-annual, communion and have seen it as a relic of Roman Catholicism. Brown admits that these recommendations were not always put into practice (most notably in Scotland) but maintains that these ecclesiastical standards more clearly reveal what other Protestant leaders have thought best, though they may not have been able to put their reforms into practice.[226] As a scholar, Brown was well read in church history. He speculates on possible reasons for the rise of communion infrequency. Brown admits his reconstruction "from the hints of the history of these times" is speculative but maintains that it was a pretended regard for the "solemnity of the ordinances" which led the clergy to establish infrequent communion. Here it is impossible to miss the implied attack on current Scots Reformed sentiment, as regard for "solemnity" is one of the chief concerns of those who were defending the *status quo* in Scotland.[227]

As one seeking a further reformation of the Scottish church, similarly to Mason, Brown posits that greater frequency has been practiced, or advocated, in more pure churches, or eras of church history. Conversely, infrequent communion tends to accompany unfaithfulness in churches.[228] This is because infrequent communion leads to "looseness" in morality, since people can go for long periods of time without the "awe and dread of God" which accompanies communion. Ministers who administer communion infrequently encourage their congregations to partake infrequently, and so perpetuate a vicious cycle.[229] The Lord's Supper is "most calculated for communicating spiritual supplies of grace" and more frequent communion bestows more spiritual blessings. The Apostolic church and the Scottish Presbyterians in north Ireland are sterling examples of spiritual fervor, fueled by frequent communion. Brown refers here to the Scottish immigrants to the Ulster region of Scotland. Under the ministries of, most notably, Robert Blair (1593–1666) and John Livingstone (1603–1672), revivals broke out repeatedly during mid-1600s. These revivals took place during sacramental observances and formed and important impetus for the spread of the Scottish communion seasons, as Scots traveled between Northern Ireland and Scotland, and eventually the New World.[230]

As indicated, the section of answers to objections contains valuable insights into the debate and concerns of those opposed to frequent communion. They will be summarized here because of their historical value, and since many of these objections occur regularly in the literature, it is helpful to see Brown's responses to

---

226 Brown, *An Apology*, 7–8.
227 Brown, *An Apology*, 12.
228 Brown, *An Apology*, 12–15.
229 Brown, *An Apology*, 15.
230 Westerkamp, *Triumph of the Laity*, chap. 1.

them. They will be categorized according to whether the arguments are (1) historical, or (2) practical, related to issues of spirituality and preparation. Of course, these categories overlap at some points, but an attempt will be made nonetheless to group them according to their main concern.

There are several historical objections. First, the early Christians practiced frequent communion because they lived in a time of persecution. When every Sunday might be their last, it was commendable for them, given their circumstances.[231] Answer: We ought to live as if every Sabbath were our last. If the early Christians celebrated communion frequently, in times of danger, how much more should we celebrate it frequently, in times of peace and leisure?[232]

Secondly, the primitive church and Reformation eras were times of spiritual vitality. But now we live in a time of spiritual decay, and so frequent communion is unnecessary.[233]

Answer A: The Lord's Supper is a means of grace which revives our languishing spirits. It is a remedy to our spiritual decay. Do we withhold milk from a sickly child? Do we water a garden less frequently because it is dry?[234] Answer B: Should we not also abstain from other means of grace, such as reading, praying, self-examination, preaching, and meditation? Why do we engage frequently in these, but not in the Lord's Supper?[235]

Thirdly, the Independents also have frequent communion, and we do not want to be like them.[236] Answer: The "Papists" instituted infrequent communion, and so the Scots are following their pattern. The "bloody Episcopalians and backsliding Presbyterians" also practice infrequent communion, and we surely do not want to conform to their pattern.[237] Lastly, various respected Protestant leaders did not practice frequent communion.[238] Answer: Brown appeals to a list of other Protestant leaders and churches which advocated frequent communion and asks whether the opinion of a few leaders should outweigh all of these.[239]

Brown deals with a number of objections based on practical issues, or questions of preparation, and the spirituality of those taking communion. A common concern, and one we have seen repeatedly in these debates, was that frequency would lead to

---

231 Brown, *An Apology*, 19.
232 Brown, *An Apology*, 20.
233 Brown, *An Apology*, 21.
234 Brown, *An Apology*, 21–22.
235 Brown, *An Apology*, 23.
236 Brown, *An Apology*, 42.
237 Brown, *An Apology*, 42.
238 Brown, *An Apology*, 43.
239 Brown, *An Apology*, 43.

decreased solemnity in communion.[240] Answer A: Where does Scripture command infrequency as a guarantee of solemnity? Answer B: The "Papists" also tried to preserve solemnity through infrequency, and so Reformed churches that hold communion infrequently are really following Roman Catholic practices.[241] Answer C: Why not make communion even more solemn and special by holding it even more infrequently, such as every "ten, twenty, thirty, fifty, or an hundred years?"[242]

Answer D: Why not apply this concern to other means of grace? Why not perform baptisms only twice a year or pray, read, or meditate infrequently, to increase solemnity?[243]

Another objection maintained that, since people don't communicate "conscientiously" it is better to have communion infrequently.[244] Answer: Again, why not have communion even *more* infrequently, to minimize the occurrences of communicating unworthily? We should also do away with the other "gospel ordinances," such as prayer, reading the Bible, and sermons, because they are abused as well.[245]

In response to the argument that those who desire frequent communion can travel to "occasions" in other parishes,[246] Brown asks if this is practical, especially if parishes are far away from each other. What about the poor and the weak?[247] Answer B: Ministers set the tone in their parishes. If they hold communion infrequently, what will inspire their people to desire it more frequently?[248] Answer C: If large crowds are so necessary to a proper communion, then why did Jesus establish the first communion in an "upper room," with just his disciples?[249] Answer D: The great emphasis placed on "fast" days and "thanksgiving" days is really "popery," because these are man-made traditions."[250] Answer E: What if a man were to establish a fast day, preparation day, and thanksgiving day in order to hear sermons twice a year? What, if he had opportunity to hear sermons once a week, yet refused, because he could not observe his days of preparation and thanksgiving?[251] Answer F: Why do we exalt the Lord's Supper over the sacrament of baptism? Why do we not carefully prepare for baptism?[252]

---

240 Brown, *An Apology*, 23.

241 Brown, *An Apology*, 23–24.

242 Brown, *An Apology*, 25.

243 Brown, *An Apology*, 25–27.

244 Brown, *An Apology*, 28.

245 Brown, *An Apology*, 29.

246 Brown, *An Apology*, 31.

247 Brown, *An Apology*, 31–32.

248 Brown, *An Apology*, 32.

249 Brown, *An Apology*, 33.

250 Brown, *An Apology*, 36.

251 Brown, *An Apology*, 36–37.

252 Brown, *An Apology*, 37.

A further objection lends weight to one of the main research questions of this study (1.2), regarding the relationship of the structures of Reformed ecclesiastical discipline to ideals for frequent communion. As Brown reports this objection, some ministers felt they could not visit with every family and examine them before communion if it is held frequently.[253] Answer: What command from God requires visiting every family before communion? Because visitations are infrequent, there is more for the ministers to work through when they actually do visit families.[254] On the other end of the spectrum, some clergy felt burdened financially by communions and used this as an excuse for infrequency. Answer: The collections at communions are always enough to cover the costs. Also, clergy should consider how much of the communion costs are necessary costs or are unnecessary additions to what should be a very simple rite.[255]

Brown finally deals with the argument that, since the Passover was observed annually, and since the Lord's Supper replaces Passover, it also should be annual.[256] Answer: If the Passover is our model, we should only administer communion once a year. Surely the Apostles knew that the Passover was a yearly event, so why did they then celebrate communion so often?[257]

Brown's pamphlet ends, rather abruptly, on this note. It is probable that he would have added more to bring it to a more persuasive conclusion, had he lived longer. Although this pamphlet was published posthumously, it is still an admirable statement of the frequent communion position. Brown's fame and popularity as a writer no doubt contributed to the desire to publish it after his death. It is refreshing that Brown does not attack other authors personally. His work is free from the invective and rhetorical excesses of Mason and Thomson. The amount of attention devoted to church history and historical arguments and explanations distinguishes Brown's work from others surveyed here. The chief value of this tract lies in its summation of the standard objections to frequent communion. It gives us a window into the frequent communion debate in the Scots Reformed church at the beginning of the nineteenth century.

6.1.9 James W. Alexander (1804–1859)

An important voice critiquing the Scottish communion traditions, and advocating more frequent communion, was the American pastor and theologian James W.

253 Brown, *An Apology*, 38.
254 Brown, *An Apology*, 39.
255 Brown, *An Apology*, 39–40.
256 Brown, *An Apology*, 41.
257 Brown, *An Apology*, 41–42.

Alexander (1804–1859). As the son of Archibald A. Alexander, pastor and professor at Princeton Theological Seminary, and a staunch defender of Reformed orthodoxy, James W. Alexander carried a mantle of authority. He expressed his dissatisfaction with the patterns of the traditional Scottish Presbyterian season in a review of Samuel Bayard's *Letters on the Sacrament of the Lord's Supper*, published in 1840.[258] He cites the work of John Mason approvingly, as having shown that "the multiplicity of our week-day services is incompatible with such a frequency of communion as is our indispensable duty."[259] According to Alexander, "all services which render the celebration of the Lord's Supper protracted or wearisome, and all instructions and ceremonies which invest it with an unscriptural mystery or awfulness, have a necessary tendency to infrequent communion. Instead of being an attractive and delightful ordinance, it thus becomes fearful and repulsive."[260] Alexander argues that misinterpreting 1 Cor. 11 leads people to fear approaching the Lord's Table, viewing it rather with a superstition similar to how "heathens" regarded the rites of their mystery religions.[261] The early church celebrated the Lord's Supper every Lord's Day (Acts 20:7), and the early patristic church continued this practice. However, the increase in the "power of religion" and the growth of a sacramental understanding of communion produced dread and fear in people that prevented them from coming to the Lord's Table. Alexander appeals to Calvin and other examples in the Reformed tradition that promoted more frequent (or at least more frequent than what had become the standard Scottish practice of annual) communion.[262] In his view, the sheer length of communion services in the Scottish Presbyterian tradition is exhausting and makes more frequent communion impracticable.[263]

The argument that a ritual is more "solemn" or "affecting" is not a good reason to accept innovations in the communion rite. Those who argue for the continuance of the Scottish infrequent communion seasons claim that these events are "solemn" and affect people deeply. But that argument is what led to the creation and widespread use of the "anxious bench" in revivalism which has turned "almost

---

258 "The Scottish Presbyterians, and their descendants in America, have, as we cannot but think, fallen into a serious error, in adding to the length and the number of the services connected with the Lord's Supper." James W. Alexander, "The Sacrament of the Lord's Supper," *Biblical Repertory and Princeton Review*, XII, January 1840, 18.

259 Alexander, "The Sacrament of the Lord's Supper," 18.

260 Alexander, "The Sacrament of the Lord's Supper," 18.

261 Alexander, "The Sacrament of the Lord's Supper," 19.

262 Alexander, "The Sacrament of the Lord's Supper," 19. Alexander's historical examples are all drawn from Mason's *Letters on Frequent Communion*, and do not add any original material to the debates summarized thus far.

263 Alexander, "The Sacrament of the Lord's Supper," 20.

into a sacrament."[264] The question is not whether it is "solemn," but whether it is "commanded" by Scripture.[265]

In his *Plain Words to Young Communicants*, Alexander stresses the importance and spiritual value of the Lord's Supper. Written for those coming to communion for the first time, Alexander details the process of preparation and self-examination, and provides examples of how to focus one's thoughts before, during, and after communion. But he also mentions that more frequent communion is desirable.[266] It is especially helpful for people who experience various trials and challenges, such as spiritual doubts, hardships, loneliness, struggles with sin, and those about to die.[267]

Alexander is an appropriate figure to end this survey, as he resisted the innovations of revivalists like Charles Grandison Finney (1792–1875), while also critiquing the established rhythms of infrequent communion in the American Presbyterian church. But Alexander also saw the value of the Scottish communion seasons. In his 1856 introduction to Philip Doddridge's *Thoughts on Sacramental Occasions*, Alexander offered a nostalgic lament for the lost sacramental piety of the Scottish communion seasons. In contrast to the many "young ministers" that come to the "most solemn rite" of their religion with less preparation than they give to "an ordinary sermon," the Scottish communion seasons were high points of devotion, conversion, and spiritual experience.[268] While Alexander admits the old Scottish communion services were too long and "burdensome," he believes that, with their decline, the church "lost much that was comely, and glowing, and delightful."[269] The infrequent, large gatherings were "best fitted to awaken high emotions, and cultivate kindly affections."[270] Much good came from the Scottish tradition:

> These were times of revivals; and it is by means of the extraordinary assemblages, and penetrating influence of such communions, that the chief advances of our church were made. These were days of gladness, when the beauty of Zion was admired of her sons, and when thousands were brought to acknowledge Christ. And, whatever may be thought

---

264 Alexander, "The Sacrament of the Lord's Supper," 27.
265 Alexander, "The Sacrament of the Lord's Supper," 27.
266 "It is supposed by many learned men, that the early Christians commemorated Christ's death at least every Lord's Day. In America there is a general disposition to celebrate this sacrament oftener than was customary with our forefathers." *Plain Words to a Young Communicant* (New York: Anson D.F. Randolph & Company, 1854), 64.
267 Alexander, *Plain Words to a Young Communicant*, 65–66.
268 James W. Alexander, "Introduction" to *Thoughts on Sacramental Occasions, Extracted from the Diary of the Rev. Philip Doddridge, D.D.* (Philadelphia: William S. Martien, 1846), 15–16.
269 Alexander, "Introduction," 16.
270 Alexander, "Introduction," 17.

of the admission, I hesitate not to own, that we have gained nothing as a church, by magnifying the convenience and the decorum of ordinances, at the expense of fervour and joyfulness and life.[271]

Although Alexander advocated more frequent communion and did not wish to re-instate the traditional Scottish communion seasons, he still acknowledged the many benefits that the seasons had brought.[272] The seasons had served a valuable purpose at a particular period in history. But the times had changed, and Alexander believed that it was now possible to follow what he believed was the more Scriptural practice of frequent communion. But he wanted to retain the "more careful, earnest, and affectionate observance of the Lord's Supper" as well.[273] Perhaps because he was removed from the high point of the frequency debates, Alexander could articulate a more judicious assessment of the value of both infrequent and frequent communion. In this respect, he provides an appropriate ending point for this survey.

6.2   Comparative Analysis of Arguments

Although the distinctions between the various types of arguments surveyed so far are permeable, and they sometimes merge quite easily with each other, the main arguments will be divided into various categories, in order to examine more closely the foundational claims and presuppositions on both sides of the frequency debates. First, Biblical arguments will be analyzed (6.2.1), focusing on which Biblical texts are used as key texts and considering the theological claims made about the Eucharist. Next (6.2.2), theological arguments will be summarized. Following that, the different authors' attitudes toward church history will be examined (6.2.3), especially focusing on which eras of history they view as normative and which authors they appeal to in support of their position on communion frequency. In the next section (6.2.4), the focus will be on the issues of "preparation," and "solemnity." These are all issues of pastoral theology, where eucharistic theology becomes quite practical.

Much of the argumentation surveyed thus far is historically specific to the Scottish situation. However, elements of the debate continued to affect communion

---

271 Alexander, "Introduction," 17–18.
272 "Tradition informs us of the vast assemblages which were attracted to sacramental services, under the ministry of the Tennents, Blairs, and Smiths, of a former day. These were times of great increase to our church, and they were connected with blessings on communion-services." Alexander, "Introduction," 20.
273 Alexander, "Introduction," 21.

observance in the Americas. The system of "humiliation days" (for spiritual preparation) and "thanksgiving days" (for review and retrospect) is especially important as an element of the larger question of how much time and effort is required to commune in the proper manner. That is a question that has persisted beyond the early Scots Reformed context and continues to impact current discussions.

6.2.1 Biblical and Theological Arguments

A common trope in pro-frequency polemics is the appeal to the "dying words of Jesus" (Matthew 26:26-27). In the Scots Reformed context, we first find this appeal in Willison. This is both a Biblical argument, as well as a pathos-laden rhetorical appeal. Willison and other pro-frequency authors take Jesus' words at the Last Supper as self-evidently necessitating frequent communion.[274] Thomson responds to Mason, noting that Jesus' last words are not as clear as Mason would like them to be, a point Mason concedes in passing.[275] Duncan appeals to the "dying words" of Jesus to support his view that the Lord's Supper is "peculiarly solemn" and so should be observed infrequently.[276]

Before moving into the question of communion in the Book of Acts and the apostolic example, it is noteworthy that, among the voices surveyed here, only John Erskine appeals to Luke 24 (although John Brown of Haddington does reference it in a footnote). As we saw, John Anderson dismisses Luke 24 in a reference note. Thus, while Erskine finds eucharistic implications in Luke 24, Anderson rejects this idea, and sees it simply as an ordinary meal.

Regarding New Testament texts, Acts and 1 Corinthians are the key sources. For the pro-frequency writers, Acts 2:42, 46 are clear examples that the early church gathered frequently, and that communion was a part of these gatherings. The central claim is that "breaking bread" in these texts is a eucharistic term.[277] Neither Thomson nor Anderson respond to these claims from Acts 2. Duncan claims that "breaking bread" in Acts 2 refers to the fellowship between early Christians, in the contexts of common meals—not the Lord's Supper.[278] However, they all interact with Acts 20:7. Again, pro-frequency authors claim that Acts 20:7 describes an ecclesial gathering, which included the Eucharist. It is another instance of the

---

274 Willison, *A Sacramental Catechism*, viii; Randall, *A Letter*, 66; Mason, *Letters on Frequent Communion*, 15–16.
275 Thomson points out that the real focus of Mason's position (and the pro-frequency position) is appealing to the apostolic example, as exemplified in Acts. Thomson, *Letters Addressed to Rev. John Mason*, 18–19; Mason, *Letters on Frequent Communion*, 15–16.
276 Duncan, *A Disquisition*, 47–51, 87.
277 Willison, *A Sacramental Catechism*, 85; Erskine, *An Attempt*, 18–19; Randall, A Letter, 7–8.
278 Duncan, *A Disquisition*, 92.

apostolic pattern.[279] A key theological point that flows from this is: if we follow the apostolic example in the transfer and change of the Sabbath to "Lord's Day"/Sunday, we should follow their example in observing the Lord's Supper frequently.[280] For proponents of infrequent communion, the text is not so transparent. The fact that the early disciples had communion during this gathering does not mean they had communion every time they gathered on the first day.[281] Thomson and Anderson view the pro-frequency interpretation as an argument from silence. Duncan believes that Acts 20:7 does refer to a communion observance, but that it is not enough to lay down a definitive pattern for weekly communion.[282]

Another exegetical battleground is 1 Corinthians 11. This is perhaps where the authors on both sides work the hardest to make the Biblical texts support their own position. There are some hermeneutical gymnastics on both sides of the issue. Erskine and others argue that Paul's censure in 1 Cor. 11:20-21 assumes that the purpose of gathering was to eat the Lord's Supper. Since he censures them for not eating properly, that suggests that a primary purpose of their gathering was to eat the "Lord's Supper."[283] In contrast, Thomson grants that the "irregularities" Paul rebukes could not have occurred except when the Corinthians came together as the church, but he questions whether these "irregularities" occurred every single time they gathered as the church. In other words, "irregularities" when they communed does not prove they communed every time they gathered.[284] Anderson develops the case further, with a series of counterexamples of how to interpret the passage in a way that does not equate "gathering together" as the church and "breaking bread" in communion.[285] Duncan grants that 1 Cor. 11 does contain instances of the Lord's Supper, but argues that this supports the practice of multiple congregations gathering together for a large communion service.[286]

1 Cor. 11:25-26 is another key point of contention. Pro-frequency authors see a clear indication that communion should be frequent in Jesus' words "as often."[287] Thomson does not interact with this passage, but Anderson attempts to show other New Testament examples where the same (or similar) Greek expressions

---

279 Willison, *A Sacramental Catechism*, 85; Erskine, *An Attempt*, 22–23; Randall, A *Letter*, 8; Mason, *Letters on Frequent Communion*, 35; Alexander, "The Sacrament of the Lord's Supper," 19.

280 Erskine, *An Attempt*, 15; Randall, *A Letter*, 32; Mason, *Letters on Frequent Communion*, 35.

281 Thomson, *Letters Addressed to Rev. John Mason*, 19–20; Anderson, *Communion Seasons Defended*, 20–21.

282 Duncan, *A Disquisition*, 92–94.

283 Erskine, *An Attempt*, 23; Randall, *A Letter*, 9; Mason, *Letters on Frequent Communion*, 36–37; Alexander, "The Sacrament of the Lord's Supper," 19.

284 Thomson, *Letters Addressed to Rev. John Mason*, 20.

285 Anderson, *Communion Seasons Defended*, 21–22.

286 Duncan, *A Disquisition*, 94–112.

287 Willison, *A Sacramental Catechism*, 85; Erskine, *An Attempt*, 12–14; Brown, *An Apology*, 5–6.

meaning "as often" are used to describe events that do not happen weekly. He also notes that Jesus and Paul do not explicitly state *how* often is "often."[288] Although both Anderson and Thomson desire to see more frequent communion in the Church of Scotland, they do not believe the Biblical text clearly mandates weekly communion. They believe that churches have latitude to establish their own patterns of frequency.[289] Duncan interprets the Greek ὁσάκις to mean "whensoever," instead of "as often" and emphasizes Paul's warnings to observe the Supper correctly.[290]

A chief concern of the "careful frequency" authors is that communicants need to partake in a "worthy" manner. Drawing on 1 Cor. 11:27-28, Thomson accuses Mason of not taking seriously Paul's warnings about communing without proper self-examination.[291] Anderson and Duncan also stress the need for proper preparation before communion, which necessitates a certain amount of time between communions. Duncan focuses on 1 Cor. 11:28, while Anderson bases his reasoning about preparation both on 1 Cor. 11:28 and on Old Testament texts, which leads into the next important difference between the pro-frequency and the "careful frequency" camps.[292]

Anderson, Thomson, and Duncan rely heavily on the Old Testament. They see a direct correlation between Israel and the Church. They argue that, since the Jews had to undergo ritual purification before eating the Passover, so too should Christians undergo a process of spiritual preparation before the Lord's Supper. This provides their chief Biblical support for the "days of humiliation," although Anderson also finds support in a typological reading of Ezek. 45:21, 25.[293] Thomson builds his entire theology of communion on the Old Testament, where he finds a distinction between "ordinary" and "extraordinary" religious duties. The "extraordinary" duties were infrequent, and Passover was an "extraordinary" duty. Since Passover is fulfilled in the Lord's Supper, it follows that the sacrament should be infrequent.[294] Thomson also justifies emphasizing "solemnity" during communion, because of the "solemnity" that accompanied Passover. Furthermore, Thomson draws correlations between the Scots Reformed days of fasting/humiliation with the days of preparation before the Passover.[295] Duncan also stresses the primary

---

288 Anderson, *Communion Seasons Defended*, 19.

289 Thomson, *Letters Addressed to Rev. John Mason*, 16, 18; Anderson, *Communion Seasons Defended*, 5, 23–24.

290 Duncan, *A Disquisition*, 87–88.

291 Thomson, *Letters Addressed to Rev. John Mason*, 11.

292 Duncan, *A Disquisition*, 170–172; Anderson, *Communion Seasons Defended*, 9.

293 Anderson, *Communion Seasons Defended*, 8–9.

294 Thomson, *Letters Addressed to Rev. John Mason*, 25–26.

295 Thomson, *Letters Addressed to Rev. John Mason*, 27, 30–32.

symbolic and typological referent of Passover to understand the meaning of the Lord's Supper, especially its "solemnity."[296]

Apparently, Erskine heard similar sentiments when he wrote fifty years earlier. He states the following consideration as a possible objection to his argument: "Because the Jews had to undergo various purifications and preparations before they could worship God properly, so we should purify and prepare ourselves."[297] His response is that we should not want to return to the "bondage" of the Old Covenant system.[298] He also rebuts the annual communion/annual Passover point by referring to the daily sacrifices of the Jews, which supply a pattern for frequency.[299]

When they deal with Scripture to prove the necessity of frequency, pro-frequency writers interact primarily with the New Testament, unless they are refuting objections to frequent communion. "Careful frequency" authors, in contrast, draw most of their positive evidence for infrequency from the Old Testament, which is perhaps indicative of differing hermeneutical priorities. Erskine deals with the Old Testament chiefly when he is refuting possible objections to frequent communion. However, he does make one comment which seems to illustrate the general attitude of the pro-frequency writers. Arguing from the relationship between the Old and New Covenants, he notes that the Jews had clear direction on how often to offer the Paschal sacrifice—if God did not give us clear direction about the frequency of observing the fulfillment of this rite, then the New Covenant is *not* more clear than the Old.[300] Since the New Covenant is more clear revelation than the Old, we should expect to find clear directives about communion frequency. Whatever their precise motivations and hermeneutical concerns, pro-frequency authors focus almost exclusively on the New Testament, while "careful" frequency authors focus primarily on the Old when they seek to prove their positions.

Ironically, both Erskine and Randall seem to admit that the New Testament texts are not as clear as they would like, and resort to some interesting hermeneutical moves. After interacting with 1 Cor. 11:25-26, Erskine concludes: "It is more probable their [the apostles] practice was founded upon a New Testament precept, plain to them, though to us dark and obscure."[301] Erskine is so sure that weekly communion was the apostolic practice (drawing mainly from texts in Acts), that he assumes the Apostles knew of some clear New Testament "precept" which would sanction weekly communion. Interestingly, we see again the almost exclusive focus on the New Testament in the pro-frequency authors of this time. Was there nothing in the

---

296 Duncan, *A Disquisition*, 12, 14, 47–51.

297 As stated by Erskine, *An Attempt*, 55.

298 Erskine, *An Attempt*, 55.

299 Erskine, *An Attempt*, 49. Cf. Brown of Haddington's response to the Passover argument on §6.1.8.

300 Erskine, *An Attempt*, 12.

301 Erskine, *An Attempt*, 15.

Old Testament to give direction for the Apostles? This is a curious hermeneutical dynamic that continues throughout discussions of worship and communion in Reformed churches.

Randall goes even further, and basically suggests that frequent communion was special revelation to the apostles. Based on his reading of 1 Cor. 14:37, Randall claims that Jesus did not teach directly on everything but revealed some things to the apostles through the Spirit. Because of this theological assumption, Randall can view the communion practices of the apostolic church as divinely instituted.[302] Although Randall is a Protestant, this sounds curiously similar to Roman Catholic claims that tradition is a special source of revelation, in addition to Scripture.

6.2.2 Theological Arguments

Moving from biblical to theological arguments, a central question has to do with the essential nature of the Lord's Supper—is it a "fast" or a "feast"? Pro-frequency writers emphasize the "feast" aspect, while "careful" frequency authors insist that it is a "fast." Indeed, defining communion as essentially a "fast" or "feast" will have implications for frequency. Much here depends, however, on how the writers define these terms. "Careful frequency" authors stay focused on Old Testament definitions and solemn ritual practices, while pro-frequency writers adopt a broader meaning of "feast."

Erskine points out that, in the Old Testament, the Day of Atonement was the only annually recurring "fast day," whereas the other Jewish holy days were days of "joy and thanksgiving."[303] Should we have fewer days of thanksgiving, and more fasts, now that we live in light of Jesus' coming?[304] While Willison, like Erskine, can easily refer to communion as a blessed feast, Thomson and Anderson shy away from the term, again focusing on Old Testament examples.[305] For Thomson, Anderson, and Duncan, the Passover is the primary reference point for their eucharistic theology. For Thomson, the bitter herbs, fasting, and solemnity which characterized Passover should also characterize the Lord's Supper. Therefore, the dominant mood of communion should be that of "fasting" with the emphasis on preparation and solemnity. As he argues, does the New Testament sacrament call for *less* preparation than the Old Testament meal?[306] It is important to note here that these authors are

---

302 See Randall, *A Letter*, 4–7. Erskine hints at this possibility (that the apostles knew something we did not about God's will for communion frequency) in *An Attempt*, 15.

303 Erskine, *An Attempt*, 55.

304 Mason also interacts with this argument, from analogy with the Day of Atonement, in more detail than Erskine. See §6.1.4, f.n. 95.

305 Willison, *A Sacramental Catechism*, viii.

306 Thomson, *Letters Addressed to Rev. John Mason*, 27, 31–32; Duncan, *A Disquisition*, 148.

using the terms "fast" and "feast" rather imprecisely. The focus is on the dominant emotional mood that should surround the observance of the Lord's Supper. Careful frequency authors stress the idea of "fasting" to emphasize the aspects of self-denial and spiritual solemnity. Pro-frequency authors put the emphasis on the idea of "feasting" with its connotations of joy and thanksgiving.

Another central issue in these debates is the role of other means of grace, such as baptism and the preaching of the gospel, in relation to the Lord's Supper. In particular, baptism often surfaces as either a rhetorical point, or subject of comparison. Pro-frequency authors acknowledge that baptism and communion are different. Primarily, baptism is for initiation, but Supper is for spiritual nutrition, which we need often.[307] Thus, they acknowledge a difference in the sacraments in some respects. At other times, pro-frequency authors ask why churches observe communion with such "solemnity," and preparation, without observing baptism in the same way. For instance, when arguing against fasting before communion, Mason asks why we should not also fast before other religious duties, including baptism?[308]

Some of the pro-frequency authors in this period put forward ideas that tended towards a "leveling" of the sacraments, even as they argued for more frequent communion. This can be seen most strikingly in John Mason. To argue against the Lord's Supper being a "special" duty (therefore requiring "special" preparation), Mason tends to reduce the Supper the same level as all other religious "duties." As he challenges his readers:

> I would, therefore, beg the Christian to point out a single blessing to be supplicated or expected at the holy communion, which he does not, or at least ought not, to supplicate and expect in *every* approach to God through the faith of Jesus.[309]

Mason also asks why so much time must be spent in preparation? The theological motivation underlying the emphasis on lengthy and soul-searching preparation is that, since we come nearer to God in communion, we need more time to prepare.[310] So, then, communion is on a higher theological plane than the other religious duties of prayer, Bible reading, and Sabbath observance.

This is another instance where Mason seems to downplay the importance of communion, even while he argues for frequency.[311] He acknowledges that commu-

---

307 Willison, *A Sacramental Catechism*, 84.

308 See Mason, *Letters on Frequent Communion*, 62.

309 Mason, *Letters on Frequent Communion*, 66.

310 Mason, *Letters on Frequent Communion*, 51.

311 Others have noted this tendency in Mason's argumentation. See Schmidt, *Holy Fairs*, 188 and Hughes, "Holy Communion in the Church of Scotland in the Nineteenth Century," 60–61.

nion offers the believer "sweet and joyous communion with his God," but denies that this quality of communion is only attainable in the Lord's Supper. He defines "communion" as "the reciprocation of love between [God] and his people," and defines "nearness to God" as "a realizing view, by faith, of his [God's] most glorious perfections, accompanied with a sense of his favour as our reconciled God in Christ," and then attempts to show that both of these qualities are equally accessible in other religious duties. He writes:

> Nay, is it not evident, that, if you except the social acts of eating and drinking, the symbolical bread and wine, the exercises of a communion-table are, or ought to be the very same with those which should mark other duties of devotion?[312]

The "levelling" of sacramental communion and other religious exercises is important because this reveals a subtle shift in Mason's sacramental theology. Even while arguing for more frequent communion, Mason stresses that the grace received in communion is no different than the grace received in any other spiritual exercise. To combat stress on the "extraordinary" nature of the Supper, Mason seems to emphasize the "ordinary" nature of communion to a degree not present in earlier treatments. This same "leveling" occurs in John Brown of Haddington.[313]

Thomson rejects this coupling of baptism and communion. He believes Mason is unjust when he attempts to fault traditionalists for not observing baptism with the same amount of preparation and solemnity as the Lord's Supper. Thomson denies that there is any Biblical warrant for solemnity or preparation for circumcision, but we do see Biblical warrant for preparation and solemnity in observing the Passover.[314] For Anderson as well, the two sacraments have important differences that preclude comparing them in the way that pro-frequency writers do. Anderson maintains that the Lord's Supper is a more intensely individual sacrament, and so it requires more preparation. He also appeals to the Old Testament strictures for circumcision, noting that there were no stated requirements for "preparing" for circumcision.[315]

As with baptism, the relation of the preached Word and communion are also a point of contention. Writers like Thomas Randall tend to "level" preaching and communion, arguing that, since they are both means of grace, why do the Scots Reformed place a greater emphasis on preaching?[316] In defense of the traditional

---

312 Mason, *Letters on Frequent Communion*, 53.
313 Brown, *An Apology*, 23, 25–27, 37.
314 Thomson, *Letters Addressed to Rev. John Mason*, 26.
315 Anderson, *Communion Seasons Defended*, 14.
316 Randall, *A Letter*, 8.

scheme, John Thomson charges that John Mason "exalts the Lord's supper at the expense of the preached gospel." Thomson maintains that the "gospel" is the "daily bread of the Christian," and "will by no means give place in the Christian life to the Lord's supper."[317]

When Anderson addresses this issue, he maintains that, because of the priority of the preached Word (the "testament"), people must be carefully instructed through the Word, before they partake of the Supper (which is the "seal" of the testament). Anderson also claims that pro-frequency writers link the benefits of communion too closely to the actual, "outward," act of partaking. On the contrary, he compares communion to baptism, and argues that spiritual benefits continue far beyond the actual time of baptism, or communing.[318]

6.2.3 Historical Arguments

Regarding attitudes to church history, we again find a clear difference of opinion. Pro-frequency authors appeal often to the early church, to the Reformers, and quote other theological authorities. In contrast, "careful frequency" authors dismiss appeals to history, maintaining that appealing to the past can prove almost anything. Instead, they endeavor to rely solely on Biblical argumentation.

Willison appeals to the Westminster Directory, and to various Scottish ecclesial statements, which he claims express the "mind" of the Scots Reformed church in regard to frequency.[319] Erskine follows a more typical Protestant polemic method, by appealing to the "first four centuries" of church history as a standard of "primitive purity." He appeals to various church fathers as well, no doubt reflecting his wide reading.[320] Erskine also brings in the example of the "purest Reformed churches" for additional support.[321] Randall also maintains that frequent communion prevailed for the first "four or five hundred Years after Christ," and blames the corruptions of the Roman Catholic church for disrupting this ancient norm.[322] Erskine and Randall set a template for the pro-frequency authors who followed them, and when we compare all of them, we see a consistent pattern emerge:

---

317 Thomson, *Letters Addressed to Rev. John Mason*, 17–18.

318 "The benefit of baptism, once received, is continued to the end of life; so the benefit of the Lord's Supper does not pass away with the transient act of receiving, but is abiding and operative afterwards." Anderson, *Communion Seasons Defended*, 20.

319 Willison, *A Sacramental Catechism*, vii–ix.

320 See Yeager, *Enlightened Evangelicalism*, chap. 8.

321 Erskine, *An Attempt*, 25–34.

322 Randall, *A Letter*, 17–27. See also Alexander, "The Sacrament of the Lord's Supper," 19.

1. Appeal to the first four or five hundred years of the early church, as a time of purity (and more frequent communion), and citations of church fathers.[323]
2. Description of the medieval, or Roman Catholic, degeneration and corruption of the church.[324]
3. Appeal to John Calvin and other Reformers on the issue of communion frequency.[325]
4. Appeal to the "purest Reformed churches" and their communion practices.[326]
5. Appeal to the early Scots Reformed church and her ecclesial standards.[327]

In response to this, "careful frequency" authors choose, for the most part, to simply *not* respond. For Thomson and Anderson, appeals to church history are spurious and possibly dangerous. Thomson undercuts Mason's appeals to church history by claiming that the early church quickly fell away from apostolic purity (citing the seven letters to the churches in Revelation as descriptive of periods of church history). Additionally, he notes that Roman Catholic apologists also base their arguments on appealing to antiquity, so Thomson remains skeptical of any appeals to church history.[328] Thomson also chides Mason for appealing to antiquity whereas he elsewhere states that antiquity is a "wretched" standard for truth.[329] Thomson himself will only appeal to true "antiquity," which is the Old Testament. He also dismisses Mason's appeal to various authors who support more frequent communion with his own appeal to current opinion. Thomson maintains that the "greater number of respectable ministers" are content to follow the current Scots Reformed communion practices.[330] Duncan interacts more carefully with evidence from church history, but reinterprets much of it, and presents evidence that demonstrates that authors in the past cared about examination, preparation, and solemnity.[331]

---

323 Erskine, *An Attempt*, 24–31; Randall, *An Attempt*, 17–22; Mason, *Letters on Frequent Communion*, 37–38; Brown, *An Apology*, 6–7, 14.
324 Erskine, *An Attempt*, 31–33; Randall, *An Attempt*, 22–28; Mason, *Letters on Frequent Communion*, 38–41; Brown, *An Apology*, 9–12.
325 Erskine, *An Attempt*, 36, 56–59; Randall, *A Letter*, 29–31; Mason, *Letters on Frequent Communion*, 41–43; Brown, *An Apology*, 7, 14.
326 Erskine, *An Attempt*, 33–37; Randall, *An Attempt*, 31–33; Mason, *Letters on Frequent Communion*, 44; Brown, *An Apology*, 7–9.
327 Erskine, *An Attempt*, 37–42; Randall, *An Attempt*, 33–35; Mason, *Letters on Frequent Communion*, 44–46; Brown, *An Apology*, 18–19.
328 Thomson, *Letters Addressed to Rev. John Mason*, 23–24.
329 Thomson, *Letters Addressed to Rev. John Mason*, 38.
330 Thomson, *Letters Addressed to Rev. John Mason*, 40.
331 Duncan, *A Disquisition*, 113–124.

Anderson also focuses on Biblical argumentation, rather than appealing to history. The core of his case for "careful" frequency centers on principles and application from the Old Testament. Yet, he does quote noted Protestant authorities (such as Witsius, James Durham, John Owen, and Thomas Boston) who support his view. As with Thomson, Anderson warns against appealing to the early church, because of the "corruptions" that crept in so quickly. He maintains that Scripture should be our only norm. He recognizes Calvin desired more frequent communion but cautions against pursuing frequency at the expense of solemnity.[332] Duncan goes further and appeals to Calvin on the priority of ensuring that the entire congregation is prepared before having communion.[333]

Appeals to church history are also used when pro-frequency authors respond to objections. Brown anticipates and answers the objection that, whereas the early church and Reformation were times of greater spiritual vitality and more frequent communion, in times of spiritual decay (nearly all the writers on both sides of the issue agree that they were living in such a time) we should commune less frequently. In reply, Brown asks if we should water a garden less when it is dry or when it is wet?[334] Thomson utilizes a similar approach when he attempts to relativize the early church's communion practices. For Thomson, it is apparent that the early church lived in a fervent state of expecting the second coming of Christ and were also suffering persecution. Both historical circumstances justified frequent communion; however, Thomson believes the church no longer lives in such a time. Additionally, he believes that Matt. 9:15 suggests that the church would later live in a time of "fasting."[335] Obviously, biblical and historical considerations merge here.

Another point at issue is the history of the days of preparation and thanksgiving. Again, we see pro-frequency authors at pains to detail the history of these days. Why this effort? Their motivation seems to be to relativize the "days" as man-made traditions that have crept into the "pure" worship envisioned by the early Scottish Reformers. Additionally, pro-frequency writers highlight how current Scots Reformed communion practices emerged from both political and ecclesiastical divisions.[336] Mason's treatment is quite thorough.[337] He surveys all of church history, highlighting canons and confessions on the issue of fasting and worship. His actual treatment of the development of the Scots Reformed "days" of fasting is short (compared to the rest of Letter 6, spanning only four and a half pages). Mason's goal is to show how the current Scots Reformed traditions are at odds with much of the

---

332 Anderson, *Communion Seasons Defended*, 24.
333 See Duncan, *A Disquisition*, 120, 123.
334 Brown, *An Apology*, 21–22. Erskine deals with the same objection in *An Attempt*, 48–49.
335 Thomson, *Letters Addressed to Rev. John Mason*, 22.
336 Erskine, *An Attempt*, 43–48; Randall, *A Letter*, 72–73, 83–86.
337 Mason, *Letters on Frequent Communion*, 68–88.

earlier Christian tradition, and not so much to show how, or when, they developed. For Mason, it is enough to state that "they are clearly of *modern* date."[338]

Again, we see Thomson, Anderson and Duncan dismissing the discussion as mostly irrelevant to the debate. Thomson maintains that the "days" are helpful, but not required, and since he finds an example of "days" of preparation before the Passover in the Old Testament, he does not concern himself with the history of the Scots Reformed days of preparation and thanksgiving. Anderson addresses the issue more directly when he states that he has no "leisure for enquiring into the manner in which humiliation days before communion days were introduced," nor does he care to enquire since he is arguing "not for the observation of the days, but the observation of the exercises that ought to attend our communicating."[339] In other words, Anderson feels no need to defend or justify the historical development of the "days," since he is not defending the "days," as such, but only the necessity of careful, serious, preparation before communion, which could take various forms. Duncan presents the most thorough defense of the "days" in the literature surveyed, but not as something required by Scripture.[340] After this survey of theological and historical arguments, it is legitimate to ask what practical implications resulted from these different conceptions of the Lord's Supper.

6.2.4 Frequency, Preparation, and Solemnity

In these trans-Atlantic debates, the tension between "preparation" for communion and the spiritual value of communing often continued to be a central issue. Both sides used "weak faith" in their argumentation. Pro-frequency authors stress the spiritual efficacy of frequent communion. Willison argued that more frequent communion would soften hearts, fortify against sin, and increase love for Jesus Christ.[341] Additionally, he maintains that communing frequently will help people to remember Christ more often. Frequent communion, in other words, is an antidote to "spiritual deadness" and "weakness of faith."[342] Similar claims abound in the other pro-frequency authors surveyed.[343] Randall summarizes the pro-frequency approach well when he emphasizes the spiritual blessings of communion to such a

---

338 Mason, *Letters on Frequent Communion*, 84.
339 Anderson, *Communion Seasons Defended*, 17.
340 See Duncan, *A Disquisition*, 124–25, 134, 137, for a defense of the "days."
341 Willison, *A Sacramental Catechism*, vii-viii.
342 Willison, *A Sacramental Catechism*, 85.
343 Erskine, *An Attempt*, 48–49; Randall, *A Letter*, 14; Mason, *Letters on Frequent Communion*, 118; Brown, *An Apology*, 15–16.

degree that he argues we should ask ourselves how "often" we can partake of the Supper, rather than how "seldom."[344]

By contrast, Thomson and Anderson point to weak faith as a primary reason *not* to commune frequently. For proponents of "careful" frequency, the dangers of "formality" far outweigh the possibility of spiritual blessing through communing. Thomson and Duncan both maintain that frequency will breed "formality."[345] Their fear is that frequency will detract from the "solemnity" of communion. Their fundamental claim is that, since communion is the closest approach we can make to God, it requires solemn preparation.[346] Without enough time to prepare, people cannot commune effectively.[347] They believe it is impossible to obey Paul's command (in 1 Cor. 11:27) to "examine" ourselves and commune in a "worthy" manner, without adequate preparation.[348]

In response, advocates of frequent communion realize the magnitude of the charge, realizing it is the chief objection to frequency.[349] However, they maintain that formality is a danger to any religious duty.[350] Frequency does not obviate the need for spiritual preparation.[351] Alexander, especially, exemplifies this, since he both advocates frequent communion, and provides extensive guidance on how young people coming to communion for the first time should prepare before, during, and afterwards.[352]

Randall's responses are typical, and so are worth summarizing. He admits that frequent communion does not bring automatic spiritual benefits. We must prepare intentionally. However, the possibility of formality should not dissuade us from pursuing what God has commanded. Although we might observe communion frequently (and poorly), this should not dissuade us from pursuing frequent communion.[353] Christianity is different from other religions, in that it does not rely on an outward "display" in order for its rites to be "solemn." The solemnity of the meal comes from the spiritual realities and symbolism, not from a large crowd partaking together.[354] Randall argues that since the early Christians managed to

---

344 Randall, *A Letter*, 6.
345 Thomson, *Letters Addressed to Rev. John Mason*, 10; Anderson, *Communion Seasons Defended*; Duncan, *A Disquisition*, 72.
346 As stated by Erskine, *An Attempt*, 54.
347 Thomson, *Letters Addressed to Rev. John Mason*, 17; Anderson, *Communion Seasons Defended*, 9.
348 Thomson, *Letters Addressed to Rev. John Mason*, 11, 34; Anderson, *Communion Seasons Defended*, 11, 17.
349 Randall, *A Letter*, 49.
350 Randall, *A Letter*, 49.
351 Willison, *A Sacramental Catechism*, 85.
352 Alexander, "The Sacrament of the Lord's Supper," 64.
353 Randall, *A Letter*, 57–58.
354 Randall, *A Letter*, 54.

combine frequency with fervency, perhaps frequency is a "Remedy of the Holy Ghost" against formalism.[355] Randall encourages the churches to be more diligent in the exercise of church discipline, in order to heighten peoples' spiritual and moral awareness. Since discipline relates to the Supper, more frequent communion could well be a God-ordained means of bringing revival.[356] Similar points are found in the other pro-frequency authors surveyed.[357]

The emphasis on preparation reinforced infrequent communion, even when there might be a preference for frequency. This is illustrated by James Oliphant's *A Sacramental Catechism* (1798), where the author seems to acknowledge the propriety of frequent communion:

Q *How OFT are we to shew forth the death of Christ?*
A. The first Christians seem to have done it every Sabbath, and we ought so to do as oft as we have opportunity.[358]

However, Oliphant introduces his catechism with the sincere desire that readers will "peruse the same carefully before each dispensation of the Lord's Supper," and given the fact that his catechism runs to a mere sixty four pages, one wonders how contemporary Scots could come close to the apostolic example? Those agitating for more frequent communion still acknowledged the need for preparation, while those who argued against greater frequency, and for the Scottish pattern of infrequent communion in large gatherings stressed the importance of not neglecting the sacrament. Although both sides could sound similar themes, there was a definite sense of change and a growing dissatisfaction with the Scottish pattern of communion observance. *What was really at stake was the survival of the multi-parish communion seasons.*

Schmidt summarizes the result of the John Mason vs. John Thomson debate, in the context of the growing movement towards communion frequency:

Mason's book itself, though indebted to earlier formulations, marked something of a turning-point: it was among the fullest, most influential treatises on the subject ... But more important than Mason's specific tract was the weight of opposition to the traditional practices: the number of works for frequency simply dwarfed the number for festivity ... If after 1800 the process of moving from festivity to frequency still often remained slow, it

355 Randall, *A Letter*, 58.
356 Randall, *A Letter*, 60–62.
357 Willison, *A Sacramental Catechism*, viii, 85, Erskine, *An Attempt*, 50–55; Mason, *Letters on Frequent Communion*, 51–52; Brown, *An Apology*, 23–29.
358 James Oliphant, *A Sacramental Catechism, Designed for Communicants Old and Young* (Edinburgh: J. Guthrie, 1798), 41.

was nonetheless all but inexorable … As the logic of frequency triumphed, semiannual and quarterly communions gradually came to supplant the annual festivities of the summer season.[359]

However, the growth of quarterly communion did not automatically mean more frequent communion in each parish. Under the old system of "sacramental seasons," people could, and did, attend multiple "communion fairs" in neighboring parishes. When these "communion fairs" disappeared, some people actually communed less, confined to their parish's quarterly observances.[360] For the advocates of more frequent communion, the communion seasons and "days" were the chief obstacle standing in the way. For defenders of the status quo, the multi-parish gatherings were a glorious time of spiritual refreshment, as well as visible demonstration of the unity of the Body of Christ. Neither side was willing to compromise, and both sides accused each other of being "popish," "Independent," or generally misguided.[361]

Opponents of the traditional "days" and communion "seasons" point to a number of practical factors. Willison notes that acts of the General Assembly had already aimed to limit the number of ministers who could gather to assist during communion.[362] Willison also objects to large communion gatherings because they are an economic burden.[363] Erskine simply gives a rambling listing of various practical difficulties and objections. He quotes extensively from Randall, so Randall is the more important source.[364] Randall lists a number of advantages following from more frequent communion, within one parish, rather than multi-parish gatherings.[365] The ministers would not have to travel to other parishes, and neglect their own.[366] Church discipline would improve, because parishioners would be forced to examine themselves more often.[367] Christian unity would deepen within a parish, as "real" Christians are separated from nominal, or hypocritical, Christians.[368] Since the "holy fairs" were satirized and critiqued by outsiders, ceasing to engage in them would take away grounds for criticizing the church.[369]

---

359 Schmidt, *Holy Fairs*, 190.
360 Schmidt, *Holy Fairs*, 190–91.
361 Brown, *An Apology*, 36; Thomson, *Letters Addressed to Rev. John Mason*, 40–41.
362 Willison, *A Sacramental Catechism*, vii–ix.
363 Willison, *A Sacramental Catechism*, vii–ix; Brown, *An Apology*, 39–40.
364 Erskine, *An Attempt*, 63–72.
365 See also Mason, *Letters on Frequent Communion*, 89–105.
366 Randall, *A Letter*, 35–36.
367 Randall, *A Letter*, 41–42; Brown, *An Apology*, 38–39.
368 Randall, *A Letter*, 44; Mason, *Letters on Frequent Communion*, 120.
369 Randall, *A Letter*, 45–46; Mason, *Letters on Frequent Communion*, 117.

While noting that there were abuses in the traditional Scots Reformed "days" and "seasons", Thomson, Anderson, and Duncan still defended them as spiritually advantageous. Thomson points out that people can commune more often by traveling to other parishes.[370] He objects that Mason's plan for frequent communion within each parish would restrict and interfere with the broader fellowship and spiritual friendship and intimacy engendered by the multi-parish "sacramental communion of saints." Thomson speaks from personal experience and extolls the spiritual blessings of the large communion gatherings.[371] In his view, God used those "occasions" mightily to nourish his people, and so the benefits outweigh any of the criticisms. Likewise, for Anderson, these large communion gatherings embody and graphically represent the reality of the church as the "mystical body" of Christ. He sees many spiritual and practical benefits from these large gatherings. He also sees the multi-parish gatherings as a partial foretaste of the prophecies of Zechariah (8:21; 14:16), where God's people will stir each other up to worship in large congregations.[372]

In conclusion, Reformers and traditionalists were arguing about a specific pattern of eucharistic performance and spirituality. The cycles of "communion fairs," and the multi-parish gatherings, with the "days" of preparation and thanksgiving, formed a controversial context for the issue of communion frequency. The debates were not just about Biblical texts, or historical exemplars, in the abstract, but about shared rhythms of life that many people loved, some hated, and formed the inescapable context of the discussion. The issue of communion frequency impinged on a wide array of other priorities and preconceptions. At its heart, the debate was about the best way to gather as the people of God, in the central rite of the Church. It was precisely because the rite was so meaningful to all parties that the debate provoked such animated responses from those on both sides of the issue.

6.2.5 Legacies of the Frequency Debates

Although the communion frequency reformers were ultimately successful, their success came at a cost. It was not as if advocates of frequent communion won a decisive battle in the courts of public opinion, or in ecclesiastical assemblies. While it is true that those arguing for frequent communion overwhelmed the opposition by the sheer volume of their publications, the patterns of infrequent communion and sacramental festivity also died out because of other, more mundane, causes. Many of these causes did not just make communion more frequent; they also

---

370 Thomson, *Letters Addressed to Rev. John Mason*, 15.

371 Thomson, *Letters Addressed to Rev. John Mason*, 37, 40.

372 Anderson, *Communion Seasons Defended*, 24.

undermined many of the cornerstones of the sacramental piety that had evolved in the Reformed tradition, from the sixteenth-century Reformers to the American frontier.

other
factors

One cause of the decline was the growth of American revivalism. Recent scholarship has highlighted the continuity between the Great Revival, or Second Great Awakening, of the 1790s and early 1800s with the First Great Awakening (1625–1760).[373] Many preachers of this second movement retained a sacramental focus in their preaching, and many of the notable occurrences of emotional outbursts, conversions, and exuberant worship occurred at large sacramental occasions that continued the trajectory of the Scottish communion seasons.[374] This movement grew and expanded into a new form of worship and evangelism—one which was not focused on the Lord's Supper. Although this point is beyond the scope of this book, later revivalists moved away from the communion season, but retained the practices of large gatherings, characterized by emotional outbursts. These later revivalist meetings became focused on conversion and did not culminate in a communion observance.[375]

Another cause was the inherent "Scottishness" of the communion seasons. They had served for a time to protect and reinforce the communal identities of Scots-Irish immigrants. But in the context of the colonies and the developing United States, they seemed more and more like relics of another country, and another time. The revivals also became an inter-denominational movement, and many Presbyterians withdrew from participation in it.[376] So, the process of attaining more frequent communion came at the cost of losing many of the distinctive traditions and the overall sacramental piety of the Scots-Irish tradition.

Eventually, even the critics of the Scottish communion seasons, like J.W. Alexander, came to realize that something was lost when more frequent communion prevailed. It was difficult to maintain and promote a serious and emotional theol-

---

373 According to Bracken Long, "scholars have brought to light the relationship between the revivals of the late eighteenth and early nineteenth century and Scots-Irish sacramental occasions." *The Eucharistic Theology of the American Holy Fairs*, 63, citing Paul Conkin, *Cane Ridge: America's Pentecost* (Madison: University of Wisconsin Press, 1990). Longfield, *Presbyterians and American Culture*, observes that "[t]he revivalism of this Awakening was different from that which exercised the colonies in the 1730s and 1740s but was 'not so significantly different as to require a distinction between the two eras of social history,'" quoting Donald G. Matthews, "The Second Great Awakening as an Organizing Process, 1780–1830: An Hypothesis," *American Quarterly* 21, no. 1 (1969): 26.

374 Schmidt has shown the intimate connections between the Great Revival (also sometimes called the "Second Great Awakening") and the Scots-Irish sacramental traditions. In particular, see Schmidt, *Holy Fairs*, 65–66.

375 Winter, "American Churches and the Holy Communion," 433.

376 Longfield, *Presbyterians and American Culture*, 56.

ogy of the Eucharist without the intensity of the communion seasons.[377] Schmidt also notes the decrease in sacramental fervor which accompanied greater frequency. The growth of quarterly communion did not automatically mean more frequent communion in each parish. Under the old system of "sacramental seasons," people could, and did, attend multiple "communion fairs" in neighboring parishes. When these "communion fairs" disappeared, some people actually communed less, confined to their parish's quarterly observances.[378] A rise in frequency also led to a decline in broader Christian fellowship. John Thompson had already lodged this complaint in his exchange with John Mason. Thompson saw that, once people stopped traveling to other towns to participate in communion seasons, then social bonds would be severed and fractured.[379]

Bracken Long suggests that the Scottish communion season tradition has important spiritual and theological resources for the development of sacramental piety in the contemporary church. As an increasing number of Presbyterian and Reformed churches adopt the practice of weekly, or more frequent, communion, the deep and fervent spirituality of the communion seasons is a reminder to come to the Lord's Table with appreciation and anticipation.[380] In the same vein, Todd Billings offers the Scottish communion seasons as an example that has features worthy of emulation, despite their flaws and excesses.[381] As this survey of the communion frequency debates of the 1700s and early 1800s has demonstrated, the issue of communion frequency raises fundamental questions about Reformed theology,

---

377 "Successful in reforming the traditional communion season, proponents of the new scheme awaited a eucharistic revival that never came. As Thompson had feared and Mason had hoped, the profound—or superstitious—awe and mystery that the old way had evoked were gradually lost. Significantly lessening the solemnity of the Lord's Supper, the acceptance of frequency put an end to sacramental festivity." Schmidt, *Holy Fairs*, 190.

378 Schmidt, *Holy Fairs*, 190–191.

379 "Frequency, in other words, was at cross-purposes with the community, sociability, and mutuality that came in the communion season. Frequency, according at least to its more far-seeing critics, was a handmaiden in the decline of traditional forms of community." Schmidt, *Holy Fairs*, 192. See Thomson, *Letters*, 37.

380 "As modern-day Presbyterians move toward more frequent celebrations, a new embracing of the power of the sacraments is in order. Although the church need not return to the practices of the American frontier, it must consider how sacramental celebrations might be enriched so that the communicants might experience spiritual vitality, intellectual understanding, emotional fervor, and physical engagement." Bracken Long, *The Eucharistic Theology of the American Holy Fairs*, 143.

381 See also Billings, *Remembrance, Communion, and Hope*, 45–56, especially 55–56: "However, the holy fairs movement (along with similar movements in English Puritan and Dutch *Nadere Reformatie* contexts) is deeply instructive and provides a window into post-Reformation Reformed thought and practice … It shows that an emphasis upon transformed, affective perception—made possible by the Spirit—is not only a broadly catholic theme but also one that can thrive in the Reformed tradition."

tradition, and eucharistic practice. The authors surveyed are a rich resource for the
continuing development of Reformed eucharistic practice.

Conclusion

This study summarized and contextualized patterns of communion frequency in the English, Scottish, and early American Puritan Reformed communities. It illuminated the political and ecclesial factors that played important roles in shaping patterns of communion frequency in these Reformed communities. Beginning with the origins of the tradition in the Swiss Reformed churches of the sixteenth century, it surveyed developments in the English and Scottish Reformations, as well as early American Reformed communities. Although the desire for more frequent communion was shared by many authors, pastors, and theologians, it was tempered by the pastoral and political realities, structures of church discipline, and by the stress on preparing properly before participating in communion. These patterns and dynamics are also found in other Christian traditions, and so this study lays the foundations for further analysis and comparison across denominational and ecclesiastical boundaries.

From the very beginning, the Reformed tradition has wrestled with the question of communion frequency. In the context of the late medieval period, the first generation of Reformers all urged more frequent communion than the typical annual observance. But this ideal always existed in tension with another conviction of the reform movements—that all adults in the community should participate in communion. This pastoral goal was complicated by the conviction that moral purity and spiritual sincerity were required of those who came to the Lord's Table. This was not a new tension in the history of the Christian church, but rather one that extends back to the foundations of the apostolic church. Paul's rebuke to the Corinthians demonstrates his desire that they come to the Table in the proper manner, and with the right attitude (1 Corinthians 11). One can infer that Paul is stressing purity, rather than frequency.

This same concern was central to the development of ideals for church discipline and maintaining a pure Christian community in the Reformed communities of Basel, Strasbourg, and Geneva. However, the persistence of human sin and the complex relationships between church and civic leaders made reformers like Calvin compromise on their ideals for communion frequency. Indeed, although Calvin favored frequent communion, he was also willing to compromise for the sake of purity, and to ensure that people were coming to the Table in a unified way, understanding the importance of the sacrament. Calvin also instituted a system of ecclesiastical discipline in Geneva that made it practically impossible to hold communion weekly, because of the demands placed on both the consistory and the people.

Other reformers also stressed the need for preparation before communion, while also advocating that communion be celebrated more frequently than in the late medieval period. Johannes Oecolampadius was one of the first reformers to argue for "fencing" the Table, even as his writings indicate that the Lord's Supper should be observed as near to weekly as possible. Martin Bucer's writings also evidence a desire for frequent communion, but his concern for purity and preparation led him to argue for more structures of church discipline, and the practice of pre-communion examinations, to ensure proper participation in the Lord's Supper.

The Zurich tradition, represented by Zwingli and Bullinger, took a different approach by instituting quarterly communion which was still more frequent than before the Reformation. While there are aspects of communion spirituality in Zwingli's thought and liturgical prescriptions that are under-appreciated, it is also true that he did not stress frequency to the same extent as the reformers of Basel, Strasbourg, and Geneva. Bullinger continued Zwingli's trajectory by holding a middle position. He recognized the theological validity of weekly communion but was reluctant to upset the delicate political and ecclesiastical balance in Zurich.

As the Genevan model spread into England and Scotland, ecclesiological commitments about how to prepare for communion, and who was worthy to receive communion, directly impacted communion frequency. The Scots Reformed developed the Genevan priority of church discipline, while also emphasizing preparation. So, although the First Book of Discipline (1561) recommended quarterly communion, the tradition of infrequent, but intense, communion celebrations developed. The Scottish Reformed church also instituted patterns of church discipline, penance, and reconciliation, that made frequent communion impractical. Other factors influenced communion frequency in Scotland, such as a shortage of ministers, political and ecclesiastical upheavals, and the financial burden of the celebration itself, as well as the accompanying traditions that developed around it.

The English and American Puritans emphasized preparation but were not able to fully implement their ideals for church discipline. In focusing more on the issue of preparation, rather than frequency, Puritans continued to carry forward Calvin's pastoral concern, but they tended to over-emphasize this point. While many Puritans, such as Lewis Bayly, Arthur Hildersham, William Bradshaw, Stephen Charnock, Thomas Doolittle, and Matthew Henry, exhorted their readers to not neglect the Lord's Supper, they also prescribed a rigorous regimen of self-examination, to ensure coming to communion properly. This emphasis, and this tension, was exported to the New World in colonies influenced by the Puritan movement.

In the American Puritan colonies, churches and communities endeavored to fully carry out their ideals for reform. They stressed the need for identifying the effects of God's grace in the lives of those who professed saving belief. The boundaries between those who were part of the church, and those who were outside of it—and so outside of the political community as well—were clearly drawn. This was starkly obvious when people came to the Lord's Supper. A minority of the churches generally felt qualified, or were deemed qualified by the church leaders, to participate in communion. Although Solomon Stoddard challenged this conception, and opened up access to the Lord's Supper, other American Puritans like Edward Taylor opposed Stoddard and defended the status quo. Taylor and Samuel Willard combined a rich eucharistic theology with exhortations about the necessity of coming to the Supper fully prepared. Jonathan Edwards wrestled with his grand-father Solomon Stoddard's legacy, and carried on the Puritan emphasis on proper preparation, while indicating his preference for more frequent communion. Edwards serves as a connecting point for the trans-Atlantic revivals and the movement to hold fast to Reformed orthodoxy, as exemplified by his friendship and correspondence with the Scottish theologian, John Erskine.

Erskine was one of the main voices in Scotland calling for more frequent communion. Along with John Willison and Thomas Randall, Erskine challenged what had become the standard Scottish practice of infrequent, but large and festive, communion gatherings. The emphasis on preparation was not lost, though. John Willison, in particular, emphasized the duty of preparing for the Lord's Supper in his sacramental writings, which were popular on both sides of the Atlantic. The later 1700s and early 1800s witnessed many connections between Scotland and the United States, as seen in the career of John Mitchell Mason and John Anderson. Both had Scottish roots but ministered for most of their careers in the American context. While Mason argued stridently for weekly communion, he was just as stridently opposed by John Thompson, John Anderson, and Alexander Duncan. The pamphlets written by authors on both sides of the frequency issue display differing theological presuppositions, exegetical strategies, understandings of church history, and even the nature of pastoral and practical theology. While both sides scored points against each other, the tradition of Scottish communion seasons gradually died out. The influence of the Scots-Irish communion traditions is especially important in the development of revivalism, as it developed in the Second Great Awakening. Although the Lord's Supper was central to the efforts of earlier revival preachers, it moved to the periphery and was largely abandoned by later revivalists. It was this later neglect of the Supper that contributed to the growth of movements like the Mercersburg Theology which pursued the recovery of liturgical worship, and the restoration of the Lord's Supper to a more central role in Reformed worship.

While the history of those movements is outside the scope of this book, it is helpful to draw some final observations on what contemporary churches and church leaders can learn from the history of communion frequency practices and polemics in the Reformed tradition. First, the example of Calvin is instructive for contemporary church leaders who are examining the issue of communion frequency. Both proponents and opponents of weekly communion tend to appeal selectively to the Reformers of the sixteenth century. More caution should be used, and the original situations and challenges faced by the Reformers should be considered. It does seem, however, that contemporary proponents of weekly communion have almost entirely turned away from the rigorous demands of spiritual preparation and church discipline espoused by the Reformers.[1] How do we determine which group is truly representing the "Reformed" tradition, when we find differences of opinion in the Reformers themselves? Are churches truly "Reformed" if they practice weekly communion, but abandon the strict moral guidelines and ecclesiastical control that Calvin also fought for? These are all questions that continue to shape the debates about communion frequency in Reformed churches, even into the present day.

When Wolterstorff claims there is "no more fundamental liturgical issue facing the Reformed churches today" than the issue of weekly communion, he correctly highlights the centrality of this question.[2] If this were not an important question, the various authors surveyed here would not have labored to argue their respective points of view. Authors on both sides of the issue of communion frequency debates believed that the Lord's Supper is a deeply meaningful event. But, as this study has shown, there is a continuing tension between the priorities of preparation and purity, and the priority of frequency. It is a fair criticism that the Reformed tradition has stressed purity and preparation beyond what the average Christian can bear, but it should always be remembered that these concerns flowed from a serious desire for people to experience the fullest measure of God's grace. In the arc of history, one can also appreciate the renewed emphasis and attention being paid to the Lord's Supper in Reformed churches. However, authors who critique the Reformed tradition on the issue of communion infrequency tend to ignore the traditions of communion festivity and practices of spirituality that also characterized Reformed communion observance in various contexts—most notably in the Scottish Reformed tradition.

To return to our initial research question, (*What patterns of communion frequency characterized the sixteenth-century Swiss Reformed, English Puritan, Scottish Reformed, and early American Reformed communities?*), various patterns of communion frequency have characterized these communities. There is no single pattern of frequency that can be labeled as "truly" Reformed, as if all others were sub-standard and relics of the medieval church. In their best moments, all the writers surveyed here have granted that point. Communion frequency is a matter of inference, best judgement, and pastoral wisdom. There are many Biblical and historical considera-

---

1 "Congregations where the Lord's Supper is celebrated on a weekly basis without any form of communicant examination or without sufficient emphasis on personal self-examination have departed significantly from the sacramental theology and practice of Calvin." Adam M. Kuehner, *Calvin, Weekly Communion, and the Scottish Reformed Tradition* (Grand Rapids: Torwood Press, 2013), 29.

2 Nicholas P. Wolterstorff, "The Reformed Liturgy," in *Major Themes in the Reformed Tradition*, ed. Donald McKim (Grand Rapids: Eerdmans, 1992), 295.

tions that must be taken into account, but churches should view the traditions and practices of others with charity.

At the same time, this study has shown how traditions can quickly assume a sanc- tified and exalted status, rendering them immune from criticism. The development of infrequent communion in the Scottish Reformed church is a prime example of this phenomenon. Since the Reformed tradition finds its core convictions in measuring everything by the Word of God, churches and church leaders should be willing to hold up their own communion traditions to the light of criticism and scrutiny. This study has demonstrated that patterns of communion frequency were often shaped and impacted by historical, political, and ecclesial considerations. Churches today need to be willing to look at the various factors that have contributed to their own patterns of communion frequency and be courageous in making any changes necessary—as were many of the authors surveyed here.

A further research question concerned the role of church discipline and proper participation. These have been key concerns for Reformed communities and the stress laid on them made more frequent communion difficult, if not impossible, to achieve. Because the early Reformed communities, and those following in their wake, placed such a high priority on the mechanisms of church discipline, examination by elders, penance, self-examination, and preparation, these all tended to overshadow desires for frequent communion. In many cases, it was simply a matter of the time needed for all these activities. Hours, if not days, were required, and so patterns of monthly, quarterly, or even annual communion fit best within these structures. The issue of church discipline, and its role in the present, is likewise beyond the scope of this book, but it is noticeable that the rise of the frequent communion movement corresponds with a lowering of standards and expectations within many churches, both in areas of traditional morality and in the specific area of preparation for communion.

This survey has shown that there was a constant tension between the ideals of purity, proper preparation, and communion frequency in the Reformed tradition. It is notable that contemporary proponents of frequent communion downplay the demands of the sixteenth-century reformers and those continuing their legacy, in the matter of church discipline, examination, and spiritual preparation. Although pastors and theologians are free to adapt and appropriate various aspects of their own traditions in the best way suited to their own contexts, this study has shown that the Reformed tradition, particularly in its ideals of creating a holy community and a profound experience of communion, contains many resources that can enrich contemporary observance of the Lord's Supper.

The issue of communion frequency also has ecumenical dimensions. As noted in Chapter 1 (1.1), communion frequency has been an area of disagreement, and a cause for concern, in Roman Catholic, Orthodox, Lutheran, and Anglican churches. This is something that every Christian church must deal with at some point. It is supremely ironic that the sacrament of unity has often been source of disunity. By helping churches to re-examine their own past and understand what has helped to shape their own practices of communion, perhaps a foundation can be laid for greater progress, and greater unity.

Many authors, especially the Puritans, who argued for communion frequency also devoted many pages to warning people to prepare themselves thoroughly and to approach the Lord's Supper with a serious and earnest sense of the magnitude of what they were doing. This aspect of preparation is missing in some current discussions of frequent communion. Contemporary advocates risk departing from what we might tentatively call a "catholic consensus" of the church regarding the necessity of spiritual preparation for the Eucharist. Although there are undoubtedly many salutary aspects of how some contemporary Reformed churches and theologians are pursuing, practicing, or advocating weekly communion, it would be nearsighted to ignore the wisdom of the past regarding proper observance of the Lord's Supper. What might it mean for us to prepare more fully for this rite? How might a renewed attention to this aspect of eucharistic spirituality help to restore this central sign of union and communion, which has so often been the site of division? Writers in the past knew that there was much at stake in the observance of the Lord's Supper. By learning from communion frequency debates in the past, perhaps we can have more productive debates in the present, and in the future.

Bibliography

Primary Sources

Acts of the General Assembly of the Church of Scotland 1638–1842. Edited by Church Law Society. Edinburgh: Edinburgh Printing & Publishing Co 1843. British History Online. Accessed April 24, 2021. http://www.british-history.ac.uk/church-scotland-records/acts/1638-1842.

A Directory for the publique worship of God, throughout the three kingdoms of England, Scotland, and Ireland together with an ordinance of Parliament for the taking away of the Book of common-prayer, ... die Jovis, 13. Martii, 1644. London: Printed for Evan Tyler, Alexander Fifield, Ralph Smith, and John Field ..., 1644; Ann Arbor: Text Creation Partnership, 2011. http://name.umdl.umich.edu/A36061.0001.001.

Alexander, James W. "The Sacrament of the Lord's Supper." *Biblical Repertory and Princeton Review,* XII (January, 1840): 14–20.

— *Plain Words to a Young Communicant.* New York: Anson D.F. Randolph & Company, 1854.

— "Introduction" to *Thoughts on Sacramental Occasions, Extracted from the Diary of the Rev. Philip Doddridge, D.D.* Philadelphia: William S. Martien, 1846.

Anderson, John. *Communion Seasons Defended: A Scriptural Response to John M. Mason's "Letters on Frequent Communion".* Edited by Sean McDonald. Grand Rapids: Torwood Press, 2013.

— *Vindicae Cantus Dominici. In two parts: I. A discourse of the duty of singing the book of Psalms in solemn worship. II. A vindication of the doctrine taught in the preceding discourse. With an appendix: containing essays and observations on various subjects.* Philadelphia: David Hogan, 1800.

An Address to the Christian People, under the Inspection of the Reformed Presbytery, Concerning the More Frequent Dispensing of the Lord's Supper. Glasgow: n.p., 1795.

An apologeticall narration, humbly submitted to the Honourable Houses of Parliament. By Tho: Goodwin, Philip Nye, Sidrach Simpson, Jer: Burroughes, William Bridge. London: Printed for Robert Dawlman, M.DC.XLIII. [1643]; Ann Arbor: Text Creation Partnership, 2011. http://name.umdl.umichap.edu/A85427.0001.001.

Aktensammlung zur Geschichte der Basler Reformation in den Jahren 1519 bis Anfang 1534, 6 vols. Edited by Emil Dürr and Paul Roth. Basel: Verlag der historischen und antiquarischen Gesellschaft Universitätsbibliothek Basel, 1921–50. Vol. 3, Nr. 473.

Bayly, Lewis. *The Practice of Piety: Directing a Christian How to Walk, that He May Please God.* [1611?]. Grand Rapids: Soli Deo Gloria Publications, 2019.

Brown, John. *An Apology for the More Frequent Administration of the Lord's Supper; with Answers to the Objections Urged Against It.* Edinburgh: J. Ritchie, 1804.

— *Compendium View of Natural and Revealed Religion*, originally published in 1782; republished as *The Systematic Theology of John Brown of Haddington*, Introduced by Joel R. Beeke and Randall J. Pederson. Ross-shire: Christian Focus Publications; Grand Rapids: Reformation Heritage Books, 2002.

Bucer, Martin. *Ein Summarischer vergriff der Christlichen lehre vnd Religion die man zu Strasburg hat nun in die xxviij jar gelehret...* [Strasbourg: Wendelin Rihel, 1548]. = Seebass, Bucer Bibliographie Nr. 183.

— *Von der waren Seelsorge vnnd dem rechten Hirten dienst wie der selbige inn der Kirchen Christi bestellet vnnd verrichtet werden solle ...* (Strasbourg: Wendelin Rihel, 1538). = Seebass, Bucer Bibliographie Nr. 81.

— *Martin Bucers Deutsche Schriften*, ed. Robert Stupperich et al., 17 vols. Gütersloh, 1960–, v.

— *Martini Buceri Opera Omni*, ed. Robert Stupperich, Series 2, Vol. 15, *De Regno Christi Libri Duo*, ed. Francois Wendel. Paris: Presses Universitaires de France; Gütersloh, Bertelsmann, 1955.

— *Concerning the True Care of Souls.* Translated by Peter Beale. Edinburgh and Carlisle: The Banner of Truth Trust, 2009; repr. 2016.

Bradshaw, William. *A Direction for the Weaker Sort of Christians, Shewing in What Manner They Ought to Fit and Prepare Themselves to the Worthy Receiving of the Sacrament of the Body and Blood of Christ.* Reprinted as *Preparing for the Lord's Supper*. Edited by Lesley A. Rowe. Grand Rapids: Reformation Heritage Books, 2019.

Bullinger, Henry. *The Decades of Henry Bullinger, Minister of the Church of Zurich*, The Fifth Decade. Translated by H.I. Edited by Thomas Harding. Cambridge: The University Press, 1852. Reprint, New York: Johnson Reprint Corporation, 1968.

Calvin, John. *Commentary on the Epistles of Paul to the Corinthians*, Vol. 1. Edinburgh: Calvin Translation Society, 1848. Reprint, Grand Rapids: Baker Books, 2005.

— *Calvin: Theological Treatises.* Edited and Translated by J.K.S. Reid. Library of Christian Classics, Vol. XXII. Philadelphia: The Westminster Press, 1965.

— *Commentary on the Epistles of Paul the Apostle to the Corinthians.* Translated by John Pringle. Edinburgh: Calvin Translation Society. Reprint, Baker Books, 2005.

— *Commentary on the Gospel of John.* Translated by William Pringle. Edinburgh: Calvin Translation Society. Reprint, Grand Rapids: Baker Book House, 2005.

— *Calvin's Ecclesiastical Advice.* Translated and Edited by Mary Beaty and Benjamin W. Farley. Louisville: Westminster John Knox, 1991.

Charnock, Stephen. *The Complete Works of Stephen Charnock, B.D.* vol. IV. Edinburgh: James Nichol, 1865. Reprint, Edinburgh: The Banner of Truth Trust, 1985.

Churchwardens' Accounts of Pittington and Other Dioceses in the County of Durham, 1580–1700, Vol. 84. Edinburgh: Surtees Society, 1888.

Collections of the Massachusetts Historical Society, 4th ser., Vol. 8. Boston: Wiggin and Lunt, 1868. https://archive.org/details/collectionsmass27socigoog/page/n96/mode/2up.

Cotton, John. *The Way of the Churches of Christ in New England*. London, 1645.

— *The Way of Congregational Churches Cleared*. London: 1648.

Davies, Samuel. *Sermons on Important Subjects*, 5 vols. Baltimore: Mason L. Weems, 1816.

Doolittle, Thomas. *A Treatise Concerning the Lord's Supper; with Three Dialogues For the More Full Information of the Weak in the Nature and Use of This Sacrament*. 1665. Reprint Aberdeen: George and Robert King, 1844. Reprint, Ravenbrook Publishers, 2016.

Duncan, Alexander. *A Disquisition on the Observance of the Lord's Supper with a View to the Defence of the Presbyterian Plan of Administrating That Ordinance*. Edinburgh: Thomas Turnball, 1805. Reprint, Carlisle: George Kline, 1807.

Edwards, Jonathan. *The Works of Jonathan Edwards, With a Memoir by Sereno E. Dwight*, Edited by Edward Hickman. Edinburgh and Carlisle, PA: The Banner of Truth Trust, 1834; republished, 1974. Reprint, 1995. https://www.ccel.org/ccel/edwards/works1.i.xviii.html.

Erskine, John. *An Attempt to Promote the Frequent Dispensing of the Lord's Supper*. Kilmarnock: J. Wilson, 1783.

Furnivall, F. James, et al., *Harrison's Description of England In Shakspere's Youth: Being the Second And Third Books of His Description of Britaine And England*. London: Pub. for the New Shakspere society, by N. Trubner & co., 1877–81, vol. I.

Gillespie, George. *Aarons Rod Blossoming, Or, The Divine Ordinance of Church Government Vindicated* (London, 1646).

Geree, John. *The Character of an old English Puritan, or Non-Conformist* (London: A. Miller, 1646), in Lawrence A Sasek, ed., *Images of English Puritanism: A Collection of Contemporary Sources 1589–1646* (Baton Rouge and London: Louisiana State University Press, 1989.

Henderson, Alexander. *The Government and Order of the Church of Scotland*. Edinburgh: s.n., 1641; Ann Arbor: Text Creation Partnership, 2011. http://name.umdl.umichap.edu/A43314.0001.001.

Henry, Matthew. *The Communicant's Companion. By the Rev. Matthew Henry. With An Introductory Essay; By the Rev. John Brown, Edinburgh*. Boston: Crocker and Brewster, 1828.

— *An Account of the Life and Death of Mr. Philip Henry, Minister of the Gospel, Near Whitchurch in Shropshire*, 1712. Reprint, Edinburgh: Banner of Truth Trust, 1974.

Hooker, Thomas. *A Survey of the Summe of Church Discipline. Wherein the Way of the Congregationall Churches of Christ in New-England, is Warranted and Cleared, by Scripture and Argument, and all Exceptions of weight made against it by sundry Learned Divines*. London: John Bellamy, 1648.

Lechford, Thomas. *Plain Dealing, or, News From New England*. London, 1642. Reprint, Boston: J.K. Wiggin and Wm. Parsons Lunt, 1867.

Mason, John. *Letters on Frequent Communion, Addressed Particularly to the Members of the Associate-Reformed Church in North-America*. New-York: T. & J. Swords, 1798.

— *Letters on Frequent Communion*. In *The Writings of the Late John M. Mason, D.D.* New York: Ebenezer Mason, 1832.

— *Letters on Frequent Communion.* In *The Complete Works of John M. Mason, D.D.* New York: Baker and Scribner, 1849.

Mather, Cotton. *Ecclesiastes: The Life of the Reverend & Excellent Jonathan Mitchel.* Boston, 1697; Ann Arbor: Text Creation Partnership 2011. http://name.umdl.umich.edu/N00651. 0001.001.

— *A Monitor for Communicants. An Essay To Excite and Assist Religious Approaches to the Table of the Lord. Offered by an Assembly of the New-English Pastors, unto their own Flocks, and unto all the Churches in these American Colonies; with A Solemn Testimony to that Cause of God, and Religion, in them.* 1715. Reprint, Boston: S Kneeland, 1750.

— *Magnalia Christi Americana.* 2 vols. London, 1702. Reprint, Hartford: 1820.

Mather, Richard. *A Platform of church discipline gathered out of the Word of God.* Cambridge, MA: S.G. at Cambridge in New England, 1649; Ann Arbor: Text Creation Partnership 2011. http://name.umdl.umichap.edu/A55001.0001.001.

Morice, William. *Coena quasi Koine: or the Common Right to the Lords Supper Asserted, Wherein That Question is Fully Stated.* London, 1660.

Oliphant, James. *A Sacramental Catechism, Designed for Communicants Old and Young.* Edinburgh: J. Guthrie, 1798.

Owen, John. *The Works of John Owen*, Vol. XV, ed. William H. Goold (Johnstone & Hunter, 1850–53. Reprint, Edinburgh and Carlisle, PA: The Banner of Truth Trust, 1965; 1998.

Prynne, William. *Foure serious Questions of Grand Importance, Concerning Excommunication, and Suspension from the Sacrament; propounded to the Reverend Assembly, and all Moderate Christians, to prevent Schismes, and settle Unity among us, in these divided Times; by a Lover both of Peace and Truth.* London: s.n., 1644?; Ann Arbor: Text Creation Partnership, 2011. http://name.umdl.umich.edu/A56165.0001.001.

— *A Seasonable Vindication of the frequent Administration of the Holy Communion, to all Visible Church-members, Regenerate or Unregenerate.* London, 1656; Ann Arbor: Text Creation Partnership, 2011. http://name.umdl.umich.edu/A91267.0001.001.

— *A Vindication of foure Serious Questions of Grand Importance Concerning Excommunication and Suspension from the Sacrament of the Lords Supper.* London, 1645; Ann Arbor: Text Creation Partnership, 2001. http://name.umdl.umich.edu/A91314.0001.001.

Quick, John. *The Young Mans claim unto the Sacrament of the Lords Supper.* Boston, 1700.

Randall, Thomas. *A Letter to A Minister from his Friend, Concerning Frequent Communicating, Occasioned by the late Overture of the Synod of Glasgow and Air upon that Subject.* Glasgow, 1749.

Reformed Confessions of the 16th and 17th Centuries in English Translation: Volume 1, 1523–1552. Edited by James T. Dennison, Jr. Grand Rapids: Reformation Heritage Press, 2008.

Rutherford, Samuel. *The Divine Right of Church Government and Excommunication.* London, 1646.

Sewall, Samuel. *The Diary of Samuel Sewall*, M. Halsey Thomas, ed., (New York: Farrar, Straus & Giroux, 1973), I.

Shepherd, Thomas. *The First Principles of the Oracles of God*. London: Printed for John Rothwel, 1655; Ann Arbor: Text Creation Partnership, 2011. http://name.umdl.umich.edu/A59663.0001.001.

Stoddard, Solomon. *Three sermons lately preached at Boston. I. Shewing the vertue of Christs blood to cleanse from sin. II. That natural men are under the government of self-love. III. That the Gospel is the means of conversion. : To which a fourth is added, to stir up young men and maidens to praise the name of the Lord. / By Solomon Stoddard A.M. Pastor of Northampton*. Boston, 1717. Reprint, Gale, Sabin Americana Print Editions 1500–1926, n.d.

— *The Safety of Appearing*. Boston: Samuel Green, for Samuel Phillips, 1687; Ann Arbor: Text Creation Partnership, 2011. https://quod.lib.umichap.edu/e/evans/N00357.0001.001/1:3.7?rgn=div2;view=fulltext.

— *The Inexcusableness of Neglecting the Worship of God*. Boston, 1708.

Taylor, Edward. *Edward Taylor's Treatise Concerning the Lord's Supper*. Norman S. Grabo, ed. Michigan State University Press, 1966.

Tennent, Gilbert. *The Duty of Self-Examination Considered in a Sermon on 1 Corinthians 11:28 … Before the Celebration of the Lord's Supper*. Boston: n.p., 1739.

Tennent, Gilbert et. al., *Sermons on Sacramental Occasions by Divers Ministers*. Boston: J. Draper, 1739.

Tennent, William "Sermon on 1 Corinthians 11:26." Edited by Thomas C. Pears. *Journal of the Presbyterian Historical Society*, 19 (June 1940): 76–84.

The First and Second Prayer Books of Edward VI. Edited by Douglas Harrison. Everyman's Library. London: Dent, 1910.

The Rector's Book, Clayworth. Edited by H. Gill and E.L. Guilford. Nottingham, 1910.

Weld, Thomas. *A brief narration of the practices of the churches in New-England*. London: Printed by Matth. Simmons for John Rothwell, 1645; Ann Arbor: Text Creation Partnership, 2011. http://name.umdl.umich.edu/A96168.0001.001.

Willard, Samuel. *Some Brief Sacramental Meditations, Preparatory for Communion at the Great Ordinance of the Supper*. Boston: B. Green, 1711.

Willison, John. *A Sacramental Catechism: Or, A Familiar Instructor for Young Communicants*. Glasgow: David Niven, 1794.

Winthrop, John. "A Modell of Christian Charity," *MHSC*, 3rd ser., 7 (1838).

Wilburn, Percival. *A Checke or Reproofe of M. Howlet's Untimely Screeching*. London, 1581.

Secondary Sources

Adams, Doug. *Meeting House to Camp Meeting: Toward a History of American Free Church Worship From 1620 to 1835*. Saratoga: Modern Liturgy-Resource Publications and Austin: The Sharing Company, 1981.

Ansdell, Douglas. *People of the Great Faith: The Highland Church 1690–1900*. Stornoway, 1998.

Bancroft, Eric. "We Celebrate the Lord's Supper Frequently But Not Weekly," April 18, 2012.http://www.thegospelcoalition.org/article/we-celebrate-the-lords-supper-frequently-but-not-weekly.

Baker, J. Wayne. "Church Discipline or Civil Punishment: On the Origins of the Reformed Schism, 1528–1531." *Andrews University Seminary Studies*, no. 4 (1985): 3–18.

— "Church, State, and Dissent: The Crisis of the Swiss Reformation, 1531–1536." *Church History*, (June 1988): 135–152.

Ballor, Ballor, and W. Bradford Littlejohn, "European Calvinism: Church Discipline." In European History Online (EGO), published by the Leibniz Institute of European History (IEG), Mainz 2013-03-25. URL: http://www.ieg-ego.eu/ballorj-littlejohnw-2013-en URN: urn:nbn:de:0159-2013032507 [2017-05-05].

Bannerman, W. Bruce, ed. *Miscellanea Genealogica et Heraldica*. Vol. 5, third series. London: Mitchell Hughes and Clarke, 1904.

Bagchi, David and David C. Steinmetz, eds. *The Cambridge Companion to Reformation Theology*. Cambridge: Cambridge University Press, 2004. Reprint, 2013.

Bauer, Walter. *A Greek-English Lexicon of the New Testament and Other Early Christian Literature*. Translated and revised by W.F. Arndt, F.W. Gingrich, and F.W. Danker. Chicago: University of Chicago Press, 1979.

Beeke, Joel R. and Mark Jones. *A Puritan Theology: Doctrine for Life*. Grand Rapids: Reformation Heritage Books, 2012.

Benedict, Philip. *Christ's Churches Purely Reformed: A Social History of Calvinism*. New Haven: Yale University Press, 2002.

Bennett, James B. "'Love to Christ'"—Gilbert Tennent, Presbyterian Reunion, and a Sacramental Sermon." *American Presbyterians*, (Summer 1993): 77–89.

Billings, J. Todd. *Remembrance, Communion, and Hope: Rediscovering the Gospel at the Lord's Table*. Grand Rapids, MI: Eerdmans, 2018.

Bossy, John. *Christianity in the West 1400–1700*. Oxford: Oxford University Press, 1985.

— *Peace in the Post-Reformation*. Cambridge, 1998.

Boulton, J.P. "The Limits of Formal Religion: The Administration of Holy Communion in late Elizabethan and Early Stuart London." *London Journal*, 10 (1984): 135–154.

Bozeman, Theodore Dwight *To Live Ancient Lives: The Primitivist Dimension in Puritanism*. Chapel Hill, N.C., 1998.

— *The Precisianist Strain: Disciplinary Religion & Antinomian Backlash in Puritanism to 1638*. Chapel Hill: University of North Carolina Press, 2004.

Bracken Long, Kimberly. *The Eucharistic Theology of the American Holy Fairs*. Louisville: Westminster John Knox Press, 2011.

Bradley, James E. and Richard A. Muller. *Church History: An Introduction to Research, Reference Works, and Methods*. Grand Rapids: Wm. B. Eerdmans Publishing Co., 1995.

Bremer, Francis J. *The Puritan Experiment: New England Society from Bradford to Edwards*, rev. ed. Hanover and London: University Press of New England, 1976; 1995.

— *Shaping New Englands: Puritan Clergymen in Seventeenth-Century England and New England*. New York: Twayne Publishers, 1994.

— *Congregation Communion: Clerical Friendship in the Anglo-American Puritan Community, 1610–1692*. Boston: Northeastern University Press, 1994.

Burnet, G.B. *The Holy Communion in the Reformed Church of Scotland*. Edinburgh and London: Oliver and Boyd, 1960.

Burnett, Amy Nelson. *The Yoke of Christ: Martin Bucer and Christian Discipline*. Kirksville: Sixteenth Century Publishers, 1994.

Burnett, Amy Nelson. "The Myth of the Swiss Lutherans: Martin Bucer and the Eucharistic Controversy in Bern." *Zwingliana* 32, (2005): 45–70.

— *Teaching the Reformation: Ministers and Their Message in Basel, 1529–1629*. Oxford: Oxford University Press, 2006.

— "The Social History of Communion and the Reformation of the Eucharist." *Past & Present*, no. 211, (2011): 77–119.

Byars, Ronald P. *Come and See: Presbyterian Congregations Celebrating Weekly Communion*. Eugene: Cascade Books, 2014.

Cameron, Euan. *The European Reformation* 2nd ed. Oxford: Oxford University Press, 2012.

Canlis, Julie. *Calvin's Ladder: A Spiritual Theology of Ascent and Ascension*. Grand Rapids: Wm. B. Eerdmans Publishing Co., 2010.

Chung-Kim, Esther. *Inventing Authority: The Use of the Church Fathers in Reformation Debates over the Eucharist* Waco: Baylor University Press, 2011.

Chung-Kim, Esther and Todd R. Hains, eds., *Reformation Commentary on Scripture: Acts*. Downers Grove: IVP Academic, 2014.

Coffey, John and C.H. Lim. *The Cambridge Companion to Puritanism*. Cambridge: Cambridge University Press, 2008.

Collinson, Patrick. *The Elizabethan Puritan Movement*. Oxford: Clarendon Press, 1967. Paperback, 1990.

Conkin, Paul. *Cane Ridge: America's Pentecost*. Madison: University of Wisconsin Press, 1990.

Cowan, Ian B. *The Scottish Reformation: Church and Society in sixteenth century Scotland*. New York: St. Martin's Press, 1982.

Cunnington, Ralph. "Calvin's Doctrine of the Lord's Supper: A Blot Upon His Labors as a Public Instructor?" *WTJ*, 73 (2011): 215–36.

Davies, Horton. *Worship and Theology in England*, vol. 1, *From Cranmer to Baxter and Fox, 1534–1690*. Grand Rapids: William B. Eerdmans Publishing Company, 1970, 1975; combined edition 1996.

— *The Worship of the English Puritans*. 1948; repr., Morgan, PA: Soli Deo Gloria Publications, 1997.

Davis, Thomas J. *The Clearest Promise of God: The Development of Calvin's Eucharistic Teaching*. AMS Studies in Religious Tradition 1. New York: AMS Press, 1995.

— *This Is My Body: The Presence of Christ in Reformation Thought.* Grand Rapids: Baker Academic, 2008.

— ed. *John Calvin's American Legacy.* Oxford: Oxford University Press, 2010.

Dawson, Jane E.A. "'The Face of Ane Perfyt Reformed Kirk': St Andrews and the Early Scottish Reformation." In *Humanism and Reform: the Church in Europe, England, and Scotland, 1400–1643.* Edited by James Kirk. Oxford: Blackwell Publishers, 1991.

Dougherty, Joseph. *From Altar-Throne to Table: The Campaign for Frequent Holy Communion in the Catholic Church,* ATLA Monograph Series, No. 50. Lanham, MD: The Scarecrow Press and American Theological Library Association, 2010.

Drummond, A. L. *The Kirk and the Continent.* Edinburgh: Saint Andrew Press, 1956.

Duffield, G.E. ed., *John Calvin,* Courtenay Studies in Reformation Theology. Appelford: The Sutton Courtenay Press, 1966.

Duffy, Eamon. *The Stripping of the Altars: Traditional Religion in England 1400–1580.* New Haven: Yale University Press, 1992; 2nd ed. 2005.

Duffy, Eamon. *Reformation Divided: Catholics, Protestants and the Conversion of England.* London: Bloomsbury, 2017.

Dublanchy, E. "Communion eucharistique (fréquente)." *Dictionnaire de théologie catholique.* Paris: Letouzy et Ané, 1929.

Eire, Carlos. *Reformations: The Early Modern World, 1450–1650.* New Haven: Yale University Press, 2016.

Ellwood, Christopher. *The Body Broken: The Calvinist Doctrine of the Eucharist.* New York: Oxford University Press, 1999.

Fast, Heinhold. *Heinrich Bullinger und die Täufer. Ein Beitrag zur Historiographie und Theologie im 16. Jahrhundert.* Weierhof [Pfalz], 1959.

Fisher, Jeff. "The State of Research of the Basel Reformer, Johannes Oecolampadius with a Focus on the History of Biblical Interpretation." Unpublished paper, 2009. https://www.academia.edu/986421/The_State_of_Research_on_the_Basel_Reformer_John_Oecolampadius_1482-1531_with_a_Focus_on_the_History_of_Biblical_Interpretation.

— *A Christoscopic Reading of Scripture: Johannes Oecolampadius on Hebrews.* Göttingen: Vandenhoeck & Ruprecht, 2016.

Fisk, William Lyons. *The Scottish High Church Tradition in America: An Essay in Scotch-Irish Ethnoreligious History.* Lanham, MD: University Press of America, 1995.

Forrester, Duncan, and Douglas Murray. *Studies in the History of Worship in Scotland.* T. and T. Clark, Edinburgh, 1984.

Fudge, Thomas A. "Icarus of Basel? Oecolampadius and the Early Swiss Reformation." *JRH,* vol. 21, no. 3, (October 1997): 268–284.

Gaffin, Richard B. Jr. *Calvin and the Sabbath: The Controversy of Applying the Fourth Commandment.* Mentor: Ross-shire, 1998. Reprint, 2008.

Gibson, Jonathan and Mark Earngey, eds., *Reformation Worship: Liturgies from the Past for the Present.* Greensboro: New Growth Press, 2018.

Gerrish, B.A. "Discerning the Body: Sign and Reality in Luther's Controversy with the Swiss." *Continuing the Reformation: Essays on Modern Religious Thought.* Chicago: University of Chicago Press, 1993.

— *Grace and Gratitude: The Eucharistic Theology of John Calvin.* Eugene: Wipf and Stock, 2002; 1st ed. 1993.

— "Gospel and Eucharist: John Calvin on the Lord's Supper." In *The Old Protestantism and the New: Essays on the Reformation Heritage.* Chicago: The University of Chicago Press, 1982.

Gordon, Bruce. *The Swiss Reformation.* Manchester: Manchester UP, 2002.

Gordon, Bruce and Emidio Campi, eds. *Architect of Reformation: An Introduction to Heinrich Bullinger, 1504–1575.* Grand Rapids: Baker Academic, 2004.

Graham, Michael F. "Social Discipline in Scotland, 1560–1610." In *Sin and the Calvinists: Morals Control and the Consistory in the Reformed Tradition.* Edited by Raymond A. Mentzer. Sixteenth Century Essays & Studies, Volume XXXII. Kirksville, MO: Sixteenth Century Journal Publishers, Inc., 1994:129–157.

— *The Uses of Reform: 'Godly Discipline' and Popular Behavior in Scotland and Beyond, 1560–1610.* Leiden: E.J. Brill, 1996.

Green, Ian. *Print and Protestantism in Early Modern England.* Oxford: Oxford University Press, 2000.

Gregory, Jeremy *Restoration, Reformation, and Reform, 1660–1828: Archbishops of Canterbury and Their Diocese*, Oxford Historical Monographs. Oxford: Clarendon, 2000.

Gribben, Crawford. *John Owen and English Puritanism: Experiences of Defeat.* New York: Oxford University Press, 2016.

Grosse, Christian. *Les rituels de la cène: le culte eucharistique réformé à Genève (XVIe–XVIIe siècles).* Geneva: Librairie Droz, 2008.

Guggisberg, Hans R. *Basel in the Sixteenth Century: Aspects of the City Republic before, during, and after the Reformation.* St. Louis: Center for Reformation Research, 1982.

Gunnoe, Charles. *Thomas Erastus and the Palatinate: A Renaissance Physician in the Second Reformation.* Brill's Series in Church History, vol. 48. Leiden: Brill, 2011.

Hageman, Howard. *Pulpit and Table: Some Chapters in the History of Worship in the Reformed Churches.* 1962. Reprint, Eugene: Wipf and Stock Publishers, 2004.

Hall, David D. *The Faithful Shepherd: A History of the New England Ministry in the Seventeenth Century.* Chapel Hill: University of North Carolina Press, 1972.

— *The Puritans: A Transatlantic History.* Princeton: Princeton University Press, 2019.

Haigh, Christopher. *English Reformations: Religion, Politics, and Society under the Tudors.* Oxford: Clarendon Press, 1993.Harding, Matthew Scott. "A Calvinist and Anabaptist Understanding of the Ban." *Perichoresis*, vol. 10, issue 2, (2012): 165–193.

Hambrick-Stowe, Charles E. *The Practice of Piety: Puritan Devotional Disciplines in Seventeenth-Century New England.* Chapel Hill: The University of North Carolina Press, 1982. Reprint, 1985.

Hazlett, Ian. "The Development of Martin Bucer's Thinking on the Sacrament of the Lord's Supper in its Historical and Theological Context." Ph.D. diss, Westfälische Wilhelms-Universität zu Münster, 1975.

Harman, Allan. *Matthew Henry: His Life and Influence.* Fearn, UK: Christian Focus Publications, 2012.

Hendrix, Scott H. *Recultivating the Vineyard: The Reformation Agendas of Christianization.* Louisville: Westminster John Knox Press, 2004.

Hesselink, I. John ed. *Calvin's First Catechism. A Commentary.* Translated by Ford Lewis Battles. Louisville: Westminster John Knox, 1997.

Holifield, E. Brooks. "The Intellectual Sources of Stoddardeanism." *The New England Quarterly*, (Sep., 1972): 373–392.

— *The Covenant Sealed: The Development of Puritan Sacramental Theology in Old and New England.* New Haven and London: Yale University Press, 1974.

— "Peace, Conflict, and Ritual in Puritan Congregations." *The Journal of Interdisciplinary History*, Vol. 23, No. 3 (Winter, 1993): 551–570.

Horton, Michael S. "At Least Weekly: The Reformed Doctrine of the Lord's Supper and of Its Frequent Celebration." *MJT*, 11 (2000): 147–169.

— *People and Place: A Covenant Ecclesiology.* Louisville: Westminster John Knox Press, 2008.

Hughes, Kenneth. *Holy Communion in the Church of Scotland in the Nineteenth Century.* PhD diss., University of Glasgow, 1987.

Hunt, Arnold. "The Lord's Supper in Early Modern England." *Past & Present*, (November 1998): 39–83.

Hurlbut, Stephen A. ed. *The Liturgy of the Church of Scotland Since the Reformation, Part II. The Book of Common Order.* Charleston: The St. Alban's Press, 1950.

Janse, Wim. *Albert Hardenberg als Theologe. Profil eines Bucer-Schülers* [SHCH 57]. Leiden/New York/Köln: E.J. Brill, 1994.

— "Calvin's Eucharistic Theology: Three Dogma-Historical Observations." In *Calvinus sacrarum literarum interpres: Papers of the International Congress on Calvin Research.* Edited by Herman J. Selderhuis. Göttingen: Vandenhoeck & Ruprecht, 2008.

— '12. The Sacraments.' In *The Calvin Handbook.* Edited by Herman J. Selderhuis. Grand Rapids: William B. Eerdmans, 2009: 344–355.

— 'Controversy and Concordance between Calvin and Westphal on the Communion of the Sick.' In *Calvinus clarissimus theologus. Papers of the Tenth International Congress on Calvin Research* Göttingen: Vandenhoeck & Ruprecht, 2012.

— "Calvin's Doctrine of the Lord's Supper." *Perichoresis*, Vol. 10, Issue 2 (2012): 137–163.

Jenkins, G.H. *Literature, Religion and Society in Wales 1660–1730.* Cardiff: University of Wales Press, 1978.

Jones, Chelsyn, Geoffrey Wainwright, and Edward J. Yarnold, eds. *The Study of Liturgy.* New York: Oxford University Press, 1978.

Joo, Jong Hun. "Communion with God as Word-Centered Piety: Exploring the Pastoral Concern and Thought of Matthew Henry (1662–1714)." *TTJ*, 16.1 (2013): 73–85.

— *Matthew Henry: Pastoral Liturgy in Challenging Times.* Eugene, OR: Pickwick/ Wipf and Stock Publishers, 2014.

Kidd, Thomas S. *The Great Awakening: The Roots of Evangelical Christianity in Colonial America.* New Haven and London: Yale University Press, 2007.

Kingdon, Robert. "Calvin and the Government of Geneva." In *Calvinus Ecclesiae Genevensis Custos.* Edited by Wilhelm Neuser. Frankfurt am Main: Verlag Peter Lang, 1984.

Kingdon, Robert. "A New View of Calvin in Light of the Registers of the Geneva Consistory." In *Calvinus Sincerioris Religionis Vindex: Calvin as Protector of the Purer Religion.* Edited by Wilhelm H. Neuser and Brian G. Armstrong. Kirksville, MO: Sixteenth Century Journal Publishers, 1997.

— "The Genevan Revolution in Public Worship." *Princeton Seminary Bulletin,* 20, No. 3, (1999): 264–280.

— "Calvin and Church Discipline." In *John Calvin Rediscovered: The Impact of His Social and Economic Thought.* Edited by Edward Dommen and James D. Bratt. Louisville: Westminster John Knox Press, 2007, 29–31.

Kittelson, James. *Toward an Established Church: Strasbourg from 1500 to the Dawn of the Seventeenth Century* Mainz: Verlag Philipp von Zabern, 2000.

Kirk, James. *Patterns of Reform: Continuity and Change in the Reformation Kirk.* Edinburgh: T&T Clark, 1989.

Knoll, Mark. *A History of Christianity in the United States and Canada.* Grand Rapids: William B. Eerdmans Publishing Company, 1992.

Kuehner, Adam M. *Calvin, Weekly Communion, and the Scottish Reformed Tradition.* Grand Rapids: Torwood Press, 2013.

Kuhr, Olaf. "Calvin and Basel: The Significance of Oecolampadius and the Basel Discipline Ordinance for the Institution of Ecclesiastical Discipline in Geneva." *Scottish Bulletin of Evangelical Theology,* 16 (1998), 19–33.

— *Die Macht des Bannes und der Busse: Kirchenzucht und Erneuerung der Kirche bei Johannes Oekolampad* 1482 – 1531). Bern New York: P. Lang, 1999.

Lambert, Frank. *Inventing the Great Awakening.* Princeton: Princeton University Press, 1999.

Landsman, Ned C. *Scotland and Its First American Colony, 1683–1765.* Princeton, NJ: Princeton University Press, 1985.

Lane, Anthony N. S. *John Calvin: Student of the Church Fathers.* Grand Rapids: Baker Books, 1999.

Lee, Jung-Sook. "Spiritual Renewal Through Worship Reform in Calvin's Geneva." *Torch Trinity Journal* 7 (2004): 123–139.

Leithart, Peter J. *The Kingdom and the Power: Rediscovering the Centrality of the Church.* Phillipsburg: P&R Publishing, 1993.

Leishman, Thomas. *Ritual of the Church of Scotland,* Vol. 5 of Robert Herbert Story, ed., *The Church of Scotland, Past and Present.* London: William Mackenzie, 1891.

Lewis, Peter. *The Genius of Puritanism.* Haywards Heath: Carey Publications, 1975.

Lindberg, Carter. *The European Reformations,* 2nd ed. Chichester: Wiley-Blackwell, 2010.

Longfield, Bradley J. *Presbyterians and American Culture: A History*. Louisville: Westminster John Knox Press, 2013.

Lugioyo, Brian. *Martin Bucer's Doctrine of Justification: Reformation Theology and Early Modern Irenicism*. Oxford: Oxford University Press, 2010.

Maag, Karin. *Lifting Hearts to the Lord: Worship with John Calvin in Sixteenth-Century Geneva*. Grand Rapids: Wm. B. Eerdmans Publishing Co., 2016.

MacCulloch, Diarmaid. *The Reformation: A History*. New York: Penguin Books, 2003.

— *Thomas Cranmer: A Life*. New Haven: Yale University Press, 1996.

MacLeod, Ian. "The Sacramental Theology and Practice of the Reverend John Willison (1680–1750)." PhD diss., University of Glasgow, 1994.

Macleod, John. *Scottish Theology in Relation to Church History Since the Reformation*. 1943. Reprint, Edinburgh: Banner of Truth, 2015.

Marsden, George M. *Jonathan Edwards: A Life*. New Haven: Yale University Press, 2003.

Marshall, Peter. *Heretics and Believers: A History of the English Reformation*. New London: Yale University Press, 2017.

Matthews, Donald G. "The Second Great Awakening as an Organizing Process, 1780–1830: An Hypothesis." *American Quarterly* 21, no. 1 (1969): 23–43.

Mathison, Keith A. *Given for You: Reclaiming Calvin's Doctrine of the Lord's Supper*. Phillipsburg: P&R Publishing, 2002.

Mayor, Stephen. *The Lord's Supper in Early English Dissent*. 1972. Reprint, Eugene: Wipf and Stock, 2016.

Maxwell, William. *The Liturgical Portions of the Genevan Service Book*. Westminster: Faith Press, 1931. Reprint, 1965.

McClelland, Joseph C. *The Visible Words of God: An Exposition of the Sacramental Theology of Peter Martyr Vermigli A.D. 1500–1562*. Grand Rapids: Wm. B. Eerdmans, 1957.

McEwan, James S. *The Faith of John Knox*. London: Lutterworth, 1961.

McKee, Elsie Ann. "Reformed Worship in the Sixteenth Century." In Lukas Vischer, ed., *Christian Worship in Reformed Churches Past and Present*. Grand Rapids: William B. Eerdmans Publishing Company, 2003: 3–31.

— "Places, Times, and People in Worship in Calvin's Geneva," *Journal of the Institute for Christianity and Culture of the International Christian University*, No. 41 (2010): 101–20.

— *The Pastoral Ministry and Worship in Calvin's Geneva*. Genève: Librairie Droz S.A., 2016.

McMillan, William. "Medieval Survivals in Scottish Worship." *Church Service Society Annual*, 4 (1931–1932): 21–34.

McNeill, John T. *The History and Character of Calvinism*. New York: Oxford University Press, 1954.

Meyer, John R. "*Mysterium Fidei* and the Later Calvin." *SJT*, 25 (1972): 393–411.

Meyers, Jeffrey J. *The Lord's Service: The Grace of Covenant Renewal Worship*. Moscow: Canon Press, 2003.

Miles, Margaret R. *Image as Insight: Visual Understanding in Christianity and Secular Culture*. 1985; Reprint, Eugene: Wipf and Stock Publishers, 2006.

— "Vision: The Eye of the Body and the Eye of the Mind in Augustine's *De Trinitate* and Other Works." *Journal of Religion*, No. 2 (April 1983): 125–42.

Melton, Julius. *Presbyterian Worship in America: Changing Patterns Since 1787*. WMJK/ Pickwick Publications, 1967/1984. Reprint, Eugene: Wipf and Stock Publishers, 2001.

Miller, Ed L. "Oecolampadius: The Unsung Hero of the Basel Reformation." *Iliff Review*, 39, No. 3 (1982): 5–24.

Miller, James P. *Biographical Sketches and Sermons of Some of the First Ministers of the Associate Church in America*. Albany: Hoffman and White, 1839.

Moeller, Bernd. *Imperial Cities and the Reformation: Three Essays*. Edited and translated by H.C. Erik Midelfort and Mark U. Edwards, Jr. Fortress Press, 1972. Reprinted, Durham, NC: Labyrinth Press, 1982.

Morgan, Edmund S. *Visible Saints: The History of a Puritan Idea*. New York: New York University Press, 1963. Reprint, Ithaca, N.Y.: Cornell University Press, 1965.

Muller, Richard A. "From Zürich or from Wittenberg? An Examination of Calvin's Early Eucharistic Thought." *CTJ*, 45 (2010): 243–255.

Nichols, James Hastings. *Corporate Worship in the Reformed Tradition*. Philadelphia: The Westminster Press, 1968.

Njoto, Ricky F. "The Lord's Supper in the Hands of a Sensitive Preacher: The Bible in Edwards' Sermons on 1 Corinthians 10." *Jonathan Edwards Studies*, Vol. 9, No. 2 (2019): 28–59.

Northway, Eric W. "The Reception of the Fathers & Eucharistic Theology in Johannes Oecolampadius (1482–1531), with Special Reference to the *Adversus Haereses* of Irenaeus of Lyons." Ph.D. diss., Durham University, 2008.

Old, Hughes Oliphant. "Henry, Matthew," *Dictionary of Major Biblical Interpreters*, Donald McKim ed. Downers Grove, IL and Nottingham, UK: InterVarsity Press, 2007.

— *Holy Communion in the Piety of the Reformed Church*, Jon Payne ed. Powder Springs, GA: Tolle Lege Press, 2013.

Opitz, Peter. "At the Table of the Lord: To Zwingli's View on the Lord's Supper." Accessed December 12, 2016. https://www.academia.edu/5802889/At_the_Table_of_the_Lord_To_Zwinglis_View_on_the_Lords_Supper.

Ottomar, Fredrick Cypris, "Basic Principles: Translation and Commentary of Martin Bucer's *Grund und Ursach*, 1524." Th.D. diss., Union Theological Seminary, 1971.

Pauck, Wilhelm, ed. *Melanchthon and Bucer*. Philadelphia: The Westminster Press, 1969.

Pelikan, Jaroslav. *Historical Theology: Continuity and Change in Christian Doctrine*, Theological Resources. New York: Corpus Instrumentorum, 1971.

Pears, Thomas C. and Elizabeth Freeman Reed, "Sessional Records of the Presbyterian Church of Booth Bay, Maine, 1767—1778." *Journal of the Department of History (The Presbyterian Historical Society) of the Presbyterian Church in the U.S.A.* 16, no. 5 (1935): 203–40. Accessed January 30, 2021. http://www.jstor.org/stable/23323779.

Pederson, Randall J. *Unity in Diversity: English Puritans and the Puritan Reformation, 1603–1689*. Leiden: Brill, 2014.

Pettegree, Andrew. *Foreign Protestant Communities in Sixteenth-Century London.* Oxford: Clarendon Press, 1986.

Piotrowski, Nicholas. "Johannes Oecolampadius: Christology and the Supper." *MAJT*, 23 (2012): 131–137.

Pauw, Amy Plantinga. "Practical Ecclesiology in Calvin and Edwards." In *John Calvin's American Legacy*, edited by Thomas Davis, 91–110. Oxford: Oxford University Press, 2010.

Price, James. "Letters of Rev. John Anderson, D.D., and Matthew Henderson." *Journal of the Presbyterian Historical Society* (September, 1902): 341–343.

Riggs, John W. *The Lord's Supper in the Reformed Tradition.* Columbia Series in Reformed Theology. Louisville: Westminster John Knox: 2015.

Robertson, A.T. "John Brown of Haddington or Learning Greek Without a Teacher." In *The Minister and His Greek New Testament.* 1923. Reprint, Vestavia Hills, AL: Solid Ground Christian Books, 2008.

Rubin, Miri. *Corpus Christi: The Eucharist in Late Medieval Culture.* Cambridge: Cambridge UP, 1991.

Rupp, Gordon. *Patterns of Reform.* Philadelphia: Fortress Press, 1969.

Ryrie, Alec. *The Age of Reformation: The Tudor and Stewart Realms 1485–1603.* New York: Routledge, 2013.

Savage, Theodore F. *The Presbyterian Church in New York City.* New York: Presbytery of New York, 1949.

Scannel, Thomas. "The History of Daily Communion." In *Report of the Nineteenth Eucharistic Congress, Held at Westminster from 9th to 13th September 1908.* London: Sands, 1909.

Scarisbrick, J.J. *The Reformation and the English People.* Oxford: Oxford University Press, 1984.Schaff, Philip. *History of the Christian Church.* Vol. VIII, 3rd ed., revised. Charles Scribner's Sons, 1910. Reprint, Grand Rapids: Wm. B. Eerdmans Publishing Company, 1977.

—, ed., rev. David S. Schaff. *The Creeds of Christendom*, Vol. III. Harper and Row, 1931. Reprinted, 1983; Grand Rapids: Baker Books, 1998.

Schmemann, Alexander. *The Eucharist: Sacrament of the Kingdom.* Translated by Paul Kachur. Crestwood, NY: St. Vladimir's Seminary Press, 1987.

Schmidt, Leigh Eric. *Holy Fairs: Scotland and the Making of American Revivalism.* Grand Rapids: Wm. B. Eerdmans Publishing Co., 1989; 2nd ed. 2001.

Senn, Frank C. *A Stewardship of the Mysteries.* New York: Paulist Press, 1999.

Sirota, Brent S. *The Christian Monitors: The Church of England and the Age of Benevolence, 1680–1730.* New Haven, CT: Yale University Press, 2014.

Smylie, James H. *A Brief History of the Presbyterians.* Louisville: Geneva Press, 1996.

Soderberg, Gregory. "Ancient Discipline and Pristine Doctrine: Appeals to Antiquity in the Developing Reformation." M.A. thesis, University of Pretoria, 2006.

— "Weekly Communion: A Criterion of Catholicity? A Short Survey of Historical Claims in Reformed Debates." In *Reforming the Catholic Tradition: The Whole Word for the Whole Church*, edited by Joseph Minnich. Leesburg: The Davenant Institute, 2019: 153–197.

Speelman, Herman A. *Calvin and the Independence of the Church*. Göttingen: Vandenhoeck & Ruprecht, 2014.

— *Melanchthon and Calvin on Confession and Communion: Early Modern Protestant Penitential and Eucharistic Piety*. Göttingen: Vandenhoeck & Ruprecht, 2016.

— Speelman, "Weekly at the Lord's Table: Calvin's Motives for a Frequent Celebration of the Holy Communion." In *Liturgy and Ethics: New Contributions from Reformed Perspectives*, edited by Pieter Vos,. Leiden: Brill, 2018.

Spinks, Bryan D. *Sacraments, Ceremonies and the Stuart Divines: Sacramental theology and liturgy in England and Scotland 1603–1662*. Aldershot: Ashgate Publishing Limited, 2002.

Sprague, William Buell. *Annals of the American Pulpit; or Commemorative Notices of Distinguished American Clergymen*. Vol. IV. New York: Robert Carter & Brothers, 1859.

Sprott, George W. *The Worship of the Church of Scotland, During the Covenanting Period 1638–1661*. William Blackwood and Sons: Edinburgh and London, 1893. Reprint, Lexington: Forgotten Books, 2012.

Spurr, John. "Religion in Restoration England." In Lionel K.J. Glassey, ed., *The Reigns of Charles II and James VII & II*. New York: St. Martin's Press, 1997.

— *The Post-Reformation: Religion, Politics and Society in Britain 1603–1714*. Essex: Pearson Education Limited, 2006.

Staehelin, Ernst. *Das Theologische Lebenswerk Johannes Oekolampads*, QFR 21. New York: Johnson 1939.

— *Briefe Und Akten Zum Leben Oekolampads: Zum Vierhundertjahrigen Jubilaum der Basler Reformation herausgegeben von der Theologischen Fakultät der Universität Basel*, QFR, Bd. 10, 19. Leipzig, 1927; Reprint, New York, London: Johnson, 1971.

Stewart, Kenneth J. "The Frequency of Communion Calmly Considered," April 18, 2012 http://www.thegospelcoalition.org/article/the-frequency-of-communion-calmly-considered. Accessed May 5, 2015.

— "Accelerating the Rhythm: Two Eighteenth Century Scottish Presbyterians on the Frequency of the Lord's Supper." In Ian Clary and Steve Weaver, eds. *The Pure Flame of Devotion: The History of Christian Spirituality: Essays in Honor of Michael A. G. Haykin on his Sixtieth Birthday*. Joshua Press, 2013.

— *In Search of Ancient Roots: The Christian Past and the Evangelical Identity Crisis*. Downer's Grove: IVP Academic, 2017.

Strange, Alan D. "Jonathan Edwards and the Communion Controversy in Northampton," *MJT*, 14 (2003): 57–97.

Sykes, Stephen and John Booty, eds. *The Study of Anglicanism*. London: SPCK/ Fortress Press, 1988.

Taft, Robert A. "The Frequency of the Eucharist Throughout History." In *Between Memory and Hope: Readings on the Liturgical Year*, edited by Maxwell Johnson, 77–96. Collegeville, MN: The Liturgical Press, 2000.

Tanner, Norman P. *Decrees of the Ecumenical Councils*, Vol. I. London: Sheed & Ward, 1990.

Terlouw, Arjen. "'Naturally More Vehement and Intense': Vehemence in Calvin's Sermons on the Lord's Supper." *Reformation & Renaissance Review*, 20:1, (2018): 70–81, DOI: 10.1080/14622459.2017.1419802.

Todd, Margo. *The Culture of Protestantism in Early Modern Scotland*. New Haven and London: Yale University Press, 2002.

Thompson, Bard. *Liturgies of the Western Church*. 1961. Reprint, Philadelphia: Fortress Press, 1980.

Thomson, John. *Letters addressed to the Rev. John Mason, M.A. of New-York, in Answer to his Letters on Frequent Communion*. Glasgow: William Paton, 1799. Reprint, Troy: R. Moffitt & Co., 1801.

Trinterud, Leonard J. *The Forming of an American Tradition: A Re-examination of Colonial Presbyterianism*. Philadelphia: Westminster, 1949.

Thurian, Max. *The Eucharistic Memorial*. Translated by J.G. Davies. Ecumenical Studies in Worship, No. 7 and 8. Richmond: John Knox Press, 1960.

Tylenda, Joseph. "The Ecumenical Intention of Calvin's Early Eucharistic Thought." In B.A. Gerrish, ed., *Reformatio Perennis: Essays on Calvin and the Reformation in honor of Ford Lewis Battles*. Pittsburgh: The Pickwick Press, 1981.

van de Poll, G.J. *Martin Bucer's Liturgical Ideas: The Strasbourg Reformer and His Connection with the Liturgies of the Sixteenth Century*. Assen: Koninklijke Van Gorcum, 1954.

van den Brink, Gijsbert and Johan Smits. "The Reformed Stance: Distinctive Commitments and Concerns." *Journal of Reformed Theology*, 9 (2015): 325–47.

van Dixhoorn, Chad B. "Unity and Diversity at the Westminster Assembly (1643–1649): A Commemorative Essay." *The Journal of Presbyterian History*, (Summer, 2001): 103–117.

Van Neste, Ray. "Three Arguments for Weekly Communion," April 18, 2012 http://www.thegospelcoalition.org/article/three-arguments-for-weekly-communion. Accessed May 5, 2015.

van 't Spijker, Willem. *The Ecclesiastical Office in the Thought of Martin Bucer*. Translated by John Vriend and Lyle D. Bierma. Leiden: E.J. Brill, 1996.

van Vetchen, Jacob. *Memoirs of John M. Mason, D.D., S.T.P. with Portions of his Correspondence*. New York: Robert Carter and Brothers, 1865.

Viladesau, Richard. *The Triumph of the Cross: The Passion of Christ in Theology and the Arts*. Oxford: Oxford University Press, 2008.

Vermigli, Peter Martyr. *The Oxford Treatise and Disputation on the Eucharist*. Translated and edited by Joseph C. McClelland. The Peter Martyr Library, ser. 1, v. 7, Sixteenth Century Essays & Studies, Vol. 55. Kirksville, MO: Truman State University Press, 2000.

von Allmen, J.-J. *Worship: Its Theology and Practice*. New York: Oxford University Press, 1965.

Wainwright, Geoffrey and Karen Westerfield Tucker, eds., *The Oxford History of Christian Worship*. Oxford: Oxford University Press, 2006.

Wakefield, Gordon S. *An Outline of Christian Worship*. Edinburgh: T&T Clark, 1998.

Wallace, Dewey D. *Puritans and Predestination: grace in English Protestant theology 1525–1695*. Studies in Religion. Chapel Hill: University of North Carolina Press, 1982.

Wallace, Ronald S. *Calvin's Doctrine of Word and Sacrament*. 1953. Reprint, Eugene: Wipf and Stock, 1997.

Wandel, Lee Palmer. *The Eucharist in the Reformation*. Cambridge: Cambridge University Press, 2006.

Watkins, Owen C. *The Puritan Experience: Studies in Spiritual Autobiography*. New York: Schocken Books, 1972.

Watt, Jeffrey R. *The Consistory and Social Discipline in Calvin's Geneva*. Rochester: University of Rochester Press, 2020.

West, Jim, ed and trans. *Huldrych Zwingli: The Implementation of the Lord's Supper*. Occasional Publications of the Pitts Theological Library. Accessed December 29, 2016. http://pitts. emory.edu/files/publications/ZwingliLordsSupper.pdf.

West, W. Morris S. "John Hooper and the Origins of Puritanism." *The Baptist Quarterly*, 15, Issue 8 (1954): 346–368.

Westerkamp, Marilyn J. *Triumph of the Laity: Scots-Irish Piety and the Great Awakening, 1625–1760*. New York: Oxford University Press, 1988.

White, James F. *The Sacraments in Protestant Faith and Practice*. Nashville: Abingdon Press, 1999.

Whitford, David M. ed., *Reformation and Early Modern Europe: A Guide to Research*. Kirksville: Truman State University Press, 2008.

Wieting, Kenneth W. *The Blessings of Weekly Communion*. Saint Louis: Concordia Publishing House, 2006.

Williams, John Bickerton. *Memoirs of the Life, Character, and Writings of the Rev. Matthew Henry*. 3rd edition. London: Joseph Ogle Robinson, 1829.

Winter, Robert Milton. "American Churches and the Holy Communion: A Comparative Study in Sacramental Theology, Practice, and Piety in the Episcopal, Presbyterian, Methodist, and German Reformed Traditions." PhD diss., Union Theological Seminary, 1988.

Winship, Michael P. *Hot Protestants: A History of Puritanism in England and America*. New Haven: Yale University Press, 2018.

Wolterstorff, Nicholas P. "The Reformed Liturgy." In *Major Themes in the Reformed Tradition*. Donald McKim, ed. Grand Rapids: Eerdmans, 1992.

Wotherspoon and J.M. Kirkpatrick, *A Manual of Church Doctrine according to the Church of Scotland*. 1919. Revised and enlarged by T.F. Torrance and Ronald Shelby Wright. London: Oxford University Press, 1960.

Wright, D.F., ed. *Common Places of Martin Bucer*. Abingdon: Sutton Courtenay Press, 1972.

— *Martin Bucer: Reforming Church and Community*. Cambridge: Cambridge UP, 1994.

Wriedt, Markus. "How to Bring About a Reformation: A critical re-consideration about most recent theories in Historiography." Public Lecture: Marquette University, Milwaukee WI, October 13, 2005.

Yates, Nigel. *Preaching, Word and Sacrament: Scottish Church Interiors 1560–1860*. London and New York: T&T Clark, 2009.

Yeager, Jonathan M. *Enlightened Evangelicalism: The Life and Thought of John Erskine*. Oxford: Oxford University Press, 2011.

Index

Index of person

A

Alexander, James W. 199, 230

B

Bayly, Lewis 110, 112, 113, 115, 136, 252
Bradshaw, William 113–115, 117, 136, 252
Brown, John of Haddington 184, 224, 233, 239
Bucer, Martin 22, 32, 33, 35, 36, 57, 60–62, 66, 71, 76, 123, 177, 252
Bullinger 76
Bullinger, Heinrich 31, 43, 44, 56, 57, 59, 75, 76, 152, 252

C

Calvin, John 14, 17, 22, 28, 30, 31, 37, 43, 45, 47–49, 51, 52, 54, 55, 59, 60, 63–66, 68–71, 73, 77, 82, 86, 94, 108, 109, 123, 152, 176, 177, 213, 214, 217, 221, 225, 230, 241, 242, 251–253
Charnock, Stephen 117, 119, 122, 123, 136, 252

D

Doolittle, Thomas 129–132, 134, 136, 252
Duncan, Alexander 13, 184, 199, 204, 215, 217–222, 224, 233–235, 237, 241, 243, 244, 247, 253

E

Edwards, Jonathan 147, 157, 172, 174–176, 189, 253
Erskine, John 13, 147, 176, 184, 188, 190–195, 198, 200, 201, 203, 204, 233, 236, 237, 240–243, 245, 246, 253

H

Henry, Matthew 129, 132, 135, 136, 225, 252
Hildersham, Arthur 113, 116, 117, 136, 252

L

Luther, Martin 14, 28, 32, 38, 40, 50, 61, 70, 75, 77

M

Mason, John Mitchell 13, 184, 199–204, 206–209, 211, 215, 216, 224, 226, 229, 233, 235, 238, 240–245, 247, 249, 253
Mather, Cotton 129, 147, 156, 167, 168, 171

O

Oecolampadius, Johannes 22, 30, 56, 59, 63, 71, 252

R

Randall, Thomas 13, 176, 184, 190, 195, 203, 219, 239, 253

Index of subjects

A

Anabaptist 36, 39, 41, 57, 59, 61, 66
Anglican 18, 79, 100, 110, 149, 155, 183, 193, 219, 255
  – Church of England 99, 100, 110, 129, 136, 155, 193
annual communion 102, 236

B

Baptist 11, 103, 207
Basel 29–31, 56, 57, 59, 62, 251, 252
Bible 45, 64, 136, 145, 148, 152, 188, 202, 203, 208, 209, 228, 238
  – New Testament 12, 13, 104, 119, 138, 175, 190, 191, 197, 201, 203, 205, 206, 212, 218–220, 224, 225, 233, 234, 236
    – 1 Corinthians 12, 53, 118, 151, 157, 233, 251
    – Acts 12, 46, 52, 104, 119, 145, 152, 175, 187, 191, 192, 197, 201, 205, 212, 213, 221, 230, 233, 236
    – Luke 12, 174, 213, 233
    – Mark 12
    – Matthew 41, 62, 162, 163, 233
  – Old Testament 13, 58, 120, 134, 194, 203, 204, 206, 210, 213–215, 217, 223, 224, 235, 237, 239, 241, 243
  – Passover 13
British 16, 23, 25, 73, 75, 76, 82, 96, 97, 148
Bullinger, Heinrich 31

C

catechesis 60–62, 65, 71, 72, 83, 88, 91, 93, 95, 109, 137, 145
church discipline 16–18, 31, 32, 37, 45, 55, 57–60, 63, 66–68, 70–72, 81–83, 85, 87–89, 93, 94, 96, 97, 106, 124, 125, 145,
158, 163, 165, 176, 177, 197, 198, 229, 245, 246, 251, 252, 254, 255
church fathers 22, 221, 225, 240
church history 14, 120, 188, 197, 201, 203, 207, 225, 229, 232, 240, 241, 253
  – Apostolic church 14, 22, 150, 152, 197, 205, 219, 221, 237, 251
  – early church 12, 14, 22, 54, 62, 65, 77, 173, 190–192, 194, 197, 198, 206, 209, 214, 219, 221, 225, 230, 233, 240–242
  – patristic church 119, 190, 230
communion
  – annual communion 31, 42, 46, 88, 120, 144, 178, 225, 255
  – careful frequency 209, 212, 214, 215, 217, 235, 237, 240, 241
  – communion reception 28, 47, 88
  – communion seasons 140, 143, 178–181, 184, 185, 202, 208, 210, 212, 214, 226, 231, 245, 246, 248, 249, 253
  – daily communion 46, 48, 152, 202
  – frequency debates 12, 13, 16, 18, 52, 71, 73–75, 86, 87, 96, 120, 126, 128, 136–138, 140, 141, 145, 147, 177, 184, 188, 193, 195, 198, 203, 205, 209, 210, 213, 224, 227, 232, 243, 247
  – frequency polemics 13, 17, 22, 45, 52, 54, 56, 184, 186, 201, 233
  – monthly communion 31, 64, 86, 102, 103, 105, 112, 133, 134
  – oral reception 24, 26, 28, 75
  – quarterly communion 29, 41, 42, 67, 69, 70, 86–88, 105, 128, 145, 193, 208, 222, 246, 249, 252
  – visual reception 25, 26, 28, 82
  – weekly communion 11, 14, 15, 22, 27, 29–31, 33, 34, 47, 55, 63, 64, 69, 71,